The teaching materials included in this volume have been prepared in committee by a distinguished group of teachers working on the primary, secondary, and college levels. Their names and schools are listed in the front matter of the ENRICHED CLASSICS titles. Every effort has been made to address the questions (in the objective tests and the report or discussion sections) to the important features of the books to which they apply. Inquiry into petty detail has been avoided; instead, the stress is on pivotal elements in plot and theme development, characterization, structural and style techniques, evaluation of motives and attitudes, and relevance to the reader's emerging sense of values and understanding of human relations. The committee was also mindful of the grade in which a title is usually studied, and adjusted the sophistication of its analysis to appropriate maturity levels.

Books by Harry Shefter

Faster Reading Self-Taught*
How to Prepare Talks and Oral Reports*
Shefter's Guide to Better Compositions*
Shortcuts to Effective English*
Six Minutes a Day to Perfect Spelling*
A Teacher's Guide to Supplementary Reading**
Teaching Aids for 40 Enriched Classics**

* Published by POCKET BOOKS
** Published by WASHINGTON SQUARE PRESS

Teaching Aids

for

40

Enriched Classics

HARRY SHEFTER, Editor

Professor of English, New York University

WASHINGTON SQUARE PRESS
POCKET BOOKS • NEW YORK

TEACHING AIDS FOR 40 ENRICHED CLASSICS

Washington Square Press edition published May, 1975

L

Published by
POCKET BOOKS, a division of Simon & Schuster, Inc.,
630 Fifth Avenue, New York, N.Y.

WASHINGTON SQUARE PRESS editions are distrib-
uted in the U.S. by Simon & Schuster, Inc., 630 Fifth
Avenue, New York, N.Y. 10020, and in Canada by Simon
& Schuster of Canada, Ltd., Markham, Ontario, Canada.

Standard Book Number: 671-48762-0.
Front cover illustration by Howard Koslow.
Printed in the U.S.A.

CONTENTS

Introduction   1
    I. The Reader's Supplement   2
   II. Teaching Aids   9
The Adventures of Huckleberry Finn / Mark Twain   19
The Adventures of Tom Sawyer / Mark Twain   31
And Then There Were None / Agatha Christie   42
Anne Frank: The Diary of a Young Girl /
    Anne Frank   50
Billy Budd / Herman Melville   61
The Bridge of San Luis Rey / Thornton Wilder   71
The Caine Mutiny / Herman Wouk   81
The Call of the Wild / Jack London   94
Crime and Punishment / Fyodor Dostoevsky   104
Dr. Jekyll and Mr. Hyde / Robert Louis Stevenson   113
Don Quixote / Miguel de Cervantes   123
Fathers and Sons / Ivan Turgenev   133
The Good Earth / Pearl S. Buck   145
Great Expectations / Charles Dickens   156
Gulliver's Travels / Jonathan Swift   169
Heart of Darkness / Joseph Conrad   180
Jane Eyre / Charlotte Brontë   192
Kon-Tiki / Thor Heyerdahl   204
Life with Father / Clarence Day   216
The Little World of Don Camillo /
    Giovanni Guareschi   227
Lost Horizon / James Hilton   237
Lust for Life / Irving Stone   250
The Mayor of Casterbridge / Thomas Hardy   263

Moby Dick / Herman Melville   275
Mutiny on the Bounty /
     Charles Nordhoff and James Norman Hall   289
Oedipus the King / Sophocles   302
Of Human Bondage / W. Somerset Maugham   315
Oliver Twist / Charles Dickens   326
Pride and Prejudice / Jane Austen   340
Pygmalion / George Bernard Shaw   352
The Red Badge of Courage / Stephen Crane   362
The Return of the Native / Thomas Hardy   373
The Scarlet Letter / Nathaniel Hawthorne   386
Silas Marner / George Eliot   397
A Tale of Two Cities / Charles Dickens   405
Tess of the D'Urbervilles / Thomas Hardy   415
Treasure Island / Robert Louis Stevenson   427
Vanity Fair / William Makepeace Thackeray   439
War and Peace / Lev Tolstoy   451
Wuthering Heights / Emily Brontë   461

INTRODUCTION

This collection of *Teaching Aids* has been prepared for use with the forty titles in the ENRICHED CLASSICS series, published in paperback by Washington Square Press. The series features forty-eight- to sixty-four-page *Reader's Supplements* bound into each book, designed to help the student read with greater understanding and appreciation. The *Teaching Aids* include:

- Objective tests in three forms
- Thought-provoking cluster questions for written or oral book reports or class discussions
- Vocabulary study of selected words located in the text by page references.

It is suggested that teachers planning to use the ENRICHED CLASSICS also secure copies of *A Teacher's Guide to Supplementary Reading,* available from the same publisher. Together, the *Aids* and the *Guide* can serve as the framework within which stimulating lesson plans can be developed for individualized instruction, supplementary reading programs, or the in-depth analysis of single classics. Herewith are brief outlines of the contents of the *Reader's Supplements* and the *Teaching Aids,* including suggestions for integrating the various sections into sound classroom experiences.

I. THE READER'S SUPPLEMENT

A. *Biographical Background*

1. *Contents*

In addition to a picture of the author, there is a brief sketch of his career, with deliberate emphasis on the circumstances that led to the writing of the particular book under discussion.

2. *Application*

a. Volunteers can be asked to do research to supply additional details about the "human interest" aspects of the author's motivation in choosing the narrative stucture and themes; for example, the acting career of Charles Dickens and its relevancy to the creation of the Sidney Carton character in *A Tale of Two Cities*.

b. Some students may wish to investigate the reputation of the author during his own lifetime, his standing in the political community (for example, Jonathan Swift), the extent of his financial rewards for his creative efforts, his romantic involvements, and so forth.

c. In some instances, it may be possible to secure additional illustrations of the writer's residence(s), activities during varying stages of his or her life, appearances with other famous people, travels, and so forth. Exposure to actual visual records establishes greater rapport between reader and author.

d. The artists in the class may wish to create line drawings of details in the author's life for bulletin board display.

B. *Historical Background*

1. *Contents*

The setting of the story, in terms of both time and background detail, is identified through descriptions of actual events of the period so that the reader can evaluate the authenticity of the writer's references to clothing, exterior and interior decoration, political or social movements, and general public attitudes. For example, an understanding of events prior to the outbreak of World War II is essential for a full appreciation of the tragedy that befell Anne Frank.

2. *Application*

a. Space limitations within the *Reader's Supplements* necessarily confine the discussions of the background elements to highlights of the setting as they relate to plot and character structure. Students may be motivated to explore certain aspects in greater depth. For example, a reader of *Treasure Island,* interested in ships and the sea, might report to the class on the many nautical terms used by Stevenson. A partial list is typical:

Note: An entry like *4T* next to a word is a page reference to the text of the novel—meaning p. 4 Top (M-middle, B-bottom).

cove 4T
swabs 17M
latitude, longitude 41B
fathoms 42M
quays 51M
boatswain (bo's'n) 51B
keel 59T
lanyard 67M
bowsprit 70M

mizzen-top 78M
luff 78M
foresail 78M
scuppers 87B
three bells 109T
gunwale (gun'l) 115T
yawed 157B
starboard 176M
shrouds 181T

Illustrations accompanying the explanations will, of course, be most helpful.

b. With certain books, an evaluation of background elements as they compare or contrast to current conditions would lead to a challenging group discussion. Students who are disturbed by Mark Twain's references to Jim in *The Adventures of Huckleberry Finn* might want to investigate the extent, if any, of the author's racism or the desirability of eliminating racial epithets from established literary masterpieces.

C. *Pictorial Background*

1. *Contents*

At least seventeen, and as many as twenty-five, illustrations are reproduced from authentic graphic sources of the period dealt with in the book (photographs, line drawings, woodcuts, etchings, paintings, lithographs). The illustrations are arranged in the order of plot chronology, each representing a key background element in a highlight of the narrative. Stress is laid on buildings, dress, implements, conveyances, social customs, significant historical events—all aimed at helping the reader *see* people, places, and things, as well as read about them.

2. *Application*

a. The inherent appeal of illustrations makes a more attractive book, especially as this factor applies to the less eager reader.

b. With the details of the setting clearly established, students get the reassurance they need to try to read books that might otherwise seem far removed from their interests and environment, or too remote in time and place.

c. The illustrations can serve as the initial sources for student reproductions that become stimulating bulletin board displays. Moreover, this section is a great source of ideas for original book jacket layouts and blurbs.

d. Here is a built-in *sampler* to help the student choose a book that he hopes will be right for him. The teacher can use the illustrations to support suggestions made during individual book conferences.

e. For class or school dramatizations of scenes derived from literature, the illustrations supply important information about costumes and stage sets.

f. At the head of each illustration is a substantial quotation from the book, pointing up the pertinence of both the picture and the plot highlight. A specific page reference makes it possible to locate the quotation in the text. Thus, readers have a quick means of reviewing the entire story line—or only those portions that preceded the point at which they stopped reading.

g. For creative students, a proposed extension of the number of illustrations might prove to be a challenging departure from the routine report. The guide questions might be:

If we were to add twelve more illustrations, where would you suggest they be inserted? Why?

What detail of the plot segment would you select as symbolizing the main point?

If you were drawing the picture yourself, what would you include in the pictorial detail? (Some students may prefer to do the actual drawings!)

h. Some teachers, seeking alternatives to standard written reports, may find the illustrations fruitful sources for composition projects, in-class essay tests, or research assignments.

i. The illustrations aid in developing greater insight into character development and cultural differences. Various suggested after-reading activities can thereby be enriched: "Letters Between Characters," "The Complete Confession," "Diary of a Character," "This Is Your Life," "Round-table Discussions," and "Script Possibilities," to cite a few examples.

j. Students who need help in determining the important elements of plot and theme can use the illustrations as guides for this purpose.

D. *Visual Glossary*

1. *Contents*

This section is omitted in some titles because of the paucity of challenging terms. However, where the *Visual Glossary* does appear, words are selected that would be difficult to define but would be readily understood if visually presented. Original line drawings are prepared. Preference is given to items of apparel, implements, weapons, and so forth. For example, words like *hyssop, troika, halbert, quarterdeck, portmanteau,* and *cob* come alive through the drawings.

2. *Application*

a. Several of the suggestions made in connection with the illustrations of plot highlights are equally applicable here.

b. Space limitations have often prevented the representation of more than twelve background words. Certainly, the class artists may want to go through the book to look for additional line-drawing possibilities.

c. This may sound like an overly ambitious project, but it is quite possible of completion with superior students. Working in committees (writers and artists), several classes can concentrate on a substantial number of books commonly read by their colleagues, extract words worthy of line representation, and ultimately develop a modest picture dictionary! (In lieu of reports!)

d. During vocabulary instruction periods, teachers can use this section to demonstrate how important it is to look for an illustration of a word whenever possible; how meanings are retained more easily if they can be visually associated; how even abstract words can be mastered through symbolic image (for example, *anarchy* associated with the classic picture of the bewhiskered bomb-thrower).

E. *Literary Allusions and Notes*

1. *Contents*

Selected literary allusions, name and fact references, and foreign expressions are explained, and the precise reason for the author's use of these terms is carefully indicated in each instance.

2. *Application*

a. Again, space limitations have prevented an exhaustive treatment of all such terms. Students can be asked to complete the lists instead of preparing reports.

b. Discussions of, or reports on, style can be enriched by an analysis of the extent to which the author uses allusions and his skill in doing so.

F. *Critical Excerpts*

1. *Contents*

Brief excerpts, rarely more than a paragraph in length, are quoted from pieces written by outstanding critics who have analyzed the book and the author's strengths and weaknesses. Excerpts are grouped around specific writing skills—characterization, style, plot development, verisimilitude—and, wherever possible, conflicting critical views are juxtaposed. Often, original editorial comments are added, directing the reader to do his own analysis of the skills and ideas in question. Specific page references send the reader back to selected passages to verify or refute a critic's statement. No conclusions are drawn for the student, but he is stimulated into making independent decisions about literary values.

2. *Application*

a. This section can be used extensively to achieve the aim of helping students to develop their own critical judgments of the books they read.

b. Frequent examination of the critical matter in various ENRICHED CLASSICS can also lead toward a greater appreciation and understanding of the differing literary types.

c. Interesting oral reports can be delivered in which the students attempt to refute the findings of respected critics.

d. If the activity "Author Meets the Critics" is used, the excerpts can become the sources for the questions by the "critics."

e. Similarly, in round-table discussions, the critical comments can generate a flow of ideas channeled into specific areas of investigation.

f. In connection with the guide questions (see *A Teacher's Guide to Supplementary Reading*) for directing the preparation of creative written book reports, the excerpts can help the students find some of the answers they need to produce an original piece.

g. The superior readers may be motivated to further reading in the original sources from which the excerpts were taken.

h. Regular examination of the critical material should enable many students to apply some of the approved writing techniques to their own compositions.

II. TEACHING AIDS

A. *Objective Tests*

1. *Contents*

Testing material for each book is presented through twenty-five multiple-choice questions on the plot highlights, a ten-unit matching exercise, and fifteen fill-ins.

2. *Application*

a. By duplicating the tests, for which the publisher's permission is granted, teachers can simultaneously test groups of ENRICHED CLASSICS read by the students. This procedure can offer a change from reports or activities.

b. Teachers interested in using individual titles in class sets have a means of testing the reading before proceeding with the more creative activities associated with group study of a great book.

B. *Ideas for Written or Oral Book Reports or Class Discussions*

1. *Contents*

At least ten searching problem questions are presented to stimulate depth analysis of the features of the book. As the title of this section implies, the questions are suited for almost any activity involving writing or speaking skills. It might be added that few of the questions can be answered without a thorough reading of the entire book.

2. *Application*

a. "In-class themes" can quite readily be developed from the problem questions listed in this section.

b. Instead of the standard report, answers to several of the questions might provide a sound basis for training in writing "professional" reviews.

c. By having any single set of problem questions duplicated for distribution to the students, the teacher can thereby train students in preparing analytical questions on the books they are reading. Subsequently, another variation from standard reports might be the preparation by a student of a similar set for his book.

C. *Vocabulary Study*

Research indicates that it is unrealistic to expect students to add more than a handful of new words to their vocabularies as the result of reading any single book. Progress in this area is relatively slow and should be handled as a cumulative process rather than a feat of memory in mastering long word lists. Each vocabulary group is presented, therefore, in the form of a diagnostic test. It is suggested that the diagnosis for an individual title should lead to the compilation of a list of perhaps twenty-five to thirty words for general class study. It is further suggested that, for individual word study, teachers may wish to duplicate the following "Vocabulary Building Guide" (based on the words found in Robert Louis Stevenson's *Dr. Jekyll and Mr. Hyde*) so that all students will have a copy for their own purposes.

1. *Vocabulary Building Guide*

Your best means of increasing your vocabulary is through extensive reading. Because the textual background

frequently makes their meanings clear, strange words gradually become familiar to you and eventually become part
of your functional vocabulary. However, it is unwise to attempt to learn every new word you come across in a
book. In general, you might follow these practices:

a. If you meet a word for the first time, do your best
to work out its meaning from the sense of the sentence or
paragraph in which it appears. If this is imposssible, don't
worry about it. Even if you miss a word here and there,
you will still be able to follow the main ideas.

For example, the following words are not likely to appear very often in your reading. Page references have been
supplied so that you can reexamine the context in which the
word is used.

catholicity (p. 2M):	universality, comprehensive quality
distained (p. 4T):	discolored
holograph (p. 11B):	document wholly handwritten by author
presentment (p. 12B):	appearance, representation
conveyancing (p. 14M):	drawing up transfers of property
troglodytic (p. 20B):	like a caveman or ape, coarse, brutal
pede claudo **(p. 23T):**	with lame or halting foot
insensate (p. 31M):	unfeeling, blind
farrago (p. 80B):	mixture
bull's eye (p. 83T):	lantern
transcendental (p. 87B):	superhuman, visionary, abstract
bravos (p. 98T):	daring villains, hired assassins

b. If you come across a word that looks vaguely familiar (perhaps you've seen it two or three times before),
circle it lightly in pencil, or jot it down on a piece of paper
if the book is not yours, *but keep on reading!* Don't destroy the continuity of your reading by rushing to a dictionary to look up each new word. Again, do what you

can to work out the general meaning from the context, and if you have some spare time later, consult a dictionary for the precise meanings, and take another look at how the word is used in the original sentence. That's all!

The following list contains words you may have seen before and will see again. Some of them you may know rather well, and you would prefer to transfer them to the third group below. Otherwise, study the meanings carefully, check again with the original sentences, and make no further special efforts to learn them.

balderdash (p. 14T):	nonsense
concourse (p. 16B):	assemblage, gathering
baize (p. 38T):	coarse fabric that resembles felt
carbuncles (p. 41B):	shiny red stones
sedulously (p. 43B):	diligently, industriously
amities (p. 49T):	friendly relations
diaphanous (p. 58B):	of delicate and transparent texture
debility (p. 83M):	weakness, feebleness
accoutrement (p. 84M):	attire, dress
minims (p. 86T):	smallest liquid measure, each about a drop
ebullition (p. 86M):	bubbling, boiling
prodigy (p. 87T):	miracle, wonder
turpitude (p. 88B):	vileness, depravity
aura (p. 92B):	distinctive atmosphere
effulgence (p. 92B):	brilliance, splendor
vicarious (p. 98B):	enjoyed by one person through his sympathetic participation in the experience of another person
obsequiously (p. 111T):	servilely, fawningly
amorphous (p. 114M):	formless, shapeless

c. There will be some words that you will meet for perhaps the fifth or sixth time. These are the ones worth doing something about, because you have proof that they are used frequently. *Underline each of them,* or jot them down, but keep on reading! After you have finished the book, select thirty or fewer of this group (don't try to be overly ambitious!) and proceed in an orderly fashion to learn as many of them as time permits. Here's how:

- Look up each word in a dictionary that has good etymological references.
- Note the spelling; say the word aloud. Unless you make yourself familiar with the word *visually and orally,* your mind will tend to reject it for use.
- Check the source of the word, its etymology, its breakdown into prefix, stem or root, and suffix (if any).
- Go back to the original sentence in the book, and decide what meaning the author had in mind when he used the word.
- Now divide the set of words into three groups:

    ——those that can most easily be remembered because their interesting history provides a clue to their meaning

    > *Example:* **pecuniary**—from the Latin *pecunia* (money); originally, property in cattle, from *pecus* (cattle or livestock)
    > In early days, a man's wealth was measured by the number of cattle he owned. Only later did a man's wealth depend on the amount of money he had.

    ——those that come from a family of words, all of which have a common root and can best be remembered by association with one another

    > *Example:* **impending**—*im* (in) $+$ *pendere* (to hang)
    > hanging over, menacing, threatening
    > SEE: append, appendix, depend, ex-

pend, pendant, suspend, independent, pending, pendulum,
perpendicular, suspense

——those that had best be mastered directly, but for
which you can perhaps invent your own clue or
association

Example: **imperious**—lordly, domineering
CLUE: like an emperor in behavior

- After you have arranged your words into appropriate
groups and have worked out the memory aids, construct brief paragraphs containing five or more of the
words. Use only spaces and definitions in the paragraph, and list the words underneath. Later, for review, you can practice inserting the proper word in
the space before its definition, thus:

Poole seemed _____ (notably) qualified to be Dr.
Jekyll's butler. Although he was careful about _____
(correct behavior), he _____ (habitually) regarded Mr.
Hyde with _____ (strong dislike). Often he _____
(meditated) about the _____ (difference) between his
master and the apparently _____ (evil) Mr. Hyde. At
a _____ (later) time, when he feared his master had
been _____ (treacherously) murdered, Poole proved
himself very _____ (shrewd) in seeking Mr. Utterson's
help.

repulsion	malign	insidiously
ruminated	disparity	inveterately
astute	subsequent	
proprieties	eminently	

Note: At first, you may have some difficulty
doing these paragraphs. However, as
you acquire experience with them, you
will find the exercise an interesting

challenge, gradually easier to do, and, of course, immensely valuable for making the words a part of your everyday vocabulary. There is no better way of mastering new words than by forcing yourself to use them in speech and writing.

• For further review, you might try a daily reminder trick. Write a word on a card; on the reverse side list the derivation, family connection (if any), other memory prods, and a sentence using the word. One way or another, make it your business to use that word that day at least two or three times. The most unlikely words can be slipped in somewhere, even if it means using a friend or associate as your guinea pig.

2. Diagnostic Test

Here is a list of words taken from *Dr. Jekyll and Mr. Hyde*. They have been arranged in self-test fashion so that you can eliminate those that you already know and can concentrate on the ones that require intensive study as outlined above.

1M	eminently	scantily	notably	partially
3B	sinister	worthy	straight	evil
3B	sordid	vile	candid	excellent
7B	proprieties	owners	mistakes	correct behavior
14M	protégé	protector	marvel	one under another's care
23T	condoned	pardoned	completed	accused
23T	iniquity	virtue	wickedness	unfairness
26M	heresies	rumors	accepted doctrines	unauthorized opinions
26M	blatant	noisy	hesitant	quiet
26M	ruthlessly	kindly	pitilessly	carelessly
34T	hypocrisy	honesty	cruelty	false pretense

35T	connoisseur	playboy	tasteless one	critical judge
39B	ruminated	argued	meditated	acted rashly
42B	elicited	hid	drew forth	acted illegally
51T	inscrutable	unhappy	understood	incomprehensible
53M	repulsion	reform	attraction	strong dislike
68T	malefactor	maker	evildoer	sympathetic friend
73T	blasphemies	lies	pious remarks	irreverencies
78B	morbid	glum	unwholesome	healthful
81B	pungent	bland	penetrating	punishing
83B	incipient	final	receipt	beginning
84M	disparity	difference	disposition	likeness
86M	metamorphoses	changes	marvels	constancies
86M	scrutiny	scolding	oversight	close examination
87M	enigmas	riddles	proofs	evident truths
87B	derided	ridiculed	separated	praised
88M	incredulous	gullible	unbelievable	unbelieving
89M	imperious	lordly	impish	humble
89B	duplicity	variety	deception	sincerity
90T	inveterately	habitually	seldom	youthfully
91T	incongruous	comic	harmonious	inconsistent
91T	denizens	foreigners	inhabitants	tourists
91T	infallibly	unsteadily	mistakenly	unerringly
91B	extraneous	foreign	additional	applicable
95M	lethal	deadly	permissive	curative
98T	pecuniary	intellectual	monetary	peculiarly
99T	malign	evil	envious	virtuous
99T	avidity	coldness	indifference	greediness
99M	insidiously	sideways	treacherously	scrupulously
99M	infamy	dishonor	youth	high repute
99M	connived	made	denounced	cooperated secretly
100B	comely	ugly	good-looking	hearty
105M	propensity	tendency	propriety	disinclination
108T	beneficent	blissful	charitable	barbarous
108B	subsequent	later	underneath	previous
111T	astute	shrewd	naïve	harsh
113M	impending	blessing	menacing	elapsing
114T	phenomena	events	hopes	tricks
114T	poignant	unfelt	touching	steely
115M	acquiescence	rejection	acceptance	acquisition

Teachers interested in using the ENRICHED CLASSICS with their students, or in learning more about them, are invited to write to the publisher for available brochures that give details about educational discounts and examination copies. Address all mail to:

Washington Square Press
Educational Division—ENRICHED CLASSICS
630 Fifth Avenue, New York, N.Y. 10020

Teaching Aids

for

THE ADVENTURES OF
HUCKLEBERRY FINN

Ernest Hemingway said: ". . . all modern American literature comes from one book by Mark Twain called *Huckleberry Finn.*" Here is a rollicking story that evokes a period of romantic excitement and dangerous adventure along the mighty Mississippi River. It was a time and place Mark Twain knew well. His recreation of the riverboats, the country folk, the lynch mobs, the thieves and shysters, and, particularly, his creation of Huckleberry Finn and the runaway slave, Jim, have made this book his masterpiece. It has a twofold appeal: on the surface, the uproarious episodes that provide the flavor of a picaresque novel; and underneath, profound observations on the seamier side of mankind.

I. *Objective Test*

In the space provided at the left, insert the *letter* of the correct choice from among those offered; for example:

....c....   The name of the author of this book is (a) Charles Dickens (b) Tom Jones (c) Mark Twain (d) Nathaniel Hawthorne

.... 1. Tom proved his honesty early by (a) leaving five cents for the "borrowed" candles (b) telling the truth about Huck (c) refusing to aid Jim (d) returning what the gang stole

.... 2. Jim became a celebrity when he (a) told how the witches rode him (b) did tricks with a rope (c) found a treasure (d) joined Tom's pirates

.... 3. Miss Watson's comments about religion and Providence (a) persuaded Huck to remain with the Widow Douglas (b) influenced Pap to reform (c) attracted Tom's attention (d) were unattractive to Huck

.... 4. Huck's father forbade the boy's (a) smoking (b) drinking (c) stealing (d) going to school

.... 5. Huck, before being taken away by Pap, discovered that he (a) hated all adults (b) could bear the Widow's ways (c) really liked the old man (d) was glad to leave

.... 6. Huck failed to convince Mrs. Loftus that he was a girl because he (a) walked like a boy (b) talked like a boy (c) had fixed his hair poorly (d) brought the needle to the thread

.... 7. When Huck's father's body was found (a) Huck was glad Pap was dead (b) Judge Thatcher became Huck's legal guardian (c) Jim covered the body to spare Huck (d) Huck realized he would miss Pap

.... 8. Jim expressed doubt about Solomon's wisdom because (a) Jim knew nothing about the biblical king (b) Solomon had suggested a baby be cut in two (c) Solomon lived too lavishly (d) Jim opposed all kings

.... 9. Huck saved Jim from the hunters of runaway slaves by (a) claiming Jim was his property (b) hiding Jim in the wigwam (c) pretending not to know Jim (d) suggesting that there was smallpox on the raft

.... 10. Huck felt commendable regret when he (a) lied to Aunt Sally (b) quarreled with Tom (c) hoodwinked the Duke (d) fooled Jim

.... 11. Jim was eager to get to Cairo because he (a) craved travel (b) had friends there (c) thought he could get to "free territory" from there (d) knew he would be safe

.... 12. Emmaline Grangerford was (a) Harney's secret love (b) Huck's close friend (c) refined and inquisitive (d) morbidly fascinated by death

.... 13. The reason for the Grangerford-Shepherdson feud had been (a) a jilted bride (b) Col. Grangerford's secret (c) an accidental killing (d) forgotten

.... 14. The King was a (a) confidence man (b) forger (c) murderer (d) bank robber

.... 15. When the King told the camp meeting he was a reformed pirate, the people (a) threatened him with violence (b) contributed to a fund to reform other buccaneers (c) refused to believe him (d) demanded he share his loot

.... 16. The attempted lynching of Col. Sherburn was precipitated by (a) the Royal Nonesuch (b) the death of Boggs (c) Jim's escape (d) the disappearance of the gold

.... 17. The King managed to seem very well informed about Peter Wilks by (a) studying old newspapers (b) getting information from one of his contacts (c) observing the Duke's discoveries (d) "pumping" a gullible native

.... 18. Huck didn't report the King and the Duke because (a) he was afraid they would make trouble for Jim (b) they reminded him of Pap (c) he feared reprisals against himself (d) he was impressed with their rank

.... 19. Huck resigned himself to damnation when he (a) tore up his letter to Miss Watson (b) allowed the Duke and the King to be apprehended (c) helped with the Royal Nonesuch (d) decided to give Jim up

.... 20. Tom rejected Huck's escape plan for Jim because it (a) was impractical (b) was too simple (c) was inconsiderate of the Phelpses (d) had been tried before

.... 21. As a feature of the escape, Jim had to sleep (a) on the floor (b) with a grindstone under his mattress (c) in an upright position (d) in the tool shed

.... 22. One of the more extreme features of Tom's escape plan was (a) subduing one of the guards (b) letting the Phelpses know when Jim was to escape (c) drugging the dogs (d) stealing ammunition

.... 23. Aunt Sally stopped interrogating Huck when (a) she saw the butter (b) he collapsed (c) she heard the commotion (d) Tom appeared

.... 24. Jim was freed through a (a) shooting (b) purchase (c) will (d) sacrifice

.... 25. At the end, Huck decided to (a) return to the Widow Douglas (b) go with Aunt Polly (c) run away again (d) go into partnership with Tom

Answers

1-a, 2-a, 3-d, 4-d, 5-b, 6-d, 7-c, 8-b, 9-d, 10-d, 11-c, 12-d, 13-d, 14-a, 15-b, 16-b, 17-d, 18-a, 19-a, 20-b, 21-b, 22-b, 23-a, 24-c, 25-c

II. *Alternate Objective Tests*

A. Matching

Before each number in the column on the left, write the *letter* of the item in the column on the right that matches:

.... 1. Miss Sophia
.... 2. Jim
.... 3. Bridgewater
.... 4. Mr. Wilks's brothers
.... 5. Miss Watson
.... 6. Dauphin
.... 7. Tom's idea of ransomed
.... 8. Uncle Silas Phelps

a. the King
b. dead
c. was shot
d. runaway
e. the Duke
f. murderers
g. Englishmen
h. Harney Shepherdson

.... 9. Boggs

...... 10. Bill and Jake

i. Huck's aunt

j. gullible

k. Jim's owner

l. was lynched

Answers

1-h, 2-d, 3-e, 4-g, 5-k, 6-a, 7-b, 8-j, 9-c, 10-f

B. Fill-ins

From the column on the right, select the item that best completes each statement below, and write it in the space provided:

1. Huck tried to fool Jim by claiming that he had not left the _____.
2. The leader of the mob that threatened Col. Sherburn was _____.
3. Mary Jane gave her money to _____.
4. Huck admired Tom's _____.
5. Tom had gotten some of the ideas he talked to Huck about from _____.
6. Huck had a struggle with his _____.
7. Huck hid Wilks's money in a _____.
8. Tom "let on" the Sunday school picnic was a group of _____.
9. The new judge in town was frustrated in his efforts to reform _____.
10. A determined enemy of the bogus uncles from the beginning was _____.
11. Peter Wilks's body was exhumed to examine a _____.
12. The character who felt guilty over the way a child was treated was _____.
13. Jim was sure they would have bad luck because of a _____.
14. Huck masqueraded as _____.

style

freedom

Pap

Dr. Robinson

snakeskin

George Jackson

spoons

Jim

Miss Watson

Don Quixote

Aunt Sally

Davy Crockett

raft

the King

conscience

Buck Harkness

Arabs

coffin

candles

tattoo

15. Because of the boys' pranks, Aunt
Sally had trouble counting her _____.

Answers

1-raft, 2-Buck Harkness, 3-the King, 4-style, 5-Don Quixote,
6-conscience, 7-coffin, 8-Arabs, 9-Pap, 10-Dr. Robinson, 11-tattoo,
12-Jim, 13-snakeskin, 14-George Jackson, 15-spoons

III. *Ideas for Written or Oral Book Reports or Class Discussions*

1. Mark Twain once said, "Humor must not professedly teach, and it must not professedly preach, but it
must do both if it would live forever." You can understand
that it is possible to read *The Adventures of Huckleberry
Finn* and be aware merely of the humor, the adventures,
the characters, and the good story. Now that you have finished the book, see whether or not you can find the teaching and the preaching. What lessons does Mark Twain,
despite his humor, try to teach? What does he preach
against? What character traits, behavior patterns, and attitudes does he seem to favor?

2. The relationship between Huck and Tom is an interesting one. Tom, being watched over by his Aunt Polly,
was once threatened with severe punishment if he associated with Huck, the ragged son of the town drunkard.
Yet Tom continues to seek Huck's company. Why? You
notice that Huck always seems to be happy with Tom.
Why? While Huck often says that he "takes no stock in"
many of Tom's wild ideas, he follows Tom's instructions
and admires Tom's brains and his methods of handling
situations. Why? Analyze the basis of this friendship, and
decide whether or not it is a friendship that is destined to
last through the years.

3. As the book progresses, we get to know Jim very
well—to know him and to love him. At first, he seems to
us merely a simple, unlettered person, beset by superstitions and by his enslaved position. Later, we see other

facets of Jim's character, such as his loyalty, his affectionate regard for Huck, his tender concern for the sick Tom, and his willingness to follow Tom's ridiculous instructions at the risk of his own safety and freedom. While Jim called Huck his best friend, surely Huck had no better friend than Jim. How could Huck have managed without Jim? Consider Jim's words and actions throughout the book, and try to compose an accurate sketch of his character.

4. It has been said that most of us are creatures of habit, custom, and law. What does this statement mean? Why do some of us play the game of life according to the rules, never questioning them? How do some of us find release from regulation and control, even though outwardly we seem to be conforming? Finally, what makes some of us rebel completely at a certain point and just take off in search of what we hope will be complete personal freedom? To what extent is one's basic acceptance or rejection of so-called responsible behavior influenced by each of the following: parents, home life, neighborhood, economic or social status, education, friends or associates, the nature of the world? Why do many readers identify with Huck, even though his adventures took place at another time and in another place? How does reading about Huck enable us to test our theories of an individual's response to responsibility in terms of circumstance, important influences, and maturity?

5. In considering the question of young people's desire to escape from responsibilities, regulations, and perhaps overbearing adults, an important distinction must be drawn. How does the *desire* to escape under certain conditions differ from the *need* to escape under other conditions? For example, analyze Huck's relationship with his father. Why is Pap so opposed to education? Why does he, during his drunken delirium, regard Huck as the "Angel of Death"? Reviewing all that Huck has to endure living with his father, why is running away the only sensible thing he can do? What segments of our population, like Huck, cannot even begin to solve their problems until they have escaped from their immediate environment? In summary,

when is escape an act of cowardice or stupidity; when is it an act of courage or good sense?

6. In recent years, some people have expressed the idea that when a law or attitude is morally wrong one should refuse to accept it. What examples can you give of people who have acted on this principle? What do you think of the idea generally? How does Huck handle the idea in respect to Jim? To what extent is his decision not to turn Jim in attributable to a belief that slavery is wrong? To what extent is it attributable only to his affection for Jim? In either case, why does it take strength of character to act as Huck does? How is his basic decency revealed even more sharply when it is contrasted to the behavior of the men looking for runaway slaves? On the other hand, the Grangerfords and the Shepherdsons live strictly by the code of chivalry, and conduct their feud with what they consider to be great strength of character. What label would you apply to their actions—*courageous* or *stupid*? Why? How is Huck able to defy laws and attitudes whereas the feudists can't seem to break with tradition? Which of the actions shows greater strength of character? Why?

7. In his description of the activities of the swindlers and their intended victims, Mark Twain presents some of his sharpest criticism of mankind. What does the account of the practices of the Duke and the Dauphin tell us about the people who were taken in by them? What does the Boggs incident with Col. Sherburn tell about the ordinary man in the small town of that day? What motivates many people when they act in a mob such as the one that threatened Col. Sherburn? How would the two scoundrels have handled the problem Huck faced about turning in Jim as a runaway? How often do confidence men take advantage of people today? What is the best way to protect oneself against them? To what extent is the pessimism Mark Twain exhibited in later life already evident in this book?

8. An author has developed a character successfully when he includes change and, in the case of a youngster, growth toward maturity. In considering whether or not Huck has been well developed by Twain, include answers to these questions:

a. What additional knowledge about people and the problems of life has Huck acquired by the time he get to the Phelpses' farm?

b. What decision does Huck finally come to about his relations to society when he decides to help Jim escape again?

c. How is Huck's agreeing to Tom's nonsensical plan of escape an example of a backward step we all take as we move toward maturity?

d. What evidence can you offer from the text to support the view that, although Huck abdicates leadership to Tom, Huck's more mature grasp of the realities of this and other situations is still clear?

Find other examples of change and growth toward maturity in Huck, and make a final estimate of Twain's effectiveness in developing the character of Huck.

9. In analyzing Mark Twain's style of writing, critics often refer to the literary devices he used to enrich his narrative. Look up the meaning of each of the following terms, think about the example offered, and find at least one other example for each literary device:

satire (the description of the people at the camp meeting)

irony (the way the two confidence men "pay" for their escape)

symbolism (the broader meaning of the river, the raft, Jim, Huck)

allegory (the journey downriver, the story of the Duke and the Dauphin)

foreshadowing (Huck's early thoughts about helping a runaway slave).

One other device is worthy of consideration: *point of view,* that is, through whose eyes and mind the reader is receiving the story. In this case, of course, it is a first-person narrator (Huck). What advantages or disadvantages did the author have in adopting this point of view? How might the story have been different if Tom had told it, or Jim?

10. Some critics have expressed disappointment at the way the book reaches its concluding episodes after Huck arrives at the Phelpses' place. They have gone as far as to say that the book goes downhill then, that Mark Twain deserted his artistic purpose to introduce conventional or melodramatic elements that detract from the quality of the central development. What are your feelings about the concluding chapters? To what extent did you experience a letdown? On the other hand, perhaps you feel that the ending was perfectly reasonable, consistent with the general direction of the novel, and well conceived. Take either position and defend it with specific references to details and structure.

IV. *Vocabulary Study*

Diagnostic Test

16B	ingots	logs	metal bars	bones
17T	ambuscade	charge	hidden attack	surrender
29B	temperance	moderation	excess	anger
36M	nabob	guide	salesman	rich man
37M	infernal	hellish	sleepy	devout
39T	wallowed	floundered	strode	drowned
44B	slough	plateau	mudhole	pavement
52B	brash	timid	saucy	genuine
66M	reticule	handbag	fence	medicine
68T	rummaged	lost	searched	drank
71T	calico	cotton cloth	wool	rayon
82B	harrow	broom	buggy	cultivating tool
83M	thicket	plain	dense shrubbery	swamp
88M	shrivel	swell	wither	drop
92M	careened	raised	straightened	tilted
125M	wince	draw back	laugh	cry
130B	pensive	thoughtless	thoughtful	rash
132B	impaired	improved	redone	damaged
146M	cavorting	romping	standing	sleeping

156T	phrenology	coin collecting	witchcraft	head shape analysis
156T	mesmerism	truism	hypnotism	prism
156M	degraded	upgraded	dug	debased
157B	lineal	of direct descent	curving	interrupted
157B	felons	cures	heroes	criminals
159M	premature	too late	too early	too old
163M	haughty	proud	bashful	lowly
165M	histrionic	plain	theatrical	musical
168B	contrite	glad	regretful	tight
169B	benefactor	good health	enemy	helper
175B	contumely	praise	courage	scorn
176M	ponderous	light	lively	heavy
178T	illustrious	unknown	famous	dull
187B	acquit	condemn	set free	approve
194T	capered	drew lines	stood still	jumped
196T	gaudy	showy	plain	poor
215B	obsequies	payments	funeral rites	attacks
226M	valid	sound	useless	illegal
235M	raspy	grasping	harsh	soothing
250M	ingenious	stupid	inventive	foreign
278B	stile	set of steps	cabin	hanger
284T	distracted	calmed	refused	confused
293M	audacious	polite	bold	cowardly
304T	contrive	copy	invent	hide
329M	scutcheon	box	knife	metal shield
329M	couchant	standing	lying down	running
329M	azure	blue	gray	tan
331M	tedious	interesting	different	boring
339M	blithesome	gay	somber	heavy
346M	fidgety	calm	sad	restless
353M	singular	strange	ordinary	loud

Answers

ingots-metal bars, *ambuscade*-hidden attack, *temperance*-moderation, *nabob*-rich man, *infernal*-hellish, *wallowed*-floundered, *slough*-mudhole, *brash*-saucy, *reticule*-handbag, *rummaged*-searched, *calico*-cotton cloth, *harrow*-cultivating tool, *thicket*-dense shrubbery, *shrivel*-wither, *careened*-tilted, *wince*-draw back, *pensive*-thoughtful, *impaired*-damaged, *cavorting*-romping, *phrenology*-head shape analysis, *mesmerism*-hypnotism, *degraded*-debased, *lineal*-of direct descent, *felons*-criminals, *premature*-too early, *haughty*-proud, *histrionic*-theatrical, *contrite*-regretful, *benefactor*-helper, *contumely*-scorn, *ponderous*-heavy, *illustrious*-famous, *acquit*-set free, *capered*-jumped, *gaudy*-showy, *obsequies*-funeral rites, *valid*-sound, *raspy*-harsh, *ingenious*-inventive, *stile*-set of steps, *distracted*-confused, *audacious*-bold, *contrive*-invent, *scutcheon*-metal shield, *couchant*-lying down, *azure*-blue, *tedious*-boring, *blithesome*-gay, *fidgety*-restless, *singular*-strange

Teaching Aids

for

THE ADVENTURES OF
TOM SAWYER

Here is the greatest story of American boyhood ever told and a beloved classic wherever books are read. Based on Mark Twain's own adventurous youth, it immortalizes a Mississippi River town and the vigorous characters he knew as a boy. Abounding with the lusty sense of fun so typical of this wonderful American humorist, this book is for all ages and all times. Whether whitewashing a fence, hiding in a graveyard at night, or simply showing off, Tom Sawyer embodies a love of life peculiar to us all, and in his antics we relive our youth or recognize marvelous portraits of the days we are still enjoying.

I. *Objective Test*

In the space provided at the left, insert the *letter* of the correct choice from among those offered; for example:

....b....　　The author of this book is (a) Charles Dickens (b) Mark Twain (c) Edgar Allan Poe (d) Thomas Hardy

.... 1. Tom won a Bible prize by (a) borrowing tickets from Sid (b) emptying his bank account (c) reciting a poem (d) cashing in the rewards of the "whitewash privileges"

.... 2. In the graveyard, Huck and Tom planned to

31

(a) find dead cats (b) frighten Muff Potter
(c) run away (d) get rid of warts

.... 3. During their first date, Becky became angry at
Tom because he (a) said he had been in love
(b) had lied to her father (c) would not give
up his friendship with Huck (d) refused to give
the door knob

.... 4. Injun Joe's grudge against Dr. Robinson involved (a) an old debt (b) a stolen horse (c)
an incurable disease (d) the refusal of food

.... 5. Tom and Huck sealed an oath not to tell what
they had seen in the graveyard by (a) giving
the pirate sign (b) signing a paper in blood
(c) hiding bark under a rock (d) turning
around twice each

.... 6. Some villagers wanted to tar and feather Injun
Joe for (a) being friendly to Muff Potter (b)
threatening Tom (c) hiding evidence (d)
body-snatching

.... 7. Aunt Polly stopped giving Tom the Painkiller
after he (a) became sicker than before (b)
poured it down a crack in the floor (c) gave
some to the cat (d) hid the bottle

.... 8. Joe Harper went to Jackson's Island because he
(a) wanted pirate treasure (b) hated school
(c) loved Becky, too (d) had been whipped
for drinking cream

.... 9. The villagers fired a cannon over the water to
(a) warn the countryside (b) help search for
bodies (c) celebrate a holiday (d) get ready
for a picnic

.... 10. When Tom returned home secretly from Jackson's Island, he (a) left a note (b) told Becky
(c) kissed Aunt Polly (d) obtained supplies

.... 11. The biggest threat to the boys on the island was
(a) homesickness (b) wild animals (c) lack
of food (d) the eerie darkness

.... 12. On the island, Huck Finn taught the boys how
to (a) find rattlesnakes (b) swim under water
(c) smoke pipes (d) build a campfire

.... 13. The three "dead" boys came marching up the church aisle (a) at the beginning of the funeral oration (b) following the services (c) after they were discovered by Aunt Polly (d) as the mourners sang hymns

.... 14. Becky used Alfred Temple to (a) run errands for her (b) make Amy jealous (c) do her lessons (d) make Tom jealous

.... 15. Aunt Polly was convinced of Tom's love for her when (a) she found the piece of bark in his pocket (b) he apologized (c) he agreed to go to Sunday school (d) Sid told her about the visit

.... 16. Tom was punished by the teacher because he (a) spilled ink on Becky's book (b) became fresh in class (c) lied about the torn page for Becky (d) threw a spitball

.... 17. The schoolmaster's wig was snatched off by (a) an irate parent (b) a suspended cat (c) Joe Harper (d) a melancholy girl

.... 18. The boys helped Muff Potter in jail by (a) giving him little gifts (b) promising to testify (c) supplying him with money (d) getting him a lawyer

.... 19. Muff Potter was saved from hanging by (a) Huck Finn's statement (b) Tom's evidence (c) Injun Joe's confession (d) the lawyer's cleverness

.... 20. Huck Finn saved the Widow Douglas from Injun Joe by (a) calling the sheriff (b) warning her in time (c) telling the Welshman about Injun Joe's plan (d) scaring off Injun Joe

.... 21. Becky and Tom were saved from tragedy in the cave when (a) Tom used a kite line (b) the rescuers found a secret passage (c) the sound of the cannon guided them out (d) Tom found an old map

.... 22. Injun Joe died in the cave when (a) his escape was prevented by an iron door (b) he

34 *Teaching Aids for 40 Enriched Classics*

committed suicide (c) he was killed by his partner (d) the sheriff's posse shot him

.... 23. The treasure in the cave (a) amounted to $600 (b) was never recovered (c) amounted to $12,000 (d) was given to the state

.... 24. Each boy's share of the treasure was (a) put out at interest (b) donated to charity (c) used to pay debts (d) returned to the owner

.... 25. Huck consented to being adopted by the Widow Douglas (a) after Tom promised to admit him to the robber gang (b) because he was tired of roaming (c) when he found school attractive (d) after his father agreed

Answers

1-d, 2-d, 3-a, 4-d, 5-b, 6-d, 7-c, 8-d, 9-b, 10-c, 11-a, 12-c, 13-b, 14-d, 15-a, 16-c, 17-b, 18-a, 19-b, 20-c, 21-a, 22-a, 23-c, 24-a, 25-a

II. *Alternate Objective Tests*

A. Matching

Before each number in the column on the left, write the *letter* of the item in the column on the right that matches:

.... 1.	Judge Thatcher	a. Tom's cousin
.... 2.	Mrs. Harper	b. Huck's share at 6 percent
.... 3.	Dr. Robinson	c. A picnic for youngsters
.... 4.	Huck Finn	d. Tom's first love
.... 5.	Amy Lawrence	e. tattletale
.... 6.	Mary	f. Muff Potter's knockout
.... 7.	Joe Harper	g. denied housing Tom and Becky
.... 8.	Sid	h. the Terror of the Seas
.... 9.	Aunt Polly	i. testified against Injun Joe
...... 10.	Widow Douglas	j. lost in the cave
		k. Tom's kiss
		l. the Red-Handed

Answers

1-c, 2-g, 3-f, 4-l, 5-d, 6-a, 7-h, 8-e, 9-k, 10-b

B. Fill-ins

From the column on the right, select the item that best completes each statement below, and write it in the space provided:

1. Tom was curious to see how _____ had reacted to his "death."   Jackson's Island
   tavern
2. Becky and Tom were lost in _____ for three days and nights.   Black Avenger
   wig
3. The boys were afraid that _____ would murder them for revenge.   three
   cry
4. _____ assumed he had committed a murder.   Injun Joe
   Aunt Polly
5. Injun Joe, posing as the _____, dug up the treasure in the haunted house.   hogshead
   blood
   McDougal's Cave
6. His knowledge of the murder, plus the _____ caused Tom to have a miserable summer.   Spaniard
   Muff Potter
7. Tom hopefully expected _____ would have a big funeral.   knife
   smoke
8. _____ was three miles below St. Petersburg.   measles
   boredom
9. The password to the Pirate Crew's greeting was _____.   shovel
   Judge Frazer
10. When Tom played pirate, he called himself the _____.   two
    chalk
11. Huck often slept in a _____.
12. Mr. Dobbins lost his _____ while drawing a map.
13. Joe Harper was the first to _____ on the island.

14. Tom and Huck hid near the _____ to solve Number Two.
15. Injun Joe tried to make his way out of the cave with a _____.

Answers

1-Aunt Polly, 2-McDougal's Cave, 3-Injun Joe, 4-Muff Potter, 5-Spaniard, 6-measles, 7-Judge Frazer, 8-Jackson's Island, 9-blood, 10-Black Avenger, 11-hogshead, 12-wig, 13-cry, 14-tavern, 15-knife

III. *Ideas for Written or Oral Book Reports or Class Discussions*

1. Mark Twain's attitude toward society, especially its weaknesses, is quite clear in the story. Find examples of his distaste for false holiness, snobbery, excessive sentimentality, harsh religious doctrines, fake modesty, lack of feeling for children, uninteresting classrooms. How does the author's rather sharp attack against "sappy women" (p. 253B) compare with some modern attitudes toward being too lenient with criminals? It's easy to find examples of what Twain dislikes about people. What are some characteristics of young people and adults that he obviously finds worthy of hearty approval? Give examples from the story.

2. Most of us, although we pretend not to, have a pet superstition or two. However, the young people and adults of St. Petersburg seemed to have been superstitious about almost everything. Select at least a half-dozen superstitions mentioned in the novel, try to explain their possible origin, and indicate which are retained by some people even today. Incidentally, what superstitions, if any, still bother you? If none, how have you been able to get rid of them?

3. Aunt Polly obviously loved Tom, and, in his own way, the boy returned the affection. What did Aunt Polly offer Tom, scoldings and all, that drew him to her? What was there about Tom that made it difficult to remain angry with him for any length of time? To what extent was Sid

aware of the relationship, and how did he show his displeasure? How did the relationship influence Tom's attitude toward home life, school, and other people? Contrast Huck Finn's attitude toward life, and explain why he probably felt so differently about things.

4. During the course of our daily existence, all of us at times seek escape from the problems that face us. Sometimes we read an exciting book, go to a movie, listen to our favorite music on radio, watch television, or engage in sports. Tom didn't seem particularly interested in sports and certainly didn't have available to him the electronic marvels we enjoy today. What were his main means of escape from scoldings, punishment in school, or being bored? In what ways did his escape devices show his leadership qualities? Apart from following Tom's lead, what were some of the things Huck Finn thought of when he felt the need to escape? How do you account for the differences between the two boys in their attempts to get relief from their problems?

5. Without question, Mark Twain understood the boys and girls about whom he wrote. Consider Tom's fight in the opening chapter, the whitewashing scene, the various activities he suggests involving pirates and robbers, his relationship with Becky Thatcher, even his reactions to the graveyard tragedy. In what respects did he behave like a typical boy? How did his behavior differ, if at all, from that of boys today? How well did the author seem to understand girls, especially in the way he dealt with Becky Thatcher or Amy Lawrence? In relation to Tom's experiences in school, how often do similar incidents occur today?

6. Mark Twain was, of course, known as a humorist. Now, humor can be developed by a writer through situation, character, or language. Find several examples of each technique, and explain how Mark Twain achieved his efforts. What makes most of the humor just as enjoyable today as it was at the time it was first created? *Satire* is a literary device in which the weaknesses, stupidities, and abuses of mankind are held up to ridicule. *Caricature* is another device in which there is deliberate distortion of the

major characteristics of a person, situation, or idea in order, again, to amuse, expose, or make the subject instantly recognizable. Find at least one example of satire and another of caricature; explain how the effect is achieved in each instance.

7. One of the tests of an effective character portrayal is the extent to which the individual grows, changes, achieves greater maturity. Explain how Tom showed growth and increasing maturity in each of the following:

   a. his early meetings with Becky and his handling of the cave danger
   b. his gradual awareness and display of affection for Aunt Polly
   c. his decision to keep the secret about the murder, and then his testimony
   d. his advice to Huck early in the story and toward the end
   e. his early fears of Injun Joe and his later sympathy (p. 251B) at the villain's death.

8. Mark Twain's style of writing has often been praised. Note that he suggests what is wrong with the art of composition (p. 167B)! In his own right, he was a master at introducing color, sound, and selected detail in his descriptions. For example, reread the paragraph in which the coming of morning is described (pp. 115–116). Find other examples of this ability to draw pictures with words. Observe how effectively repetition is used to develop humor, emotional tone, and reality (pp. 107 and 113), as the pirate names of the boys are inserted. Where else is this technique used? Comment on the dialogue used in the story. How believably do the boys and girls speak as boys and girls, and the adults as adults? Judging from what you have read or heard on television, how faithfully have the accents and dialect of the region and period been reproduced?

9. The murder of Dr. Robinson involves a practice that was unfortunately common before this century. Charles Dickens also refers to it in describing Jerry Cruncher's

activities in *A Tale of Two Cities*. What did the towns-people mean when they accused Injun Joe of body-snatching? Who was really responsible for the plan to commit a graveyard robbery? What has replaced the former practice of stealing corpses in order to conduct medical investigation and research? To what extent did the fact that Dr. Robinson was himself participating in a crime decrease your sympathy for him when he was killed?

10. In his early plans for the book, Mark Twain had included a scheme for taking Tom on a "Battle of Life in many lands." This suggests that the original intention was to follow the adventures of Tom Sawyer into adulthood. What do you suppose made Mark Twain change his mind and end the story as he did? How did this change achieve greater unity in the theme and narrative structure? Why would the story have been spoiled if it had continued much beyond where it went? On the other hand, if you believe otherwise, what might it have gained?

IV. *Vocabulary Study*

Diagnostic Test

1B	perplexed	calm	clear	puzzled
4T	contemplate	sleep	consider	ignore
5T	sagacity	wisdom	story	idiocy
6M	unalloyed	mixed	unmixed	united
17T	dilapidated	new	shiny	ruined
19T	intrepid	unafraid	warm	fearful
21M	grotesque	slow	weird	beautiful
28M	disconcerted	upset	calmed	deafened
31B	inevitable	uncertain	unavoidable	unruly
33B	prodigious	extra	ordinary	wonderful
36T	preposterous	silly	sound	long
39M	simpering	controlled	crying	self-conscious
48T	mortified	embarrassed	cemented	exalted
55B	alacrity	sloth	greed	eagerness
57M	animosity	good will	ill will	health
57M	perceptible	vague	lawful	visible
59M	jubilant	joyful	dour	sweet

68B	zephyr	storm	soft breeze	auto
70M	grisly	greasy	lovely	horrible
71M	incantation	silence	chant	estate
74B	accouter-ments	clothes	skins	lies
82T	inarticulately	unclearly	clearly	artfully
89B	lugubrious	happy	stern	sad
91B	colossal	puny	huge	short
94M	ostentatiously	showily	shyly	deeply
98B	infatuated	turned off	carried away	fattened
100T	consternation	delight	star	dismay
101B	apprehensive	brave	fearful	fortunate
105B	succumb	chew	charge	give up
113M	imminent	threatening	delayed	ended
113M	purloined	released	stolen	offered
116T	conflagrations	waters	duties	big fires
117T	ravenous	black	very hungry	birdlike
132M	plausible	untrue	crooked	believable
132B	charily	boldly	cautiously	cleanly
134M	inundation	flood	waste	base
149M	soliloquize	shout	speak to self	debate
152B	vindictive	kind	bright	vengeful
153T	lacerate	soothe	wound	sew
156B	ingenious	inventive	stupid	young
163T	languidly	spiritedly	lazily	quickly
168M	inveterate	fickle	experienced	unchanging
186M	obliterate	draw	erase	unfold
205B	palpable	mushy	cloudy	obvious
211M	catastrophe	style	disaster	blessing
217T	massive	feathery	crowded	heavy
217B	labyrinth	maze	line	lip
233M	reverberations	echoes	silences	words
266T	laudations	complaints	praises	prayers
270B	insipid	tasteless	artistic	lively

Answers

perplexed-puzzled, *contemplate*-consider, *sagacity*-wisdom, *unalloyed*-unmixed, *dilapidated*-ruined, *intrepid*-unafraid, *grotesque*-weird, *disconcerted*-upset, *inevitable*-unavoidable, *prodigious*-wonderful, *preposterous*-silly, *simpering*-self-conscious, *mortified*-embarrassed, *alacrity*-eagerness, *animosity*-ill will, *perceptible*-visible, *jubilant*-joyful, *zephyr*-soft breeze, *grisly*-horrible, *incantation*-chant, *accouterments*-clothes, *inarticulately*-unclearly, *lugubrious*-

sad, *colossal*-huge, *ostentatiously*-showily, *infatuated*-carried away, *consternation*-dismay, *apprehensive*-fearful, *succumb*-give up, *imminent*-threatening, *purloined*-stolen, *conflagrations*-big fires, *ravenous*-very hungry, *plausible*-believable, *charily*-cautiously, *inundation*-flood, *soliloquize*-speak to self, *vindictive*-vengeful, *lacerate*-wound, *ingenious*-inventive, *languidly*-lazily, *inveterate*-unchanging, *obliterate*-erase, *palpable*-obvious, *catastrophe*-disaster, *massive*-heavy, *labyrinth*-maze, *reverberations*-echoes, *laudations*-praises, *insipid*-tasteless

Teaching Aids

for

AND THEN THERE WERE NONE

Ten bodies are found by Scotland Yard inspectors on a deserted island—not another soul in sight, not a single clue! The last line of a nursery jingle had come to a baffling conclusion. A taut drama of a small group of people at the mercy of a vindictive, almost pathological killer, this novel has become a modern classic of the mystery story and has been made into a highly popular motion picture and successful Broadway play.

I. *Objective Test*

In the space provided at the left, insert the *letter* of the correct choice from among those offered; for example:

....b.... The name of the author is (a) Bond (b) Christie (c) Chandler (d) Gardner

.... 1. The original owner of the island had been a millionaire (a) Englishman (b) actress (c) American (d) prince

.... 2. Marston makes quite an impression with his (a) car (b) clothes (c) money (d) speech

.... 3. Vera has been hired by Mrs. Owen as a (a) governess (b) hostess (c) companion (d) secretary

.... 4. Hanging on the wall in each guest room is a (a) sword (b) poem (c) painting (d) bell

.... 5. *The Voice* comes from a (a) window (b) microphone (c) gramophone (d) radio

.... 6. Blore confesses that he is really a (a) detective (b) peddler (c) salesman (d) musician

.... 7. The attitude of Lombard and Marston toward their "crimes" is (a) suspicious (b) casual (c) concerned (d) guilty

.... 8. Macarthur had learned about his wife from a (a) friend (b) fellow officer (c) newspaper account (d) letter

.... 9. Each death is matched by the disappearance of one of the (a) chairs (b) figures (c) coats (d) cups

.... 10. The first murder to convince all that they were being stalked like animals is that of (a) Marston (b) Mrs. Rogers (c) Mr. Rogers (d) Macarthur

.... 11. Just before Miss Brent is found dead, Blore accuses (a) Vera (b) Miss Brent (c) Lombard (d) Rogers

.... 12. The guests become suspicious of Armstrong when they can't find his (a) bag (b) scalpel (c) hypodermic (d) gun

.... 13. Vera is terribly frightened by (a) seaweed (b) a cry (c) a prowler (d) strange noises

.... 14. Miss Brent's wool is used to make a (a) scarf (b) sweater (c) stocking (d) wig

.... 15. In the dead of night, Blore hears (a) voices (b) footsteps (c) growls (d) music

.... 16. A red herring signals the end of (a) Armstrong (b) Blore (c) Rogers (d) Lombard

.... 17. A clock spells the doom of (a) Blore (b) Vera (c) Lombard (d) Armstrong

.... 18. While they are alone near the rocks, Vera manages to take away Lombard's (a) stone (b) knife (c) gun (d) dagger

.... 19. The last one left seems to be (a) Blore (b) Vera (c) Lombard (d) Armstrong

.... 20. The last victim is conquered by a rope and (a) scarf (b) drug (c) club (d) chair

.... 21. Wargrave is shot in the (a) back (b) chest (c) head (d) stomach

.... 22. It turns out that the island was purchased for Owen by (a) Forbes (b) Morris (c) Claythorne (d) Lombard

.... 23. The inspectors from Scotland Yard find (a) several clues (b) no clues (c) a confession (d) a survivor

.... 24. The mystery is finally solved through (a) an eyewitness (b) a trunk (c) records (d) a bottle

.... 25. The master murderer turns out to be the (a) inspector (b) judge (c) doctor (d) secretary

Answers

1-c, 2-a, 3-d, 4-b, 5-c, 6-a, 7-b, 8-d, 9-b, 10-d, 11-b, 12-c, 13-a, 14-d, 15-b, 16-a, 17-a, 18-c, 19-b, 20-d, 21-c, 22-b, 23-b, 24-d, 25-b

II. *Alternate Objective Tests*

A. Matching

Before each number in the column on the left, write the *letter* of the item in the column on the right that matches:

.... 1. Wargrave   a. General
.... 2. Vera Claythorne   b. butler
.... 3. Lombard   c. flashy car
.... 4. Emily Brent   d. Colonel
.... 5. Macarthur   e. policeman
.... 6. Armstrong   f. Justice
.... 7. Tony Marston   g. hosts
.... 8. Blore   h. elderly spinster
.... 9. Thomas Rogers   i. adventurer
...... 10. Owens   j. villager
                          k. Doctor
                          l. teacher
                          m. "South Africa"
                          n. actress

Answers

1-f, 2-l, 3-i, 4-h, 5-a, 6-k, 7-c, 8-m, 9-b, 10-g

B. Fill-ins

From the column on the right, select the item that best completes each statement below, and write it in the space provided:

1. Most of the action occurs on _____ island.	Vera
2. Mr. Blore's assumed name is _____.	robe
3. Lombard receives _____ to pay for his services on the island.	Wargrave
4. Armstrong had once been a witness before _____.	Swan Song
5. When *The Voice* is heard, _____ faints.	Lombard
6. The title of the record is _____.	a letter
7. Vera thinks frequently of her lover _____.	50 pounds
8. The first one to die is _____.	Hugo
9. Armstrong and Blore join _____ to search the island.	Macarthur
10. Most of the guests begin to believe that _____ has gone mad.	Indian
11. The guests are disappointed when _____ fails to appear with his boat.	Fred
12. The murder of Miss Brent is symbolized by a _____.	Dying Swan
13. At one point, Lombard's _____ disappears.	Davis
14. The missing bathroom curtain becomes a _____.	gun
15. Vera's guilt concerns the boy, _____.	Cyril

100 guineas
Marston
bee
Mrs. Rogers
mysterious
rug

Answers

1-Indian, 2-Davis, 3-100 guineas, 4-Wargrave, 5-Mrs. Rogers, 6-Swan Song, 7-Hugo, 8-Marston, 9-Lombard, 10-Macarthur, 11-Fred, 12-bee, 13-gun, 14-robe, 15-Cyril

III. *Ideas for Written or Oral Book Reports or Class Discussions*

1. The plot hinges on the idea that one person decides to punish a group of people. In a real sense, then, the master avenger is acting as judge, jury, and executioner. To what extent was this person justified in doing so? What would you do if you discovered that someone had committed a crime for which he or she could not be punished?

2. We have already noted that the mystery writer does not attempt deep character analysis. Thus, the backgrounds of the guests, as well as of the two servants, are sketched rather hastily. However, each little summary of a challenging moment in a character's life suggests interesting story elements in its own right (for example, Macarthur and the love triangle). Select any one of the background sketches, and expand it into a short story. For a climax, you might try to invent some turn of events that brings exposure of the crime and some sort of punishment. Read a story like "The Telltale Heart" by Edgar Allan Poe for ideas.

3. A mystery story is often called a *whodunit*—a rather inelegant way of suggesting that the main interest for the reader is in solving the problem of "who did it," with *it* referring to the major act of violence in the story. If you were successful in following the clues here and identifying the master avenger before the end of the story, tell when you first began to suspect a particular individual. Trace each of the clues up to the point where you were sure, and justify your reasons for your early decision.

4. This book does not contain Agatha Christie's favorite detective character, Hercule Poirot. Read any one of

the mysteries in which he does appear. Then describe what Poirot might have done had he been one of the guests and decided there was "funny business" going on, after Mrs. Rogers suddenly died.

5. General Macarthur's past suggests that sometimes military commanders use their positions to take personal vengeance on someone who has fallen into their disfavor. What other story have you heard or read that involved a similar situation? You might read *Paths of Glory* by Humphrey Cobb if you have no ideas on this subject.

6. Young Marston is characteristic of many drivers whose recklessness leads to injury and death of others. What can be done to control the opportunities such thoughtless persons have for becoming highway menaces? To what extent does driver education help? What additional laws should be passed?

7. *And Then There Were None* features a lonely island. You have doubtless read or heard other stories in which the scene is a haunted house, an out-of-the-way inn or hotel, a vacation cottage in the off-season, or a room in a strange neighborhood of a city. What characteristics do such places have that lend themselves readily to mystery and intrigue? How important is *mood* in a mystery? Explain.

8. We have already mentioned Hercule Poirot. Other famous sleuths include Perry Mason (Erle Stanley Gardner), Ellery Queen, the Thin Man (Dashiell Hammett), and Philip Marlowe (Raymond Chandler), to mention a few. Select any two of these (or two others of your own choosing) and compare their techniques, indicating which one uses sounder and more believable methods of crime detection.

9. Dr. Armstrong bungles an operation and is responsible for the death of a patient. What safeguards should be used to cut down instances of faulty medical treatment? How is this problem related to periodic publicity given to improper manufacture or use of new drugs?

10. What are your ideas on stories featuring murder and violence? To what extent do they exert harmful influences on readers? Why do they have almost irresistible

appeal? What would you say if someone suggested that all such stories be banned?

IV. *Vocabulary Study*

Diagnostic Test

3M	strenuous	weak	vigorous	straight
12T	recumbent	reclining	stretching	returning
14T	imperceptibly	obviously	unnoticeably	nearly
16M	malevolence	benevolence	innocence	ill will
16B	evasive	straight-forward	not straight-forward	direct
17M	fraternizing	being friendly	avoiding	pledging
18M	dispassion-ately	hotly	calmly	lovingly
24T	fantasy	statue	plume	illusion
24B	reptilian	snaky	bland	clumsy
25M	hussy	wagon	betrothed	loose woman
27M	caustic	soft	sarcastic	lively
29M	bizarre	salable	normal	odd
34M	interposed	removed	joined	inserted
37M	verisimilitude	dream	reality	newness
38T	disembodied	massed	noiseless	bodiless
40T	epistolary	letter writing	printing	religious
40M	iniquitous	clean	equal	sinful
40B	concurred	objected	agreed	climbed
46M	ferret	hide	search out	carry
49T	inert	motionless	light	dear
51T	predatory	escaping	plundering	leaving
51M	capricious	unpredictable	steady	bluish
60T	desultory	tangy	disconnected	steady
61M	ironic	expected	metallic	contradictory
67B	chaotic	orderly	disorderly	frozen
68M	condone	forgive	charge	eat
70M	feasible	useless	changeable	workable
74T	forte	weakness	number	strong point
78M	aversion	fondness	dislike	parody
79M	spasmodically	smoothly	twitchingly	richly
82B	impassive	animated	barred	expressionless
87M	noncommittal	declared	untruthful	position unstated

98M	idiosyncrasy	normalcy	oddity	stupidity
101M	reiterate	restate	continue	conclude
102M	grimace	smile	wry face	weapon
106T	tenacious	releasing	numerous	clinging to
106T	clichés	epigrams	groups	wornout sayings
110B	affably	angrily	pleasantly	obscurely
118M	gimlet	boring tool	plane	shoe
118M	congealed	strained	matched	thickened
126T	meticulously	sloppily	neatly	lightly
126B	lethal	deadly	gassy	gentle
147B	conjuring	prayerful	magical	closing
152T	abortive	successful	surgical	fruitless
155M	lassitude	weariness	energy	desire
160B	feline	canine	slothful	catlike
173T	sadistic	decent	loud	enjoying cruelty
175M	inexorable	unrelenting	forgiving	outside
176M	assuage	ruffle	soothe	scratch
176M	maudlin	gay	tearful	solemn

Answers

strenuous-vigorous, *recumbent*-reclining, *imperceptibly*-unnoticeably, *malevolence*-ill will, *evasive*-not straightforward, *fraternizing*-being friendly, *dispassionately*-calmly, *fantasy*-illusion, *reptilian*-snaky, *hussy*-loose woman, *caustic*-sarcastic, *bizarre*-odd, *interposed*-inserted, *verisimilitude*-reality, *disembodied*-bodiless, *epistolary*-letter writing, *iniquitous*-sinful, *concurred*-agreed, *ferret*-search out, *inert*-motionless, *predatory*-plundering, *capricious*-unpredictable, *desultory*-disconnected, *ironic*-contradictory, *chaotic*-disorderly, *condone*-forgive, *feasible*-workable, *forte*-strong point, *aversion*-dislike, *spasmodically*-twitchingly, *impassive*-expressionless, *noncommittal*-position unstated, *idiosyncrasy*-oddity, *reiterate*-restate, *grimace*-wry face, *tenacious*-clinging to, *clichés*-wornout sayings, *affably*-pleasantly, *gimlet*-boring tool, *congealed*-thickened, *meticulously*-neatly, *lethal*-deadly, *conjuring*-magical, *abortive*-fruitless, *lassitude*-weariness, *feline*-catlike, *sadistic*-enjoying cruelty, *inexorable*-unrelenting, *assuage*-soothe, *maudlin*-tearful

Teaching Aids

for

ANNE FRANK: THE DIARY OF A YOUNG GIRL

This is the true story of a young Jewish girl who lived with seven other people in a secret nest of rooms in Amsterdam. Her diary reveals the life of this group of Jews hiding from the Nazis. It has been called "one of the most moving documents to come out of World War II," and is truly a warm, heartrending revelation of extreme insight and talent; bubbling with amusement, love, and discovery; fresh with the dew of adolescence. Translated into nearly twenty languages, it has been read and loved by more than five million people all over the world.

I. *Objective Test*

In the space provided at the left, insert the *letter* of the correct choice from among those offered; for example:

....b....   *Anne Frank* is a (a) novel (b) biography (c) play (d) short story

.... 1. Anne decides to keep a diary because she (a) doesn't want to hurt her parents' feelings (b) has always kept a diary (c) wants to remember important events of her life (d) has no real friend in whom to confide

.... 2. Anne's family moves from Germany to Holland in 1933 because (a) the Nazis are persecuting

Jewish people (b) her father's company transfers him (c) her father takes a new position in Holland (d) the Franks prefer the Dutch climate

.... 3. Anne leaves the Montessori School because of (a) poor scholarship (b) laws against Jews (c) dislike for the school (d) parental disapproval of the Montessori methods

.... 4. The choice of possessions Anne packs into her school satchel to take into hiding best indicates that she is (a) sentimental (b) intelligent (c) practical (d) stupid

.... 5. Daddy and Anne do most of the unpacking because (a) Mummy and Margot arrive two days late (b) Anne begs to help (c) Mummy and Margot are too upset to work (d) Mummy and Margot are busy preparing meals

.... 6. If Anne were to describe her first impressions of Peter, she would most likely include the words (a) handsome, strong, brave (b) intelligent, studious, quiet (c) shy, gawky, lazy (d) amusing, boisterous, gay

.... 7. According to Anne, the most frequent topic of the quarrels between the Van Daans and the Franks is (a) the cat Mouschi (b) the dishes and linens to be used (c) the use of the living room (d) Anne herself

.... 8. Anne feels most hurt when she is scolded by (a) Daddy (b) Mummy (c) Mrs. Van Daan (d) Mr. Dussel

.... 9. Qualities in her mother that Anne especially dislikes include (a) bad temper, laziness, bad table manners (b) impatience, lack of religion, preference for Margot (c) untidiness, sarcasm, lack of sweetness (d) dependence on Daddy, fearfulness, stupidity

.... 10. Anne's major reaction to Dussel's reports of the sad fate of Jewish friends is one of (a) pride that her father is wiser than others (b) guilt that she has a warm bed (c) joy that she is safe (d) anger at Dussel for telling the stories

.... 11. Mr. Dussel agrees to let Anne have additional use of the table primarily because (a) Anne argues with him (b) Anne refuses to talk to him (c) Daddy talks with him (d) he feels Anne's schoolwork is important

.... 12. When an air raid comes in the night, Anne shows (a) courage and independence (b) lack of concern (c) a degree of fear (d) more fear than any other resident of the "Secret Annexe"

.... 13. Daddy's reaction to Anne's attempts to discuss Mummy with him is usually (a) an unwillingness to discuss the subject (b) an explanation to Anne of Mummy's problems (c) sympathy with Anne's feelings (d) anger at Anne for mistreating Mummy

.... 14. Anne learns that the best thing to do when Mummy annoys her is to (a) cry (b) argue (c) keep quiet (d) go to Daddy

.... 15. Anne's growing love for Peter Van Daan at first makes her (a) miserable (b) puzzled (c) happy (d) angry

.... 16. Anne decides that blame for the Frank-Van Daan quarrels rests on (a) Mrs. Van Daan (b) Mummy (c) Anne herself (d) both families

.... 17. A good excuse for Anne to see Peter is her need to (a) chase the cat in the warehouse (b) get potatoes from the attic (c) do work in the private office (d) read in the kitchen

.... 18. If you are unhappy, Anne's advice would probably be (a) sleep (b) pretend to be gay (c) think of others' unhappiness and feel thankful (d) go outdoors and enjoy nature

.... 19. In her analysis of the past, Anne decides that she used jokes and pranks to (a) entertain others (b) get attention (c) drive away feelings of emptiness (d) prepare to be an actress

.... 20. Anne wants to be a writer because she (a)

hopes to live after her death (b) wishes to be rich (c) longs to prove to Mummy that she has talent (d) dislike mathematics

.... 21. After Daddy receives and is hurt by Anne's letter, Anne herself feels (a) angry (b) hurt (c) ashamed (d) satisfied

.... 22. The important event that occurs on D-Day is (a) the landing of British and American forces in France (b) the landing of British and American forces in Italy (c) the surrender of Hitler (d) the surrender of Japan

.... 23. Anne's advice to one wishing happiness would probably be (a) work and you can earn it (b) you'll get it if you are lucky (c) copy someone else who is happy (d) reveal your true personality to your friends

.... 24. Anne very much admires Winston Churchill for his (a) wisdom (b) ability to express himself well (c) handsomeness (d) courage

.... 25. In her lifetime, Anne reveals her deeper, purer self only to (a) her diary (b) her diary and Peter (c) her diary and Daddy (d) her diary and Margot

Answers

1-d, 2-a, 3-b, 4-a, 5-c, 6-c, 7-d, 8-a, 9-c, 10-b, 11-c, 12-c, 13-a, 14-c, 15-a, 16-d, 17-b, 18-d, 19-c, 20-a, 21-c, 22-a, 23-a, 24-d, 25-a

II. *Alternate Objective Tests*

A. Matching

Before each number in the column on the left, write the *letter* of the item in the column on the right that matches:

.... 1. Boche   a. Het Achterhuis
.... 2. Kitty   b. Mr. Van Daan
.... 3. Pim   c. Henk

```
........  4. Secret Annexe            d. cat
........  5. His Lordship             e. typist
........  6. Miep                     f. goat
........  7. Putti                    g. diary
........  8. Elli                     h. peas
         9. Kerli                     i. furs
......  10. skimming pods             j. Daddy
                                      k. Mrs. Van Daan
                                      l. Dussel
```

Answers

1-d, 2-g, 3-j, 4-a, 5-l, 6-c, 7-b, 8-e, 9-k, 10-h

B. Fill-ins

From the column on the right, select the item that best completes each statement below, and write it in the space provided:

1. For the first four months, there are _____ occupants in the hiding place.
2. At first, _____ people are *not* told of the hiding place.
3. Each resident chooses a place for his _____.
4. Mr. Dussel, a (an) _____, joins the group later.
5. The "rules" of the hideout are prepared by _____.
6. Peter gets bitten by a (an) _____.
7. A problem created by Mouschi is _____.
8. Anne thinks often of her former girl friend _____.
9. Anne upsets her father with a (an) _____.

strawberries
letter
midwife
dentist
rat
Mr. Van Daan
long speech
Lies
seven
Anne
fleas
dog
journalist
bathing
loose hairs
Mr. Frank
wine
three

10. Memories of former wealth are stirred when _____ describes an engagement party.

11. Anne hopes one day to become a (an) _____.

12. A wager on the invasion is made with bottles of _____.

13. There is great activity when boxes of _____ arrive.

14. "Little bunch of contradictions" means _____.

15. The only survivor after the group is arrested is _____.

Miep
yoghurt
apples
eight
talking

Answers

1-seven, 2-three, 3-bathing, 4-dentist, 5-Mr. Van Daan, 6-rat, 7-fleas, 8-Lies, 9-letter, 10-Miep, 11-journalist, 12-yoghurt, 13-strawberries, 14-Anne, 15-Mr. Frank

III. *Ideas for Written or Oral Book Reports or Class Discussions*

1. Anne says of her mother and sister (p. 27B): "Margot's and Mummy's natures are completely strange to me. I can understand my friends better than my own mother —too bad!" What causes such an attitude toward the family among some teenagers? Why is it sometimes easier to get along with friends than with parents, brothers, or sisters? What in particular do parents do that young people consider objectionable? Draw up a list of your major complaints, and then compare them to what Anne enumerates in the March 17, 1944 entry (pp. 160–161). On the other hand, what are the ingredients that enable family members to get along with complete understanding and affection?

2. The constant quarrels with and by the Van Daans are discussed repeatedly by Anne. She asks whether or not

there would be trouble with "whoever one shared a house with." What do you think? What experience have you had or heard about that would seem to support the idea that close quarters under one roof by more than one family inevitably leads to friction? What are the main reasons for such conflict? How much did the fact that they were hiding contribute to the tension, or might it have happened even under normal circumstances? Explain. Which occupants in the Secret Annexe, if any, were rarely responsible for arguments? Why?

3. Anne describes her first big "crush" (p. 119). Which of Anne's attitudes toward boys are typical of most girls her age, and which are not? Give examples. Which are commendable, and which are not? Again, examples. How long do we tend to remember the faces and personalities of those whom we grew fond of in our early years? Why? What story can you tell about an early love that was never realized but never forgotten? How might the memory of an early love influence our behavior in later life?

4. In her March 19, 1944 entry, Anne describes her first opportunity to "talk things out with Peter." Why was it easier to talk "beside the open window in the semidarkness"? What made it such a "wonderful evening"? Why do boys feel differently about kissing parents than do girls? What other teenage reactions are indicated that are typical of adolescents of the ages of Anne and Peter? Incidentally, why do Peter's shyness and "clumsiness" (p. 151M) attract Anne? How do you account for Anne's gradually declining interest in Peter as the story progresses?

5. For one of the rare times in the *Diary,* Anne finds that her father has failed her (pp. 234B–235). What are some of the things about his daughter that Mr. Frank apparently didn't understand? Why do teenagers fear laughter more than anything else under certain conditions? To what extent do we never reveal our inner selves to anyone? What cure is there, if any, for this apparent desire to erect walls between ourselves and other people, however close they may be? How much of Anne's critical appraisal of her father is reasonable, how much unfair? In connection with walls between people, how strange is it that Anne

and Margot find it necessary to communicate with each other through letters? To what extent does the same situation apply to Anne's letter to Daddy, which offended him so much? To complete the analysis of Anne's feelings about the individual members of her family, to what extent do you agree with Anne's description of what a mother should be (pp. 115B–116)?

6. As you read about Mr. Koophuis, Miep, Elli, Henk, and the others "on the outside," you get some idea of the risks taken by many natives in occupied countries in their efforts to help their persecuted friends during the Nazi occupation. What leads some people to consider it their duty to resist all enemies of democracy and human dignity, while others look on either indifferently or even approvingly at acts of discrimination and violence? What is the chief flaw in human nature that accounts for the existence of prejudice and active hostility toward racial minorities? In what respects could the courage exhibited by Anne and the other occupants of the Secret Annexe be compared to the courage of the Dutch underground and similar groups in other occupied countries at the time?

7. Anne speaks of herself as a "little bundle of contradictions" (p. 239M). Why are most human beings at least two, sometimes more, different people? What qualities of character and circumstance cause Anne to become a judge of herself? What evidence is there that confinement leads to her increasing tendency toward self-analysis? Why is this to be expected? How accurate are Anne's own judgments about her greatest assets and liabilities? How do you relate her self-awareness with her ability to remain relatively cheerful during a period of most difficult confinement? How does her self-awareness help those with whom she is living? How important is it for every person to establish self-awareness? Why?

8. The best evidence that one is growing emotionally and developing maturity is the change that occurs in attitudes and beliefs. Select at least five of the following subjects that Anne discussed from time to time, and show how a definite change occurred during her years in the Secret Annexe:

parents	self-analysis
love	career
religion	friendship
education	loneliness
war	boys
nature	fate.

What are the most powerful influences that induce change and increasing maturity?

9. Anne says, "Again and again I ask myself, would it not have been better for us if we had not gone into hiding, and if we were dead now and not going through all this misery, especially as we shouldn't be running our protectors into danger any more" (p. 218T). Knowing as you do the fate of Anne and her companions in the Secret Annexe, how would you answer her question? As you develop your answer, bear in mind that if Anne had not been spared, however briefly, the world would not have had the record of her confinement. Consider, too, the possibility that the ultimate triumph belonged to Anne!

10. It is difficult to analyze the style of the writer of this diary, of course, because it comes to us in translation. However, certain aspects of the writing are worthy of consideration. What were Anne's main reasons for keeping this personal record? What does she reveal about herself, not in what she says in her self-analysis but in what she says about others? What evidences are there that the author has a sense of humor? If you did not know Anne's age, how could you tell that she was not yet an adult, roughly judging her age entirely on the basis of her writing? Again, judging her on the abilities she reveals in the diary, what might Anne have become in later life had she not died in a concentration camp?

IV. *Vocabulary Study*

Diagnostic Test

3T	enhance	disgrace	enrich	cheapen
3B	capitulation	victory	prominence	surrender

4B scrounging	stealing	saving	dividing
5T blithely	moodily	lazily	happily
14B chattels	property	windows	losses
18M loathe	love	hate	load
22B hypochondria	pain	health-anxiety	dope
22B piqued	tested	ignored	stimulated
23B enthralling	routine	fascinating	confining
25M ludicrous	serious	proud	laughable
27T surreptitiously	secretly	openly	proudly
29M bickering	coaxing	quarreling	following
33T urchins	choir boys	puppies	ragamuffins
45T rendezvous	hiding place	meeting place	restaurant
46T ingenuity	cleverness	stupidity	youth
48T trundle	slide	bounce along	sink
50M pall	excite	heave	become dull
51T veritable	imagined	false	real
53B incoherent	balanced	disconnected	weighty
59M staid	sober	giddy	restless
70B incendiary	explosive	fire-causing	heavy
75M clandestine	visible	close	secret
79B pedantic	wise	mentally petty	soggy
82B gruesome	solemn	lovely	ghastly
84B coquetry	act of flirting	rejection	cookery
90T irrevocable	tense	unalterable	favorable
104T impenetrable	open	high	not to be pierced
116M fatuous	silly	solemn	overweight
131T furbelows	toys	showy decorations	rags
132B stagnant	unmoving	swift	crumbling
137M rummaging	neglecting	searching thoroughly	drinking
144M boisterous	noisy	dull	restful
153M confidant	certain	sharer of secrets	positive
159M incessantly	rapidly	endlessly	briefly
168T precautions	postponements	advance measures	emergencies
169M disparaging	belittling	uplifting	spreading
174M precarious	safe	risky	high
177T quelled	urged	rang out	checked
179B interlude	delay	time filler	debate
191M scandalous	worthy	shocking	tall
196T jocular	gay	sad	tough

204B	inaccessible	porous	unapproach-able	extra
213T	incalculable	uncountable	readable	measurable
216T	abyss	peak	card	deep pit
223M	scoff	praise	jeer	scrape
230B	purgatory	place of atonement	school	Hades
233T	finicky	careless	too hard	too fussy
238M	impeccable	flawless	lovable	sinful
239B	exuberant	asleep	stingy	lively
241T	supercilious	haughty	humble	supreme

Answers

enhance-enrich, *capitulation*-surrender, *scrounging*-stealing, *blithely*-happily, *chattels*-property, *loathe*-hate, *hypochondria*-health-anxiety, *piqued*-stimulated, *enthralling*-fascinating, *ludicrous*-laughable, *surreptitiously*-secretly, *bickering*-quarreling, *urchins*-ragamuffins, *rendezvous*-meeting place, *ingenuity*-cleverness, *trundle*-bounce along, *pall*-become dull, *veritable*-real, *incoherent*-disconnected, *staid*-sober, *incendiary*-fire-causing, *clandestine*-secret, *pedantic*-mentally petty, *gruesome*-ghastly, *coquetry*-act of flirting, *irrevocable*-unalterable, *impenetrable*-not to be pierced, *fatuous*-silly, *furbelows*-showy decorations, *stagnant*-unmoving, *rummaging*-searching thoroughly, *boisterous*-noisy, *confidant*-sharer of secrets, *incessantly*-endlessly, *precautions*-advance measures, *disparaging*-belittling, *precarious*-risky, *quelled*-checked, *interlude*-time filler, *scandalous*-shocking, *jocular*-gay, *inaccessible*-unapproachable, *incalculable*-uncountable, *abyss*-deep pit, *scoff*-jeer, *purgatory*-place of atonement, *finicky*-too fussy, *impeccable*-flawless, *exuberant*-lively, *supercilious*-haughty

Teaching Aids

for

BILLY BUDD

The extraordinary story of a "natural" man by Herman Melville has achieved the status of a masterpiece since its publication in 1924. Everyone who has witnessed the conflict between unsophisticated youth and passion-ridden maturity will sympathize deeply with the plight of young Billy, who finds himself assailed by uncontrollable forces, which even an impartially administered justice cannot appease. For all those who feel themselves threatened by a hostile and inflexible environment, there is special significance in this haunting story of a handsome sailor who becomes a victim of man's intransigence.

I. *Objective Test*

In the space provided at the left, insert the *letter* of the correct choice from among those offered; for example:

....b....   The author of this book is (a) Hawthorne (b) Melville (c) Poe

.... 1. Our first glimpse of Billy Budd was (a) on the docks of Liverpool (b) on board the *Rights-of-Man* (c) rowing in a cutter

.... 2. Billy Budd was also referred to as (a) "Board-her-in-the-smoke" (b) Baby Budd (c) Handsome Budd

.... 3. Billy's farewell to his ship was (a) genial (b) sorrowful (c) bitter

.... 4. When asked who his father was, Billy answered that only one knew: (a) Captain Graveling (b) Captain Vere (c) God

.... 5. Billy had but one defect: (a) a stutter (b) a lame foot (c) a scar on his cheek

.... 6. Billy's enlistment on the *Indomitable* was (a) voluntary (b) arbitrary (c) ill-natured

.... 7. Captain Vere was a man markedly (a) nautical (b) tolerant (c) intellectual

.... 8. Claggart's former life was considered by his shipmates to be (a) notorious (b) ostentatious (c) mysterious

.... 9. The only one who warned Billy of Claggart's ill-will was (a) Red Pepper (b) the Dansker (c) the chaplain

.... 10. Billy's first unpleasant encounter with Claggart involved an incident of (a) spilled soup (b) a sailor's whipping (c) stowing a bag

.... 11. Melville's description of Claggart as having a "depravity according to nature" was drawn from (a) Montaigne (b) Plato (c) the Bible

.... 12. An adjective that might be used to describe the Dansker is (a) eccentric (b) gloomy (c) petulant

.... 13. Claggart's persecution of Billy was (a) open (b) vicious (c) indirect

.... 14. One of the afterguard approached Billy to sound him out about (a) mutiny (b) murder (c) money

.... 15. Vere's first reaction to Claggart's accusation of Billy was one of (a) doubt (b) anger (c) fear

.... 16. Billy's reaction to Claggart's accusation was hampered by his (a) sense of guilt (b) speech impediment (c) ready anger

.... 17. Vere referred to Billy immediately after Claggart's death as a(n) (a) snake (b) felon (c) angel

.... 18. The main feeling of the court in response to

Billy's testimony before them was one of (a) disbelief (b) sympathy (c) repulsion

.... 19. The final judgment of the court upon Billy was prompted by their strict adherence to (a) their consciences (b) the Scriptures (c) the king's law

.... 20. Vere's relationship with Billy in the private interview preceding execution was likened by Melville to the relationship between (a) David and Jonathan (b) God the Father and God the Son (c) Abraham and Isaac

.... 21. When the chaplain spoke to Billy, Billy's attitude toward death was one of (a) irrational fear (b) innocence (c) indifference

.... 22. Billy's final words to Vere came in the form of a (a) benediction (b) curse (c) prophecy

.... 23. The surgeon stated that the absence of spasm in Billy's hanged body was (a) phenomenal (b) unimportant (c) usual

.... 24. Billy's burial was marked by the appearance of (a) stormy seas (b) birds (c) great winds

.... 25. The newspaper account of Billy's execution was (a) inflammatory (b) distorted (c) factual

Answers

1-b, 2-b, 3-a, 4-c, 5-a, 6-b, 7-c, 8-c, 9-b, 10-a, 11-b, 12-a, 13-c, 14-a, 15-a, 16-b, 17-c, 18-b, 19-c, 20-c, 21-b, 22-a, 23-a, 24-b, 25-b

II. *Alternate Objective Tests*

A. Matching

Before each number in the column on the left, insert the *letter* of the item in the column on the right that matches.

.... 1. *Jemmy Legs* a. Ship's pharmacist
.... 2. *Rights-of-   b. The Great Mutiny
       Man*   c. Ship's dining area

.... 3. Trafalgar   d. Warship
.... 4. Grog   e. Where Billy encountered Clag-
.... 5. Apothecary   gart's emissary
.... 6. *Athéiste*   f. Ship on which Billy served
.... 7. Foretop   g. Claggart
.... 8. Forechains   h. Where Billy was positioned in
.... 9. *Indomitable*   the ship
...... 10. Mess   i. Ship from which Billy was im-
         pressed
      j. Rum drink
      k. Nelson
      l. Ship firing shot that killed Vere

Answers

1-g, 2-i, 3-k, 4-j, 5-a, 6-l, 7-h, 8-e, 9-f, 10-c

B. Fill-ins

From the column on the right, select the item that best completes each statement below, and write it in the space provided:

1. Billy Budd had a reputation aboard   three
   the *Rights-of-Man* as a (an) _____.   *Victory*
2. The Dansker had received his scar on   Bristol Molly
   board the _____.   captain's cabin
3. "And handsome is as handsome did it   peacemaker
   too!" was spoken by _____.   "King's
4. Billy was known throughout the story   bargain"
   by another name, that of the _____.   knife
5. The first man to view Claggart's body,   *Agamemnon*
   aside from Billy and Vere, was the   Claggart
   _____.   hammock
6. Captain Vere was regarded by many   musketball
   as a (an) _____.   Handsome
7. Nelson's ship was called the _____.   Sailor
8. Billy was considered a capital invest-   pedant

ment at small outlay, known in naval
parlance as a (an) _____.

9. The drum-head court was convened in
the _____.

10. Billy killed Claggart by means of a
(an) _____.

11. Billy was first called "Baby" by
_____.

12. Vere was killed by a (an) _____.

13. According to the news report of the
affair, Claggart was killed by a (an)
_____.

14. The drum-head court was advised by
Vere to adhere to the law of the
_____.

15. In the ballad, Billy was given a sweetheart called _____.

surgeon
blow
Dansker
upper gundeck
purser
rattan
Mutiny Act

Answers

1-peacemaker, 2-*Agamemnon,* 3-Claggart, 4-Handsome Sailor, 5-surgeon, 6-pedant, 7-*Victory,* 8-"King's bargain," 9-captain's cabin, 10-blow, 11-Dansker, 12-musketball, 13-knife, 14-Mutiny Act, 15-Bristol Molly

III. *Ideas for Written or Oral Book Reports or Class Discussions*

1. Throughout the story, Melville uses the device of *symbolism;* that is, the representation by an object, name, or person of a concept much broader than the original. For instance, a flag may symbolize loyalty, patriotism, a cause, and so forth. What is there symbolic about the names of the ships involved in Billy's transfer—the *Rights-of-Man* and the *Indomitable?* What symbolism is implied in the fact that Billy was a foretopman, that Claggart was a master-at-arms, and that the backgrounds of both were obscure? Why do you suppose critics have suggested that Billy symbolizes Adam in "The Fall of Man," or Jesus

Christ, or, conversely, a pagan hero? Find other examples of symbolism in the narrative, and indicate the author's purpose in their use.

2. Quite apart from the symbolic interpretations that are associated with Billy Budd, consider his good looks in terms of real-life situations. Why does an extremely handsome and well-built man often become the innocent target of men less favorably endowed by nature? If a good-looking man is single and is part of a group of married couples, what effect may his mere presence have on the husbands? On the other hand, why do some women deliberately avoid becoming interested in very attractive men? What do all these reactions to handsome men suggest about the feelings of security of their challengers or detractors? To what extent does this hostility toward the physically favored have relevance to Claggart's attitude toward Billy?

3. The book presents an interesting relationship between youth and age. Why did the Dansker take an immediate liking to Billy? What elements in Billy's background may have influenced Billy to be drawn to the Dansker and to confide in him? Why did the Dansker see through Claggart's motives so much more clearly than did Billy? What evidence is there that the Dansker was right when he suggested that Claggart had arranged for the afterguardsman to speak of mutiny to Billy?

4. Captain Vere is described as a gallant naval officer, an aristocratic bachelor, one who was "mindful of the welfare of his men, but never tolerating an infraction of discipline," a scholar with a marked leaning toward everything intellectual, and a commander outraged at recent incidents of mutiny. Taking these characteristics in turn, explain how each exerted a profound influence on Captain Vere's handling of the problem between Billy and Claggart when he was first informed of the suspected mutinous conduct, after the fatal confrontation, and during the subsequent final judgment.

5. Melville, in describing the emotional characteristics of Claggart, uses a definition by Plato: "Natural Depravity: a depravity according to nature." What is your interpretation

of this definition? Look up the definitions of the psychological terms *paranoia* and *schizophrenia*. In what respects might either or both of these terms have applied to Claggart? In the light of your answer to the last question, what effect did the soup-spilling incident have on Claggart? What do you think of the fact that Captain Vere, for all his wisdom and suspicions that the charge of mutiny was false, permitted only Claggart to testify in the cabin hearing and didn't ask some of the seamen to appear, perhaps including the Dansker?

6. The surgeon and several other officers thought that the drum-head court should not have been convened aboard ship; instead, the case should have been referred to the admiralty for final adjudication. What is the likelihood that Captain Vere would have accepted this view under other circumstances? Shortly after the surgeon pronounced Claggart dead, Captain Vere exclaimed: "Struck dead by an angel of God! Yet the angel must hang!" How did this remark serve as a prediction of the captain's basic position and his subsequent testimony against Billy?

7. It can be argued that the author's invention of a speech defect in Billy Budd creates a serious flaw in the structure of the story. Had Billy been able to speak readily, he might have refuted Claggart's charge of mutiny rather easily, and the death blow would not have occurred at all in Captain Vere's presence. Therefore, the central climax of the narrative hinges on a coincidence contrived by Melville. However, it can also be argued that a fatal confrontation between Billy and Claggart might have eventually occurred anyway, considering how mentally sick and relentless Claggart was. Evaluate Melville's use of the speech defect, and explain whether it was plausible or weak as a structural device, supporting your point of view with specific references to the text.

8. Two striking details about Billy's behavior at the end invite speculation. What prompted the condemned man to say, without stuttering, "God bless Captain Vere"? What was phenomenal about the fact that there was no spasmodic twitching of the body after the hanging?

9. Consider the commentary of critic James E. Miller, Jr.,

on *Billy Budd:* ". . . Some have read the story as a commentary on the impersonality and essential brutality of the modern state, exacting death penalties of the innocent. Still others have found the tale an affirmation of the need, even at the risk of injustice, for society to protect itself and to insure order for the general welfare." Where do you place yourself in a reading of the story? Discuss the similarity of the problem faced by Captain Vere and the court to some of the problems with which today's society is faced. See, for example, Captain Vere's statement on war (p. 73T). What parallel do you see between this statement and the modern-day question of pacifism versus duty in times of war? What of private conscience versus law in the civil rights question? What other contemporary problems can you see that are relevant to the problem faced by Vere?

10. *Billy Budd* has been called a tragedy. There are two concepts of tragedy—the classic and the modern. The classic definition of tragedy is that of Aristotle. ". . . imitation of an action that is serious, complete, and of a certain magnitude; in language embellished with each kind of artistic ornament . . . in the form of action, not of narrative; with incidents arousing pity and fear, herewith to accomplish its catharsis of such emotions." Further, according to the Aristotelian concept, the tragic hero must be noble and must have a tragic flaw; he must experience a reversal of fortune in his life, and he must recognize the reason for his downfall.

The modern concept of tragedy can be found in the ideas of Arthur Miller, who wrote on the nature of tragedy and whose *Death of a Salesman* is generally considered an example of contemporary tragedy. Miller says that the audience is witnessing a tragedy when the characters are wholly and intensely realized so that the audience's belief in their reality is all but complete. The demeanor of the story is so serious that fear for the people involved is as though for the audience itself. "Tragedy is the most accurately balanced portayal of the human being in his struggle for happiness." The characters end in sadness, and the audience understands both why and how they might have avoided their end.

To what extent does *Billy Budd* fit into the mold of classic or modern tragedy? If there is no clear-cut way of classifying Melville's story, which elements of *Billy Budd* could be called classic in nature, and which modern in nature? Give reasons.

IV. *Vocabulary Study*

Diagnostic Test

6T	motley	many-colored	pale	similar
6T	retinue	container	solitary	escort
11M	genial	harsh	cordial	wizard
11M	decorum	nonconformity	propriety	appearance
16M	arbitrary	reasonable	judging	dictatorial
18T	insurrection	revolt	compliance	wakening
18B	pugnacious	quarrelsome	doglike	peaceable
20M	bravado	cowardice	defiance	ruffian
23T	infraction	violation	impertinence	immobility
23B	deference	submission	affliction	insubordination
24T	appellation	anonymity	name	abstraction
25B	innovators	introducers	conservatives	diplomats
27M	pallor	presence	ruddiness	paleness
27M	amber	yellowish	auburn	amethyst
28M	squeamish	callous	disgusted	wiggling
33M	ascetic	medicinal	wanton	austere
34M	cynicism	respect	contempt	sinfulness
35M	aridly	drily	wickedly	moistly
36B	enigma	revelation	puzzle	sign
36B	antipathy	affinity	dislike	absence
37M	unimpeach-ably	questionably	totally	faultlessly
37M	labyrinth	entrance	maze	passage
38B	auspicious	ominous	unfortunate	favorable
39M	innate	unacquired	inborn	insufficient
40M	vindicate	absolve	punish	condemn
41M	felonious	criminal	righteous	playful
41M	comely	unpleasing	handsome	becoming
43B	usurer	spendthrift	shopkeeper	money-lender

44T	clandestine	secret	open	purposeful
46T	confounded	unperturbed	confused	astonished
46M	impediment	hindrance	clearance	task
47T	interloper	solitary	meddler	peddler
47M	parley	conference	pardon	argument
49M	pithy	loquacious	wise	terse
50T	oblique	deviating	direct	opaque
51B	orbs	glances	eyes	paths
55B	subservience	servant	submissiveness	disservice
57T	ostentatious	modest	mysterious	showy
61B	transfixed	motionless	crucified	active
64M	immured	confined	unsecluded	indifferent
74B	abhorrence	attraction	loathing	tolerance
75M	flagrant	notorious	flaming	renowned
77B	stoical	impassive	enduring	sensitive
82T	diabolical	satanic	angelic	desperate
87B	hypothesis	proof	judgment	theory
89B	pinions	wings	bones	limbs
90B	martinet	slacker	disciplinarian	drillmaster
92M	remorse	regret	horror	unrepentance
93B	peevish	patient	foolish	cross
93B	superannuated	revised	outdated	destroyed

Answers

motley-many-colored, *retinue*-escort, *genial*-cordial, *decorum*-propriety, *arbitrary*-dictatorial, *insurrection*-revolt, *pugnacious*-quarrelsome, *bravado*-defiance, *infraction*-violation, *deference*-submission, *appellation*-name, *innovators*-introducers, *pallor*-paleness, *amber*-yellowish, *squeamish*-disgusted, *ascetic*-austere, *cynicism*-contempt, *aridly*-drily, *enigma*-puzzle, *antipathy*-dislike, *unimpeachably*-faultlessly, *labyrinth*-maze, *auspicious*-favorable, *innate*-inborn, *vindicate*-absolve, *felonious*-criminal, *comely*-handsome, *usurer*-moneylender, *clandestine*-secret, *confounded*-confused, *impediment*-hindrance, *interloper*-meddler, *parley*-conference, *pithy*-terse, *oblique*-deviating, *orbs*-eyes, *subservience*-submissiveness, *ostentatious*-showy, *transfixed*-motionless, *immured*-confined, *abhorrence*-loathing, *flagrant*-notorious, *stoical*-impassive, *diabolical*-satanic, *hypothesis*-theory, *pinions*-wings, *martinet*-disciplinarian, *remorse*-regret, *peevish*-cross, *superannuated*-outdated

Teaching Aids

for

THE BRIDGE OF SAN LUIS REY

After the cables of a rickety old bridge in Peru suddenly snap as five people are crossing a gorge, a Franciscan friar takes on the task of recording the life histories of the unfortunate victims of the accident. He asks thousands of questions and fills scores of notebooks "in his effort at establishing the fact that each of the five lost lives was a perfect whole." Yet Brother Juniper's enormous research reveals little of the central passions of his subjects. An omniscient narrator, however, probes more deeply into the "spring within the spring." In this ingeniously constructed novel, Thornton Wilder has created one of the priceless gems of twentieth-century literature.

I. *Objective Test*

In the space provided at the left, insert the *letter* of the correct choice from among those offered; for example:

....b....　　　The name of the author is (a) Jones (b) Wilder (c) Dickens (d) Hardy

....　1. Manuel wrote letters for the Perichole because (a) she didn't want Pio to know about the letters (b) she wanted to hurt Manuel (c) he wrote better (d) she was too busy

....　2. Uncle Pio originally discovered the Perichole (a) in a convent (b) working in the Viceroy's

71

palace (c) visiting the Marquesa (d) singing in a tavern

.... 3. Jaime suffered because of his (a) lack of education (b) epilepsy (c) isolation (d) smallpox

.... 4. Manuel died of (a) a broken heart (b) poor nutrition (c) blood poisoning (d) typhoid fever

.... 5. The Marquesa's last letter (a) infuriated her daughter (b) changed the daughter's outlook (c) was never received (d) was lost

.... 6. When the Perichole came to apologize, the Marquesa (a) sent her away (b) scolded her (c) asked her to go to the Viceroy (d) praised her

.... 7. Uncle Pio believed that the Perichole could never be a perfect actress because she (a) had never studied in Spain (b) came from the lower classes (c) became upset easily (d) had never really loved

.... 8. Esteban wanted Alvarado to give the Abbess all of Esteban's wages (a) to use for the convent (b) because of her kindness to him (c) to make up for Pepita's death (d) as a memorial to his brother

.... 9. The Marquesa made a pilgrimage to the shrine (a) to pray for her as yet unborn grandchild (b) because she had sinned (c) to make the Abbess feel better (d) because Pepita asked her to do so

.... 10. The Perichole gave up the theater (a) after Pio criticized her severely (b) because she could not become *the* leading actress (c) when she caught smallpox (d) to become a grand lady

.... 11. Manuel stopped loving the Perichole when (a) she scorned him (b) his love made his brother suffer (c) she became self-centered (d) Uncle Pio came between them

.... 12. The Abbess believed the true meaning of the

Bridge disaster was (a) a lesson of love (b) Tempt not fate (c) Lack of faith angers God (d) Be not too scientific

.... 13. *One* of these statements about Alvarado's daughter is correct. Which one? (a) She was drowned. (b) She died of a fever. (c) We are not told how she was lost. (d) She was a friend of Doña Clara.

.... 14. The Abbess sent Pepita to the Marquesa to (a) teach her humility (b) spy on her (c) write letters (d) free her from household cares

.... 15. Uncle Pio was happy when a new actress joined the company because (a) the Perichole performed better (b) he liked younger women (c) attendance was greater (d) he wanted gossip from Spain

.... 16. How many people died when the Bridge fell? (a) Four (b) Five (c) Six (d) Seven

.... 17. Esteban learned the truth about Manuel's love for the Perichole (a) from her (b) during Manuel's delirium (c) when he saw his brother visit her (d) when he wrote her letters

.... 18. Which one statement is *not* true about the Marquesa? (a) Once the people tried to have her locked up. (b) She was denounced by the Inquisition. (c) She had married a ruined nobleman. (d) She had been an attractive girl.

.... 19. The Marquesa studied, observed, and mixed with society (a) to maintain her position (b) to escape her family (c) because Uncle Pio encouraged her (d) to write entertaining letters

.... 20. Brother Juniper was burned at the stake because he (a) defied the Archbishop (b) went too far (c) proved there was a scientific explanation for the deaths (d) attacked the Inquisition

.... 21. Which *one* character did the Marquesa compare to "a soiled pack of cards"? (a) The Arch-

bishop (b) The Viceroy (c) Uncle Pio (d)
Manuel

.... 22. The Archbishop (a) could not understand the
twins' language (b) was a tall, lean man (c)
punished any priest who did not act properly
(d) refused to attend the Viceroy's dinners

.... 23. Which *one* of these people died when the
Bridge fell? (a) Pepita (b) The Viceroy (c)
The Abbess (d) Captain Alvarado

.... 24. Which phrase describes the Marquesa? (a)
thoughtless and egotistic (b) cruel and re-
vengeful (c) mild and forgiving (d) stupid
and impractical

.... 25. Which *one* statement about the Perichole is
true? (a) She could read and write. (b) She
was the best actress in the Spanish world. (c)
She traveled with a theatrical group in Spain.
(d) She sent money secretly to the Abbess.

Answers

1-a, 2-d, 3-b, 4-c, 5-b, 6-d, 7-d, 8-c, 9-a, 10-d, 11-b, 12-a, 13-c,
14-d, 15-a, 16-b, 17-b, 18-d, 19-d, 20-b, 21-c, 22-a, 23-a, 24-a, 25-b

II. *Alternate Objective Tests*

A. Matching

Before each number in the column on the left, write the
letter of the item in the column on the right that matches.

.... 1. An eccentric who wrote   a. Manuel
         long letters   b. the Perichole
.... 2. Talent scout and dramatic   c. Madre María
         coach   d. Uncle Pio
.... 3. Burned at the stake   e. Pepita
.... 4. The Directress of the   f. the Viceroy
         convent   g. Esteban

.... 5. Son who was going to Lima for an education

.... 6. The brother who pretended he was another man

.... 7. She finally learned to love her mother.

.... 8. The servant who taught her mistress a lesson

.... 9. "He was a widower, and childless, he had collected coins, wines, actresses, orders, and maps."

...... 10. She was disfigured by illness in later life.

h. Brother Juniper
i. the Archbishop
j. Doña Clara
k. the Marquesa
l. Jaime
m. Alvarado

Answers

1-k, 2-d, 3-h, 4-c, 5-l, 6-g, 7-j, 8-e, 9-f, 10-b

B. Fill-ins

From the column on the right, select the item that best completes each statement below, and write it in the space provided:

1. Uncle Pio was a frequent morning visitor to _____.

2. She was ugly; she stuttered; she was the daughter of a _____.

3. _____ deliberately accepted a marriage offer that made her move.

4. After Camila became a great lady, Pio tried to get her back to _____.

5. He wept under the window of _____.

6. The _____ hoped smallpox would spoil the Perichole's beauty.

cloth merchant
acting
Pepita
heretical
the Marquesa
townspeople
love
faith
Doña Clara
Manuel
theater
Brother Juniper

7. "It wasn't . . . it wasn't . . . brave" was said by _____.

8. The bridge of _____ does not fall.

9. Captain Alvarado saved Esteban from _____.

10. Esteban could not face life without _____.

11. _____ had been a propagandist.

12. Brother Juniper's book was declared _____.

13. _____ arranged for Esteban to go on a sea voyage.

14. All Manuel's errands seemed to lead him past the _____.

15. Uncle Pio scolded the Perichole for her speech to the _____.

the Abbess
suicide
prisoner
the Perichole
the Viceroy
city
Uncle Pio

Answers

1-the Viceroy, 2-cloth merchant, 3-Doña Clara, 4-acting, 5-the Perichole, 6-townspeople, 7-Pepita, 8-love, 9-suicide, 10-Manuel, 11-Uncle Pio, 12-heretical, 13-the Abbess, 14-theater, 15-prisoner

III. *Ideas for Written or Oral Book Reports or Class Discussions*

1. Essential to an understanding of this novel, to what Wilder was trying to tell us, is the degree to which chance controls our lives and the degree to which design (or intent) controls us. Is there any way you can resolve this matter? How? Try to show to what extent the lives of the chief characters were determined by each factor—chance and design. Remember how diligently Brother Juniper searched for a pattern in the lives of the five people who died. He tried to decide what was cause and what was effect. Yet as a man of faith, why did he look for evidence? You may recall that he said, "the discrepancy between faith and fact is greater than is generally assumed."

2. Wilder says that for Uncle Pio the Perichole "was the great secret and reason of his life" (p. 136T). Why does he say this? It has been said of the Perichole that her suffering was intensified by a failure to "integrate" her life. What does this mean?

3. A critic has commented that "this novel is *full* (a) *of life,* (b) *of interesting sidelights on an interesting period,* and above all (c) *of excellent character sketches.*" Prove the truth of these three statements.

4. The scene in which the Viceroy ordered the Perichole to apologize for slandering the Marquesa at the theater seems rather curious. How would you answer the following questions for a friend who did not understand this scene?

   a. Why didn't the Marquesa take offense at the insults?
   b. Why did the Viceroy order the actress to apologize at all? And why in bare feet and a black dress?
   c. How do you account for the misinterpretation that the Marquesa put on the whole affair?
   d. What would your reaction have been if the Perichole had directed the "topical songs" in the theater to you?

5. *The Bridge of San Luis Rey* has often been called a novel about love. How many different kinds of love are treated in the story? What motivates the person doing the loving in the various relationships? What does love demand of a person if his experience is to be rewarding and his emotion reciprocated? To what extent is it possible for love to be motivated by selfishness? Cite examples. What effect can selfishness have upon the person loved and the person loving? Which of the loves, if any, dealt with in this book did you consider reasonably healthy and rewarding? Why? If none, what was wrong in each instance?

6. Wilder is known for his awe of what he calls the mystery of human beings and for his disdain for the attempts to explain or dispel this mystery. Where in Part 1 and Part 2 do you find evidence for these feelings? On

p. 67M, Wilder says of Manuel and Esteban, ". . . there existed a need of one another so terrible that it produced miracles as naturally as the charged air of a sultry day produces lightning." Can this phenomenon be explained logically, or is it part of that mystery of human beings that fascinates Wilder? Explain.

7. No study of this book would be complete without some analysis of the author's extraordinary skill as a stylist. Examine each of the following illustrations of a specific writing technique of Thornton Wilder, and then find other examples throughout the book that show the same characteristics:

    a. *clean, striking descriptions:* "It was a mere ladder. . . ." (p. 3M)
    b. *clarity:* "Yet it was rather strange that this event . . ." (p. 4M)
    c. *gentle humor:* "He knows the answer. He merely wanted to . . ." (p. 8T)
    d. *mild satire:* "Not often, but several times . . ." (p. 8B)
    e. *poetic imagery:* ". . . the very sparrows do not lose . . ." (p. 10B)
    f. *sense of authenticity:* ". . . that is found in Letter XXII . . ." (p. 22B).

In each of your examples, explain how the effect is achieved. If you can discover other style tendencies not mentioned, discuss them.

8. "As he approached twenty, Uncle Pio came to see quite clearly that his life had three aims" (p. 114B).

    a. What were these aims?
    b. Explain whether or not he achieved them before he died.

9. By which technique do you learn more about the characters in this novel—by what they say and do or by what the narrator tells about them? Which way is more effective in revealing character? Explain with illustrations.

10. One often hears the question, "What makes a classic?" Certainly, an important consideration is the ability of the work to say things that can be applied to human problems at any time anywhere. Select at least two statements, two general ideas, and two themes presented by the author, and explain how they can apply to most of us today. To what extent do you agree with the critics who have called *The Bridge of San Luis Rey* a modern classic because of the timelessness of its ideas and themes?

IV. *Vocabulary Study*

Diagnostic Test

3T	osier	branch	willow	drug
4M	hallucination	actuality	delusion	light
4B	usury	high interest	treasure	low interest
7M	savants	fools	scholars	magicians
7B	skepticism	doubt	dilemma	certainty
14B	obsequious	rejecting	heavy	fawning
19T	baroque	simple	ornate	nautical
21B	ignoble	lofty	royal	dishonorable
26B	flamboyance	craft	showiness	flame
31T	regimen	soldier	chaos	system
31T	assiduously	carelessly	diligently	bitterly
32B	perfunctory	matter-of-fact	enthusiastic	formal
34M	magnanimity	closeness	generosity	greatness
35T	maudlin	oversentimental	musical	cold
45B	mitigate	make milder	make harsher	insure
46T	ruse	plan	charge	trick
46B	propitiation	defiance	correction	appeasement
49M	officious	withdrawing	meddlesome	efficient
50B	stoic	foolish	sensitive	emotionless
50B	jocose	sad	wild	humorous
53T	amulets	rings	bracelets	charms
56M	stupefaction	revelation	bewilderment	demise
65M	stolid	dull	excitable	secure
67T	tacit	stated	delicate	unspoken
72T	blandishments	insults	flatteries	ointments
78M	incantation	chant	growl	prophecy

93B	reticence	boldness	quiet reserve	relief
103T	banal	unusual	forbidden	commonplace
107M	coterie	dish	enemies	group
110M	lachrymose	tearful	joyous	odd
110B	polyphony	monotone	sound mixture	giant
113M	calumny	slander	praise	salve
114B	omniscient	ignorant	all-knowing	scientific
126T	penury	wealth	weight	poverty
127M	implacable	relentless	forgiving	selfish
129T	puerile	mature	pure	childish
132T	ruefully	shyly	sorrowfully	joyfully
132T	poignant	piercing	tasteless	shrewd
132B	libertine	ethical	equal	immoral
133T	Epicurean	tough	pleasure-loving	loud
134B	symposium	conference	agreement	research
136B	repertory	performance	specialty	collection
137B	cursory	deliberate	insulting	hurried
138M	usurpation	overthrow	fallacy	treatment
138M	magdalenism	guilt	repentance	holy
139B	rachitic	healthy	twirling	having rickets
162B	votive	evil	consecrated	balloting
168B	heretical	straight	unorthodox	round
170M	furtively	stealthily	directly	richly
176M	languorous	snappy	sluggish	level

Answers

osier-willow, *hallucination*-delusion, *usury*-high interest, *savants*-scholars, *skepticism*-doubt, *obsequious*-fawning, *baroque*-ornate, *ignoble*-dishonorable, *flamboyance*-showiness, *regimen*-system, *assiduously*-diligently, *dissimulating*-pretending, *magnanimity*-generosity, *maudlin*-oversentimental, *mitigate*-make milder, *ruse*-trick, *propitiation*-appeasement, *officious*-meddlesome, *stoic*-emotionless, *jocose*-humorous, *amulets*-charms, *stupefaction*-bewilderment, *stolid*-dull, *tacit*-unspoken, *blandishments*-flatteries, *incantation*-chant, *reticence*-quiet reserve, *banal*-commonplace, *coterie*-group, *lachrymose*-tearful, *polyphony*-sound mixture, *calumny*-slander, *omniscient*-all-knowing, *penury*-poverty, *implacable*-relentless, *puerile*-childish, *ruefully*-sorrowfully, *poignant*-piercing, *libertine*-immoral, *Epicurean*-pleasure-loving, *symposium*-conference, *repertory*-collection, *cursory*-hurried, *usurpation*-overthrow, *magdalenism*-repentance, *rachitic*-having rickets, *votive*-consecrated, *heretical*-unorthodox, *furtively*-stealthily, *languorous*-sluggish

Teaching Aids

for

THE CAINE MUTINY

An engrossing portrait of a nation at war, *The Caine Mutiny* has become a modern American classic. Its vivid action and unforgettable characters—especially the controversial Captain Queeg—have made it one of the most popular of all contemporary novels. The story of a mutiny against a neurotic captain and the subsequent court-martial raises important questions of "right" versus "wrong" in situations of extreme danger and personal hardship.

I. *Objective Test*

In the space provided at the left, insert the *letter* of the correct choice from among those offered; for example:

....b.... The name of the author is (a) Roth (b) Wouk (c) Singer (d) West

.... 1. At the outset, it seems quite clear that Willie is (a) completely used to independence (b) rather overprotected by his mother (c) eager to get into the war (d) quite fit for Navy duty

.... 2. The first meeting of Willie and May occurs when she is (a) serving pizzas at a bar (b) reading a novel by Dickens (c) auditioning for a singing job (d) working in a candy store

.... 3. Willie risks his life trying to (a) recover a flying mainspring (b) climb a wall (c) catch a taxi for May (d) sneak into his room unobserved

.... 4. At Furnald Hall, Willie impresses his classmates by his ability to (a) assemble firing pieces (b) run the obstacle course (c) embarrass Ensign Brain about submarines (d) memorize ordnance information

.... 5. Willie is moved to tears by (a) news from May (b) a letter from his father (c) the death of a classmate (d) an order from Captain Matson

.... 6. During his first few days aboard the *Caine,* Willie is (a) amused at its informal atmosphere (b) curious about the crow's nest (c) shocked at its filthy condition and poor crew discipline (d) interested in the engine room

.... 7. Willie is puzzled by Captain de Vriess, who is careless about minor regulations but amazingly (a) neat in his personal habits (b) efficient in handling the ship (c) strict about shore leave privileges (d) concerned about proper sleeping quarters

.... 8. The first time Queeg maneuvers the *Caine* out of the harbor, he (a) runs it aground (b) discovers a leak in the hull (c) rams a tugboat (d) impresses the men with his abilities

.... 9. The *Caine* cuts its target tow line because (a) Stilwell disobeys the captain (b) Willie fails to signal properly (c) Queeg is not watching the ship's course (d) the exec is not on the bridge

.... 10. Queeg demands that all members of the crew (a) use their initiative in emergencies (b) discard formal saluting (c) be informed of official orders (d) always keep their shirttails tucked in

.... 11. The crew is deprived of three days' shore leave in San Francisco because they (a) ignore orders to assemble (b) are not properly dressed for general drill (c) do not salute the captain properly (d) do not take proper care of gunnery equipment

.... 12. After the *Caine* docks in San Francisco, Willie proposes to May and (a) sets a marriage date

(b) receives his mother's approval (c) is convinced by his mother to wait (d) buys a diamond ring

.... 13. In an attempt to make herself more acceptable to Willie's mother, May (a) changes her name (b) finds a steady job (c) invites Mrs. Keith to tea (d) enrolls for courses at Hunter College

.... 14. While discussing Stilwell's leave without the captain's consent, Queeg (a) orders an immediate court-martial (b) puts both Stilwell and the exec on report (c) admits that he cut the target tow line (d) denies holding a grudge against Stilwell

.... 15. Immediately after the incident involving the yellow dye marker, (a) the crew calls Queeg a coward (b) Keefer suggests that Queeg is a coward (c) it is clear that Urban was at fault (d) Maryk supports Keefer's criticism

.... 16. At Stilwell's court-martial, the court finds the defendant (a) guilty and gives him a dishonorable discharge (b) innocent of the charge (c) not guilty because of a forced confession (d) guilty, but recommends only a token punishment

.... 17. During the invasion of Saipan, Willie again sees Queeg (a) drinking heavily (b) avoiding the shoreline side of the bridge (c) worrying about the welfare of another ship (d) giving precise gunnery commands

.... 18. Some missing strawberries prompt Captain Queeg to (a) order a new supply from the *Bridge* (b) confine Urban to quarters (c) direct a massive search for a phantom key (d) refuse to let Ducely leave

.... 19. Before Maryk goes to see Admiral Halsey, he (a) informs the captain of his intentions (b) is positive that Queeg is mentally ill (c) seeks advice from a doctor on the *New Jersey* (d) asks Keefer to read his "medical log"

.... 20. Maryk takes command of the *Caine* during the typhoon because (a) he thinks it is the best time to get rid of Queeg (b) Queeg asks him to take command (c) he believes Queeg has lost control of the ship (d) Queeg hits his head and passes out

.... 21. At Maryk's court-martial, Barney Greenwald uses the testimony of the psychiatrists to (a) prove that Queeg is really insane (b) show that Queeg might have been insane during the typhoon (c) inform the court that Keefer was to blame (d) prove that Maryk was qualified to judge Queeg's insanity

.... 22. When Barney Greenwald makes his speech at the party after the court-martial, he (a) speaks out in defense of Queeg (b) says that Queeg should not be commanding a ship (c) accuses the Navy of having low standards for commanding officers (d) voices pride in having won the acquittal

.... 23. When Keefer becomes captain of the *Caine,* he (a) shows extraordinary competence (b) behaves like Queeg in some respects (c) refuses to give any authority to Willie (d) develops a closeness with the crew

.... 24. As a result of his actions during the mutiny, Willie is (a) awarded the Bronze Star (b) appointed captain (c) demoted (d) given an official reprimand

.... 25. When Willie assumes command of the *Caine,* he discovers that (a) a ship's captain is truly isolated from the crew (b) the job of the captain is impossibly difficult (c) Queeg was a better captain (d) Keefer was a brave captain

Answers

1-b, 2-c, 3-a, 4-d, 5-b, 6-c, 7-b, 8-a, 9-c, 10-d, 11-b, 12-c, 13-d, 14-c, 15-b, 16-d, 17-b, 18-c, 19-d, 20-c, 21-b, 22-a, 23-b, 24-d, 25-a

II. *Alternate Objective Tests*

A. Matching

Before each number in the column on the left, write the *letter* of the item in the column on the right that matches:

.... 1. Willie Keith
.... 2. Marie Minotti
.... 3. Tom Keefer
.... 4. Captain Queeg
.... 5. Barney Greenwald
.... 6. Steve Maryk
.... 7. strawberries
.... 8. ball bearings
.... 9. Urban
...... 10. Horrible

a. author of *Multitudes, Multitudes*
b. Measuring experiment
c. wine in Keefer's face
d. prayers in a typhoon
e. casualty in fireroom
f. a Navy nurse in Honolulu
g. last captain of the *Caine*
h. commander of the *Moulton*
i. rescues the red float
j. "Kay, kay . . ."
k. Walter Feather
l. help calm Queeg's nerves

Answers

1-g, 2-k, 3-a, 4-j, 5-c, 6-i, 7-b, 8-l, 9-d, 10-e

B. Fill-ins

From the column on the right, select the item that best completes each statement below, and write it in the space provided:

1. Before he joins the Navy, Willie works as a (an) _____.

2. Willie's father is a (an) _____.

3. Willie observes a startling contrast to the *Caine* aboard the *Moulton,* whose captain is called _____.

4. Captain de Vriess reprimands Willie for failing to deliver _____.

5. Stilwell is confined to the ship for six months because he was _____ while on watch.

6. Queeg appoints Willie the _____ officer in order to improve the physical appearance of the crew.

7. Queeg uses his officer's ration coupons to buy _____ in Hawaii.

8. Against the captain's orders, _____ gives Stilwell permission for a three-day leave in the States.

9. The officers give Queeg the nickname _____ because of his behavior in combat.

10. Queeg places a ban on _____ for forty-eight hours after an officer is transferred.

11. Immediately after Queeg refuses to help protect the *Stanfield,* _____ becomes the object of Queeg's scorn.

12. Roland Keefer dies a hero after a (an) _____ attack on his ship.

13. Maryk wants to show his "medical log" to _____, but decides not to at Keefer's urging.

14. Barney Greenwald agrees to defend Maryk when he discovers that _____ is really the guilty party.

15. Ducely informs Willie that Queeg has been placed in charge of a (an) _____ in Iowa.

missile base
Admiral Halsey
Keith
the Iron Duke
liquor
Keefer
sleeping
morale
engineering
piano player
reading
Maryk
doctor
cigarettes
water
supply depot
kamikaze
Old Yellowstain
a message
taxi driver

Answers

1-piano player, 2-doctor, 3-the Iron Duke, 4-a message, 5-reading, 6-morale, 7-liquor, 8-Maryk, 9-Old Yellowstain, 10-water, 11-Keith, 12-kamikaze, 13-Admiral Halsey, 14-Keefer, 15-supply depot

III. *Ideas for Written or Oral Book Reports or Class Discussions*

1. To understand the mutiny aboard the *Caine,* the reader must, of course, understand Captain Queeg in terms of his personality, his sense of responsibility and competence as a naval officer, and his relations with his officers and crew. What elements in Queeg's background might explain his feelings of insecurity, his compulsive need to cover up mistakes, his paranoid behavior, as Keefer terms it (p. 337M)? How would the incidents involving the water ban (pp. 319–325), the strawberries (pp. 368–373), and the search for a phantom key (pp. 373–395) tend to support Keefer's diagnosis? What evidence is there that Queeg is incompetent and cowardly under fire? On the other hand, in what respects would the Navy have supported some of Queeg's demands of his men—including the "my way" speech (p. 164M), the shirttail fuss (p. 192T), and the Stilwell court-martial (pp. 329–340)? Of all the captains covered in some detail in the story, which one among de Vriess, Queeg, Sammis (the Iron Duke), Keefer, and Keith seems to be most effective for his ship and crew under the circumstances in which each serves? Give reasons for your choice.

2. Quite obviously, the mutiny occurs under emergency conditions, but the seeds have been planted long before the typhoon strikes. To what extent is Keefer responsible for the mutiny? Why does Greenwald come to the conclusion that Keefer, not Maryk, should have been court-martialed? To what extent are Queeg's personality and behavior as a naval officer, as well as a certain basic disloyalty of his subordinate officers, responsible for the mu-

tiny? What is the likelihood that a mutiny might have occurred anyway, even if the typhoon had not brought matters to a head when it did? Which factor, then, is the major cause of the mutiny—concern for personal safety, a sense of responsibility for the survival of the ship and crew, or a subconscious desire to get even with Queeg? Explain.

3. The principles of psychology and psychiatry are prominent features of this novel. How does Greenwald use the testimony of the two psychiatrists to win his case? Although the doctors all agree that Queeg is not legally insane, how do they differ in analyzing his emotional problems? Whose analysis do you find most reasonable? Why? How accurate was Keefer's diagnosis prior to the trial? What evidence, if any, does the author provide to raise the question of mental imbalance by Queeg during the typhoon? How do you account for Keefer's weak testimony at the court-martial? What foreshadowing of this surprising turnabout has already been provided in the visit to Admiral Halsey's ship (pp. 398–405)? Why does Greenwald call his own tactics "phony legal tricks" (p. 573T)? Why does he toss the wine into Keefer's face? How reasonable is it to call the verdict for acquittal of Maryk a "miscarriage of justice"?

4. Much of the novel is devoted to tracing Willie Keith's growth from a callow youth to a mature man. What evidence is offered in the early chapters to prove that Willie has not yet grown up, especially in his relations with his mother and May Wynn, as well as his attitude toward the war and his own career objectives? How much of an influence on Willie does his father's letter have (pp. 72–76)? What are the first signs that Willie is maturing? To what extent does he prove to be "tough enough at the core" (p. 73M)? How do Willie's views about what he wants out of life change from what they are before the war and after his service on the *Caine*? Why do you suppose Dr. Keith says, "Had I had one such experience in my younger years I might not be dying a failure" (p. 74B)? How likely is it that Willie will be more successful? Explain.

5. Most of the adverse criticism directed against *The Caine Mutiny* has centered around the love story between Willie and May (Marie). How justified are those who consider it a weak element in the novel, literally an intrusion on the splendid action material and character study? In what respects might modern readers consider the behavior of the two principals in the romance old-fashioned? However, looking at the affair from the author's point of view, why might this material, together with that about Willie's mother, have been absolutely essential in helping the reader measure the growth of a spoiled, irresponsible nightclub pianist into a mature human being? Express your views on whether or not, if you were Herman Wouk, you would revise the book, omitting the romantic elements entirely.

6. No study of a book can be complete without an evaluation of the author's structural techniques and style. One of the most interesting devices used by Wouk is the imposition on the reader of the need to think more deeply about questions of *right* or *wrong*. For example, just after we have about decided that Captain de Vriess is merely a slob and a loose disciplinarian masquerading as an officer, we discover his remarkable ability to handle both his ship and his men so that they respond magnificently when "the chips are down." How is the revision of initial judgments influenced in the development of Keefer, Maryk, Greenwald, even Queeg? How effectively does the author build toward a *climax* in the court-martial scenes? Note the delightful use of *satirical* humor in the descriptions of Navy life (pp. 31M–33M, 67B–69T). What other such examples can you find? Where else does Wouk display his skill at recording *realistic dialogue,* in addition to Willie's early experiences (pp. 19M–22B, 81–82)? Wouk's skillful use of authentic *detail* and *descriptive power,* including appeals to all the senses, appear in Willie's first impressions of the *Caine* (pp. 85M, 91B–93M). Cite other examples. What is your estimate of the author's knowledge of Navy procedures, psychology, and legal practices? In evaluating Wouk's *character development,* give reasons to support your choices of the real hero and real villain

in the story. If you believe this is a novel without either, tell why you think so.

7. In a letter to May, Willie describes Keefer's novel (p. 599M). From this description, point out the important ways in which *Multitudes, Multitudes* is similar to and different from *The Caine Mutiny*. To what extent might Wouk have been using this "novel within a novel" to express subtle criticism of the many war books that appeared in the late forties and early fifties, with their emphasis on explicit sex and foul language? If you were to draw a composite prose picture of the author as revealed through his various characters, what aspects of each would you include? (Reread the "Biographical Background" in the *Reader's Supplement* to the text before you answer this question.)

8. *Point of view* refers to the manner in which the author permits his readers to "see" the details and episodes in his narrative. If the story is told in the first person or through the eyes and mind of a single character, the "view" is limited. However, if the reader can be present everywhere, he is being guided by what is known as the *omniscient* point of view. At first glance, the novel seems to be centering on Willie Keith, but he is absent at an officers' meeting (p. 163T) and at other times. What, then, is the general approach used by Wouk? What are the advantages and disadvantages of this technique? In terms of selection of a point of view, try to offer valid reasons why the author probably chose to let the reader "see" the war through the activities of an obscure minesweeper. What is your general estimate of Wouk's attitude toward the handling of historical events?

9. Some interesting questions of racial, social, and ethnic prejudices are raised in the book. On what grounds are most of Mrs. Keith's objections to May mainly based? Indeed, why is Willie himself subconsciously hesitant to take the plunge toward marriage until the very end? What evidences of overt and covert prejudice in the Navy are touched upon by the author? What was Wouk trying to say about the kitchen (mess) help's being referred to as "boys," "colored," "Negro," and their speech being ren-

dered in heavy southern drawls? How does Queeg reveal his prejudices in the furor raised over the stolen strawberries? How does "the brass" show prejudice toward Maryk? How does Greenwald use the problem of racism in explaining his defense of Queeg and attack on Keefer and the other mutineers? How reasonable would it be to say that the end of World War II marked the *beginning* of more wholesome attitudes toward racial and social differences in and out of the armed forces?

10. One cannot ignore the fact that *The Caine Mutiny* is a story about the Navy, written by an author who had firsthand experience in its complex organization and procedures. Keefer tells Willie that "the Navy is a master plan designed by geniuses for execution by idiots" (p. 121B). If this is true, how would it explain the seemingly endless series of rules and regulations that define Navy life? How important is strict adherence to discipline and centralized control in protecting the welfare of officers and men? In what ways might the rigid rules encourage mediocrity and discourage creativity? Other than abolishing war, what are the alternatives toward improving conditions in the armed forces, assuming that a nation must at present maintain an alert fighting force? In general, how does the Navy image fare at the hands of Herman Wouk?

IV. *Vocabulary Study*

Diagnostic Test

4M	sanctuary	protection	exposure	blessings
21T	vitiates	enhances	enlivens	spoils
22M	kiosk	corner	newsstand	fountain
25M	surreptitious	acknowledged	secret	reputation
31B	oracle	larynx	idiot	wise man
44M	harangue	speech	dessert	silence
56B	billet	dance	weapon	berth
64M	opaque	jeweled	obscure	readable
77M	countermand	undo	support	return
121M	heresy	skepticism	agreement	belief
127M	cadenza	short phrase	long phrase	rhythm

129M	dithyrambic	calm	measured	emotional
147M	penance	money	reward	punishment
161M	khaki	gabardine	tan	blue
182M	doughty	bold	timid	frumpy
198T	languorous	working	sticky	lazy
201B	surmise	surprise	failure	guess
209B	cognizant	aware	alike	asleep
227M	incredulity	acceptance	disbelief	anger
249B	desultory	casual	serious	degrading
252B	gamboled	looked	smelled	leaped
265T	palatable	tasty	agreeable	difficult
284M	procreative	sterile	productive	original
291B	histrionics	intellect	snobbishness	theatrics
306B	poltroon	hero	soldier	coward
320M	miasma	net	swamp	smog
327T	supine	human	servile	brave
357T	comatose	unconscious	alert	spiteful
377B	doldrums	inaction	speed	agitation
395T	perfunctory	animated	mechanical	abrupt
411B	dank	smelly	hot	clammy
421T	crockery	crystal	earthenware	utensils
432M	yawed	straightened	zigzagged	tired
460T	turbulent	disordered	calm	vibrant
465B	taciturnity	swearing	understanding	silence
475B	pleurisy	insanity	heart disease	lung disease
486B	peccadilloes	little faults	amusements	felonies
488B	martinet	puppet	disciplinarian	animal
517T	flummery	nonsense	pomp	fatuousness
524M	trauma	chemicals	injury	lesions
526M	zealous	careless	envious	eager
530M	procurement	hiring	education	dismissal
535B	invidious	useful	hateful	interesting
546T	extenuating	stretched	intense	diminished
547B	vindicated	ignored	hated	confirmed
564B	impugning	slandering	confirming	challenging
571M	vermin	yellow	pests	pets
586M	procrastinated	screamed	delayed	hurried
594B	deference	respect	put off	shame
615T	poltergeist	evil spirit	boat	magnet

Answers

sanctuary-protection, *vitiates*-spoils, *kiosk*-newsstand, *surreptitious*-secret, *oracle*-wise man, *harangue*-speech, *billet*-berth, *opaque*-

obscure, *countermand*-undo, *heresy*-skepticism, *cadenza*-long phrase, *dithyrambic*-emotional, *penance*-punishment, *khaki*-tan, *doughty*-bold, *languorous*-lazy, *surmise*-guess, *cognizant*-aware, *incredulity*-disbelief, *desultory*-casual, *gamboled*-leaped, *palatable*-agreeable, *procreative*-productive, *histrionics*-theatrics, *poltroon*-coward, *miasma*-smog, *supine*-servile, *comatose*-unconscious, *doldrums*-inaction, *perfunctory*-mechanical, *dank*-clammy, *crockery*-earthenware, *yawed*-zigzagged, *turbulent*-disordered, *taciturnity*-silence, *pleurisy*-lung disease, *peccadilloes*-little faults, *martinet*-disciplinarian, *flummery*-nonsense, *trauma*-injury, *zealous*-eager, *procurement*-hiring, *invidious*-hateful, *extenuating*-diminished, *vindicated*-confirmed, *impugning*-challenging, *vermin*-pests, *procrastinated*-delayed, *deference*-respect, *poltergeist*-evil spirit

Teaching Aids

for

THE CALL OF THE WILD

Jack London's most popular novel is set in the frozen wastelands of the Yukon. It is the story of a magnificent dog, Buck, a loyal pet until cruel men make him a pawn in their feverish search for the gold of the Klondike. Brutally clubbed and beaten into serving as a sled dog, Buck finds the blood of his wolf ancestors rising within him until he breaks free to roam the Alaskan wilderness as leader of a ferocious wolf pack. *The Call of the Wild,* a true American classic, has been called the finest dog story ever written.

I. *Objective Test*

In the space provided at the left, insert the *letter* of the correct choice from among those offered; for example:

....c....   The name of the author is (a) Melville (b) Poe (c) London (d) Cooper

.... 1. Among the other animals on Judge Miller's estate, Buck was (a) just another kennel dog (b) the acknowledged leader (c) a savage bully (d) a pampered pet

.... 2. Manuel betrayed Buck because he (a) wanted revenge on Judge Miller (b) hated dogs generally (c) loved to play Chinese lottery (d) needed money for medical bills

.... 3. When he was handed over to the kidnapper, Buck's first reaction was (a) anger (b) indifference (c) surprise (d) complete trust

.... 4. During his journey in the crate, Buck was (a) treated kindly (b) given ample food and drink (c) utterly ignored (d) teased and taunted

.... 5. After the terrible beating, the man in the red sweater (a) patted Buck's head (b) bound up his wounds (c) tied his feet with ropes (d) put him back into the crate

.... 6. Perrault considered the price he paid for Buck (a) very cheap (b) much too high (c) standard according to government regulations (d) reasonable under the circumstances

.... 7. Buck decided François was fair when the half-breed punished Spitz for (a) barking below decks (b) stealing food (c) attacking Dave (d) refusing to share his food

.... 8. The first major problem Buck faced on the trail was (a) getting something to eat (b) finding a friendly companion (c) getting out of his harness (d) finding a warm place to sleep

.... 9. Buck received his best instruction in being a good sled dog from (a) Dave and Sol-leks (b) François and Perrault (c) Spitz, the leader (d) Billee

.... 10. His first theft of food marked Buck, according to the author, as (a) "a dainty eater" (b) "fit to survive" (c) "a clever malingerer" (d) "a fool"

.... 11. Buck was unique in several respects, but the special quality most valuable to him was his (a) size (b) eyesight (c) cunning (d) memory

.... 12. Buck ran in sheer terror one day when (a) chased by Spitz (b) attacked by a wolf (c) threatened with a whip (d) pursued by mad Dolly

.... 13. The greatest danger in Alaskan travel was (a) being attacked by a bear (b) starving to death

(c) falling through the ice (d) being blinded by the sun

.... 14. As the Spitz-led team approached Dawson, Buck became a troublemaker in order to (a) avoid work (b) get more food (c) get even with François (d) undermine Spitz's authority

.... 15. François and Perrault responded to Buck's killing of Spitz by (a) punishing Buck severely (b) admiring him (c) demoting him in the line (d) vowing to trade Buck off

.... 16. In his last days, Dave exhibited a trait common to sled dogs: their (a) disregard for other dogs (b) ill-will toward the drivers (c) undying loyalty to the team effort (d) deeply imbedded wildness

.... 17. After a day's work on the mail train run to Dawson, Buck spent his most memorable moments dreaming about (a) fights he had won (b) an attack on the man in the red sweater (c) his days in sunny Santa Clara (d) an ancient, uncivilized time

.... 18. The factor that contributed most to the ultimate disaster of Hal, Charles, and Mercedes was (a) lack of money (b) lack of experience (c) cruelty to the dogs (d) severity of the weather

.... 19. Hal aroused Thornton's anger by (a) ignoring advice (b) using a club on Buck (c) slapping Mercedes (d) overturning the sled

.... 20. Both Thornton and Buck almost lost their lives in (a) a blinding snowstorm (b) a fall off a cliff (c) a sudden freeze (d) the rapids of a river

.... 21. Thornton, Pete, and Hans left Dawson to (a) return to Skagway (b) hunt bear (c) build a camp for travelers (d) look for gold

.... 22. Thornton wagered over one thousand dollars on Buck's ability to (a) fight a champion husky (b) pull a heavily loaded sled (c) swim the rapids (d) leap across a gorge

.... 23. Leaving camp one night in response to a wolf
howl, Buck gradually found himself (a) drawn
repeatedly to the wild (b) ashamed of his disloyalty (c) unable to tolerate men (d) longing
for a mate

.... 24. Buck's strategy in killing the moose was to (a)
catch him by surprise (b) join with wolves in
the attack (c) break his legs first (d) isolate
him from the herd

.... 25. In attacking the Yeehats, Buck drove them to
(a) kill one another (b) argue among themselves (c) discharge their muskets (d) hide in
the cabin

Answers

1-b, 2-c, 3-c, 4-d, 5-a, 6-d, 7-b, 8-d, 9-a, 10-b, 11-c, 12-d, 13-c,
14-d, 15-b, 16-c, 17-d, 18-b, 19-b, 20-d, 21-d, 22-b, 23-a, 24-d, 25-a

II. *Alternate Objective Tests*

A. Matching

Before each number in the column on the left, write the
letter of the item in the column on the right that matches:

.... 1. sun-kissed   a. Manuel
.... 2. Southland dog   b. Dolly
.... 3. gardener's helper   c. Matthewson
.... 4. man in the red sweater   d. Yeehats
.... 5. suddenly mad   e. Yukon River
.... 6. evil-tempered   f. Buck
.... 7. Bonanza king   g. Dyea Beach
.... 8. genuine passionate love   h. gold dust
.... 9. dancing about   i. Thornton
...... 10. yellow stream   j. club
                                         k. Santa Clara
                                         l. Black Burton

Answers

1-k, 2-f, 3-a, 4-j, 5-b, 6-l, 7-c, 8-i, 9-d, 10-h

B. Fill-ins

From the column on the right, select the item that best completes each statement below, and write it in the space provided:

1. Manuel received _____ dollars for selling Buck.
2. At Dyea Beach, Buck learned a lesson by watching _____ in a fight.
3. It was dangerous to approach _____ on his blind side.
4. Buck realized early that he would have to eat his food _____.
5. During his fight with the wild huskies, Buck was attacked by _____.
6. To relieve Buck's sore feet, François put _____ on them.
7. At Dawson City, Buck delighted in joining the _____ of the huskies.
8. Buck's showdown fight with Spitz occurred during the chase of a (an) _____.
9. At night before the fire, Buck dreamed most often of _____.
10. The dog who best symbolized devotion to duty was _____.
11. The Scotch half-breed used the team to deliver _____.
12. Mercedes was the sister of _____.
13. The sled used in Thornton's bet was loaded with _____.
14. It took Buck four days to bring down a (an) _____.

Hal
moose
flour
Spitz
daintily
rabbit
100
California
Curly
charge
cavemen
timber
Charles
50
moccasins
Buck
mail
deer
rags
Sol-leks
Thornton
quickly
song
Dave

15. To the Yeehats, _____ became
known as the Evil Spirit.

Answers

1-100, 2-Curly, 3-Sol-leks, 4-quickly, 5-Spitz, 6-moccasins, 7-song, 8-rabbit, 9-cavemen, 10-Dave, 11-mail, 12-Hal, 13-flour, 14-moose, 15-Buck

III. *Ideas for Written or Oral Book Reports or Class Discussions*

1. Early in his career as a sled dog, Buck learns that he must change or discard some of his behavior patterns that were appropriate when he was a pet in civilized society in California. What former habits and attitudes must he alter if he is to survive in his new, savage surroundings? What new skills and attitudes must he acquire? How do these changes indicate that human beings as well as animals are products of their environment? Give examples to support your point of view.

2. "Conditioning" is a learning process that develops from reactions to influences on behavior. For example, "the man in the red sweater" conditions Buck to the law of the club through repeated punishment. On the other hand, Thornton conditions Buck to respond to love by being loyal and devoted. In general, conditioning occurs as the result of repetition, punishment, or reward. How might Dave's sickness illustrate the worst results of this process? When is conditioning beneficial to an individual? When might it be disastrous?

3. Although very accurate in describing their external actions, London can only guess at the inner emotions of animals. The passages that describe how Buck felt about François and Perrault or Thornton, how he plotted the destruction of Spitz, how he had dreams of a primitive time leave the author's technique open to question about the reliability of his analysis of the thought processes of an animal. To what extent do you believe that London made

reasonable estimates of what Buck was thinking at various times? Perhaps you can support your argument by using your own pet as a comparative example.

4. Buck's dreams of a primitive life have been termed "archetypal patterns," remnants of our ancestral beginnings still retained by our subconscious, which the psychologist Carl Jung said is part of our human inheritance. To what extent do you believe that we have inherited remnants of an ancient life's "collective unconscious"? What examples can you offer? Some of our timeless legends, such as Oedipus, Job, the Flying Dutchman, are said to be archetypal stories because they seem to be repeated in different forms throughout all ages. What other similar legends, myths, or beliefs can you talk about?

5. Mercedes is the only female character in the story, and, as presented by London, she is hardly the type to inspire romantic fancies. To what extent does the book suffer because of the lack of love interest between man and woman? What would modern advocates of women's liberation have to say about London's attitude toward women as revealed in his portrait of Mercedes?

6. When Thornton bets that Buck can break out and pull the loaded sled, he risks serious injury to his dog. How justified was Thornton in using his pet to satisfy his desire for money and importance? What additional side of the man's character does this incident reveal? How is it related to the foolish risks people sometimes take in order to gain recognition?

7. Some people keep lion cubs, leopards, cheetahs, and other very savage animals as pets. What qualities are necessary in both the individual and the animal to make such a relationship possible? Do you know of anyone who has such a pet, or have you read about such a relationship? Describe the problems and the rewards, if any.

8. Ask the librarian to lend you a collection of short stories that includes Jack London's "To Build a Fire." After you have read the story, develop a comparison of the writer's theories about man and animal in the short story and the novel.

9. There are those who claim that hunting by man as a

sport is a cruel and unnecessary activity. Yet meat-eating animals cannot survive unless they seek out and kill their prey, sometimes on a daily basis. Buck, for example, does not hesitate to hunt rabbits and even brings down a moose. Of course, the differences in hunting purposes by man and animal are obvious. However, if you favor hunting for sport, what justification can you offer? If you are opposed, what arguments would you offer against it, and what laws would you like to see passed? What are your thoughts about trapping animals only for the purpose of using their skins?

10. Most critics agree that London's style of writing contributes greatly to his developing an exciting narrative. How does he use contrast in describing the death struggle between Buck and Spitz (pp. 36–39)? In the scene with the "man in the red sweater" (pp. 8–9), why is the effect heightened when the author supplies the reactions of the man and the animal as well as the details of the beating? Why does London repeat the word *pride* eight times in a single paragraph (pp. 31–32)? What other elements of London's style did you find especially attractive?

IV. *Vocabulary Study*

Diagnostic Test

2T populous	barren	well-liked	densely populated
2B imperiously	lamely	domineeringly	gently
3B progeny	offspring	ancestors	wonder
5M lacerated	healed	decorated	torn
7M metamorphosed	repeated	transformed	drugged
10M wheedling	turning	commanding	coaxing
10M weazened	swollen	shriveled	savage
13T primordial	original	copy	savage
13M vicarious	direct	substitute	holy
15B incarnation	embodiment	flower	spirit
16B disconsolate	happy	musical	sad
17M placatingly	soothingly	indifferently	irritatingly

20B	malingerer	authority	faker	officer
21B	retrogression	deterioration	advance	explosion
22M	primeval	civilized	superior	primitive
27M	maurauders	guards	plunderers	sailors
32M	prostrate	stiff	swaying	lying flat
32B	covert	open	hidden	level
33M	aurora borealis	cloud	darkness	northern lights
34M	insidious	open	sly	sweet
35T	bedlam	uproar	peace	illness
35B	wraith	branch	anger	ghost
36M	rampant	unchecked	controlled	walkway
39T	inexorable	sagging	lovable	unrelenting
41T	obdurate	stubborn	lenient	close
53T	slovenly	neat	untidy	warm
53M	remonstrance	agreement	parade	protest
58B	voracious	greedy	sated	trim
58B	cajole	reject	coax	climb
59B	amenities	insults	challenges	niceties
60B	copious	short	abundant	heady
61M	importuned	entreated	ordered	brought in
64T	innocuously	dangerously	harmlessly	quickly
64M	terse	to the point	off the point	fingered
72M	peremptorily	weakly	largely	commandingly
78M	appalled	entertained	shocked	built
79T	plethoric	scanty	overful	steady
79B	jubilant	sad	slight	joyful
82M	babel	stillness	children	tumult
84M	ramshackle	sturdy	shaky	butting
87T	salient	obscure	seaworthy	noticeable
89B	pertinacity	persistence	impatience	pretty
92M	carnivorous	vegetarian	flesh-eating	clownish
93B	quarry	hunter	mineral	prey
94M	simulated	avowed	pretended	coincided
95M	harrying	tormenting	protecting	naming
96M	shambling	trotting	breaking	moving lazily
96M	palpitant	dull	throbbing	messy
97M	excrescence	cut	outgrowth	exterior
98T	usurp	overthrow	install	swallow

Answers

populous-densely populated, *imperiously*-domineeringly, *progeny*-offspring, *lacerated*-torn, *metamorphosed*-transformed, *wheedling*-

coaxing, *weazened*-shriveled, *primordial*-original, *vicarious*-substitute, *incarnation*-embodiment, *disconsolate*-sad, *placatingly*-soothingly, *malingerer*-faker, *retrogression*-deterioration, *primeval*-primitive, *marauders*-plunderers, *prostrate*-lying flat, *covert*-hidden, *aurora borealis*-northern lights, *insidious*-sly, *bedlam*-uproar, *wraith*-ghost, *rampant*-unchecked, *inexorable*-unrelenting, *obdurate*-stubborn, *slovenly*-untidy, *remonstrance*-protest, *voracious*-greedy, *cajole*-coax, *amenities*-niceties, *copious*-abundant, *importuned*-entreated, *innocuously*-harmlessly, *terse*-to the point, *peremptorily*-commandingly, *appalled*-shocked, *plethoric*-overful, *jubilant*-joyful, *babel*-tumult, *ramshackle*-shaky, *salient*-noticeable, *pertinacity*-persistence, *carnivorous*-flesh-eating, *quarry*-prey, *simulated*-pretended, *harrying*-tormenting, *shambling*-moving lazily, *palpitant*-throbbing, *excrescence*-outgrowth, *usurp*-overthrow

Teaching Aids

for

CRIME AND PUNISHMENT

This powerful story of a young university student who sets out to prove that he is a superior human being capable of committing the perfect murder has thrilled readers ever since it was first published. With the possible exception of *War and Peace,* there is probably no Russian novel so universally read and admired as this masterpiece of Dostoevsky. It has all the ingredients of a great work of fiction: a superb story of crime and detection, a taut psychological study, and the drama of man's eternal efforts to revolt against God.

I. *Objective Test*

In the space provided at the left, insert the *letter* of the correct choice from among those offered; for example:

....b....   The author of this book is (a) Turgenev (b) Dostoevsky (c) Tolstoy

.... 1. Raskolnikov's mood when we first met him was (a) gay, lighthearted (b) somber, pensive (c) serene, calm

.... 2. On his first visit to the pawnbroker, Raskolnikov (a) pawned something (b) left a pledge (c) murdered her

.... 3. The pawnbroker was (a) sweet but old (b) young and vivacious (c) ugly and vicious

104

.... 4. Raskolnikov's *initial* reaction to Marmeladov was one of (a) disgust (b) curiosity (c) pity

.... 5. The cause of Marmeladov's misfortunes was (a) his wife (b) drink (c) ambition

.... 6. Raskolnikov became interested in Marmeladov because of (a) Sonya (b) Marmeladov's honesty (c) Marmeladov's usefulness

.... 7. Raskolnikov objected to help from his sister's suitor because he (a) wanted to study (b) would have money from the murder (c) didn't want her to sacrifice herself for him

.... 8. Which of the following traits were *not* used to describe Raskolnikov? (a) gloomy, proud (b) isolated, unsociable (c) manic, ambitious

.... 9. If we treat symbolically the dream about beating the horse, the horse stands for (a) the pawnbroker (b) Sonya (c) Marmeladov

.... 10. Raskolnikov thought of the murder as (a) humanitarian (b) unnecessary (c) exotic

.... 11. A motive that was disproved after the murder was (a) revenge (b) financial gain (c) passion

.... 12. Raskolnikov considered Luzhin (a) an intellectual (b) a successful businessman (c) a fop

.... 13. Leaving the pawnbroker's apartment after the murder, Raskolnikov looked on the world as a (a) dead soul (b) sanctuary (c) generous host

.... 14. Having taken the dying, crushed Marmeladov home, Raskolnikov came down to the street filled with (a) hate (b) disgust (c) exhilaration

.... 15. In character, Dunya was more like (a) Sonya (b) Raskolnikov (c) Razumikhin

.... 16. Raskolnikov considered himself to be (a) subhuman (b) ordinary (c) extraordinary

.... 17. The magazine article Raskolnikov wrote revealed his theory of (a) superman (b) heredity (c) socialism

.... 18. Porfiry's suspicion of Raskolnikov rested on

(a) the hidden loot (b) Raskolnikov's manner
(c) the painter's words

.... 19. Compared to the way Raskolnikov felt after the murder, when he confessed to Sonya he felt (a) the same way (b) more hatred (c) more antagonism

.... 20. Sonya asked Raskolnikov to explain his motives so she could (a) understand them (b) feel them (c) reveal them

.... 21. The first time Dunya shot at Svidrigailov (a) she killed him (b) the bullet grazed him (c) the gun exploded

.... 22. Svidrigailov had no apparent ulterior motive for helping (a) Dunya (b) Luzhin (c) the Marmeladovs

.... 23. Dunya and Razumikhin (a) married (b) separated (c) remained friends

.... 24. In the beginning, the attitude of the other prisoners toward Raskolnikov was one of (a) jealousy (b) distrust (c) admiration

.... 25. At the end of the novel, Raskolnikov (a) shot himself (b) died in prison (c) was converted

Answers

1-b, 2-a, 3-c, 4-a, 5-b, 6-b, 7-c, 8-c, 9-a, 10-a, 11-b, 12-c, 13-a, 14-c, 15-b, 16-c, 17-a, 18-b, 19-a, 20-b, 21-b, 22-c, 23-a, 24-b, 25-c

II. *Alternate Objective Tests*

A. Matching

Before each number in the column on the left, write the *letter* of the item in the column on the right that matches:

.... 1. Raskolnikov
.... 2. Razumikhin
.... 3. Sonya
.... 4. Dunya

a. shot himself
b. Luzhin's intended
c. socialist
d. barber

.... 5. Porfiry	e. married Dunya
.... 6. Marmeladov's wife	f. a fop
.... 7. Lebezyatnikov	g. government clerk
.... 8. Svidrigailov	h. pawnbroker's sister
.... 9. Luzhin	i. police officer
...... 10. Lizaveta	j. streetwalker
	k. pawnbroker
	l. priest
	m. magazine author
	n. landlady
	o. consumptive

Answers

1-m, 2-e, 3-j, 4-c, 5-i, 6-o, 7-a, 8-d, 9-f, 10-h

B. Fill-ins

From the column on the right, select the item that best completes each statement below, and write it in the space provided:

1. The time of the murder was near _____ o'clock.
2. Raskolnikov's garret was on the _____ floor.
3. The murder weapon was a (an) _____.
4. Svidrigailov died by a (an) _____.
5. Marmeladov's death was caused by a _____.
6. Sonya had a yellow _____.
7. Raskolnikov was sent to Siberia for _____ years.
8. The accuser at Marmeladov's funeral feast was _____.
9. Marmeladov's wife had won attention as a (an) _____.

gun
Luzhin
horse
dancer
cook
fainted
rape
hatchet
third
Sonya
loot
seven
eight
confessed
ticket
fifth

10. On his first visit to the police station, Raskolnikov _____.
11. Svidrigailov's intention toward Dunya was to _____ her.
12. In the police station, Porfiry planned a (an) _____ for Raskolnikov.
13. Raskolnikov gave the pawnbroker a fake _____.
14. Sonya's friend was _____.
15. Svidrigailov was *alleged* to have killed his wife by _____ her.

Lizaveta
beating
poisoning
pledge
surprise

Answers

1-seven, 2-fifth, 3-hatchet, 4-gun, 5-horse, 6-ticket, 7-eight, 8-Luzhin, 9-dancer, 10-fainted, 11-rape, 12-surprise, 13-pledge, 14-Lizaveta, 15-poisoning

III. *Ideas for Written or Oral Book Reports or Class Discussions*

1. Many aspects of life in Russia, and especially St. Petersburg, in the mid-1800s seem unusual to a twentieth-century American. Select at least three customs, habits, or attitudes described in *Crime and Punishment* that are unfamiliar to you. For instance, how do you feel about the Russian attitude toward the marriage that was to be arranged between Svidrigailov and his very young intended bride? In a full discussion of each, explain the differences time and place have brought about.

2. Some aspects of life in St. Petersburg in the mid-1800's seem quite familiar to even a twentieth-century American. Select at least three customs, habits, or attitudes described in *Crime and Punishment* that would fit very easily into our way of life. For instance, you might choose the way the Raskolnikov family tried to stick together in a time of strife. In a full discussion of each, explain the similarities that time and place have not affected.

3. In a letter in June 1865, Dostoevsky wrote, "My

novel is called *The Drunkards* and will be tied in with the current issue of drunkenness . . . [with] all its ramifications . . . shown especially [will be] scenes of family life and the education of children in such conditions, etc. . . ." Hence, *Crime and Punishment* began as a story of the Marmeladov family, but in the finished version, the family (except for Sonya) does not play a large part. Was Dostoevsky just padding *Crime and Punishment* with a part of a novel he never published? On the other hand, would the "good" side of Raskolnikov's character be complete unless we saw him helping the Marmeladov family? Analyze in detail why you think Dostoevsky decreased his emphasis on the Marmeladov family in the novel and why he built up the role played by Raskolnikov.

4. With which side of Raskolnikov's personality does Dostoevsky's sympathy lie? Did Dostoevsky really want Raskolnikov to be able to carry off the crime? Do you feel the author was unsympathetic toward Raskolnikov's weakness? If you do not, how do you explain the passage (p. 539B) where he says, "Crime? What crime? . . . Only now do I see the full absurdity of my faintheartedness, only now when I've already decided to accept this needless disgrace! I'm doing it simply because I'm worthless and a mediocrity. . . ." Take one point of view or the other, and support it by citing other passages that reveal what you consider to be the true sympathy of Dostoevsky.

5. In the alternate ending to the novel (revealed in Dostoevsky's notebooks), Raskolnikov killed himself. Do you agree with several critics that the present ending is weak? Take one point of view or the other, and support it with a vigorous written defense.

6. In July 1866, Dostoevsky wrote a letter saying that his publishers wanted to eliminate the chapter where Sonya reads the story of Lazarus to Raskolnikov (pp. 337T–339B). He said, "They aren't concerned with its literary excellence, but only with its *morality*. I'm right on this point. There is nothing immoral in this chapter; in fact, the very opposite is true. But they see it differently, and in fact see even traces of nihilism in the chapter." What is revealed in the characters of Sonya and Raskol-

nikov in this chapter? Is the chapter really necessary? Take one point of view or the other, and, making specific references to this chapter, defend your argument.

7. One of the best evidences of an author's writing skill is the extent to which he is able to develop his characters so that they grow and even change as the story progresses. Select one character in *Crime and Punishment* who is markedly different at the end from what he or she was at the beginning. Select another who remains relatively unchanged. In each instance, center your discussion on at least three characteristics that are altered by events or remain unaffected by them. Make references to the story to support your conclusions.

8. The characters who creep about in *Crime and Punishment* seem to come from (as some critics have said) an "improbable" world. The atmosphere of the novel and the weird characters who people it are so fantastic that we cannot believe they could exist. Or can we? Is there sufficient realism in the novel? Given the characters and circumstances, could the plot have happened in our world? Argue the case for or against Dostoevsky's realism, citing at least three "realistic" or "fantastic" incidents to support your point of view.

9. What was the real motivation for killing the pawnbroker? Cite at least four possible motivations and choose one which is the most convincing to you. Develop reasons for your choice of the one and your rejection of the other three.

10. In a passage in his notebooks, Dostoevsky wrote, "Svidrigailov is desperation, the most cynical. Sonya is hope, the most realizable (Raskolnikov must express this). He was passionately tied to both." Hence, these two characters are supposed to express both sides of Raskolnikov, the good and bad angels, so to speak. Do they? Is there an even balance? If not, in which direction is the scale tipped? Support your answer by citing evidence about both Sonya and Svidrigailov in their relations to Raskolnikov.

11. What is the "crime" and what is the "punishment" in *Crime and Punishment?* There is a surface answer, and

there is a profound answer. Indicate the surface answer first, and then develop a fully supported essay about the profound answer.

IV. *Vocabulary Study*

Diagnostic Test

4T	hypochondria	serpent	health-anxiety	courage
4T	drivel	nonsense	drain	wisdom
5M	scruples	unconscious	conscience	scratches
11T	premonition	scolding	mystery	forewarning
14B	penchant	hatred	stone	inclination
16B	pillory	ridicule	praise	build
22M	dissolute	melted	debauched	moral
36M	infamy	disgrace	honor	civil right
37M	supercilious	humble	silly	haughty
49B	fop	laborer	candy	vain man
54T	inordinately	numerically	excessively	moderately
68T	splay	spread	split	contract
79M	athwart	under	above	across
83B	spasmodically	twitchingly	gracefully	movingly
100M	cynicism	optimism	belief	pessimism
117M	malevolent	benevolent	masculine	ill-willed
119T	charlatan	quack	expert	knight
131M	metaphysical	clear	healthy	abstract
150T	ingenious	clever	innocent	similar
156M	platitude	epigram	commonplace	joke
159T	inveterate	casual	habitual	military
183B	mettlesome	lazy	brassy	spirited
192B	rakish	sloppy	dashing	sweeping
215B	surreptitiously	openly	steadily	stealthily
224M	impoverished	poor	rich	grand
235M	deranged	twined	insane	cooled
248M	solicitude	concern	indifference	greed
265B	retrograde	moving back	moving forward	guessing
293M	ambiguous	straight	creamy	vague
307T	elucidated	darkened	explained	puzzled
353M	buffoon	clown	ball	miser
361M	paroxysm	relaxation	sarcasm	seizure

379T heterogeneous	similar	varied	bright
388M naïveté	artlessness	intricacy	heaviness
389M ephemeral	permanent	queenly	fleeting
395T berserk	frenzied	calm	sad
407M incessant	ceaseless	short	mild
417B denouement	beginning	outcome	veil
430M enigmatically	openly	sharply	perplexingly
446T implacable	relentless	forgiving	positioned
457M morbidly	happily	deeply	gloomily
473M trepidation	fear	hope	bias
479M disingenuous	reliable	witty	insincere
485M deferential	callous	respectful	bold
491T braggadocio	shyness	skill	boastfulness
503M scowled	smiled	frowned	peered
514M vindictive	vengeful	cooperative	loose
526B petrified	softened	stunned	leveled
538M unquenchable	manageable	fiery	uncontrollable
550M ascetic	generous	self-denying	cheerful

Answers

hypochrondia-health-anxiety, *drivel*-nonsense, *scruples*-conscience, *premonition*-forewarning, *penchant*-inclination, *pillory*-ridicule, *dissolute*-debauched, *infamy*-disgrace, *supercilious*-haughty, *fop*-vain man, *inordinately*-excessively, *splay*-spread, *athwart*-across, *spasmodically*-twitchingly, *cynicism*-pessimism, *malevolent*-ill-willed, *charlatan*-quack, *metaphysical*-abstract, *ingenious*-clever, *platitude*-commonplace, *inveterate*-habitual, *mettlesome*-spirited, *rakish*-dashing, *surreptitiously*-stealthily, *impoverished*-poor, *deranged*-insane, *solicitude*-concern, *retrograde*-moving back, *ambiguous*-vague, *elucidated*-explained, *buffoon*-clown, *paroxysm*-seizure, *heterogeneous*-varied, *naïveté*-artlessness, *ephemeral*-fleeting, *berserk*-frenzied, *incessant*-ceaseless, *denouement*-outcome, *enigmatically*-perplexingly, *implacable*-relentless, *morbidly*-gloomily, *trepidation*-fear, *disingenuous*-insincere, *deferential*-respectful, *braggadocio*-boastfulness, *scowled*-frowned, *vindictive*-vengeful, *petrified*-stunned, *unquenchable*-uncontrollable, *ascetic*-self-denying

Teaching Aids

for

DR. JEKYLL AND MR. HYDE

The use of the term "Jekyll and Hyde personality" is commonplace today. It is no small tribute to the narrative skill and extraordinary insight of Robert Louis Stevenson that the title of his most famous novel has been incorporated into our language to describe man when he is harassed by struggles within himself. Readers who have not yet thrilled to the excitement of this tale of horror have a chilling treat in store for them—as well as a disconcerting glimpse into the darkest recesses of human emotions.

I. *Objective Test*

In the space provided at the left, insert the *letter* of the correct choice from among those offered; for example:

....b....   The author of this book is (a) Poe (b) Stevenson (c) Doyle

.... 1. The atmosphere of the story seemed most like that of a (a) scientific treatise (b) religious tract (c) nightmare

.... 2. The author's descriptive powers were best shown in his accounts of (a) Hyde's facial characteristics (b) London's weather (c) Lanyon's medical office

.... 3. The first story about Mr. Hyde came from (a) Dr. Lanyon (b) Mr. Enfield (c) Poole

.... 4. The captors of Mr. Hyde, including the child's father, waited all night so that in the morning they could (a) cash a check (b) notify the police (c) obtain a confession

.... 5. People who saw Mr. Hyde found him (a) easy to describe (b) difficult to describe (c) similar to a clown

.... 6. Dr. Jekyll and Mr. Utterson disagreed about Dr. Jekyll's (a) experiments (b) will (c) servants

.... 7. Poole's distinguishing characteristic was his (a) loyalty (b) dishonesty (c) envy

.... 8. It was evident that Dr. Jekyll had been born (a) into a wealthy family (b) in poor surroundings (c) in France

.... 9. Dr. Jekyll experienced despair when he lost (a) confidence in Mr. Utterson (b) Dr. Lanyon as a friend (c) control over his experiment

.... 10. After the murder, Dr. Jekyll seemed sure that Hyde would (a) never appear again (b) overcome him (c) be arrested

.... 11. The two main elements in the story seemed to be horror aroused and (a) science explained (b) moral expounded (c) methods of detection outlined

.... 12. Dr. Jekyll's final will left the bulk of his estate to (a) Hyde (b) Utterson (c) Poole

.... 13. Mr. Utterson's trustworthiness was shown by his (a) behavior in court (b) defense of his needy clients (c) locking up Dr. Lanyon's letter unread

.... 14. Their appearances made it clear that Mr. Hyde was (a) younger than Jekyll (b) older than Jekyll (c) taller than Jekyll

.... 15. Dr. Jekyll and Dr. Lanyon had disagreed on matters involving (a) medical ethics (b) wills (c) science

.... 16. Poole suspected that Dr. Jekyll had been murdered because of the (a) unpaid bills (b) uneaten food (c) sound of the voice coming from his office

.... 17. Dr. Jekyll ordered Poole to return the chemical because it (a) did not work (b) was impure (c) was too costly

.... 18. Poole felt certain that the masked man could not be Dr. Jekyll because the former was too (a) short (b) tall (c) heavy

.... 19. Dr. Lanyon's illness seemed to be a direct result of (a) old age (b) a sudden stroke (c) witnessing Dr. Jekyll's experiment

.... 20. After they found the dead body, Poole and Mr. Utterson searched for (a) the murder weapon (b) Dr. Jekyll (c) the chemical

.... 21. Dr. Jekyll wrote that he had originally postponed trying out his experiment because of fear of (a) death (b) disgrace (c) imprisonment

.... 22. One of the reactions Dr. Jekyll experienced during his first successful experiment was a feeling of (a) drowsiness (b) great peace (c) excruciating pain

.... 23. The first knowledge Dr. Jekyll had that he had turned into Hyde without using his chemicals was the sight of (a) the trampled child (b) the murdered man (c) his hand

.... 24. The only power of Dr. Jekyll's that Hyde possessed was the ability to (a) experiment scientifically (b) duplicate Jekyll's handwriting (c) believe in his religion

.... 25. The cause of Dr. Jekyll's death was (a) a bullet wound (b) a blow on the head (c) poison

Answers

1-c, 2-b, 3-b, 4-a, 5-b, 6-b, 7-a, 8-a, 9-c, 10-a, 11-b, 12-b, 13-c, 14-a, 15-c, 16-c, 17-a, 18-a, 19-c, 20-b, 21-a, 22-c, 23-c, 24-b, 25-c

II. *Alternate Objective Tests*

A. Matching

Before each number in the column on the left, write the *letter* of the item in the column on the right that matches:

....	1. Dr. Jekyll's butler	a. burn the laboratory
....	2. Hyde's penalty	b. Dr. Lanyon
....	3. Dr. Lanyon's mission	c. suicide
....	4. The man Hyde killed	d. duality
....	5. Dr. Jekyll's school friend	e. Poole
....	6. Dr. Jekyll's lawyer	f. crime
....	7. Mr. Utterson's kinsman	g. 100 pounds
....	8. Dr. Lanyon's statement	h. Mr. Utterson
....	9. Cause of Dr. Jekyll's death	i. clergyman
......	10. Subject of Dr. Jekyll's study	j. hanging
		k. deliver a drawer
		l. Enfield
		m. Sir Danvers Carew
		n. sealed letter

Answers

1-e, 2-g, 3-k, 4-m, 5-b, 6-h, 7-l, 8-n, 9-c, 10-d

B. Fill-ins

From the column on the right, select the item that best completes each statement below, and write it in the space provided:

1. Dr. Jekyll's home and laboratory had formerly belonged to a (an) _____.
2. In his normal life, Dr. Jekyll had been known for his _____.
3. The new chemicals did not work because they were _____.

hand
experiments
murdered
too pure
deformed
a dwarf

4. People who saw Hyde thought he was
   _____.

5. The first account of Hyde concerned
   his mistreatment of a (an) _____.

6. A clue left by Carew's attacker was
   part of a (an) _____.

7. Dr. Jekyll had _____ servants.

8. In comparison with Dr. Jekyll, Mr.
   Hyde seemed to be _____.

9. Early in the story, Mr. Utterson was
   worried about Dr. Jekyll's _____.

10. Dr. Jekyll finally could not _____
    his changes.

11. Poole asked _____ to help him.

12. Afraid to go to his home, Dr. Jekyll
    sought help from _____.

13. Poole seemed sure that Dr. Jekyll had
    been _____.

14. Dr. Jekyll and Dr. Lanyon had grown
    less friendly because of Dr. Jekyll's
    _____.

15. That part of Hyde's body that the
    author described in detail was his
    _____.

many
cane
surgeon
too impure
a giant
charities
beneficiary
child
checkbook
two
bring about
Utterson
Lanyon
arrested
control
face

Answers

1-surgeon, 2-charities, 3-too pure, 4-deformed, 5-child, 6-cane, 7-many, 8-a dwarf, 9-beneficiary, 10-control, 11-Utterson, 12-Lanyon, 13-murdered, 14-experiments, 15-hand

III. *Ideas for Written or Oral Book Reports or Class Discussions*

1. While we cannot believe in Dr. Jekyll's chemical theories, there is an important lesson to be learned from the book. Explain that lesson (a) in terms of Dr. Jekyll's dual personality and (b) in terms of human beings living today. Discuss whether you think the story could be more

effectively told as a believable tale of warring elements in a person's soul or as Stevenson wrote it, with the chemicals producing a physical and moral change in Dr. Jekyll.

2. What lesson do you think the author was trying to teach by having Dr. Jekyll turn more and more frequently into Mr. Hyde without benefit of his chemical potion? How can you apply this lesson to certain aspects of character development? Give an example of a person about whom you have heard or read who, having experimented with evil of some kind, fell almost unthinkingly into evil practices.

3. Why do you suppose the author chose to describe Mr. Hyde only in terms of his dwarfish stature and the appearance of his hand? If you were asked to supply a detailed description of Mr. Hyde, what would that description contain? Why do you think different readers would vary in their descriptions of Mr. Hyde? To what extent is a person's character mirrored in his appearance? What do you think the author's purpose was in making Mr. Hyde's appearance so different from Dr. Jekyll's?

4. We read very little about Dr. Jekyll's circle of friends, although we know that he had five or six old friends to dinner (p. 25T). The only two who are described at all are Dr. Lanyon and Mr. Utterson. Why do you think Dr. Jekyll considered one or the other a closer friend of his? Explain with examples from the book why you believe Mr. Utterson or Dr. Lanyon really was a true friend to Dr. Jekyll. The relationship between Dr. Jekyll and Dr. Lanyon turned out to be a stormy one. They had been companions at school (p. 77T) and had remained friends ever since. Ten years before the story began, they had disagreed on scientific matters (p. 14M). Explain whether or not Mr. Hyde's transformation in Dr. Lanyon's office could have been the cause of Dr. Lanyon's decline and death.

5. Make a comparative study of *Dr. Jekyll and Mr. Hyde* and a more recent mystery or horror story that impressed you. In a paragraph for each item, compare the two books in terms of

a. Characterization (In which of the two books do the characters seem more lifelike and fully drawn? Give reasons for your opinion.)
b. Plot (In which of the two books does the action seem to be more real and plausible? Why?)
c. Elements of mystery and horror (In which of the two books do these elements seem to be more terrifying? Why?)
d. Suspense (In which of the two books did you find the suspense greater? Why?)

In a final paragraph, analyze which of the two books you consider a more impressive novel, one which is likely to remain in your thoughts.

6. Some critics have complained that Stevenson was rather careless in permitting inconsistencies to remain in his plot details. For example, Mr. Hyde *(not as Dr. Jekyll)* cautions Dr. Lanyon to keep the secret of the potion "under the seal of our profession" (p. 87M). Obviously, Dr. Lanyon could not have known at the time that he was dealing with Dr. Jekyll and should have told Mr. Hyde that only doctors could talk about "our profession." Moreover, it seems likely that even the most bungling police officers would have connected Mr. Hyde with Dr. Jekyll in the Danvers murder. What other details in the story seemed the products of mistakes by the author or ideas hard to accept as believable? Explain. On the other hand, comment on the thought that in order to lose oneself completely in and enjoy a horror tale one must ignore mistakes and "suspend belief." Otherwise, perhaps, one loses the whole purpose of the story.

7. Stevenson's powers of description are shown mainly in his accounts of London weather at critical points in the story (pp. 16B, 29M, 31B, 33B, 41B–42M, 58B–59M, 67M, 108B) and the effect of Mr. Hyde on those who saw him (pp. 4B–5T, 9B–10T, 20M, 21B, 32M, 67T–M, 83M). Explain (a) what the descriptions of the weather add to the story and (b) why the effect Mr. Hyde made on on-lookers is or is not more impressive and chilling than an actual description of him might have been.

8. The story begins with the Sunday walk of Mr. Utterson and Mr. Enfield, during which Mr. Enfield gives his account of the evil creature who trampled the child. The book ends with two letters: Dr. Lanyon's account of the transformation in his office and Dr. Jekyll's "full statement of the case." Explain why you think Stevenson's time arrangement was more or less effective for his purposes than the same details given in chronological order.

9. In spite of the fact that we speak loosely of one person as "a perfect angel" and of another as "a perfect devil," we can probably agree with the psychologists that a human being is a mixture of both good and bad traits. After preparing a list of Dr. Jekyll's good traits and of Mr. Hyde's evil traits, explain why you do or do not believe that such opposing traits can actually exist in the same human being. Then evaluate what you think the author gained for his story by having the opposing traits embodied in two different people.

10. Although it is clear that Dr. Jekyll is the good person and Mr. Hyde, Dr. Jekyll's other self, the bad person, several things are not so clear. What may have driven the doctor to experiment in dual personalities in the first place? What may have been missing in his life that caused him to attempt changes that would give him other experiences than the ones with which he was familiar? In answering these questions, consider the hints that are supplied about the kinds of things Mr. Hyde did other than the violent crimes. In summary, how often does it happen that a rich, respected professional person, admired by his community and colleagues, is suddenly exposed as having a shady side of life that shocks everyone? What example can you offer from real life? Describe it.

IV. *Vocabulary Study*

Diagnostic Test

1M	eminently	scantily	notably	partially
3B	sinister	worthy	straight	evil

3B	sordid	vile	candid	excellent
7B	proprieties	owners	mistakes	correct behavior
14M	protégé	protector	marvel	one under another's care
23T	condoned	pardoned	completed	accused
23T	iniquity	virtue	wickedness	unfairness
26M	heresies	rumors	accepted doctrines	unauthorized opinions
26M	blatant	noisy	hesitant	quiet
26M	ruthlessly	kindly	pitilessly	carelessly
34T	hypocrisy	honesty	cruelty	false pretense
35T	connoisseur	playboy	tasteless one	critical judge
39B	ruminated	argued	meditated	acted rashly
42B	elicited	hid	drew forth	acted illegally
51T	inscrutable	unhappy	understood	incomprehensible
53M	repulsion	reform	attraction	strong dislike
68T	malefactor	maker	evildoer	sympathetic friend
73T	blasphemies	lies	pious remarks	irreverencies
78B	morbid	glum	unwholesome	healthful
81B	pungent	bland	penetrating	punishing
83B	incipient	final	receipt	beginning
84M	disparity	difference	disposition	likeness
86M	metamorphoses	changes	marvels	constancies
86M	scrutiny	scolding	oversight	close examination
87M	enigmas	riddles	proofs	evident truths
87B	derided	ridiculed	separated	praised
88M	incredulous	gullible	unbelievable	unbelieving
89M	imperious	lordly	impish	humble
89B	duplicity	variety	deception	sincerity
90T	inveterately	habitually	seldom	youthfully
91T	incongruous	comic	harmonious	inconsistent
91T	denizens	foreigners	inhabitants	tourists
91T	infallibly	unsteadily	mistakenly	unerringly
91B	extraneous	foreign	additional	applicable
95M	lethal	deadly	permissive	curative
98T	pecuniary	intellectual	monetary	peculiarly
99T	malign	evil	envious	virtuous
99T	avidity	coldness	indifference	greediness
99M	insidiously	sideways	treacherously	scrupulously

99M	infamy	dishonor	youth	high repute
99M	connived	made	denounced	cooperated secretly
100B	comely	ugly	good-looking	hearty
105M	propensity	tendency	propriety	disinclination
108T	beneficent	blissful	charitable	barbarous
108B	subsequent	later	underneath	previous
111T	astute	shrewd	naïve	harsh
113M	impending	blessing	menacing	elapsing
114T	phenomena	events	hopes	tricks
114T	poignant	unfelt	touching	steely
115M	acquiescence	rejection	acceptance	acquisition

Answers

eminently-notably, *sinister*-evil, *sordid*-vile, *proprieties*-correct behavior, *protégé*-one under the care of another, *condoned*-pardoned, *iniquity*-wickedness, *heresies*-unauthorized opinions, *blatant*-noisy, *ruthlessly*-pitilessly, *hypocrisy*-false pretense, *connoisseur*-critical judge, *ruminated*-meditated, *elicited*-drew forth, *inscrutable*-incomprehensible, *repulsion*-strong dislike, *malefactor*-evildoer, *blasphemies*-irreverencies, *morbid*-unwholesome, *pungent*-penetrating, *incipient*-beginning, *disparity*-difference, *metamorphoses*-changes, *scrutiny*-close examination, *enigmas*-riddles, *derided*-ridiculed, *incredulous*-unbelieving, *imperious*-lordly, *duplicity*-deception, *inveterately*-habitually, *incongruous*-inconsistent, *denizens*-inhabitants, *infallibly*-unerringly, *extraneous*-foreign, *lethal*-deadly, *pecuniary*-monetary, *malign*-evil, *avidity*-greediness, *insidiously*-treacherously, *infamy*-dishonor, *connived*-cooperated secretly, *comely*-good-looking, *propensity*-tendency, *beneficent*-charitable, *subsequent*-later, *astute*-shrewd, *impending*-menacing, *phenomena*-events, *poignant*-touching, *acquiescence*-acceptance

Teaching Aids

for

DON QUIXOTE

Cervantes conceived of this book as a biting satire on the Spain of his day. But his own high spirits and wealth of imagination transformed Don Quixote, a figure of ridicule, into a truly noble hero. The beloved classic, a comic masterpiece, was called by Macaulay "the best novel in the world, beyond comparison." Other critics have said: "Many generations of the most diverse sorts have taken delight in *Don Quixote,* for it suits all ages, all conditions, all temperaments, and all races. It has agreed with all of them, for, judging by the number and extraordinary variety of the translations, they do not weary of it."

I. *Objective Test*

In the space provided at the left, insert the *letter* of the correct choice from among those offered; for example:

....b....   The author of this book is (a) Twain (b) Cervantes (c) Lopez

.... 1. Don Quixote sold many acres of land to buy (a) armor (b) books (c) horses

.... 2. The prisoners freed by Don Quixote showed their gratitude to him by (a) praying for him (b) giving him food (c) stoning him

.... 3. Sancho gave up his governorship (a) of his own accord (b) when he was ordered back by the duke (c) when he was evicted by the citizens

.... 4. After Sancho had left for his island, the first mishap that befell Don Quixote was (a) the death of his horse (b) evil rumors about him (c) runs in his stockings

.... 5. Don Quixote and Sancho were alike in that (a) both loved Dulcinea (b) neither cared about her (c) neither had ever seen her

.... 6. The boy whom Don Quixote rescued from being whipped was (a) paid his wages by his master (b) whipped much more severely (c) a knight in disguise

.... 7. One characteristic that Sancho could not learn from Don Quixote was how to (a) speak better (b) talk about knights (c) act like a hero

.... 8. In judging cases on his "island," Sancho seemed to be unusually (a) silly (b) wise (c) greedy

.... 9. One habit of Sancho's that Don Quixote acquired was (a) yearning for money (b) quoting proverbs (c) worrying about his family

.... 10. Don Quixote's one victory occurred in his encounter with the (a) Knight of the Mirrors (b) Knight of the White Moon (c) hogs

.... 11. The second time Don Quixote returned home, he was (a) lying on a donkey (b) in a cage (c) on a stretcher

.... 12. The "giant" whose head Don Quixote cut off turned out to be a (a) wineskin (b) puppet (c) windmill

.... 13. Don Quixote seemed to be in the greatest danger when he wanted to attack the (a) lion (b) Knight of the Mirrors (c) enchanted head

.... 14. Don Quixote called the windmills (a) enchanters (b) devils (c) giants

.... 15. The duke and duchess looked upon Don Quixote with (a) admiration (b) hatred (c) ridicule

.... 16. Samson Carrasco was called a bachelor because

he was (a) unmarried (b) a lawyer (c) a university graduate

.... 17. Don Quixote's niece, housekeeper, and friends looked upon him with (a) anger (b) pity (c) envy

.... 18. Sancho Panza's main interest was in (a) food (b) power (c) health

.... 19. Don Quixote never met a real knight-errant because there were (a) none (b) too few (c) too many in hiding

.... 20. Don Quixote seemed to be very well acquainted with (a) science (b) literature (c) theology

.... 21. At the duke's house, Sancho was displeased with the manner used to (a) wash his beard (b) feed him (c) dress him

.... 22. At the time of the story, barbers also served as (a) surgeons (b) blacksmiths (c) cobblers

.... 23. In Part Two, we find that Don Quixote achieved fame because of (a) Sancho Panza (b) a book (c) the innkeeper

.... 24. Dulcinea was really (a) a princess (b) a peasant (c) imaginary

.... 25. Sancho showed great affection for (a) Rozinante (b) Dapple (c) Dorothea

Answers

1-b, 2-c, 3-a, 4-c, 5-c, 6-b, 7-c, 8-b, 9-b, 10-a, 11-b, 12-a, 13-a, 14-c, 15-c, 16-c, 17-b, 18-a, 19-a, 20-b, 21-a, 22-a, 23-b, 24-c, 25-b

II. *Alternate Objective Tests*

A. Matching

Before each number in the column on the left, write the *letter* of the item in the column on the right that matches:

.... 1. Knight of the White Moon   a. the duchess

.... 2. Knight of the Lions   b. windmills

.... 3. Sancho's mount   c. Dorothea
.... 4. Don Quixote's old horse   d. Samson
.... 5. He made Sancho a governor   e. Don Quixote
.... 6. Don Quixote's beloved   f. Clavileno
.... 7. She wrote to Sancho's wife   g. Rozinante
.... 8. Sancho's wife   h. Dapple
.... 9. The wooden horse   i. Dulcinea
...... 10. The giants   j. the viceroy
                                                 k. Teresa
                                                 l. the duke

Answers

1-d, 2-e, 3-h, 4-g, 5-l, 6-i, 7-b, 8-k, 9-f, 10-a

B. Fill-ins

From the column on the right, select the item that best completes each statement below, and write it in the space provided:

1. Don Quixote's letter to _____ was never delivered.

2. During most of his travels, Don Quixote regarded the _____ as his worst enemies.

3. The duchess sent Sancho Panza's wife a string of _____ beads.

4. What Don Quixote thought was giant's blood turned out to be _____.

5. Sancho's wife sent the duchess a gift of _____.

6. Don Quixote attacked _____, mistaking them for Moors.

7. Sancho enjoyed quoting _____.

8. The _____ proved to be ungrateful.

9. Don Quixote tried to be a peacemaker between rival _____.

Teresa
wine
trees
governor
Barcelona
villages
enchanters
Dulcinea
head
giants
peasant
White Moon
coral
saddle
Madrid
acorns
galley slaves
puppets

10. Don Quixote wanted the barber's basin for a (an) _____.
11. Sancho decided he was not born to be a (an) _____.
12. Sancho administered lashes to himself and _____.
13. Don Antonio was Don Quixote's host in _____.
14. Don Quixote was amazed to hear an enchanted _____ speak.
15. Don Quixote was vanquished by the Knight of the _____.

saints
glass
proverbs
Sorrowful Figure
helmet

Answers

1-Dulcinea, 2-enchanters, 3-coral, 4-wine, 5-acorns, 6-puppets, 7-proverbs, 8-galley slaves, 9-villages, 10-helmet, 11-governor, 12-trees, 13-Barcelona, 14-head, 15-White Moon

III. *Ideas for Written or Oral Book Reports or Class Discussions*

1. Critics have agreed that *Don Quixote* may be read on many different levels and that each reader may arrive at his own version of the characters and events. Analyze your reactions to the book in relation to the following topics:

a. Your own version of Don Quixote's character and actions
b. Your attitude toward other characters in the book as a result of their behavior toward Don Quixote
c. Your view of whether humor or pathos is the dominant element in the book
d. Your reasons for deciding what the author's purpose was in writing the book.

2. Don Quixote's adventure with the windmills is treated

very briefly in our text, and yet it is the episode in the story most frequently remembered and most often cited. Why do you suppose that the windmill episode remains so memorable? In what ways is it typical of other encounters of Don Quixote's? Mention at least three others. Analyze the reasons why you found Don Quixote's adventure with the windmills particularly ludicrous or particularly pathetic.

The expression "tilting with windmills" is frequently used in speech and writing. Explain what we mean when we say to a person, "Oh, stop fighting windmills!" Describe a person you have known or read about who customarily upset himself or herself in arguments against imaginary enemies or imaginary injuries.

3. Books, plays, and motion pictures have tremendous power to affect our thoughts, emotions, and even actions. Sometimes people are particularly affected by stories featuring the sensational, the romantic, the sentimental, and what is most far removed from their everyday lives. Try to explain the continuing appeal of stories of brave knights, beautiful ladies in distress, heroes of the Wild West and the faraway and long ago.

Discuss a story that once made so powerful an impression upon you that you put yourself in the place of a character in the story and thus lived for a time in your imagination. Analyze the reasons why the appeal was so strong that you delighted in imagining yourself transformed into that person in the story. Explain how an experience such as that can help you to understand Don Quixote. Then give your reasons for concluding that he was (a) mentally unbalanced (b) merely playing a part thoroughly, or (c) creating his own reality out of his dreams. Be sure to explain how the ending of the story affected your opinion.

4. Write an analysis of the character of Sancho Panza. Make specific reference to his mental capacity, his emotional balance, his courage or cowardice, and his attitude toward food, money, his family, and Don Quixote. Support each reference with brief outlines of incidents in the plot.

In light of your analysis of Sancho Panza's character,

write a paragraph in answer to each of the following questions:

    a. Why did he agree to accompany Don Quixote in the beginning?

    b. Considering all the discomforts of the journeys, why did he remain with Don Quixote?

    c. What do you think he gained or lost as a result of his long association with Don Quixote?

5. Reread the passage (pp. 26B–27T) beginning, "I know who I am." Explain why you think that Don Quixote meant that he knew he was a knight-errant or that he knew he was Señor Quisada.

Review episodes in the book to help you decide whether Don Quixote believed in them realistically or whether he knew that he was living in his imagination. Be sure to analyze such episodes as those with his armor, Dulcinea, the cave of Montesinos, the puppets, the traveling players, and the wooden horse.

6. a. Critics have said that in Part Two Don Quixote becomes more like Sancho Panza and Sancho Panza becomes more like Don Quixote. By means of reference to the text, explain this idea. Be sure to consider their manner of speaking, their use of imagination, their feelings about Dulcinea, and their attitude toward reality.

    b. Don Quixote met reality suddenly when he was defeated by the Knight of the White Moon and had to keep his promise to return home. Explain why you think he then decided to become a shepherd and lead a pastoral life. Similarly, explain why Sancho Panza's experiences as a governor made him decide that a governor's life was not for him.

7. Analyze the appeal of *Don Quixote,* and explain why you think it has remained so popular for over three hundred and fifty years. What elements in the story do you think so impressed musicians, artists, authors, and actors that there have resulted (a) over eighty musical settings, operas, and ballets, (b) copious illustrations in various artistic media throughout the centuries, and (c) plays, mo-

tion pictures, and the widely acclaimed musical hit *Man of La Mancha?* Why do you think *Don Quixote* would or would not be effective as a new motion picture? What players would you select for the roles?

8. Explain why the duke and duchess went to so much trouble to entertain Don Quixote and Sancho Panza. Consider such items as the fine clothing, the washing of the beards, the boar hunt, the elaborate parade at night, the wooden horse and all the attendant activities, Sancho's governorship, and the duchess's communication with Sancho's wife. What benefits did the duke and duchess expect to gain as a result of all their efforts? To what extent were they satisfied or disappointed with the results of their activities? What light did their actions throw upon their characters? Why would you choose or reject them as friends? Compare their behavior with that of at least three other persons who had dealings with Don Quixote.

9. Assess Sancho Panza as a governor in light of each of the following questions:

a. Which aspects of his life, both before and after he became Don Quixote's squire, helped him? hindered him? Why?

b. Which of his decisions and actions as governor did you find praiseworthy? which undesirable? Give reasons in each case.

c. Again referring to Sancho's past, as well as his future prospects, what were his strongest reasons for deciding to leave his office of his own accord? To what extent did you agree with his self-analysis?

10. Samson Carrasco is an interesting character. Trace his relationship with Don Quixote, and assess his qualities as a person and as a friend of Don Quixote's. Explain in detail why you think that Samson Carrasco or Sancho Panza was a truer friend to Don Quixote. Describe a person you have known who demonstrates friendship as either of these two did. Explain why you would prefer to have Samson Carrasco or Sancho Panza as a friend.

IV. *Vocabulary Study*

Diagnostic Test

7M	mellifluous	bitter	fluent	honeyed
7M	harbinger	reaper	forerunner	rear guard
8M	descried	detected	shrieked	overlooked
9B	accoutrements	images	equipment	useless ideas
11M	risible	deplorable	easily seen	laughable
13T	tribunals	courts	injustices	jails
15T	temerity	caution	rashness	cowardice
16M	intrepidity	bravery	instability	lack of valor
19B	disburse	collect	oppress	pay
24M	imputing	urging	charging	disclaiming
38T	ruminated	sickened	meditated	acted rashly
43B	miscreant	villain	mistake	hero
45T	trenchant	precious	cutting	smoothing
45T	choleric	lovable	soothing	hot-tempered
49M	enjoined	ordered	refused	married
69B	succinctly	cruelly	concisely	at length
70M	chimera	duck	valid idea	foolish fancy
105M	exigency	need	egress	uselessness
105M	expedient	fast	harmful	advantageous
125B	importuned	landed	forbade	urged persistently
161B	vagaries	oaths	rambling	direct paths
175B	billet-doux	club	love letter	harsh charge
186T	maledictions	curses	transgressions	blessings
194M	adulation	wave	denouncement	excessive praise
194M	ingenuous	tricky	stupid	artlessly frank
195M	calumny	praise	slander	heavy weight
195M	aspersions	details	compliments	injurious remarks
202T	fastidious	fickle	easily pleased	difficult to please
210T	vicissitudes	changes	storms	constant states
212M	ignominy	honor	disgrace	lack of wisdom
214B	tractable	capable	easily managed	hard to handle
218B	inveighing	railing	envying	praising
222T	adroitly	skillfully	underhandedly	clumsily
223M	prevarications	difficulties	lies	truths

228M soliloquy	dialogue	actor	act of talking to oneself
238M impunity	falsehood	freedom from harm	risk of danger
241T disparage	undervalue	display	overpraise
260B cavil	agree	envy	raise frivolous objections
261T parsimoniously	strangely	frugally	lavishly
261M insidious	treacherous	mysterious	benign
291M execration	blessing	dismissal	curse
294B penurious	poor	jealous	wealthy
306T pristine	original	snobbish	future
337B solicitous	begging	full of concern	uncaring
342B indigence	wealth	indecency	poverty
360B sagacity	renown	shrewdness	stupidity
406M prerogative	privilege	prescience	punishment
421M torpor	energy	anger	sluggishness
427M obdurate	ugly	unyielding	relenting
446M salutary	beneficial	harmful	greeting

Answers

mellifluous-honeyed, *harbinger*-forerunner, *descried*-detected, *accoutrements*-equipment, *risible*-laughable, *tribunals*-courts, *temerity*-rashness, *intrepidity*-bravery, *disburse*-pay, *imputing*-charging, *ruminated*-meditated, *miscreant*-villain, *trenchant*-cutting, *choleric*-hot-tempered, *enjoined*-ordered, *succinctly*-concisely, *chimera*-foolish fancy, *exigency*-need, *expedient*-advantageous, *importuned*-urged persistently, *vagaries*-ramblings, *billet-doux*-love letter, *maledictions*-curses, *adulation*-excessive praise, *ingenuous*-artlessly frank, *calumny*-slander, *aspersions*-injurious remarks, *fastidious*-difficult to please, *vicissitudes*-changes, *ignominy*-disgrace, *tractable*-easily managed, *inveighing*-railing, *adroitly*-skillfully, *prevarications*-lies, *soliloquy*-act of talking to oneself, *impunity*-freedom from harm, *disparage*-undervalue, *cavil*-raise frivolous objections, *parsimoniously*-frugally, *insidious*-treacherous, *execration*-curse, *penurious*-poor, *pristine*-original, *solicitous*-full of concern, *indigence*-poverty, *sagacity*-shrewdness, *prerogative*-privilege, *torpor*-sluggishness, *obdurate*-unyielding, *salutary*-beneficial

Teaching Aids

for

FATHERS AND SONS

Ivan Turgenev was one of the giants of Russian literature, and this is his greatest novel. Through the philosophy and character of Bazarov, the nihilist, we see the clash of the nobility with the peasants and the rising middle class—a conflict that grew in intensity during the nineteenth century and led to revolution in the second decade of the twentieth century. At issue, too, are the ever-widening differences that develop between parents and children as old attitudes and beliefs are challenged by youthful idealism and cynicism. To the modern reader, for whom the term "generation gap" has become almost a cliché, it would seem that the book must have been written yesterday.

I. *Objective Test*

In the space provided at the left, insert the *letter* of the correct choice from among those offered; for example:

....b.... The author of this book is (a) Tolstoy (b) Turgenev (c) Gogol (d) Pushkin

.... 1. Arkady and Bazarov had formed a friendship (a) in the army (b) at the university (c) during service in the diplomatic corps (d) while working in Moscow

.... 2. On their arrival in the province where both lived, (a) Arkady went to Bazarov's home (b)

each went his separate way (c) Bazarov decided to return to Moscow (d) Bazarov stopped off at Arkady's home

.... 3. Nikolai Petrovich had named his country estate after (a) a famous nobleman (b) one of the czars (c) his beloved first wife (d) a younger son

.... 4. Arkady learned that his father had (a) had a child with Fenichka (b) decided to sell the estate (c) become interested in Katya (d) ordered Pavel to leave

.... 5. Nikolai's brother Pavel had become embittered by (a) heavy losses on the exchange (b) a tragic love affair (c) failure to advance in the service (d) rejection of his manuscript

.... 6. Pavel showed early hostility toward Bazarov because of the young man's long hair, dress, and inclination to (a) drink heavily (b) be impolite to Nikolai (c) dissect frogs (d) curse excessively

.... 7. In a discussion with Pavel, Arkady explained that a nihilist like his friend Bazarov was one who (a) respected nothing (b) regarded everything critically (c) refused to obey the law (d) wanted all aristocrats executed

.... 8. Arkady's attitude toward Bazarov could most accurately be described as (a) secretly antagonistic (b) rather patronizing (c) obviously hero-worshiping (d) basically indifferent

.... 9. In his early conversations with Bazarov, Pavel Petrovich soon discovered that about most things they (a) disagreed violently (b) were not too far apart (c) agreed heartily (d) needed further information

.... 10. As a farmer, Nikolai was (a) active and efficient (b) interested only in mechanical equipment (c) careless and inefficient (d) pleased with his grounds

.... 11. Arkady disagreed with Bazarov about the (a) virtues of marriage (b) trends in politics (c)

beauty of Fenichka (d) lack of interest in music by Nikolai

.... 12. Pavel was furious when he learned that Bazarov had said of Nikolai that (a) "his mind is a blank" (b) "he should have married her" (c) "he should read Pushkin" (d) "his singing days are over"

.... 13. It was clear that Pavel was interested in Fenichka because she (a) was his brother's wife (b) gave him sly encouragement (c) reminded him of a former love (d) seemed to agree with his politics

.... 14. Nikolai seemed to prefer to ignore the possibility that (a) his farm might go under (b) other men were attracted to Fenichka (c) Bazarov might corrupt Arkady (d) Pavel might marry again

.... 15. The young men left the estate to (a) see Nikolai's relative in town (b) take a trip abroad (c) revisit the university (d) look at a horse for sale

.... 16. Matvei Ilyich was the son of Kolyazin, who had been the (a) mayor of St. Petersburg (b) former owner of Maryino (c) commander of a brigade (d) guardian of the Kirsanov brothers

.... 17. The governor seemed to spend most of his day (a) eating heavily (b) issuing orders (c) visiting his tenants (d) entertaining ladies

.... 18. That Bazarov held the muzhiks in contempt seemed (a) oddly inconsistent with his philosophy (b) perfectly logical (c) obviously a pretense (d) prompted by his background

.... 19. Yevdoxia Kukshina represented Turgenev's satiric portrait of (a) an ultramodern young lady (b) a boorish peasant (c) an arch female conservative (d) a blue-blooded aristocrat

.... 20. When he was introduced to Odintsova at the governor's ball, Arkady soon became (a) anxious to leave (b) resentful of her haughtiness

        (c) delighted with her simplicity (d) awed by her maturity and sophistication

.... 21. Bazarov became annoyed with himself when he discovered that he had (a) agreed to visit Odintsova (b) treated Arkady coldly (c) fallen in love with Odintsova (d) avoided speaking to Timofeich

.... 22. Pavel showed great respect for Bazarov after (a) the treatment of a thigh wound (b) an unanswerable bit of logic (c) a laboratory discovery (d) a visit from the governor

.... 23. Bazarov returned to his father's house and began to (a) organize the muzhiks (b) seek religious instruction (c) help in medical practice (d) study agriculture

.... 24. Arkady married Katya (a) against the objections of her sister (b) despite his father's disapproval (c) in a secret ceremony (d) during a double wedding ceremony

.... 25. Bazarov died as the result of (a) a savage duel (b) an accident with a machine (c) typhus contracted from a patient (d) execution by the state

Answers

1-b, 2-d, 3-c, 4-a, 5-b, 6-c, 7-b, 8-c, 9-a, 10-c, 11-a, 12-d, 13-c, 14-b, 15-a, 16-d, 17-b, 18-a, 19-a, 20-d, 21-c, 22-a, 23-c, 24-d, 25-c

II. *Alternate Objective Tests*

A. Matching

Before each number in the column on the left, write the *letter* of the item in the column on the right that matches:

.... 1. Maryino   a. Nikolai and Pavel

.... 2. Nikolai   b. Bazarov

.... 3. Pavel   c. borzoi

.... 4. "old Kirsanov boys"   d. matured by love

.... 5. Odintsova   e. Nikolai's estate
.... 6. Medical skill   f. perfumed mustache
.... 7. Fenichka   g. 'cello player
.... 8. Katya   h. servant girl
.... 9. Mitya   i. mistress, mother, wife
...... 10. Fifi   j. Pavel's son
                    k. "oh-ho-ho"
                    l. baby

Answers

1-e, 2-g, 3-f, 4-a, 5-k, 6-b, 7-i, 8-d, 9-l, 10-c

B. Fill-ins

From the column on the right, select the item that best completes each statement below, and write it in the space provided:

1. Nikolai was often given loans by _____.

2. The elder Bazarovs' attitude toward their son was a mixture of love and _____.

3. Sitnikov's father was a (an) _____.

4. Pavel spent four years abroad fruitlessly following _____.

5. Bazarov expressed admiration for the intellectual achievements of the _____.

6. Fenichka was found to be embarrassingly attractive not only to Pavel but also to _____.

7. Odintsova's father had been a (an) _____.

8. Bazarov's impulsive kiss led to a _____.

9. Katya played the piano for _____ when they first met.

trial
English
deep thinker
gambler
Odintsova
warmly
   receptive
Sitnikov
fathead
peasants
panic-stricken
arrogance
Germans
Bazarov
aiming
Pavel
warning
Arkady
fear

10. Bazarov considered Sitnikov to be a (an) _____.
11. Odintsova seemed _____ when Bazarov declared his love.
12. _____ decided finally that Bazarov and Arkady were two boors.
13. Bazarov shot at Pavel without _____.
14. Strangely, the _____ regarded Bazarov as something of a fool.
15. On his deathbed, Bazarov sent a note to _____.

tax farmer
Princess R—
boors
duel

Answers

1-Pavel, 2-fear, 3-tax farmer, 4-Princess R—, 5-Germans, 6-Bazarov, 7-gambler, 8-duel, 9-Arkady, 10-fathead, 11-panic-stricken, 12-Sitnikov, 13-aiming, 14-peasants, 15-Odintsova

III. *Ideas for Written or Oral Book Reports or Class Discussions*

1. Nearly every other individual in *Fathers and Sons* has a decided opinion about the nature of Bazarov's character. What is yours? Does he deserve the admiration, almost the hero-worship, of an Arkady or, rather, the contempt, even the hatred, of a Pavel Petrovich? Why? Or do you, perhaps, admire Bazarov for certain traits in his character and despise him for others? If this is so, list those aspects of Bazarov's character that you find worthy of praise and those you find deserving of condemnation. Explain.

2. Sometimes in a literary work, a writer will give us two figures with distinctly opposing personalities; we then say that one character is a "foil" for the other. It is through the use of this foil that the contrast between the characters is seen with greater distinctness. The generosity of a philanthropist is more noticeable because his foil is a miser; the evil in a villain impresses us more because of its contrast with the goodness of his foil. In what ways is

Pavel Petrovich Kirsanov the best foil that Turgenev could have chosen for Bazarov? Why do you suppose Turgenev did not present us with an out-and-out Russian autocrat as a foil to Bazarov, the kind of person associated in our minds with the absolute and tyrannical rule of the czar? Is it, indeed, possible to say that through the portrait of Pavel Petrovich, Turgenev was picturing—and criticizing—a whole class of people in the Russia of the 1850s and the 1860s? Which class? And how—or for what—did Turgenev, in his portrait of Pavel Petrovich, criticize the members of this class?

3. The thoughts of Nikolai Petrovich (pp. 59–61B) indicate how far he and his son had drifted apart. We read (p. 154T) that Nikolai "During meals . . . tried to turn the conversation to physics, geology, or chemistry, since all other topics, including farming, not to mention politics, were fraught with the risk of mutual annoyance, or clashes."

Of Bazarov's mother, we learn (p. 130T) that "She loved her son and feared him beyond words." As for Vasily Ivanich Bazarov, his attitude toward his son may be indicated by the remark made to Arkady (p. 133T): "But I dare not show my feelings in front of him; he doesn't like it. He has an aversion to every display of affection; many people disapprove of this hardness of his, which they regard as a sign of pride or insensibility; but men like him should not be measured by the ordinary rule, don't you think so?" Bazarov's father was himself a scientist, a doctor whose education was possibly as good as that of his son and whose experience was certainly much more extensive. How, then, can you explain the awe, the hero-worship, with which the father regarded his son?

Why was it so difficult for Nikolai Petrovich Kirsanov and Vasily Ivanich Bazarov—the fathers—to understand their sons? After all, both fathers were educated men.

4. There are those who say that Turgenev's description of Nikolai Petrovich Kirsanov, Arkady's father, is an attempt at a self-portrait. If that is so, what sort of chap does Turgenev picture himself—or Nikolai Petrovich—to

be? At the time of Arkady's and Bazarov's return from the university, Nikolai was living the life of one who in England or America would be called a gentleman farmer. What impression of this life do you get as you read Turgenev's account of life on the Kirsanov estate (Chapters 4–11)? In what respects could the Kirsanov estate be considered successful? In what ways was it a failure?

5. What is there about *Fathers and Sons*—especially in such sections as the conversation between Pavel Petrovich and Bazarov in Chapter 10—that explains why the reaction of the public to the novel when it was first published in February 1862 was almost entirely political in nature, the conservatives very largely reacting to the book in one way and the liberals in another? Why did both sides have reasons to be pleased and angered by the book? Although written more than a hundred years ago, what ideas expressed by the fathers and sons could well have been the subjects of conversation at a dinner table in some homes as recently as yesterday? Explain. Incidentally, how do you account for Bazarov's attitude toward the lower classes, considering his enormous contempt for aristocrats and distaste for all Russian political and social institutions?

6. Every woman that Turgenev describes in any detail in the book is distinctive in character, attitude, and background. Discuss each of the four women dealt with in some depth in terms of the following basic questions:

Fenichka: What was there about her that attracted three men so strongly? To what extent would it suffice to give the simple explanation that she was a very pretty young woman?

Odintsova: What influences in her background had inhibited her to the point where she practically feared love or passion?

Arina Vlasyevna (Bazarov's mother): Why did Turgenev say of her: "Such women are rare nowadays. God knows whether we should be glad of it or not"?

Katya: In what respects did she turn out to be the wisest, most stable, and most mature of all the women dealt with in detail?

7. What exactly was the relationship between Odintsova and Bazarov? Were they or were they not truly in love? If he spoke the truth when he said (p. 110M), "I love you stupidly, madly," why then did he leave her a day or two later? If she did not truly love him, if her real attitude was expressed in the thought that flashed through her mind (p. 113T), "I am afraid of that man," why did she encourage his attentions? Why did she, after receiving Arkady's letter asking for Katya's hand, ask Bazarov (p. 193M), "Why shouldn't you stay *now?* Do stay . . ."? And why did he talk about being a fish out of water who should be allowed to flop back into his own element? Why did she come to see him when he sent for her on his deathbed? Why, indeed, did he send for her? Which aspects of Bazarov's character was Turgenev able to develop more richly through Bazarov's relationship with Odintsova? Explain your answer.

8. Explain why Turgenev insisted on presenting the estates of both "fathers"—Bazarov's and Arkady's—as failures. He could just as easily have pictured them as prosperous. Yet he tells us (p. 145M) how Vasily Ivanich tremblingly counted out his banknotes to Timofeich for the day's shopping. Evidently, there were precious few of those banknotes. And there is an elaborate description (pp. 149T–150T) of the deterioration of conditions on the Kirsanov estate. How do these failures of the fathers to run their estates prosperously, or even profitably, fit the general theme of *Fathers and Sons?*

9. On the surface, it appears that Pavel Petrovich challenged Bazarov to a duel because of Bazarov's behavior toward Fenichka. What, however, seems to you the real reason for the challenge? How does the behavior of both contestants at the duel—and toward each other after the duel—enable us to penetrate even more deeply into the characters of Pavel Petrovich and Bazarov? Explain your answer by referring to incidents before and after the duel. Looking back now at events that occurred after Turgenev's death, how accurate would it be to say that the duel was a prophetic foreshadowing of the terrible violence that would one day engulf the Russians?

10. Although Turgenev's style of writing comes to us in translation, it is still possible to examine certain elements that earned him a preeminent reputation among Russian novelists. What evidences of his *descriptive power* can you find besides the passage telling about sights on the road to the Petrovich estate (pp. 11M–12) or Fenichka's room (p. 38)? Where else does the author use *symbols* (objects or persons to represent broader concepts than the original) like the dissected frogs (p. 19B), the sphinx (p. 32T), or the perfumed mustache (p. 15B)? What would you say about the *economy of narrative sequence* in the writer's ability to cover important episodes in little space? Finally, comment on his crisp use of *dialogue*.

IV. *Vocabulary Study*

Diagnostic Test

2T	obsequious	proud	stupid	servile
3T	chagrin	mortification	stubbornness	triumph
3B	decorum	rudeness	propriety	fragility
5T	beatific	pretty	melancholy	blissful
6T	protuberances	indentations	sores	bulges
11T	reveling	delighting	apologizing	exhibiting
12T	fell	kindly	savage	grasping
17T	archaism	antique	novelty	prominence
19M	brackish	sweet	plentiful	saline
24B	waddling	perfectly graceful	clumsily swaying	unusually fast
25T	furtively	stealthily	frankly	happily
26B	truculently	harshly	sweetly	intelligently
30B	avidly	eagerly	cruelly	indifferently
31M	inanities	foolish remarks	wise remarks	disputed statements
32T	inscrutable	candid	affectionate	impenetrable
34M	sallies	prophecies	doubts	witticisms
35B	enigmatic	humorous	baffling	educational
57T	execrably	beautifully	abominably	ably
57M	vaunted	boasted	controlled	modest
60B	halcyon	exciting	peaceful	fascinating
65T	kowtow	defy	neglect	bow low

66B	smirking	smiling unpleasantly	groaning inwardly	blushing
69B	languidly	awkwardly	apathetically	enthusiastically
77M	limpid	muddy	opaque	clear
78T	callow	sophisticated	bold	inexperienced
85T	plaited	curried	shortened	braided
89B	cardinal	primary	desirable	ecclesiastical
91B	spawn	quality	offspring	ancestry
93M	broached	mocked	exhausted	suggested
115B	minced	walked daintily	strode boldly	ambled
124T	incessantly	noisily	unceasingly	sporadically
125B	indolently	energetically	lazily	enthusiastically
127M	encumbered	ornamented	well dressed	weighed down
129T	sprites	ghosts	remedies	guests
131M	infusion	drug	derivative	mixture
131B	plebeian	aristocrat	common person	intellectual
133M	stinted	spent	begrudged	lavished
134T	refractory	stubborn	mild	yielding
134T	palliatives	deteriorations	panaceas	alleviators
137T	platitude	epithet	banality	epigram
143M	ruefully	regretfully	hopefully	spontaneously
153B	cilia	nuclei	muscles	hairs
154B	guile	cunning	good will	generosity
162T	copse	forest	thicket	garden
178M	predatory	philanthropic	uncivilized	preying
180B	reticent	depressed	loquacious	silent
182B	perturbation	agitation	calm	interest
188T	niches	platforms	recesses	protuberances
190T	quagmire	marsh	irrigated field	mountain
201T	cauterize	swab	soothe	burn

Answers

obsequious-servile, *chagrin*-mortification, *decorum*-propriety, *beatific*-blissful, *protuberances*-bulges, *reveling*-delighting, *fell*-savage, *archaism*-antique, *brackish*-saline, *waddling*-clumsily swaying, *furtively*-stealthily, *truculently*-harshly, *avidly*-eagerly, *inanities*-foolish remarks, *inscrutable*-impenetrable, *sallies*-witticisms, *enigmatic*-baffling, *execrably*-abominably, *vaunted*-boasted, *halcyon*-peaceful, *kowtow*-bow low, *smirking*-smiling unpleasantly, *languidly*-apathetically, *limpid*-clear, *callow*-inexperienced, *plaited*-braided, *cardinal*-primary, *spawn*-offspring, *broached*-suggested, *minced*-walked daintily, *incessantly*-unceasingly, *indolently*-lazily, *encumbered*-weighed down, *sprites*-ghosts, *infusion*-mixture, *plebeian*-common person, *stinted*-begrudged, *refractory*-stubborn, *palliatives*-alleviators, *platitude*-banality, *ruefully*-regretfully, *cilia*-hairs, *guile*-cunning, *copse*-thicket, *predatory*-preying, *reticent*-silent, *perturbation*-agitation, *niches*-recesses, *quagmire*-marsh, *cauterize*-burn

Teaching Aids

for

THE GOOD EARTH

Here is the moving story of a humble Chinese farmer who rose in his lifetime to become a wealthy landowner. Wang Lung gloried in the soil, holding it above his family, even above his gods. But soon, between Wang Lung and the kindly soil that sustained him, came flood and drought, pestilence and revolution. Through this one Chinese peasant and his wife and children, Nobel prize winner Pearl S. Buck traces the whole cycle of life, its terrors, its passions, its ambitions, and its rewards. Her brilliant novel—beloved by millions of readers—is a universal tale of the destiny of man.

I. *Objective Test*

In the space provided at the left, insert the *letter* of the correct choice from among those offered; for example:

....b.... The name of the author is (a) Poe (b) Buck (c) Hardy (d) Conrad

.... 1. When Wang Lung first sees O-lan, he is disappointed that (a) she is ugly (b) her feet are not bound (c) her face is pock-marked (d) she is too tall

.... 2. When O-lan delivers her firstborn, she is attended by (a) no one (b) a local midwife (c) the town doctor (d) a distant relative

.... 3. When the second child is born, the older boy

145

has to sleep (a) with Wang Lung (b) in the shed (c) with his grandfather (d) on the floor

.... 4. Wang Lung's uncle slaps him for (a) hiding his silver (b) harvesting too soon (c) offering a bribe (d) correcting an elder

.... 5. The word "slave" reveals the attitude toward (a) field workers (b) female children (c) kitchen stewards (d) foot soldiers

.... 6. O-lan's quiet strength is shown when she (a) beats the uncle (b) scolds Wang Lung (c) kills the ox (d) destroys the house

.... 7. The peasants go south because of (a) a great famine (b) an approaching army (c) the warmer climate (d) an order from the governor

.... 8. For a time, Wang Lung works as a (a) dock hand (b) ricksha-puller (c) vegetable peddler (d) street sweeper

.... 9. Among the city people, Wang Lung feels (a) proud and independent (b) especially privileged (c) ignorant and humble (d) wise and learned

.... 10. To earn their daily bread, O-lan teaches the children (a) how to farm (b) the art of weaving (c) how to be pickpockets (d) how to beg

.... 11. Wang Lung accidentally gets gold so that he can return to his land when (a) he finds a purse (b) the soldiers attack the city (c) a rich noble gives him a gift (d) a shopkeeper befriends him

.... 12. One of the rare times O-lan shows inner emotion occurs when she tells Wang Lung about (a) her love for the children (b) the loss of her necklace (c) the jewels she found in the city (d) the man who broke the door

.... 13. When Wang Lung goes to the great house to buy still more land, he discovers that he must now deal with (a) the Old Lord (b) a shrill-voiced woman (c) the Ancient Mistress (d) the young lords

.... 14. Wang Lung is saddened to realize that his eldest girl child is (a) not very pretty (b) loose in her ways (c) cruel and violent (d) mentally retarded

.... 15. To reward an act of generosity and steadfast loyalty, Wang Lung (a) lends money to the Old Lord (b) buys a house for his uncle (c) appoints Ching steward of the estate (d) sells some land

.... 16. The idea to send his sons to school occurs to Wang Lung mainly because (a) he can't read (b) O-lan wants educated children (c) it is suggested by the mayor (d) both boys suggest it

.... 17. Wang Lung visits the great tea house frequently because he has (a) business to transact (b) developed a taste for wine (c) grown tired of O-lan (d) fallen in love with Cuckoo

.... 18. Besides getting him to wash more often, Lotus Blossom convinces Wang Lung to (a) go on a vacation (b) steal the pearls from O-lan (c) buy the great tea house (d) cut off his braid

.... 19. Wang Lung arranges for the purchase of his new love through (a) the marriage broker (b) his uncle's wife (c) the Old Lord's son (d) his uncle

.... 20. After hearing about her husband's desire to bring another woman into the house, O-lan, for the first time in memory, (a) goes into a violent rage (b) leaves the house (c) weeps aloud (d) threatens revenge

.... 21. Wang Lung's love for Lotus becomes imperfect when she (a) curses his children (b) flirts with his uncle (c) slaps O-lan (d) says she misses the tea house

.... 22. A false red beard and red length of cloth save Wang Lung's uncle from being (a) recognized by the police (b) driven from his nephew's house (c) robbed by the band (d) set upon by the workers

.... 23. Wang Lung permits his eldest son to go south

after (a) learning of the university (b) finding him with Lotus (c) hearing O-lan's pleas (d) visiting the oracle

.... 24. Before she dies, O-lan wishes to see (a) her eldest son married (b) Lotus sent back to the tea house (c) her youngest daughter engaged (d) her pearls returned

.... 25. Wang Lung gets revenge on his uncle by (a) paying money to the robbers (b) sending for the soldiers (c) feeding him opium (d) throwing him down a well

Answers

1-b, 2-a, 3-c, 4-d, 5-b, 6-c, 7-a, 8-b, 9-c, 10-d, 11-b, 12-c, 13-b, 14-d, 15-c, 16-a, 17-c, 18-d, 19-b, 20-c, 21-a, 22-b, 23-b, 24-a, 25-c

II. *Alternate Objective Tests*

A. Matching

Before each number in the column on the left, write the *letter* of the item in the column on the right that matches:

.... 1. "Firewagon"   a. robber
.... 2. Pear Blossom   b. lucky day for burial
.... 3. Ancient Mistress   c. gold coins
.... 4. Redbeard   d. manager of tea house
.... 5. O-lan   e. Wang's daughter
.... 6. geomancer   f. military official
.... 7. "Do not kill me!"   g. ricksha
.... 8. Poor Fool   h. train
.... 9. Cuckoo   i. "fire in my vitals"
...... 10. youngest son   j. slave of Lotus
                                   k. surveyor
                                   l. last year's coat

Answers

1-h, 2-j, 3-l, 4-a, 5-i, 6-b, 7-c, 8-e, 9-d, 10-f

B. Fill-ins

From the column on the right, select the item that best completes each statement below, and write it in the space provided:

1. O-lan had been a slave in the _____.   fields
2. A teacher's favorite weapon is his _____.   daughter
3. The New Year's decorations are mostly colored _____.   uncle
4. When the rains come, it is time for _____.   fan
5. O-lan returns to the _____ after the birth of her second son.   crippled
6. The _____ ransack Wang's house for food.   villagers
7. When Wang sees O-lan's fourth child, it is _____.   wife
8. During the famine, Wang is urged by his _____ to sell his land.   revolution
9. Near the Confucian temple, Wang hears talk of _____.   vagrants
10. Wang fears that the city is teaching his sons to become _____.   dead
11. To get back to his land, Wang is told to sell his _____.   visiting
12. Wang goes into a shop to hide from _____.   third son
13. The farms are nearly destroyed by _____.   ruler
14. Wang's sons want to sell the _____.   thieves
15. The _____ wishes to learn to read.   locusts

red
soldiers
land
an earthquake
House of Hwang
blue
house

Answers

1-House, of Hwang, 2-fan, 3-red, 4-visiting, 5-fields, 6-villagers, 7-dead, 8-uncle, 9-revolution, 10-thieves, 11-daughter, 12-soldiers, 13-locusts, 14-land, 15-third son

III. *Ideas for Written or Oral Book Reports or Class Discussions*

1. Certainly one reason Pearl S. Buck wrote *The Good Earth* was to give the outside world a view of China and its people at the turn of the century, just before revolution swept the land. Consider *human relationships*. What did you find admirable or disagreeable about the treatment of elders, the attitude toward wives and children, the involvement with neighbors, and the concern for morality? What *customs* and *superstitions* did you note that were new to you? What elements in the *social structure* contained the seeds of revolution? From what you know of China today, what have been some of the important changes introduced in recent years?

2. At the birth of her third child, O-lan says, "It is only a slave this time—not worth mentioning" (p. 62M). What did this remark tell us of the attitude of women like O-lan toward themselves? Why was a word like "slave" an appropriate label for the position of women of the lower classes at the time of the story? What is your view of arranged marriages, as practiced in China in those days? Considering the nature of the times, who got more out of life, a woman like O-lan or one like Lotus Blossom? Explain. What hints did you find in the novel that, even then and especially among the sons' wives, changes were taking place?

3. O-lan, of course, is the symbol of the women of her class in old China. What elements in her background made it unthinkable that she would stand up to Wang Lung at crucial moments in the story? Despite the handicaps of her position, what evidences did you find of her courage, patience, ability to adjust, resourcefulness, pride, and, at rare moments, sensitivity? What do you really think happened at the birth of the fourth child? Why? Looking back at the earlier history of this country, what kind of women were comparable in many ways to O-lan? What was the significance of O-lan's dying statement to

Cuckoo: ". . . I have been a man's wife and I have borne him sons . . ." (p. 247B)?

4. In many respects, Wang Lung was not typical of the peasants among whom he lived. What consuming belief, bordering almost on a religious passion, made him stand out above the other farmers? How faithful was he to his belief throughout the story? Give examples. How would you evaluate his feelings for O-lan, his children, and society about him? What was more influential in his decision to take Lotus Blossom into his house—the fact that he had lost interest in O-lan or the impulse to act the part of a rich man, as was the custom? What evidence can you cite of Wang's respect of tradition, appreciation of past favors, compassion, cunning, and awareness of his own weaknesses?

5. It would seem that in a period when the father was the absolute ruler of the household and respect for elders was a paramount tradition, there would be little likelihood that a generation gap would occur. However, taking each of the sons in turn, show how their ideas and aspirations differed from those of their father at certain points in the narrative. Toward the end, what was the most shocking request made of Wang Lung by his sons? What do you think happened after Wang's death? Project the story ten years after the conclusion of the novel. Estimate the role the youngest son was playing in the important events taking place at that time.

6. In evaluating Pearl S. Buck's style of writing, it is important to note two statements she once made:

   a. "A good novelist, or so I have been taught in China, should be natural, unaffected, and so flexible and variable as to be wholly at the command of the material that flows through him."
   b. When she was awarded the Nobel prize, she said, "Oh, I wish it could have been given to [Theodore] Dreiser instead!"

For the design of her novel, Pearl S. Buck borrowed the *naturalist* technique she admired when she came under the spell of Dreiser. This meant that she tried to show the forces—natural, social, psychological—that shaped the lives of her major characters. In this connection, accident and coincidence play large roles. How did Nature influence the destiny of Wang's family from time to time? What coincidences occurred that determined the ultimate fortunes of the struggling farmer? For example, how did Wang get the money to return from the city; how did he acquire enough wealth to buy huge tracts of land? Give further examples of coincidence.

For her style of writing, Pearl S. Buck chose the *simplicity* she had learned to appreciate from hearing her father read the Bible aloud and listening to fascinating tales in storytellers' booths on the streets of China. Note her use of ancient words like *meet* (p. 157M), *builded* (p. 153T), and *digged* (p. 185M) to give the book a biblical flavor. What other examples can you cite? Note, too, her skill in creating *images* and developing *sense appeal:* the action words in the market description (pp. 104-105) and references to sound, smell, touch, sight in the description of Wang's return to farming (p. 203). Again, find other examples. Also, find additional *figures of speech* like "a body light as a bamboo" (p. 168M). In summary, give reasons to support your belief that Pearl S. Buck's style was or was not appropriate for the kind of book she wrote.

7. Although the author does not develop her minor characters in as much depth as she does Wang Lung and O-lan, each has a contribution to make to the cross-section view we get of the community. How, for example, did the Ancient Mistress and the Old Lord symbolize the decaying aristocracy soon to be destroyed by revolution? What characteristics of the uncle reminded you of the classic villain to be found almost anywhere in fiction? In what respects did Ching suggest what Wang Lung might have become had he not been blessed with better luck? How did the writer draw sympathy from both the characters in the story and the reader toward the retarded daughter? How accurate would it be to say that Cuckoo

and Lotus Blossom were victims of their times rather than basically grasping and immoral?

8. Also to be judged in terms of the climate of living of the time is the morality or lack of it shown by various characters. How justified was O-lan in teaching her children to beg in the city and winking at their occasional thefts? What did you think of Wang Lung's bullying the fat merchant into giving away his gold coins for fear of his life or of O-lan's taking the jewels from behind the loose brick? How immoral was it of the villagers to storm Wang's house in search of food? Finally, how reprehensible was Wang's scheme to rid himself of his uncle by feeding him opium?

9. Some critics, mainly American intellectuals of Chinese extraction, objected to *The Good Earth* as presenting a distorted view of China. They claimed that Pearl S. Buck overstressed the loose morals of some Chinese women, included too many characters who had villainous traits, and showed lack of understanding of basic Chinese customs and tradition. Her reply was that she had written about events and people that were real as she had known from personal experience, that it would have been wrong to have presented an ideal life-style among her peasants, and that her critics simply had too much contempt for the lower-class Chinese to accept them as normal human beings with both strengths and weaknesses. With which point of view are you inclined to agree—the critics' or the author's? Give reasons.

10. *The Good Earth* is rich in *symbolism,* which is a literary device used by writers to suggest a broad idea or concept by concentrating attention on a single thing or person. For instance, what did the two pearls symbolize for O-lan, besides the fact that they were part of the jewels she found? What symbolic meaning did the land have for Wang Lung? To what extent was it symbolic that Wang agreed to cut off his braid at Lotus Blossom's request? Find other examples of symbolism in the story, and explain their broader meanings.

IV. *Vocabulary Study*

Diagnostic Test

7M	sodden	grassy	soaked	arid
14M	impudence	solemnity	respect	sauciness
24T	volubly	talkatively	softly	forcibly
25T	consummated	unfinished	boiled	accomplished
26M	exultation	triumph	revolution	loss
26B	querulously	strangely	complainingly	approvingly
36T	transmuted	overwhelmed	unbent	changed
40M	winnowed	fished	sifted	mixed
40B	chaff	cream	legging	worthless part
49T	impassive	tunneled	unemotional	heated
49T	countenance	store	alley	facial expression
53T	maliciously	spitefully	easily	hopefully
60B	filial	from son or daughter	as of the future	musical
68T	foreboding	relief	bad omen	stitching
74T	angular	gaunt	boatlike	strange
82B	unctuously	boldly	abruptly	fawningly
97M	garbed	sailed	attired	mixed
107B	opulence	wealth	poverty	strength
115M	stolidly	proudly	feelingly	dully
122M	consternation	calmness	dismay	anger
132B	loathed	approved	disliked	ground
140B	wistfulness	sharpness	likeness	longing
155M	indignation	anger	respect	love
163T	pendulous	straight	hanging	heavy
174T	petulantly	reasonably	loosely	peevishly
182M	repine	complain	lust	pray
196M	pouted	rang	sulked	separated
204M	reek	perfume	oil	smell
213T	propitious	evil	favorable	long
230M	agape	tight	with mouth open	silent
247M	repulsion	distaste	appeal	noise
252T	acquiescent	agreeable	difficult	possessive
256M	distraught	solid	confused	certain
274B	overweening	conceited	sensitive	shy
277B	spawn	refuse	offspring	death

281B	dais	tunnel	platform	wrath
292T	bumpkin	tender	lump	yokel
303T	parsimony	generosity	stinginess	conjunction
306M	blowsy	neat	windy	slovenly
312M	coy	demure	crude	noisy
313B	haggard	fat	wild-eyed	pretty
326M	incessantly	fitfully	longingly	ceaselessly
327T	amiss	irreligious	faulty	perfect
327M	gravity	seriousness	humor	lightness
330M	begrudge	be happy	crush	grumble at
333M	coquetry	cooking	flirting	spurning
333B	surcharged	promoted	unloaded	overburdened
336T	requited	left	repaid	silenced
343B	mincing	dainty	threatening	crude
344M	scanty	ample	insufficient	shocking

Answers

sodden-soaked, *impudence*-sauciness, *volubly*-talkatively, *consummated*-accomplished, *exultation*-triumph, *querulously*-complainingly, *transmuted*-changed, *winnowed*-sifted, *chaff*-worthless part, *impassive*-unemotional, *countenance*-facial expression, *maliciously*-spitefully, *filial*-from son or daughter, *foreboding*-bad omen, *angular*-gaunt, *unctuously*-fawningly, *garbed*-attired, *opulence*-wealth, *stolidly*-dully, *consternation*-dismay, *loathed*-disliked, *wistfulness*-longing, *indignation*-anger, *pendulous*-hanging, *petulantly*-peevishly, *repine*-complain, *pouted*-sulked, *reek*-smell, *propitious*-favorable, *agape*-with mouth open, *repulsion*-distaste, *acquiescent*-agreeable, *distraught*-confused, *overweening*-conceited, *spawn*-offspring, *dais*-platform, *bumpkin*-yokel, *parsimony*-stinginess, *blowsy*-slovenly, *coy*-demure, *haggard*-wild-eyed, *incessantly*-ceaselessly, *amiss*-faulty, *gravity*-seriousness, *begrudge*-grumble at, *coquetry*-flirting, *surcharged*-overburdened, *requited*-repaid, *mincing*-dainty, *scanty*-insufficient

Teaching Aids

for

GREAT EXPECTATIONS

One of the most popular of the many famous works written by Charles Dickens, this book represents a perfect blending of the amazingly varied skills that have given the author prime rank among the world's great novelists. The story of the well-meaning young Pip, who so often does foolish things, has for some an extremely sad quality. Yet the major virtues of *Great Expectations* are found in its emphasis on forgiveness, love, and forbearance. This world, it says, may be a gloomy place, but it is not without hope that truth can be learned and souls can be enlightened.

I. *Objective Test*

In the space provided at the left, insert the *letter* of the correct choice from among those offered; for example:

....c....   The author of this book is (a) Conrad (b) Stevenson (c) Dickens (d) Eliot

.... 1. Pip steals food from Mrs. Joe's kitchen because he (a) wants to get back at her for her cruelty (b) feels sorry for the hungry convict (c) is afraid to disobey the convict (d) is very hungry

.... 2. The prison ships are introduced primarily to (a) show the thoroughness of British justice (b) accentuate Pip's sense of being a criminal

(c) evoke sympathy for the convicts (d) provide important background

.... 3. Mrs. Joe responds kindly to Pumblechook because he (a) treats her better than Joe does (b) has promised to make the Gargerys rich (c) has generous habits (d) has impressed her by his wealth and worldly ways

.... 4. Dickens makes it clear in the early chapters that Pip is most concerned about his (a) mistreatment by his sister (b) feelings of guilt for stealing (c) humiliation at the hands of Pumblechook (d) living as a pauper

.... 5. When the convict lies about having stolen food from Joe, we realize that (a) convicts are evil men (b) the sergeant has been fooled (c) the convict is not really entirely bad (d) he is just trying to protect himself

.... 6. In evaluating the educational system found at Mr. Wopsle's great-aunt's school, Dickens (a) smiles at its haphazard procedures (b) frowns at its demanding routine (c) rejoices at its appealing atmosphere for education (d) seems indifferent to it all

.... 7. Joe's story about his own childhood shows that (a) people are simply born for trouble (b) Joe is really more foolish than first supposed (c) poverty is unavoidable (d) Joe is really more sensitive than first supposed

.... 8. Dickens suggests that your attitude toward Mrs. Joe should be to (a) admire her stern approach toward rearing children (b) disapprove her poor understanding of a young boy (c) sympathize with her putting up with a nuisance (d) consider her a typical parent

.... 9. Miss Havisham wants Pip to come and "play" because she (a) is bored and wants someone to talk to (b) needs a helper to take care of some chores (c) wants to try out Estella's charms on a male victim (d) is a charitable woman

.... 10. After a few visits to Miss Havisham's house, Pip sees himself as a (a) pagan seeking God (b) poor boy needing a fortune (c) common lad needing higher social status (d) confident young man

.... 11. When Joe goes to see Miss Havisham, he talks only to Pip because he (a) is too shocked by Miss Havisham to talk to her (b) has been advised not to talk directly to her (c) thinks he would thus please Pip (d) has been told by Miss Havisham not to address her

.... 12. Pip meets Herbert Pocket (a) in an oddly accidental way (b) as a part of Herbert's deliberate plan (c) as the result of a natural coincidence (d) as a part of Pip's plan

.... 13. When Pip discloses his secret desire to become a gentleman, Biddy (a) sternly criticizes him for his ingratitude (b) encourages him to pursue his dream (c) ignores him completely (d) calmly tries to persuade him it would be unwise

.... 14. From the description of Jaggers' work, it is clear that Dickens (a) admired all police work and lawyers (b) had a rather low esteem for Scotland Yard and legal work (c) regarded the law with complete trust (d) wished he had studied to become a lawyer

.... 15. Pip mistakenly believes the source of his "great expectations" is Miss Havisham because (a) she had also given Joe a handsome sum (b) she had shown Pip the bride cake (c) Pip had first met Jaggers at Miss Havisham's house (d) Pip knew the source could not be a convict

.... 16. Which of the following thoughts troubles Pip about Joe from the early visits to Miss Havisham until late in the story? (a) Next to a gentleman, Joe appears coarse and common. (b) Though he may work well, he will never overcome his thoughtlessness. (c) Joe is becoming snobbish. (d) Joe is ungrateful and selfish.

.... 17. How does Herbert Pocket feel about Estella? (a) He needs her beauty and charm about him. (b) He envies Pip's more intimate acquaintance with her. (c) He still loves her. (d) He wants no part of her.

.... 18. Wemmick treats the prisoners at Newgate (a) with pity for their wretched condition (b) with complete indifference (c) in his usual impersonal and businesslike manner (d) with obvious disdain

.... 19. Herbert and Pip deal with their mounting debts by (a) listing them all but paying none (b) paying a few at a time (c) borrowing money from Jaggers (d) filing for bankruptcy

.... 20. When Magwitch returns to London and enters Pip's room on that stormy night, Pip most fears (a) being killed by the vicious visitor (b) being arrested for aiding a criminal (c) ruining his own status as a gentleman (d) being asked for a loan

.... 21. The most likely symbolic interpretation of Miss Havisham's death is that the fire represents the (a) consuming wrath of God for the wicked (b) burning purification of her soul (c) raging desire for revenge (d) final flames of unrequited love

.... 22. Mrs. Matthew Pocket lets the servants run her house because she (a) knows nothing about domestic life (b) knows they need jobs (c) spends most of her time with her children (d) wants to spy on them

.... 23. At the very end of the novel, the great change in Estella seems to suggest that (a) beauty is fragile and fleeting (b) love is born through suffering (c) virtue always gets its reward (d) love is totally unpredictable

.... 24. By the *tone* of the author's treatment of Biddy's life with Joe, you can assume that Dickens thinks that (a) Biddy has thrown her life away

on Joe (b) Joe is deserving of someone better
(c) both are fools (d) Biddy and Joe are well
matched

.... 25. Looking at the story as a whole, one could say
that Pip learns from his association with Magwitch to see the (a) horror of crime (b) honor
of being a gentleman (c) need for wealth
(d) real worth of a human being beneath the
surface

Answers

1-c, 2-b, 3-d, 4-b, 5-c, 6-a, 7-d, 8-b, 9-c, 10-c, 11-a, 12-a, 13-d, 14-b,
15-c, 16-a, 17-d, 18-c, 19-a, 20-c, 21-b, 22-a, 23-b, 24-d, 25-d

II. *Alternate Objective Tests*

A. Matching

Before each number in the column on the left, write the
letter of the item in the column on the right that matches:

.... 1. Biddy   a. half-brother
.... 2. Jaggers   b. Philip Pirrip
.... 3. Miss Havisham   c. actor
.... 4. Pip   d. scarred wrists
.... 5. Trabb   e. judge
.... 6. Compeyson   f. candles
.... 7. Wopsle   g. walnut shell
.... 8. Arthur   h. scented soap
.... 9. Molly   i. lifting by the hair
...... 10. Matthew   j. school teacher
                                     k. convict
                                     l. tailor

Answers

1-j, 2-h, 3-f, 4-b, 5-l, 6-k, 7-c, 8-a, 9-d, 10-i

B. Fill-ins

From the column on the right, select the item that best completes each statement below, and write it in the space provided:

1. _____ could be called a *sycophant*, one who seeks favor through flattery.

2. During her illness, _____ wants to appease Orlick.

3. Estella first hurts Pip by saying he is _____.

4. Miss Havisham uses Estella as an instrument of _____.

5. Pip first admires _____ for her pleasant competence and wisdom.

6. Jaggers deals only with those who _____.

7. _____ and Orlick are similar in that they both slouch.

8. As he approaches Walworth, Wemmick becomes more and more _____.

9. Pip admits that _____ lies at the heart of his "great expectations."

10. The court is lenient with _____ because he appears respectable.

11. Miss Havisham sees her own cruelty only after Pip tells her of his _____.

12. Unlike Pip, _____ believes love is a great pleasure.

13. After Magwitch's final capture, _____ is concerned about the convict's portable property.

14. Joe is motivated by compassion to come to _____ during Pip's illness.

15. The character who, even in the end, remains idealistic about the power of money is _____.

Joe
Biddy
Compeyson
Herbert
welfare
Drummle
Mrs. Joe
dirty
suffering
common
Estella
Magwitch
revenge
kill
London
friendly
pay
aristocrat
Wemmick
Pumblechook

Answers

1-Pumblechook, 2-Mrs. Joe, 3-common, 4-revenge, 5-Biddy, 6-pay, 7-Drummle, 8-friendly, 9-Estella, 10-Compeyson, 11-suffering, 12-Herbert, 13-Wemmick, 14-London, 15-Magwitch

III. *Ideas for Written or Oral Book Reports or Class Discussions*

1. Very early in the story, Pip is involved in an act of stealing under pressure from an escaped convict. As the narrative continues, we meet Orlick, Jaggers, Wemmick, Compeyson, and others who are involved in either breaking or upholding the law. It is now an accepted principle in literature that the writer often draws upon details of his own background in creating events and characters for his novels. How would this fact account for the rather extraordinary amount of space Dickens devoted to criminal behavior and law enforcement agents in *Great Expectations*? In the light of the way he described certain episodes and developed some of his characters, what were the author's views toward the courts, lawyers, prisons, prisoners, motivations for committing crimes, and guilt feelings that follow an illegal act? Make specific references to the text to support your conclusions.

2. One can judge the extreme distaste Dickens had for hypocritical behavior by the frequency with which he revealed this disagreeable trait in many of his characters. In what ways did Pumblechook display hypocrisy in his dealings with Pip? Why would it be reasonable to say that the Pockets behaved like typical hypocrites in the presence of a rich relative? What was there hypocritical about the behavior of Miss Havisham and Estella toward Pip through much of the story? How did Pip give evidence of this same weakness of character on an early visit from London to Joe Gargery's place and later during his return for Mrs. Joe's funeral? What is the significance of the reference to "self-swindlers" (p. 216M)? How did Joe's behavior

throughout the story serve as a sharp contrast to that of the "self-swindlers" about him?

3. A cycle of (a) sin, crime, or bad behavior (b) suffering (c) repentance and (d) atonement occurs again and again in the book. Explain the cycle as it applies in each of the following relationships:

Estella and Pip and Miss Havisham
Miss Havisham and Pip
Pip and Joe and Biddy
Magwitch and Pip and Estella
Mrs. Joe and Pip and Joe

4. Some critics have complained that Dickens in creating his less prominent characters presented them as little more than *caricatures* of real people; that is, he selected a single trait, more or less; exaggerated it to reveal the desired personality feature; and let it function in the same manner in every situation, without adding another dimension or added depth. For example, in the character of Orlick, we saw a classic portrait of the all-bad villain who spoke and acted as if driven by some inner evil force that permitted no redeeming quality to emerge. To what extent were each of the following presented in only a single dimension: Jaggers, Wemmick, Wopsle, Pumblechook, Compeyson, and Matthew Pocket? Cite successive incidents that reveal a constant sameness in speech and behavior, or offer evidence to dispute the idea that any one of the group was drawn in caricature. Incidentally, why might it have been necessary for Dickens to limit the development of certain characters, considering his purposes as a novelist?

5. Dickens seemed to believe that one can measure character by the way an individual reacts to disappointment. For instance, what would you say about the strength of Joe Gargery's character, judging by the way he reacted to the disappointments he experienced at the hands of Mrs. Joe and Pip? What effect did disappointment have on the characters of Miss Havisham and Estella? What role did disappointment play in the relationship between Pip and

Magwitch, as well as between Pip and Estella? In what respects did Pip become disappointed in himself? How favorable or unfavorable an influence did this realization have on his gradual growth toward maturity? If you were to select the one character who showed inner strength most consistently, who would it be? Explain your choice.

6. Another means Dickens used to reveal character development was to show how it is affected by love. In each of the following, answer the preliminary questions and then summarize by explaining the impact love had on the person involved:

Pip's Love
Why did Pip fall in love with Estella?
What made his love so painful?
How selfish was Pip's love?
What did he learn from this experience?

Estella's Love
How had she been trained to regard men?
How did she feel about Pip?
What had to happen before she could really love any-
  one?
What were her real feelings about Miss Havisham?

Miss Havisham's Love
Why was she jilted?
What kind of love did she have for Estella?
Why was she shocked at Estella's coldness later?

Joe's Love
Why did Joe permit his wife to exploit him?
How did he feel about Pip?
Why was it predictable that he would marry Biddy?

7. You have doubtless heard the expression: "Live and learn." What does this mean generally? For some people, the appropriate statement might be: "Suffer and learn to develop genuine feeling." How did the latter apply to both Pip and Estella? What had to happen before Miss Hav-

isham permitted a break in her bitterness? What glimpses did you get of real humanity in Jaggers, Wemmick, and Magwitch? How did Joe's activity during Pip's illness affect Pip? What experiences led Pip to feel closer to Magwitch after a while, indeed to admire certain qualities of the convict? Why do some people profit from their experiences in terms of character development and others do not?

8. No study of a book by Charles Dickens would be complete without some consideration of his style of writing, which has been the subject of much critical analysis. Consider each of the following, and offer additional examples to illustrate the technique used.

a. *Point of view:* What advantages and disadvantages did the author have in telling his story in the first person?

b. *Descriptive power:* How did Dickens use nature to reflect the themes in the story? For example, at times Pip had to make his way through a dense fog or through mists. Note also the symbolic use of light in the name Estella (Star), the gifts of jewels by Miss Havisham to Estella, the absence of daylight in Miss Havisham's house. Other examples abound.

c. *Symbolism:* In this device, the author uses an object or person to signify a concept much broader than the original. What significance did the frequent references to a file have in connection with Magwitch, or Mrs. Joe's drawing of a hammer in relation to Orlick? What about the scented soap and Jaggers? Find more examples.

d. *Suspense:* Dickens displayed a masterful ability to build suspense by withholding information until the appropriate time. Why didn't he identify the "pale young gentleman" immediately? How long did it take to learn the identity of Molly, Magwitch, Compeyson? How else did Dickens keep us guessing?

e. *Irony:* This is a device that points up a meaning or result that is opposite to what appears on the surface. What is ironic about the name *Satis House,* Pip's early attitude toward Magwitch, Estella's reactions to Miss Havisham? Where else are there examples?

9. One aspect of Dickens' writing style we have not yet considered is his broad use of humorous touches, especially in the development of some of his minor characters. Who are the people and what are the incidents that made you smile most frequently as you read the book? Considering his life, times, and understanding of psychology, why would it be accurate to say that much of the humor had a layer of tragedy or pathos beneath it? For example, what was pathetic about Pumblechook? What was sad in the description of Mr. Wemmick's father ("The Aged"); or Trabb's Boy, the assistant to the village tailor; or Old Bill Barley (Old Gruffandgrim, the drunken father of Herbert Pocket's girl friend)? What other examples can you find of humor that made the reader laugh on the outside but feel sad on the inside?

10. There are two legitimate endings to *Great Expectations* and a third suggested by George Bernard Shaw. The ending finally given to the story at the suggestion of Bulwer-Lytton, a novelist friend of Dickens, was the second choice, the one ordinarily given to popular editions of the novel, like this one. In his first ending, Dickens had a long period of time elapse before Pip saw Estella again. In the meantime, her brutal husband had died, she had married again (an indigent Shropshire doctor), and had found it necessary to support her new husband with her own funds. Pip finally met Estella in the street, after being called by a servant to speak to "a lady in a carriage," and had a talk with his former beloved one. But nothing materialized out of this, other than Pip's realization that Estella had suffered and had found "a heart to understand what my heart used to be." G. B. Shaw would have accepted the final meeting at Satis House, but would have had Pip say as the final word: "Since that parting I have been able to think of her without the old unhappiness, but I have never tried to see her again, and I know I never shall." Which ending best fits the story? Which seems most consistent with the characters? Support your choice by citing statements made earlier in the novel that offer reasonable evidence. In summary, examine your own feelings about Pip and Estella.

How much do you really *like* them by the end of the story? Why?

IV. *Vocabulary Study*

Diagnostic Test

5M	gibbet	chicken part	gallows	lynx
7T	connubial	humorous	solitary	matrimonial
8T	trenchant	forceful	flabby	deep
11B	augmented	lowered	increased	bored
20M	vicariously	viciously	directly	by proxy
33M	execrating	cursing	praising	discharging
42M	erudition	ignorance	hostility	scholarship
44M	perspicuity	dullness	clarity	density
49B	ablutions	soilings	experiments	washings
64M	caparisoned	covered	disclosed	involved
67M	rumination	emptiness	scope	meditation
70T	fortuitously	by design	by chance	by force
89B	suborned	bribed	reformed	created
98B	mollified	antagonized	soothed	chopped
100M	malevolent	kindly	loud	ill-disposed
101T	excrescence	reduction	outgrowth	cavity
112B	maudlin	cold	girlish	too sentimental
118T	aberration	consolidation	deviation	confirmation
123B	disconcerted	upset	calmed	intoned
130T	subterfuge	consent	deception	tunnel
137T	evincing	displaying	dividing	deceiving
149T	flaccid	narrow	flabby	husky
152T	discomfited	lifted	pleased	frustrated
177B	incipient	ending	beginning	middling
180M	distraught	bewildered	thirsty	peaceful
192B	homage	comfort	contempt	respect
197M	inveigled	untied	entrapped	rejected
218M	choleric	ill	genial	angry
225M	disparity	dissimilarity	likeness	hopelessness
235M	miscreant	atheist	hero	villain
256M	diffident	bold	shy	odd
265M	edifying	defiant	mysterious	instructive
266B	interment	deference	burial	resurrection
274T	cogent	convincing	healing	dubious
287T	rubicund	flat	costly	rosy

297B	untenable	obvious	slippery	indefensible
307B	repugnance	love	dislike	indifference
314M	prolix	wordy	brief	humorous
329M	extricate	catch	escape	devise
345M	credence	doubt	prayer	belief
354M	tacit	silent	loud	long
368B	necromantic	sentimental	magic	obvious
395M	obdurate	open	elegant	unmoved
404T	brazen	cowardly	bold	unfeeling
415T	vivacity	liveliness	lethargy	cheers
423M	grizzled	roasted	gray-haired	rejuvenated
432B	portentous	interesting	ominous	discounting
450T	composure	illness	music	self-possession
457M	debilitating	weakening	reviving	bedeviling
464M	avarice	hope	greed	strength

Answers

gibbet-gallows, *connubial*-matrimonial, *trenchant*-forceful, *augmented*-increased, *vicariously*-by proxy, *execrating*-cursing, *erudition*-scholarship, *perspicacity*-clarity, *ablutions*-washings, *caparisoned*-covered, *rumination*-meditation, *fortuitously*-by chance, *suborned*-bribed, *mollified*-soothed, *malevolent*-ill-disposed, *excresence*-outgrowth, *maudlin*-too sentimental, *aberration*-deviation, *disconcerted*-upset, *subterfuge*-deception, *evincing*-displaying, *flaccid*-flabby, *discomfited*-frustrated, *incipient*-beginning, *distraught*-bewildered, *homage*-respect, *inveigled*-entrapped, *choleric*-angry, *disparity*-dissimilarity, *miscreant*-villain, *diffident*-shy, *edifying*-instructive, *interment*-burial, *cogent*-convincing, *rubicund*-rosy, *untenable*-indefensible, *repugnance*-dislike, *prolix*-wordy, *extricate*-escape, *credence*-belief, *tacit*-silent, *necromantic*-magic, *obdurate*-unmoved, *brazen*-bold, *vivacity*-liveliness, *grizzled*-gray-haired, *portentous*-ominous, *composure*-self-possession, *debilitating*-weakening, *avarice*-greed

Teaching Aids

for

GULLIVER'S TRAVELS

Jonathan Swift intended *Gulliver's Travels* to be an absolutely savage attack upon man and his institutions. Much to his chagrin, it turned out to be a book that could be read with delight by children, who love imaginative tales about strange creatures. This unexpected juvenile appeal led critic Carl Van Doren to say: "As much, and in as many languages, as *Gulliver's Travels* has been read, it has, in a sense, seldom been read at all because it has too often been read too soon." Here, then, is a phenomenon—a book that must be read many times because each succeeding level of maturity brings with it increased appreciation of the contents of one of the great satires in literary history.

I. *Objective Test*

In the space provided at the left, insert the *letter* of the correct choice from among those offered; for example:

....b.... The author of this book is (a) Pope (b) Swift (c) Defoe

.... 1. Gulliver arrived in Lilliput as the result of being (a) shipwrecked (b) abandoned by his companions (c) marooned by pirates

.... 2. The Lilliputians overcame Gulliver by (a) using bows and arrows (b) stealing his weapons (c) tying him down

.... 3. The Lilliputians believed that Gulliver's most important possession was his (a) pistol (b) watch (c) spectacles

.... 4. Government officials in Lilliput were appointed as a result of (a) favoritism (b) a written examination (c) examinations in acrobatic rope and stick dancing

.... 5. Blefuscu was (a) a province of Lilliput (b) the capital of Lilliput (c) an island whose navy Gulliver captured

.... 6. Gulliver's stay in Lilliput was made uncomfortable because of (a) political enemies (b) inadequate food (c) the common people's jealousy

.... 7. In Brobdingnag, Gulliver enabled the farmer, his first master, to become wealthy by (a) teaching him British farming methods (b) allowing himself to be exhibited as a curiosity (c) urging the king to make the farmer a public official

.... 8. A constant danger to Gulliver in Brobdingnag was the (a) cruelty of the population (b) gigantic animals and insects (c) jealousy of the rulers

.... 9. Gulliver was made uncomfortable by the Brobdingnagians because their (a) faces were out of proportion (b) mild physical defects were monstrous and nauseating (c) ignorance of medicine kept them ill

.... 10. The queen's dwarf became Gulliver's (a) most active enemy (b) staunchest friend (c) profoundest admirer

.... 11. The king of Brobdingnag insisted that Gulliver keep secret the (a) history of England (b) corruption of European politics (c) existence of guns and bullets

.... 12. Gulliver left Brobdingnag when he was carried off by (a) an eagle (b) a passing Portuguese ship (c) a whale

.... 13. Laputa was an island in the middle of (a) the ocean (b) an inland sea (c) the air

.... 14. The ruling classes of Laputa were interested in (a) the sciences (b) literature (c) social problems

.... 15. The people of Laputa were so intellectual that they were (a) able to read Gulliver's thoughts (b) not surprised by tales of England (c) in need of "flappers" to awaken them to reality

.... 16. In Laputa, Gulliver was amazed that everyday tasks were performed with (a) efficiency (b) lack of efficiency (c) originality

.... 17. The Laputians feared that (a) their island would sink (b) they would float out to space (c) all the planets would be annihilated

.... 18. The experiments at the Grand Academy of Lagado impressed Gulliver because of their (a) foolishness (b) scientific advancement (c) improvement of the inhabitants' lives

.... 19. The Struldbrugs convinced Gulliver that immortality was (a) desirable (b) unattainable (c) a dreadful misfortune

.... 20. In the land of the Houyhnhnms, (a) men had domesticated horses (b) horses had domesticated men (c) Gulliver constantly sought to escape

.... 21. The Yahoos filled Gulliver with a feeling of (a) envy (b) admiration (c) loathing

.... 22. A characteristic of the Houyhnhnms that impressed Gulliver was their sense of (a) honor (b) humor (c) treachery

.... 23. When a Houyhnhnm went riding, his carriage was drawn by (a) horses (b) oxen (c) Yahoos

.... 24. Gulliver in time began to regard the Houyhnhnm with which he lived as his (a) master (b) servant (c) pal

.... 25. When Gulliver returned to England, he regarded the people as (a) loathsome (b) blessed companions (c) truly civilized

Answers

1-a, 2-c, 3-b, 4-c, 5-c, 6-a, 7-b, 8-b, 9-b, 10-a, 11-c, 12-a, 13-c, 14-a, 15-c, 16-b, 17-c, 18-a, 19-c, 20-b, 21-c, 22-a, 23-c, 24-a, 25-a

II. *Alternate Objective Tests*

A. Matching

Before each number in the column on the left, write the *letter* of the item in the column on the right that matches:

....	1. Reldresal	a.	Immortals
....	2. Blefuscu	b.	Gulliver
....	3. Queen of Lilliput's private apartments	c.	Grand Academy of Lagado
		d.	King of Brobdingnag
....	4. Little nurse	e.	Glumdalclitch
....	5. Sorrel nag	f.	Visions from past history
....	6. Struldbrugs	g.	Fire
....	7. Sunbeams from cucumbers	h.	Recommended blinding of Gulliver
....	8. Don Pedro	i.	Gulliver's "fellow servant"
....	9. Man-Mountain	j.	Traditional enemy of Lilliput
......	10. Balnibarbi	k.	Mainland under Laputa
		l.	Kindly ship captain

Answers

1-h, 2-j, 3-g, 4-e, 5-i, 6-a, 7-c, 8-1, 9-b, 10-k

B. Fill-ins

From the column on the right, select the item that best completes each statement below, and write it in the space provided:

1. Gulliver's _____ saved his eyes from the arrows.
2. Gulliver in his earlier sea voyages was employed as a (an) _____.
3. The Lilliputians drew up a list of items found in Gulliver's _____.
4. Gulliver was once dropped in a bowl of cream by a (an) _____.
5. Gulliver wove backs and seats for chairs from _____.
6. To read a book in Brobdingnag, Gulliver needed a (an) _____.
7. Gulliver was almost killed when the _____ tried to carry him off.
8. The garments of the Laputians were adorned with figures related to _____.
9. Laputa floated over _____.
10. Laputa's motion was controlled by a (an) _____.
11. In the palace of the governor of Glubbdubdrib, Gulliver saw _____.
12. After being marooned by his own men, Gulliver came to the land of the _____.
13. Gulliver developed an extreme loathing for the _____.
14. Gulliver was flattered when asked to kiss his Houyhnhnm master's _____.
15. On returning to England from the land of the Houyhnhnms, Gulliver _____ when his wife kissed him.

Balnibarbi
hoof
hair combings
magnifying glass
pockets
ghosts
fainted
hat
loadstone
spectacles
dwarf
cried
Houyhnhnms
grass
ape
brow
Yahoos
ladder
surgeon
science and music

Answers

1-spectacles, 2-surgeon, 3-pockets, 4-dwarf, 5-hair combings, 6-ladder, 7-ape, 8-science and music, 9-Balnibarbi, 10-loadstone, 11-ghosts, 12-Houyhnhnms, 13-Yahoos, 14-hoof, 15-fainted

III. *Ideas for Written or Oral Book Reports or Class Discussions*

1. a. On p. 61T, Gulliver tells us that "after the court had decreed any cruel execution, either to gratify the monarch's resentment, or the malice of a favourite, the Emperor always made a speech to his whole Council, expressing his *great lenity and tenderness, as qualities known and confessed by all the world.*"

Swift—in this sentence and in one or two of the remarks immediately following it—was obviously satirizing those in power who cloak their wicked deeds with sweet words. To what extent were all the rulers Gulliver met hypocritical?

b. Which rulers—possibly dictators—of more recent times can you think of concerning whom similar sentiments might justly be expressed? Explain your answer, furnishing as much detailed evidence as you can to prove your point.

c. What parallels in modern times prove Gulliver's wisdom in fleeing to Blefuscu rather than submitting— though he was, of course, convinced of his innocence—to a public trial?

2. Gulliver's friend, Reldresal, the principal secretary for private affairs, suggests in the king's council (pp. 58M– 59T) that Gulliver should be blinded rather than put to death. Is this Swift's way of indicating how considerate and sympathetic the Lilliputians could be, or is it rather another example of the savagery of Swift's satire? Explain your answer. Would it not have been more in character for one of Gulliver's enemies—Bolgolam, the admiral, or Flimnap, the high treasurer—to have made a suggestion of this nature? Explain why Swift chose a friend rather than an enemy of Gulliver's to make the proposal.

3. a. What was Swift's purpose in making Lilliput and Blefuscu enemy states? Both countries were prosperous. Both had enough land, enough food, enough of all the things people normally want. Why, then, the continual state of war between them? What purpose was Swift trying

to achieve that he could not have accomplished by making both countries live at peace with each other?

b. What satirical purpose could Swift possibly hope to achieve by making his Lilliputian candidates for public office go through their fantastic acrobatic rope and stick dances (pp. 24T–25B) in order to obtain appointment and hold office? Was Swift merely amusing himself with this bit of nonsense, or did he, in your opinion, have a deeply serious point in mind? Explain your answer.

4. The king of Brobdingnag "gave it for his opinion, that whoever could make two ears of corn or two blades of grass to grow upon a spot of ground where only one grew before, would deserve better of mankind, and do more essential service to his country than the whole race of politicians put together" (p. 129T). Think, first, what the royal statement implies—what broad generalization it leads to. Remember, in addition, that when we admire politicians, we often call them "statesmen." Consider, also, the very many relationships between the political situation of a country or a civilization and its productive capacity. Now you are ready to reflect seriously upon the king's statement and to explain in detail why you agree or disagree with it. Finally, compare this king to other rulers you met in the story.

5. On p. 128, Gulliver finds a serious defect in the princely qualities of the king of Brobdingnag, for when Gulliver offers to teach him the art of making guns, gunpowder, and bullets, the king would have none of it. Gulliver finds it hard to understand why the king would refuse to acquire information that would make him "absolute master of the lives, the liberties, and the fortunes of his people." Do you, too, agree that the king was foolish? Explain. Compare this king's attitude with that of other rulers you met in the story.

6. Possibly the most devastating criticism of English civilization in "A Voyage to Brobdingnag" is made (p. 125) in the king's long speech ending with the words: "I cannot but conclude the bulk of your natives to be the most pernicious race of little odious vermin that nature ever suffered to crawl upon the surface of the earth." What

sort of picture of England does Gulliver draw (pp. 119M–124B) to obtain so contemptuous a reaction from the king? From what you know of European history in general, or English history in particular, would you say that Swift made Gulliver draw an accurate picture of the civilization of his day? Or would you say that, on the contrary, the picture was exaggerated or unfair? Explain your answer. How do you think the rulers of Lilliput, Laputa, and the Houyhnhnms reacted to Gulliver's tales about England?

7. Are there people today who share Swift's opinion that a good deal of the research that is carried on is, if not fraudulent, then certainly useless or foolish or, on occasion, actually harmful? On what evidence do such people base their criticism? Do you agree with them? What should we do about the situation if these critics are right? Should research be controlled? By whom? Should it be more stringently supervised? By whom? Or should it be permitted to continue as at present? Defend your point of view.

8. In Lilliput (pp. 48T–50B), children were brought up in special nurseries, and parents could visit them only several times a year. In the land of the Houyhnhnms (pp. 268B–269T), adults "have no fondness for their colts or foals, but the care they take in educating them proceeds entirely from the dictates of *reason*. And I observed my master to show the same affection to his neighbor's issue that he had for his own." What is your opinion about the theory that intelligent, systematic, careful nurture is preferable to parental love? Are you familiar with any modern attempts—anywhere in the world—to raise children according to similar theories? How successful have these been?

9. Because *Gulliver's Travels* is full of all sorts of impossibilities—miniature human beings, giants, an island floating in the air, men serving horses as their masters, the summoning up of ghosts from the past, immortals—why does an intelligent reader not throw the book away in despair, declaring the whole a silly and fantastic concoction of nonsense? What is there about Swift's manner of telling the story—his tone, his style, his attitude toward

his material, his very subject matter—that makes the intelligent reader continue to the end despite all the impossibilities?

10. Almost at the very end of his book (p. 295B), Swift says, "I write for the noblest end, to inform and instruct mankind. . . ." How can an author who has said so many horrible things about mankind expect us to take such a remark seriously? If, however, you think he may be justified in his statement, about what did Swift want to "inform and instruct mankind"? Try to make your answer as definite as you can, and support it with evidence from various sections of the book, indicating what Swift was trying to teach mankind in his treatment of at least three of the major adventures (Lilliput, Laputa, Brobdingnag, and so forth).

IV. *Vocabulary Study*

Diagnostic Test

5T	computation	compromise	reckoning	certainty
9B	disapprobation	whimsey	consent	condemnation
22M	prudent	cautious	neglectful	insured
28B	morose	cheerful	seasick	sullen
40T	encomiums	insults	stories	praises
41M	renown	obscurity	fame	renewal
43B	abhorrence	loathing	partiality	indifference
46B	circumspection	bravado	caution	reminiscence
50B	subservience	arrogance	substitution	truckling
53T	vindicate	implicate	support	clear
57M	auspicious	stern	favorable	unfortunate
62M	alacrity	hesitancy	briskness	sloth
65T	expostulations	objections	orders	agreements
78T	supplicating	beseeching	deriding	rejecting
85B	contrived	attempted	failed	devised
86M	requite	record	compensate	receive
99M	nettled	pleased	irritated	aggravated
107B	provocation	incitement	settlement	proof
120T	felicity	misery	ease	happiness
120B	erudition	ignorance	learning	eagerness

121T	august	imposing	undistinguished	argumentative
122B	zealous	lazy	friendly	enthusiastic
125B	odious	hateful	affectionate	odoriferous
127T	ingratiate	escape	insult	gain favor
128T	grovelling	haughty	humble	stony
132M	contending	competing	proposing	intriguing
135M	sagacity	cunning	obtuseness	speed
150M	disquiets	uneasinesses	silences	noises
156T	obtrude	be reticent	be impolite	push forward
159M	impending	distant	threatening	unlikely
168T	redress	correction	continuation	worsening
176B	inclement	mild	warm	harsh
178B	diurnal	semiannual	daily	monthly
179B	foundering	struggling	sinking	floating
183T	diminution	reduction	augmentation	filling
186T	pert	pertinent	respectful	saucy
202B	clemency	harshness	leniency	foresight
204B	appellation	title	insult	praise
209M	incited	calmed	noticed	instigated
220B	strand	country	island	shore
224B	divert	concern	amuse	convert
228M	lineaments	features	organs	beauties
231T	insipid	delicious	healthful	tasteless
233M	tolerance	foolish	passable	ingenious
241M	antipathy	partiality	indifference	dislike
243T	insuperable	insurmountable	inconceivable	incomprehensible
247T	enormities	exaggerations	crimes	benefits
281T	rudiments	elements	refinements	niceties
290T	veracity	deceitfulness	thoroughness	truthfulness
294M	perused	carefully examined	referred to	composed

Answers

computation-reckoning, *disapprobation*-condemnation, *prudent*-cautious, *morose*-sullen, *encomiums*-praises, *renown*-fame, *abhorrence*-loathing, *circumspection*-caution, *subservience*-truckling, *vindicate*-clear, *auspicious*-favorable, *alacrity*-briskness, *expostulations*-objections, *supplicating*-beseeching, *contrived*-devised, *requite*-compensate, *nettled*-irritated, *provocation*-incitement, *felicity*-happiness, *erudition*-learning, *august*-imposing, *zealous*-enthusiastic, *odious*-hateful, *ingratiate*-gain favor, *grovelling*-humble, *contending*-competing, *sagacity*-cunning, *disquiets*-uneasinesses, *obtrude*-push forward, *impending*-threatening, *redress*-correction, *inclement*-harsh, *diurnal*-daily, *foundering*-sinking, *diminution*-reduction, *pert*-saucy, *clemency*-leniency, *appellation*-title, *incited*-instigated, *strand*-shore, *divert*-amuse, *lineaments*-features, *insipid*-tasteless, *tolerable*-passable, *antipathy*-dislike, *insuperable*-insurmountable, *enormities*-crimes, *rudiments*-elements, *veracity*-truthfulness, *perused*-carefully examined

Teaching Aids

for

HEART OF DARKNESS

Even as a small boy, Joseph Conrad had expressed his intention of visiting Africa one day. When, in his early thirties, he finally did get to the "dark continent," he did not find the romantic region his youthful imagination had pictured. Instead, he became painfully aware of the full horror of human exploitation and wrote *Heart of Darkness,* which has been called "an angry document." The anger raised by man's brutality to man has not yet subsided. Here, in the rich prose of a master of the English language, is a story of great significance to the modern reader.

I. *Objective Test*

In the space provided at the left, insert the *letter* of the correct choice from among those offered; for example:

....b....   The author of this book is (a) Galsworthy
             (b) Conrad (c) Wells

.... 1. Marlow secured his job with "the Company"
             through (a) passing an examination (b) the
             influence of his aunt (c) his reputation as a
             ship's officer

.... 2. Marlow got his job sooner than he expected to
             because of (a) the favorable impression he had
             made on his interviewers (b) his previous ex-

perience in Africa (c) the killing of a company captain by the natives

.... 3. The examining doctor seemed most anxious to determine Marlow's (a) physical health (b) mental condition (c) susceptibility to tropical diseases

.... 4. Sailing along the coast of Africa, Marlow was deeply moved by (a) a French man-of-war firing its cannon into the jungle (b) the maneuvers of a whole fleet of French warships (c) the sight of an ocean liner loaded with African slaves

.... 5. At one of the first company stations on the river Marlow reached, he found himself staring at a (a) railway truck lying on its back (b) carefully cultivated tropical garden (c) giant Egyptian monument

.... 6. It was at this station that Marlow saw (c) hospital patients parading in wheelchairs (b) native "criminals" chained to one another with iron collars around their necks (c) natives staggering under loads of ivory

.... 7. Native workers who had evidently become ill on company projects seemed to Marlow to be (a) sitting or lying around neglected and waiting for death (b) pensioned off and sent back to their homes and families (c) kept in modern hospitals and rest homes

.... 8. The picture of Kurtz that Marlow got from all who first mentioned him was that of a man who was remarkably (a) cruel (b) gentle (c) efficient

.... 9. Marlow discovered at the Central Station, where he was to take command of his boat, that it was (a) away on a trip (b) at the bottom of the river (c) not yet delivered by the boat builders

.... 10. The Central Station manager's employment record was highly unusual, for he was (a) frequently ill (b) never absent because of illness

(c) constantly traveling and hardly ever at his station

.... 11. Marlow was so amused by the appearance and behavior of the European employees of "the Company" that he labeled them (a) pilgrims (b) heroes (c) conquerors

.... 12. The manager and the "brickmaker"—who hoped to be appointed assistant manager— were both afraid that their jobs would be taken away from them and assigned to (a) Kurtz (b) Marlow (c) a newcomer from Europe

.... 13. In order to repair the boat, Marlow needed but didn't have (a) planks (b) tools (c) rivets

.... 14. Marlow's helmsman was killed by a (a) pilgrim's gun (b) cannibal looking for food (c) spear thrown from shore

.... 15. After his helmsman's death, Marlow felt a compulsion to throw overboard his own (a) hat (b) pants (c) shoes

.... 16. "Exterminate all the brutes" was a statement (a) constantly being repeated by the Central Station manager (b) added at the end of Kurtz's pamphlet (c) summing up Marlow's conclusions about his African experiences

.... 17. The fence posts around Kurtz's house were topped by (a) cannon balls (b) human heads (c) native carvings of animals

.... 18. Kurtz arrived on board Marlow's ship (a) carried in a stretcher (b) marching at the head of his European assistants (c) secretly at night

.... 19. The native woman who suddenly came from the jungle to the water's edge (a) asked permission to speak to Kurtz (b) surprised Marlow by addressing him in perfect English (c) raised her arms silently to heaven and disappeared again into the forest

.... 20. Marlow learned from the Russian seaman that the natives' attack on the ship had been (a) ordered by Kurtz (b) the beginning of an attempt by the natives to revolt (c) urged on the natives by the woman they had seen on shore

.... 21. At midnight Marlow, waking from an uneasy slumber, suddenly discovered that (a) the ship had struck a snag and was sinking (b) a beautiful native woman had come on board (c) Kurtz had disappeared

.... 22. The threatening natives on shore were most easily subdued by (a) the guns of the pilgrims (b) the ship's whistle (c) a few words from Kurtz

.... 23. During the time that Kurtz was on board the ship, Marlow's most vivid recollection of him was that of a man who was continually (a) talking (b) sleeping (c) laughing

.... 24. The last words of Kurtz suggested (a) peace and resignation (b) guilt and horror (c) pride and self-righteousness

.... 25. In his interview with the "Intended," Marlow found it difficult to (a) stop her weeping (b) convince her Kurtz was dead (c) tell her the truth about Kurtz

Answers

1-b, 2-c, 3-b, 4-a, 5-a, 6-b, 7-a, 8-c, 9-b, 10-b, 11-a, 12-a, 13-c, 14-c, 15-c, 16-b, 17-b, 18-a, 19-c, 20-a, 21-c, 22-b, 23-a, 24-b, 25-c

II. *Alternate Objective Tests*

A. Matching

Before each number in the column on the left, write the *letter* of the item in the column on the right that matches:

.... 1. ate rotted hippo meat   a. pigeon-fancier

.... 2. company office in   b. Central Station
       Europe   manager

.... 3. "The horror! The horror!"
.... 4. lied to the "Intended"
.... 5. long-bearded foreman
.... 6. immaculate dresser
.... 7. temporary secretary
.... 8. dressed like a harlequin
.... 9. peculiar smile
...... 10. student of psychology

c. brickmaker
d. company physician
e. cannibals
f. Kurtz
g. company accountant
h. knitting women
i. Marlow
j. Russian seaman
k. the pilgrims
l. Towson

Answers

1-e, 2-h, 3-f, 4-i, 5-a, 6-g, 7-c, 8-j, 9-b, 10-d

B.   Fill-ins

From the column on the right, select the item that best completes each statement below, and write it in the space provided:

1. The story in *Heart of Darkness* was narrated by Marlow to a group on the *Nellie,* anchored in the _____.
2. The one who told us (the readers) the story was someone who called himself _____.
3. By profession, Marlow was a (an) _____.
4. Uppermost in the minds of the "pilgrims" was the word _____.
5. The _____ seemed very anxious to measure Marlow's head.
6. Men, Marlow heard, were dying of fever at the rate of three a day on the _____.
7. Near the grove of dying _____, Marlow met the company accountant.

drawing room
Congo
physician
ivory
brickmaker
Kurtz
natives
man-of-war
Marlow's ship
seaman
Marlow
I
voice
café
uncle
paintings
bore

8. The ship Marlow was to command had been sunk by the _____.

9. The chief of the Inner Station was _____.

10. One who seemed to be an especially privileged person at the Central Station was the _____.

11. Marlow accidentally overheard a conversation between the manager and his _____.

12. When Kurtz escaped from the ship, he was brought back on board by _____.

13. While on board, Kurtz impressed Marlow as one endless _____.

14. Marlow was threatened with legal action if he didn't surrender the _____ given to him by Kurtz.

15. Marlow met the "Intended" in an elegant _____.

employers
Thames
manager
papers

Answers

1-Thames, 2-I, 3-seaman, 4-ivory, 5-physician, 6-man-of-war, 7-natives, 8-manager, 9-Kurtz, 10-brickmaker, 11-uncle, 12-Marlow, 13-voice, 14-papers, 15-drawing room

III. *Ideas for Written or Oral Book Reports or Class Discussions*

1. What does Conrad gain or lose—artistically, psychologically, or in any other way—by having his story told so indirectly: first by a narrator who introduces us to Marlow and his audience on the yawl *Nellie,* then by Marlow with occasional minor interruptions, and finally, at the very end, by the original narrator again? Why did not Conrad, in your opinion, choose to have Marlow tell his story from the very opening sentence of the book? What more could we have learned about the land, its people,

and Kurtz if the narrative had been in the third person throughout?

2. Mention at least half a dozen incidents in *Heart of Darkness* through which Conrad pictures the cruelty of the Europeans toward the natives. How does Marlow feel about this treatment, judging by what he says? How does Marlow's reaction to the death of his helmsman symbolize his general attitude toward the natives?

3. What are the characteristics of Marlow—derived from the things he does or says—that make you respect or even admire him? For which characteristics—for which words or deeds—would you criticize him? Support your answer in each case by specific references.

4. Kurtz, one of the most important characters in *Heart of Darkness,* seems to dominate the minds and influence the activities of a great many people in the book. But he says very few things to us. Marlow tells us that when Kurtz was lying ill on shipboard, he did a tremendous amount of talking, but Marlow reveals only vague hints as to what he said. How does this weaken Conrad's story? Why would the book have been more powerfully written, how would Conrad's purpose have been more effectively achieved, if, like Marlow, Kurtz had been given the opportunity to express his ideas—tell us of his adventures and explain his thoughts—in detail? Or, if you do not hold to this opinion, explain what Conrad gained in effectiveness by withholding from us so much of what Kurtz said.

5. There is a good deal of emphasis in *Heart of Darkness* on how vile Marlow finds the indifference and the cruelty of the "pilgrims" toward the African natives. There can be little question, however, that Kurtz's treatment of the natives was just as bad as, if not much worse than, that of the pilgrims. Why, then, do the pilgrims resent Kurtz—really one of themselves—so fiercely? Why, moreover, are Marlow's feelings toward Kurtz so very much different from those he has for the pilgrims? How would you explain the reasons for Marlow's high regard for a Kurtz whose attitude toward and treatment of the natives were so reprehensible? Explain what Marlow means (p. 108B) when he says that he accepted "this choice of

nightmares," as well as his remark (p. 113M), "Better his cry—much better. It was an affirmation, a moral victory. . . ."

6. What is the real meaning of *Heart of Darkness* as a term or symbol? Does it refer to the African continent, its people, what was done to them, to the souls of men like Kurtz—or to all of these at once? Note that Marlow, referring to Kurtz, says (p. 76B): "The thing was to know what he belonged to, how many powers of darkness claimed him for their own." Later, we find this (p. 108M): "The brown current ran swiftly out of the heart of darkness . . . and Kurtz's life was running swiftly, too. . . ." What was Conrad trying to suggest about man and nature in his choice of title?

7. If Kurtz's postscript to his pamphlet, "Exterminate all the brutes!" (p. 79T) and his dying exclamation, "The horror! The horror!" (p. 111T) convey his most deeply felt opinions, how, then, can you explain his escape from Marlow's ship and his attempt to get back to the natives—especially since this ship, in view of his severe illness, was perhaps his last opportunity to get back to European civilization?

8. "The heavens do not fall for such a trifle," says Marlow (p. 124T) after he tells the "Intended," "The last word he pronounced was—your name." He continues: "Would they have fallen, I wonder, if I had rendered Kurtz that justice which was his due? Hadn't he said he wanted only justice? But I couldn't. I could not tell her. It would have been too dark—too dark altogether. . . ." What was the justice that was due Kurtz? Do you think that Kurtz and Marlow had similar ideas as to what the justice consisted of? If not, how did their ideas differ? What does Marlow mean by the statement that it would have been "too dark altogether"? What is the true significance of his lie to the "Intended"? Explain why you approve or disapprove of the lie.

9. a. Telling us that a character is remarkable or funny or smart isn't enough for a novelist. The author won't convince us unless he actually shows his character doing or saying things that we, the readers, will think of as re-

markable or funny or smart. Many people talk to Marlow about Kurtz and say all sorts of complimentary things about him: the company accountant (p. 26B), the manager (p. 33T), the brickmaker (p. 37M), the Russian seaman (p. 84M), the journalist (p. 115B), and the company representative seeking Kurtz's documents (p. 114M). Marlow "affirms" (p. 112M) that Kurtz was a remarkable man. Aside, however, from what you as a reader learn from the statements of other people about Kurtz, what more substantial evidence do you find in the story—mention as much as you can discover—to convince you that all the things people said about how remarkable a fellow Kurtz was were really true? Or, on the other hand, did Conrad create an unconvincing character?

b. If so many people in *Heart of Darkness* are busy telling Marlow what a marvelous fellow Kurtz is, where, how, and from whom do we learn about the evil side of Kurtz's character? Try to draw up a list of all of Kurtz's evil characteristics and evil deeds, and indicate how you learned about each item on your list.

10. a. What does Conrad gain or lose by his apparently deliberate refusal to name things and places and people that other storytellers are almost always very careful to make quite definite? The country where his aunt lives is (p. 10T) "on the Continent"; the city where he is interviewed for his job is (p. 36B) "the sepulchral city"; the firm that hires him is called (p. 9B) "a Continental concern"; Africa is not mentioned, but is referred to (p. 9M) as "the biggest, the most blank" place; the river is (p. 8M) "that river"; and except for some incidental names of places passed, there are no names of cities or towns along the river, though he does mention a "seat of the government" (p. 20T), a Central Station (p. 27B), and an Inner Station (p. 37M), of which Kurtz is head. Even the characters—except for Marlow and Kurtz—have no names: the Director, the Lawyer, the Accountant, the Brickmaker, the Half-caste, the Aunt, the Intended, and so on. The only additional name Conrad does give us is that of a dead man—Fresleven, the one whose place Marlow takes as master of the riverboat.

b. Conrad's writing style has been admired as one of the most expressive in the English language, but it has also, on occasion—especially in *Heart of Darkness*—been severely criticized for being turgid, vague, repetitious, mannered, ineffective. Choose half a dozen passages—short ones or long ones—that strike you as particularly well written. Explain why you admire each passage. Then point out any passages that seem to you to be poorly written. Explain why you have a poor opinion of each passage. Examine especially pages 3M, 9T, 12T, 17M, 19T, 20B, 24T, 27M, 31T, 39M, 45T, 51B, 53B, 59T, 64B, 76M, 79B, 91B, 105M, 108M, 110B, 117M, 121M.

IV. *Vocabulary Study*

Diagnostic Test

1M	luminous	dark	light	wide
3T	diaphanous	translucent	magic	opaque
3M	venerable	disdained	swift-flowing	revered
4B	sedentary	active	inactive	wandering
6M	skulking	laughing	glorying	hiding
12M	ungarnished	highly decorated	unadorned	steep
13T	sanctuary	holy place	outer office	export department
13B	placidity	wisdom	excitement	calm
15M	imperturbably	boldly	calmly	agitatedly
17M	insipid	spiritless	inspired	spiritual
18M	sinister	ominous	cheerful	ostentatious
19M	lugubrious	optimistic	insane	mournful
20B	declivity	foundation	mountain	slope
22M	alacrity	speed	hesitation	difficulty
23M	wanton	accidental	senseless	unfortunate
27T	elicited	concluded	drew	drove
26T	festive	pessimistic	lugubrious	merry
30M	volubility	reticence	talkativeness	gesticulations
31T	trenchant	ponderous	clumsy	cutting
33T	jeopardy	peril	bankruptcy	economic expansion
36T	beguiled	hastened	whiled away	lost

36B	supercilious-ness	humility	indifference	haughtiness
38M	transgression	obedience	violation	transference
39M	primeval	newly formed	pungent	primitive
42B	exasperated	puzzled	infuriated	eased
46T	sordid	vile	admirable	brave
48T	bizarre	sensible	conventional	fantastic
48B	vexed	serene	agitated	puzzled
50M	sagacious	half-witted	impatient	shrewd
52T	implacable	unappeasable	pacific	pure
57T	thrall	slave	ally	master
59M	malevolently	benevolently	benignantly	maliciously
60B	immobility	restlessness	motionlessness	uneasiness
61B	incontinently	carefully	unrestrainedly	prudently
64B	inexorable	unyielding	forgiving	unforeseen
66B	boding	ordering	celebrating	predicting
70B	fusillade	multiple discharge	superbomb	exploding shell
71M	evanescent	fleeting	permanent	picturesque
78M	rites	music	rhythms	ceremonies
81T	duffer	villain	oaf	connoisseur
82T	interspersed	interlarded	interfered	intervened
86T	mimes	ladies	actors	doctors
86B	destitution	wealth	comfort	poverty
102T	incantation	rhythmic intoning	orchestral music	eloquent oratory
105T	wistfulness	certainty	yearning	crassness
105B	invoke	call upon	warn against	greet
110T	noxious	salubrious	ignorant	harmful
111T	craven	inexplicable	cowardly	fiendish
114T	flauntings	displays	reservations	diffidence
114M	circuitous	frank	indiscreet	indirect

Answers

luminous-light, *diaphanous*-translucent, *venerable*-revered, *sedentary*-inactive, *skulking*-hiding, *ungarnished*-unadorned, *sanctuary*-holy place, *placidity*-calm, *imperturbably*-calmly, *insipid*-spiritless, *sinister*-ominous, *lugubrious*-mournful, *declivity*-slope, *alacrity*-speed, *wanton*-senseless, *elicited*-drew, *festive*-merry, *volubility*-talkativeness, *trenchant*-cutting, *jeopardy*-peril, *beguiled*-whiled away, *superciliousness*-haughtiness, *transgression*-violation, *primeval*-primitive, *exasperated*-infuriated, *sordid*-vile, *bizarre*-fantastic, *vexed*-agitated, *sagacious*-shrewd, *implacable*-unappeasable, *thrall*-slave, *malevolently*-maliciously, *immobility*-motionlessness, *incontinently*-unrestrainedly, *inexorable*-unyielding, *boding*-predicting, *fusillade*-multiple discharge, *evanescent*-fleeting, *rites*-ceremonies, *duffer*-oaf, *interspersed*-interlarded, *mimes*-actors, *destitution*-poverty, *incantation*-rhythmic intoning, *wistfulness*-yearning, *invoke*-call upon, *noxious*-harmful, *craven*-cowardly, *flauntings*-displays, *circuitous*-indirect

Teaching Aids

for

JANE EYRE

Charlotte Brontë's sisters, Emily and Anne, once said that an interesting heroine had to be beautiful. Charlotte strongly disagreed. "I will prove to you that you are wrong," she promised. "I will show you a heroine as small and as plain as myself who shall be as interesting as any of yours." And so *Jane Eyre* was written! For more than a century, this extraordinary love story has proved that its author was right—that readers will respond to the true essence of romance, however plain the heroine, however flawed the hero. As the strong-minded, eighteen-year-old governess comes to Thornfield and captures the fancy of its dashing master, more than twice her age, the remarkable narrative weaves its way through awakening love, dark secrets in murky corridors, tragic separation, and a reunion that merges with regeneration.

I. *Objective Test*

In the space provided at the left, insert the *letter* of the correct choice from among those offered; for example:

....c....   The author of this book is (a) Eliot (b) Austen (c) Brontë (d) Ball

.... 1. Early in the story, it was clear that Jane (a) was John Reed's favorite (b) would not be bullied (c) never argued with Mrs. Reed (d) was treated like the other children

.... 2. Mrs. Reed was visibly upset when Jane (a) received a blow on the head (b) spent the night in the red-room (c) spoke the truth about her guardian (d) left for Lowood

.... 3. Jane's friend at Lowood was Helen Burns, who (a) was always cheerful (b) seemed to be Scatcherd's pet (c) never read books (d) bore her misery calmly

.... 4. A brief moment of happiness came to Jane at Lowood when she (a) spent an evening with Miss Temple (b) was praised by Mr. Brocklehurst (c) took part in a play (d) received a letter from Mrs. Reed

.... 5. Jane decided to seek a job as governess by (a) asking Miss Temple for help (b) using the influence of a patron (c) answering an advertisement (d) placing an advertisement

.... 6. During an early tour of Thornfield, Jane was puzzled to hear (a) loud bells at night (b) a curious, mirthless laugh (c) the sounds of hammering (d) water gushing from some source

.... 7. In Jane's first meeting with Rochester, he (a) passed her without a word (b) ordered her off the premises (c) fell from his horse (d) invited her for tea

.... 8. Rochester considered Adèle a (a) genuine daughter of Paris (b) dull but obedient child (c) cold, indifferent girl (d) thoughtful, frugal little lady

.... 9. In his early conversations with Jane, Rochester seemed most taken with her (a) shy subservience (b) extraordinary frankness (c) ill-concealed arrogance (d) reluctance to express opinions

.... 10. One night, Jane saved Rochester's life by (a) pulling him from a window ledge (b) warning him of a hidden marksman (c) intercepting a poisoned drink (d) putting out a fire in his room

.... 11. The mystery of Thornfield deepened when Jane was asked to (a) take a midnight ride (b) lock Adèle in her room (c) tend to Mason's wounds (d) keep guard over Grace Poole

.... 12. Jane demonstrated her capacity for forgiveness by (a) visiting sick Mrs. Reed (b) becoming friendly with Mrs. Fairfax (c) excusing Blanche's insults (d) disregarding Rochester's refusal to pay her

.... 13. In Rochester's proposal of marriage to Jane, the reader could detect (a) regret that he had lost Miss Ingram (b) relief that he was free at last (c) a hint of secret misgivings (d) fear that Jane would reject him

.... 14. The impending marriage between Jane and Rochester drew from Mrs. Fairfax (a) hearty congratulations (b) vague warnings (c) open hostility (d) tearful jealousy

.... 15. On the night before the wedding, Jane suddenly awoke and saw in her room (a) a wild-looking woman (b) Grace Poole with a candle (c) a ghostly figure floating in air (d) ugly bats at the window

.... 16. The wedding ceremony was interrupted by a charge that (a) Jane was too young (b) Rochester had not filed for a license (c) Mr. Mason was an improper witness (d) Rochester was already married

.... 17. Rochester finally told Jane how, in his youth, he had been (a) preferred over his brother (b) cut off without a penny (c) misled by his father (d) exiled to Madeira

.... 18. Jane decided to leave Thornfield because she (a) now hated Rochester (b) wanted to avoid temptation (c) was forbidden to speak to Rochester (d) preferred to live with her uncle

.... 19. Shortly after leaving Thornfield, Jane found it necessary to (a) beg for food (b) work as a maid (c) become a clerk in a bakery (d) accept another job as governess

.... 20. Jane found the sisters of St. John Rivers to be (a) cold and hostile (b) vain and selfish (c) friendly and affectionate (d) scheming and devious

.... 21. In her work as mistress of a village school, Jane found her pupils to be (a) obedient but uniformly dull (b) unruly and vulgar (c) as varied in abilities as the high born (d) lacking in affection

.... 22. St. John Rivers revealed that he and his sisters were actually (a) related to the Olivers (b) heirs to a huge estate (c) defrauded by Mr. Briggs (d) cousins of Jane

.... 23. Jane rejected the marriage proposal of St. John Rivers because (a) he was still in love with Rosamond (b) she didn't want to leave England (c) it would have been a loveless match (d) the sisters disapproved

.... 24. The ruins of Thornfield brought the shocking realization to Jane that (a) her former nightmare had come true (b) Mrs. Fairfax had been killed (c) Grace Poole had set the blaze (d) her departure had caused Rochester to destroy the place

.... 25. Jane was convinced that her reunion with Rochester had been prompted by (a) the letter from Diana (b) the prayers of St. John Rivers (c) the gipsy woman's prophecy (d) a moment of mental telepathy

Answers

1-b, 2-c, 3-d, 4-a, 5-d, 6-b, 7-c, 8-a, 9-b, 10-d, 11-c, 12-a, 13-c, 14-b, 15-a, 16-d, 17-c, 18-b, 19-a, 20-c, 21-c, 22-d, 23-b, 24-a, 25-d

II. *Alternate Objective Tests*

A. Matching

Before each number in the column on the left, write the *letter* of the item in the column on the right that matches:

.... 1. Gateshead Hall   a. Rochester's ward
.... 2. Mr. Brocklehurst   b. West Indies
.... 3. Miss Temple   c. rejected heiress
.... 4. Adèle Varens   d. first wife
.... 5. Pilot   e. gentle cousin
.... 6. Mason   f. London lawyer
.... 7. Bertha   g. pompous parson
.... 8. Briggs   h. village baker
.... 9. Rosamond Oliver   i. Rochester's dog
...... 10. Diana   j. Mrs. Reed
     k. Rochester's boat
     l. kindly superintendent

Answers

1-j, 2-g, 3-l, 4-a, 5-i, 6-b, 7-d, 8-f, 9-c, 10-e

B. Fill-ins

From the column on the right, select the item that best completes each statement below, and write it in the space provided:

1. Jane told Mr. Lloyd that she would not want to live with anyone _____.
2. After the _____ at Lowood, conditions improved.
3. During Jane's first tea with Rochester, he gruffly praised her _____.
4. Jane was upset to hear Blanche Ingram talk sarcastically of _____.

fall
drawings
gipsy
nurse
Thornfield
letter
plain
Jane's uncle

5. One night Rochester disguised himself as a (an) _____.

6. Mrs. Reed concealed a (an) _____ for Jane from her uncle, John Eyre.

7. Eliza Reed left home to become a (an) _____.

8. Love made Jane feel that she was no longer _____.

9. In her dream, Jane saw the destruction of _____.

10. Mr. Mason and Mr. Briggs had come to the wedding ceremony at the request of _____.

11. Mr. Oliver would have approved a match between his daughter and

_____.

12. St. John, Diana, and Mary Rivers each received 5,000 pounds from _____.

13. The fire at Thornfield was started by

_____.

14. Rochester's first wife died as the result of a (an) _____.

15. When Jane was reunited with Rochester, he was _____.

blind
piano playing
Gateshead
typhus
Jane
St. John Rivers
Mrs. Fairfax
gift
Bertha
governesses
Brocklehurst
nun
poor

Answers

1-poor, 2-typhus, 3-drawings, 4-governesses, 5-gipsy, 6-letter, 7-nun, 8-plain, 9-Thornfield, 10-Jane's uncle, 11-St. John Rivers, 12-Jane, 13-Bertha, 14-fall, 15-blind

III. *Ideas for Written or Oral Book Reports or Class Discussions*

1. Jane often found Rochester's character baffling, and so do we. He often seems moody and unpredictable, kind yet cruel, a battleground of warring emotions. Even at the end of the book, we are not sure that we have the key to his character. Why did he go to so much trouble to make

Jane believe that he was going to marry Blanche Ingram? Why did he tell Jane that he had found a position for her in Ireland? If he was so sure that Adèle was not his child, why did he provide for her and keep her in his home? Why did he keep the detested Bertha in his home when he could so easily have placed her in an asylum? If he was afraid to place her in an asylum in England because his secret might become known, why did he not place her in a West Indian asylum such as the one to which her mother had been sent? If his sheltering of Adèle and Bertha at Thornfield seems to you the deed of an admirable man, how can you justify his intention of committing the crime of bigamy? Develop an analysis of Rochester's character, taking into account all of the questions raised.

2. Jane's association with St. John Rivers and her idea of becoming a missionary in India are also baffling points. Why did she agree very early to go with him as his assistant but not as his wife? How can you account for the fact that she had finally decided to marry St. John Rivers until she suddenly thought she heard Rochester's voice calling her? Discuss these questions in light of the changes that had occurred in Jane's attitude and expectations after she left Thornfield, the reasons for these changes, and the psychology behind her fancy that a voice was calling out to her.

3. While Mrs. Reed's hatred of Jane is evidenced early in the book, her villainy reached its peak when she wrote to Jane's uncle that Jane was dead (p. 277M). Why did Mrs. Reed do that? What possible advantage did it give her? If that act was simply the climax of Mrs. Reed's enduring hatred, how can you account for the fact that she still had so strong an urge to confess her misdeed to Jane?

4. *Jane Eyre* is, of course, a first-person narrative. What advantages and disadvantages are there in telling a story from this point of view? To what extent would you have gotten a less biased understanding of the other characters if they had been described by an all-seeing narrator rather than presented solely through the mind and eyes of Jane? Cite specific examples to support your ideas. How did you feel about the author's technique of permitting her main

character to engage in extensive analyses of herself and other characters, utter numerous asides, present frequent literary and biblical references, and moralize at every turn? How much, if at all, did this "intrusion" on the narrative flow affect your enjoyment of the story?

5. Literary history tells us that by the middle of the nineteenth century a wave of realism had swept across the pages of novelists, mainly because of a reaction to the highly romantic tales that had been characteristic of late eighteenth- and early nineteenth-century writing. What are the factors in the appearance, problems, and outcomes involving the central characters that would tend to support the idea that Charlotte Brontë had chosen to develop her narrative along realistic lines?

On the other hand, one critic complained of the book that it had "too much melodrama and improbability." What are some of the incidents in the plot that might well have been labeled melodramatic or improbable? Why, then, might these episodes have been included despite the author's intention of developing a realistic novel? In your reply, consider the comments of critic Ernest Dimnet, who addresses his remarks to the "modern reader":

> You exclaim "Childish!" if a book offers somewhat extraordinary events, forgetting that extraordinary events happen every day, but that if even one of these realities were introduced into one of your "novels" of real life," it would crumble like a house of cards, whereas *Jane Eyre* stands firm.

6. Analyze the love affair between Jane and Rochester. She was relatively plain, inclined to be opinionated, rather spinsterlike in attitude, and very much controlled in her emotions, at least on the surface. Yet what were the qualities in her that attracted the master of Thornfield? Similarly, Rochester was sometimes coarse, abrupt, seemingly loose in his habits, and accustomed to the arrogant power of a wealthy landowner. What was there about him that attracted the governess? How valid would it be to say that this was simply a case of "opposites attract"? In your reply,

be sure to take into account the reasons why Jane found it difficult to fall in love with the handsome and righteous St. John Rivers, just as Rochester could not develop a serious interest in Blanche Ingram, despite her vivacity and beauty. It is important, too, to consider the influence each one's background had in determining the mutual attraction between Jane and Rochester, particularly in terms of the needs each thought the other could fill.

7. Some readers have found fault with the character and behavior of Jane Eyre as a fictional creation. They regard her as too prim, overly virtuous, much too pedantic in speech and language, excessively tight emotionally, almost vain at times, and so totally introspective as to rule out the possibility of her ever finding real happiness, even after she has been reunited with Rochester. Defend or reject this line of reasoning, being certain to cite specific examples from the text to make your conclusions reasonable. Incidentally, in your analysis of the central character, you might want to include on the positive or negative side the fact that Jane told Mr. Lloyd she was afraid of poverty (p. 22T–22M). To what extent were the reasons she offered similar to those that might be advanced by snobs or others who are insensitive to the lot of the poor? On the other hand, later in the story, Jane seemed to be rather uneasy at the prospects of her suddenly becoming wealthy or at least able to enjoy luxuries. Why would she have had misgivings about entering into a life-style that apparently she had wanted from the first?

8. It should be clear (see *Biographical Background*) that Charlotte Brontë included many autobiographical details in the development of her story about Jane Eyre. Select at least five elements of setting or narrative that probably were derived from the real-life experiences of the writer. Discuss the changes, if any, that were made in detail for the purposes of fictional interest. Indicate, too, what imaginative touches can be traced to the normal dreamworld of a lonely young woman.

9. Although she appeared relatively briefly in the story, Helen Burns was an interesting character. How can you explain her rather calm attitude toward her misery and

her fatalistic approach to her impending death? In what ways did she symbolize the lot of the poor of the period? What qualities did she have that drew Jane toward her? Why do you suppose the author stressed Helen's great interest in reading? What characteristics did Jane possess that made her a better candidate for survival in the cruel world about her?

10. One of the striking aspects of Charlotte Brontë's style of writing was her broad use of contrast in the development of her characters, a device sometimes referred to as creating one character as a "foil" for the other. For example, the obvious contrasts are Rochester and St. John Rivers, as well as Jane and Blanche Ingram. How was the technique applied to the daughters of Mrs. Reed and the sisters of St. John Rivers? What were the contrasts in the descriptions of the teachers at Lowood, among some of the servants in the various households, among the tradesmen and women Jane met, and even among certain residences? How does the use of contrast sharpen both interest and understanding for the reader?

IV. *Vocabulary Study*

Diagnostic Test

3T	vignettes	scribblings	pages	pictures
11T	opprobrium	praise	weight	reproach
11M	transitory	temporary	permanent	comfortable
14T	artifice	honesty	trickery	classic
14M	duplicity	deception	truth	imitation
18M	malevolent	friendly	charitable	ill willed
26B	hiatus	continuation	pause	sneeze
35T	irksome	troublesome	pleasant	demanding
55M	ignominious	proud	noble	disgraceful
63M	seraph	angel	devil	monster
82M	imputation	reward	entry	charge
119B	effigies	clouds	images	cries
126T	pliability	rigidity	timidity	flexibility
138T	piquant	hateful	stimulating	mild
144M	diadem	sandal	sash	crown

150M	brusque	abrupt	smooth	polite
151B	gregarious	solitary	frightful	sociable
152T	intrinsic	dependent	inherent	borrowed
156B	neophyte	veteran	vision	novice
158M	arrogate	claim unduly	give up	agree
162M	inamorata	cousin	sweetheart	enemy
163B	hieroglyphics	unreadable symbols	neat copies	machines
188M	chimeras	labels	impossible fancies	photographs
196T	ineffable	unspeakable	regular	voluble
198T	saturnine	happy	gloomy	serene
215M	meretricious	valuable	tawdry	genuine
231B	lassitude	width	vitality	weariness
247M	charlatan	quack	expert	soldier
263M	purloined	recovered	stolen	inserted
277B	quiescent	loud	forceful	quiet
282M	cynosure	center of attention	object of neglect	easy job
300T	fruition	interruption	planting	fulfillment
312T	colloquy	silence	discussion	scheme
328T	plebeian	noble	common	political
345T	altercation	agreement	change	dispute
367T	epicure	connoisseur	ignoramus	grocery
388M	lineament	drawing	feature	cover
394M	mendicant	clergyman	rich man	beggar
407M	imperturbably	rashly	heartily	calmly
423T	commodious	narrow	roomy	boxlike
432T	ingenuous	frank	secretive	brilliant
444T	inscrutable	clear	twisted	incomprehensible
455B	immutably	briefly	unchangeably	silently
463M	garrulous	mute	talkative	fat
478B	emulate	imitate	invent	strive
492M	zealots	critics	fanatics	mechanics
507B	sylvan	barren	unplanted	wooded
515T	vivacity	liveliness	sloth	dexterity
526M	supplicated	refused	lifted	beseeched
533T	encumber	help	hinder	surround

Answers

vignettes-pictures, *opprobrium*-reproach, *transitory*-temporary, *artifice*-trickery, *duplicity*-deception, *malevolent*-ill willed, *hiatus-*

pause, *irksome*-troublesome, *ignominious*-disgraceful, *seraph*-angel, *imputation*-charge, *effigies*-images, *pliability*-flexibility, *piquant*-stimulating, *diadem*-crown, *brusque*-abrupt, *gregarious*-sociable, *intrinsic*-inherent, *neophyte*-novice, *arrogate*-claim unduly, *inamorata*-sweetheart, *hieroglyphics*-unreadable symbols, *chimeras*-impossible fancies, *ineffable*-unspeakable, *saturnine*-gloomy, *meretricious*-tawdry, *lassitude*-weariness, *charlatan*-quack, *purloined*-stolen, *quiescent*-quiet, *cynosure*-center of attention, *fruition*-fulfillment, *colloquy*-discussion, *plebeian*-common, *altercation*-dispute, *epicure*-connoisseur, *lineament*-feature, *mendicant*-beggar, *imperturbably*-calmly, *commodious*-roomy, *ingenuous*-frank, *inscrutable*-incomprehensible, *immutably*-unchangeably, *garrulous*-talkative, *emulate*-imitate, *zealots*-fanatics, *sylvan*-wooded, *vivacity*-liveliness, *supplicated*-beseeched, *encumber*-hinder

Teaching Aids

for

KON-TIKI

Thor Heyerdahl, a biologist working in the Marquesas, had heard of a mythical Polynesian hero, Kon-Tiki, who had migrated to the island from the east, perhaps from as far away as Peru. Further investigation by the Norwegian scientist led him to believe that the story of the migration of a people across thousands of miles of the Pacific Ocean was fact, not myth. When his colleagues refused to accept his theory, Heyerdahl decided to prove its accuracy by duplicating the legendary voyage, limiting himself to a balsa log raft and taking along other intrepid adventurers. *Kon-Tiki* is the record of the extraordinary trip, a tale so filled with excitement, suspense, and outrageous daring that it has been called the greatest modern saga of the sea.

I. *Objective Test*

In the space provided at the left, insert the *letter* of the correct choice from among those offered; for example:

....c....   The author's first name is (a) Ian (b) Edgar (c) Thor (d) Mark

.... 1. As the story opened, the author wondered (a) whether he and the crew would survive (b) how it all came about (c) why he hadn't made a stronger raft (d) what the parrot would say next

.... 2. Early research had convinced Heyerdahl that

the Polynesians had ties with (a) mainly European races (b) ancient Asian tribes (c) the Incas of Peru (d) migrating villagers from Africa

.... 3. Heyerdahl's first effort to get museum support for his theory about the Polynesians was greeted with (a) immediate interest (b) a prompt pledge of funds (c) complete indifference (d) absolute rejection

.... 4. The problem of getting financial backing for the voyage seemed solved when (a) several contributors came forward (b) a museum finally cooperated (c) a former war pilot pledged the money (d) the Explorers Club underwrote the project

.... 5. Knut and Torstein had both formerly been active in (a) the Norwegian underground against the Nazis (b) local politics (c) the fishing industry (d) previous expeditions with Thor

.... 6. Balsa logs were difficult to get in Ecuador because (a) prices were too high (b) it was the rainy season (c) a government permit was needed (d) supplies had been exhausted

.... 7. Before a balsa tree was cut down, it had to be (a) carefully measured (b) sawed partially at the base (c) christened after a legendary hero (d) inspected by an official

.... 8. When the Peruvian officials saw the raft, they (a) expressed great admiration for its sturdiness (b) declared a public holiday (c) congratulated the Navy workers (d) demanded a signed release from responsibility

.... 9. The strength of the men on board was tested early in their efforts to (a) hold the steering oar steady (b) swing the sail around (c) prevent the boxes from sliding (d) move the rations to a safe place

.... 10. Early one morning, Torstein was awakened by a (a) gigantic squid (b) rare snake mackerel (c) lively bonito (d) school of pilot fish

.... 11. The behavior of a huge whale shark caused the men to (a) shake with fright (b) admire its grace (c) try to measure it (d) roar with laughter

.... 12. Quite by accident, the crew discovered that the ingenious steering system used by the Incas consisted of (a) twisting the steering oar laterally (b) moving the centerboards up and down (c) shifting weights on the raft surface (d) swinging the sails fore and aft

.... 13. As further evidence of his theory of Polynesian migration from Peru, the author gave considerable details about the (a) reef due westward (b) stone figures on Easter Island (c) prevailing wind directions (d) changes in sea life

.... 14. The radio operators were saddened when (a) the parrot was washed overboard (b) they couldn't contact Norway (c) their equipment became waterlogged (d) some wires were severed

.... 15. A fearful emergency arose one day when Herman fell overboard while (a) reaching for a shark's tail (b) trying to save Torstein's sleeping bag (c) emptying a refuse box (d) sliding across the deck in a storm

.... 16. As the raft approached its destination, it became less stable because (a) one of the masts gave way (b) the deck became slippery (c) the water became choppy (d) some of the ropes loosened

.... 17. Compared to the original time estimates, the *Kon-Tiki* sighted land (a) a month late (b) almost exactly on time (c) several weeks early (d) eight days past the deadline

.... 18. Nearing Angatau, the biggest problem was (a) finding gifts for the natives (b) getting the dinghy overboard (c) making a safe landing (d) getting the sails down

.... 19. The men scrambled ashore on an uninhabited South Sea island after (a) paddling through the breakers (b) abandoning the wrecked *Kon-Tiki* on a coral reef (c) swimming through the churning water (d) casting a line around a tree

.... 20. The tension for the stranded men ceased when a (a) radio message finally went through (b) steamer was sighted (c) plane flew overhead (d) smoke signal was acknowledged

.... 21. Walking along the reef, Erik and Herman (a) gashed their feet (b) slipped repeatedly (c) took further bearings (d) were attacked by eels

.... 22. The natives of Raroia were delighted to learn that (a) they would be rewarded (b) Polynesian was understood by all (c) Tiki had once actually lived (d) the raft could replace their canoes

.... 23. The funniest moment during the island feast occurred when (a) Herman fell down (b) Erik danced the hula (c) Tupuhoe did imitations (d) the pae-pae was christened

.... 24. When the expedition reached Tahiti, (a) many gifts were exchanged (b) the six men were given medical treatment (c) the *Kon-Tiki* was given the place of honor (d) no further feasts were held

.... 25. When the crew of the *Kon-Tiki* left Tahiti, they (a) saluted the officials (b) sang a native song (c) headed for Norway (d) threw six white wreaths in the water

Answers

1-b, 2-c, 3-d, 4-c, 5-a, 6-b, 7-c, 8-d, 9-a, 10-b, 11-d, 12-b, 13-b, 14-a, 15-b, 16-d, 17-b, 18-c, 19-b, 20-a, 21-d, 22-c, 23-b, 24-c, 25-d

II. *Alternate Objective Tests*

A. Matching

Before each number in the column on the left, write the *letter* of the item in the column on the right that matches:

.... 1. Tiki   a. balsa logs
.... 2. Bengt Danielsson   b. a crab
.... 3. Quevedo   c. breakfast
.... 4. Jorge   d. Raroia chief
.... 5. flying fish   e. first island sighted
.... 6. Johannes   f. a raft
.... 7. plankton   g. chief-god
.... 8. Puka Puka   h. a drink
.... 9. Teka   i. shrunken head
...... 10. pae-pae   j. red beard
                                 k. seasick
                                 l. tiny creatures

Answers

1-g, 2-j, 3-a, 4-i, 5-c, 6-b, 7-l, 8-e, 9-d, 10-f

B. Fill-ins

From the column on the right, select the item that best completes each statement below, and write it in the space provided:

1. The journey took the raft _____ from Peru across the Pacific.   sweet potato
2. The inspiration for the voyage came from an old _____ on a South Sea island.   ant   six months   penicillin
3. Heyerdahl found it amusing to be called _____ just because he was buying a chart.   nail   dolphin   Knut   long-ears

4. The initial time estimates for the voyage were from ninety-seven days to _____.

5. Many supplies were secured from the _____.

6. While cutting a balsa tree, Herman was stung by a (an) _____.

7. Not a single _____ was used in the raft.

8. Besides the six men, the only other living thing taken aboard was a (an) _____.

9. Three important Polynesian plants taken along were the coconut, the bottle gourd, and the _____.

10. Pilot fish usually swam ahead of _____.

11. The earliest Polynesian migrants were called _____.

12. Herman's life was saved by _____ in the sea.

13. Messengers from Polynesia were two large _____.

14. Herman and Knut used _____ to cure a boy's abscess.

15. The *Maoae,* a schooner carrying _____, was caught on the coral reef at Raroia.

parrot
captain
a salve
rope
westward
copra
wild onion
sharks
native
Peruvian Navy
birds
eastward
Pentagon
scorpion
four months

Answers

1-westward, 2-native, 3-captain, 4-four months, 5-Pentagon, 6-ant, 7-nail, 8-parrot, 9-sweet potato, 10-sharks, 11-long-ears, 12-Knut, 13-birds, 14-penicillin, 15-copra

III. *Ideas for Written or Oral Book Reports or Class Discussions*

1. One of the more remarkable aspects of the voyage of the *Kon-Tiki* was that six men, practically strangers to one another, were able to live together in the closest possible quarters for more than three months without ever having a serious quarrel or getting on each other's nerves. To what extent is it possible that there were disagreements but that Heyerdahl simply didn't mention them? On the other hand, considering the nature of the men—their backgrounds, personalities, and ability to respond to challenge—how likely is it that they did indeed pass through their ordeal without bothering about petty differences? What factors in the trip would have made it undesirable, perhaps even dangerous, for the men to fail to work together amicably? How accurate would it be to call these daring adventurers a *special breed* who could manage in a way that ordinary men could not?

2. Surely you must have been fascinated by some of the descriptions of the behavior of certain species that inhabit the deep sea. For example, you doubtless knew something about whales, sharks, and dolphins before. However, what did you learn about these familiar creatures that was new to you? What interesting information did you gain about various species that you had never heard of before? In addition to being informed about living things in the sea, what did you learn about seamanship, food that can be eaten by man, and human ingenuity in the midst of emergencies? How did all these discoveries contribute to your enjoyment in reading the book?

3. Heyerdahl showed extraordinary persistence in trying to get backing for an expedition to prove his theory. Why did he have such faith in the eventual success of the enterprise? In what did he put his major trust? How much of his faith was based on scientific research and analysis and how much on self-reliance and intuition? Explain. What aspects of Heyerdahl's character and training helped him succeed where another man might have failed? How

do you account for the fact that, aside from the early chapters describing his efforts to raise supplies and money, Heyerdahl wrote very little about his own accomplishments during the trying days at sea on a fragile raft?

4. It should be interesting to draw conclusions about Heyerdahl's reactions to some of the people he became involved with in his project. What subtle criticism did he suggest about some scientists and government officials? What was his attitude toward the people of Peru and Ecuador generally and toward particular persons in each country with whom he dealt directly? Some critics have said that the author seemed to show a *prejudice in favor* of the Polynesians. What characteristics did these natives reveal that are not too common elsewhere? Why is it understandable that Heyerdahl grew extremely fond of the islanders? Judging from what you have heard or read about the situation, how true is the claim that many of the problems that have affected South Sea natives *were brought to them* by the European explorers who came to their tropical paradise? How does this explain the fact that since the nineteenth century the world has witnessed fierce resistance to colonial control and interference in local affairs? Give some recent examples.

5. Some anthropologists disagree with Heyerdahl's theory about the origins of the Polynesians. They prefer to speculate that the inhabitants of the islands came originally from Asiatic territories. One went so far as to say that all Heyerdahl proved was that "it is possible to reach Polynesia from Peru on a balsa raft." Incidentally, the Norwegian scientist later said that that was all he set out to prove! However, what evidence did you find in the story that would seem to support the author's theory of migration? After checking the facts with library reference sources, indicate whether or not there is any convincing proof that the Polynesians came from Asia.

6. One of the striking aspects of Heyerdahl's style is the descriptive power shown in his writing. Very early in the story (p. 11), there is an example of the author's ability to appeal to the senses—sound, sight, smell, taste, touch— in his descriptions. Indicate, by specific references to the

passage, how the same device was used in writing about the arrival in Ecuador (p. 41). Find other passages in the book that illustrate Heyerdahl's skill in making his descriptions appeal to the reader's senses. What should you do in your own writing to make your descriptions as effective as Heyerdahl's?

7. In the tale of a dangerous trip on a flimsy craft across a threatening ocean, one would hardly expect to find much humor. Yet the book abounds in such touches. Note the sly reference to the use of "Captain" (p. 24B), the discussion about the radio (p. 31B), the "expectant little boy" phrase (p. 36T), the delightful account of the entrance to the Andes (pp. 47–49), and the meeting with the Peruvian minister of marine (p. 57). What language devices did Heyerdahl use to develop his amusing bits? Cite several other examples of the author's humorous touch. What do you suppose was Heyerdahl's purpose in adding humor to his story of a scientific expedition? What does this aspect of the writing tell us about the writer?

8. Heyerdahl refused to use any modern materials in building the raft. For instance, not a single nail was used in the construction. Why was he so insistent on duplicating the basic design of the legendary Peruvian raft to the last faithful detail? At what moments in the journey did the ancient methods of raft construction prove to be logical and advantageous? What discovery about steering the raft did the crew make after the trip had been well under way? How reasonable would it be to say that adherence to the original raft-building techniques actually saved the lives of the crew?

9. Apart from the author, each member of the crew of the *Kon-Tiki* had a distinctive personality of his own. With specific supporting references to the text, describe the outstanding contributions made to the voyage by each of the five other men—Torstein Raaby, Herman Watzinger, Knut Haugland, Bengt Danielsson, and Erik Hesselberg. Explain, with reasons, why you would prefer to have one particular man with you in an emergency. Which one would probably best keep your spirits up during a crisis? Why? How important were the radio operators? Why was Heyer-

dahl wise in deciding in advance on the skills his men would need to make the voyage successful? Why was the crew limit set at six, rather than five or less or seven or more?

10. There were those who scoffed at Heyerdahl's plans, not so much in respect to his migration theories as to the foolish idea that a crudely built raft could cross a great ocean. What is the difference between the spirit of scientific adventure and foolhardy risk in the presence of certain danger? How would you characterize the intrepid crew of the *Kon-Tiki*—devil-may-care adventurers or serious and courageous scientists? Why? What other examples can you give of men and women who took great risks to investigate or prove a theory? Why is it often said that without such people progress would be severely limited?

IV. *Vocabulary Study*

Diagnostic Test

9T	retrospect	look forward	removal	look back
9M	inevitable	possible	certain	changeable
14B	affirmation	confirmation	denial	argument
15T	monoliths	bachelors	stone blocks	sands
21T	indignantly	forgivingly	resentfully	unworthily
24T	sobriety	temperance	intoxication	skill
29M	thermody-namics	telepathy	heat energy	electronics
33M	disingenuous	charming	truthful	not frank
37B	advocate	supporter	foe	juryman
39M	impediment	tool	help	hindrance
42T	accessible	secluded	guilty	approachable
47B	undulate	billow	becalm	lapse
49T	cauldron	icebox	kettle	cupboard
54M	nonchalant	casual	worried	intense
58B	gesticulations	orations	gestures	woes
60M	migration	a move	residence	bird lore
60B	firmament	dispute	earth	the heavens
68M	intimation	secret	hint	lie
72M	exemplary	admirable	evil	expensive
77B	meager	humble	scanty	rich

81M cessation	end	beginning	middle
88M predatory	saving	foretelling	plundering
91T nocturnal	late	nightly	daily
100T perforate	mend	weave	pierce
101B gratuitous	grateful	unasked	unfounded
114M vulnerable	strong	indecent	woundable
117T voracious	stingy	greedy	foul
120B aggrieved	offended	pleased	routed
122B consummate	eaten	incomplete	perfect
126T vacillate	fall	waver	strengthen
133M sporadic	common	mean	infrequent
143M involuntary	deliberate	unintentional	welcome
152T culminate	crash	stop	reach a peak
152B antiquity	ancient times	modern times	furniture
165T primeval	sophisticated	primitive	qualified
166B impetus	driving force	holding force	retraction
171T meditate	reconcile	ponder	drop
172B insidious	often	treacherous	trustworthy
183M vehement	casual	loose	intense
191T ramshackle	firm	shaky	protruding
192B hideous	pretty	covered	ugly
197M writhing	shooting	twisting	holding
203M ecstatically	moodily	sharply	joyfully
205M malignant	promising	evil	fishy
206M lagoon	sea	shallow lake	river
217M coquettishly	sadly	flirtingly	angrily
220B ingratiate	charm	disobey	repel
225B capsizing	sailing	overturning	commanding
226B myriad	countless	few	reflective
229M quay	bird	dock	fool

Answers

retrospect-look back, *inevitable*-certain, *affirmation*-confirmation, *monoliths*-stone blocks, *indignantly*-resentfully, *sobriety*-temperance, *disingenuous*-not frank, *thermodynamics*-heat energy, *advocate*-supporter, *impediment*-hindrance, *accessible*-approachable, *undulate*-billow, *cauldron*-kettle, *nonchalant*-casual, *gesticulations*-gestures, *migration*-a move, *firmament*-the heavens, *intimation*-hint, *exemplary*-admirable, *meager*-scanty, *cessation*-end, *predatory*-plundering, *nocturnal*-nightly, *perforate*-pierce, *gratuitous*-unasked, *vulnerable*-woundable, *voracious*-greedy, *aggrieved*-offended, *consummate*-perfect, *vacillate*-waver, *sporadic*-infrequent, *involuntary*-unintentional, *culminate*-reach a peak, *antiquity*-ancient times, *primeval*-primitive, *impetus*-driving force, *meditate*-ponder, *insidious*-treacherous, *vehement*-intense, *ramshackle*-shaky, *hideous*-ugly, *writhing*-twisting, *ecstatically*-joyful, *malignant*-evil, *lagoon*-shallow lake, *coquettishly*-flirtingly, *ingratiate*-charm, *capsizing*-overturning, *myriad*-countless, *quay*-dock

Teaching Aids

for

LIFE WITH FATHER

At a time when it seems to have become almost out of fashion for the young to speak of their parents in terms of endearment, it should be a refreshing change to read a son's affectionate account of his family, with special emphasis on a father who ruled firmly, but was adored by an admiring household. The setting is the turn of the century; yet the warmth and humor are to be found today in the hearts of all people who love and respect one another. Originally selected by the Book-of-the-Month Club and later made into an enormously successful play, *Life with Father* and its unforgettable characters out of real life have won a permanent place among the great books of our time.

I. *Objective Test*

In the space provided at the left, insert the *letter* of the correct choice from among those offered; for example:

....a.... The book is mainly about the author's (a) father (b) wife (c) mother (d) nephew

.... 1. Occasionally on Saturday mornings, Father took Clarence to "the office" and (a) on a tour of Ellis Island (b) for lunch at Delmonico's (c) on the elevated train (d) for a bicycle ride

.... 2. Father's first horse was (a) a gentle bay (b) nothing but a dray (c) as stubborn as his master (d) trained to do tricks

.... 3. Father's infrequent illnesses were blamed solely on (a) incompetent doctors (b) carelessness by the household (c) the wrong pills (d) the clumsiness of God

.... 4. A crisis arose in the Day household when (a) ice was not delivered (b) the milk turned sour (c) wine was not served at dinner (d) the dog-cart broke down

.... 5. Although suffering a concussion when thrown from his horse, Father (a) refused medical aid (b) remounted and rode back to the house (c) did not lose consciousness (d) refused to stay in bed

.... 6. Several substitute cooks caused Father to (a) question Margaret's ability (b) become fond of new dishes (c) like Japanese menus (d) feel starved and poisoned

.... 7. Clarence had to take violin lessons even though he (a) had no ear for music (b) preferred the piano (c) played better than George (d) couldn't read music

.... 8. Where bills were concerned, Mother acted as if they were (a) always too high (b) complete strangers to her (c) tests of her adding ability (d) obligations to be paid at once

.... 9. Mother succeeded in keeping the money she had saved from her (a) shopping expenses (b) sale of a dresser (c) trip abroad (d) winning raffle ticket

.... 10. George announced the baseball scores by (a) tacking a notice on a wall (b) playing the piano (c) signaling with his fingers (d) drawing a coded sketch

.... 11. Clarence learned to be prompt at breakfast when he (a) was not fed (b) was put on probation by Father (c) got a gold heirloom timepiece (d) kept breaking watch crystals

.... 12. An Armenian dealer showed great acting skill in getting Mother to (a) replace her vanity mirror (b) buy a rug (c) lend him some money (d) buy a pin for Father

.... 13. Clarence had difficulties with his correspondence because (a) the mail often came late (b) postage stamps were expensive (c) he had Father's first name (d) Father read all outgoing mail

.... 14. After his freshman year at Yale, Clarence (a) received excellent grades (b) stayed in New Haven for the summer (c) took a camping trip (d) was heavily in debt

.... 15. When telephones were available, the Day family (a) couldn't wait to get one (b) had one installed in the foyer (c) didn't care to have one (d) used the neighbor's phone

.... 16. At Mother's musicale, one catastrophe involved (a) Father's noisy singing (b) a broken string on the harp (c) Clarence's violin playing (d) Miss Kregman's galoshes

.... 17. Mother worried about apoplexy when Father tried to (a) sew on a button (b) mend his socks (c) lengthen his trousers (d) repair the stove

.... 18. When Mother made social appointments, Father (a) was delighted (b) went reluctantly but enjoyed himself (c) complained about the expense (d) refused to leave the house

.... 19. Mother struck the tomb of a crusader with her parasol because she (a) wanted to show respect (b) was testing the metal (c) disapproved of his frequent marriages (d) was told to do so

.... 20. The symbols of a formal dinner at home were the (a) borrowed chairs (b) new tablecloths (c) potted palms (d) printed invitations

.... 21. When Clarence had a leg operation, Father expressed sympathy by (a) reading the Bible (b) offering painkillers (c) denouncing the doctors (d) emitting loud groans at night

.... 22. Father disapproved of Mother's (a) knowledge of current events (b) handling of the children

(c) thriftiness in her budget (d) treatment of the cook

.... 23. "Locusts that ought to be sent back to Egypt" was Father's reference to (a) bill collectors (b) house guests (c) boiler repair men (d) street beggars

.... 24. Father's reaction to President Wilson resulted in (a) arguments with Mother (b) furious letters to newspapers (c) loosened bridgework (d) telegrams of congratulation

.... 25. Father stoutly maintained that (a) all nurses were incompetent (b) his business was going to pot (c) French novels were exciting (d) he had no blood pressure

Answers

1-b, 2-c, 3-d, 4-a, 5-b, 6-d, 7-a, 8-b, 9-c, 10-b, 11-d, 12-b, 13-c, 14-d, 15-c, 16-d, 17-a, 18-b, 19-c, 20-c, 21-d, 22-a, 23-b, 24-c, 25-d

II. *Alternate Objective Tests*

A. Matching

Before each number in the column on the left, write the *letter* of the item in the column on the right that matches:

.... 1. Rob Roy a. Father
.... 2. Margaret b. harp player
.... 3. Herr M. c. World's Fair
.... 4. Clare d. political science teacher
.... 5. Chicago e. dinner guests
.... 6. Wilhelmine f. Mother
.... 7. Cousin Julie g. Father's horse
.... 8. Ormontons h. tradesmen
.... 9. Edna Gulick i. music teacher
...... 10. Vinnie j. Father's ring
  k. family cook
  l. butler

Answers

1-g, 2-k, 3-i, 4-a, 5-c, 6-j, 7-b, 8-e, 9-d, 10-f

B. Fill-ins

From the column on the right, select the item that best completes each statement below, and write it in the space provided:

1. When Father was ill, he _____ a lot.

2. Father complimented the cook on her _____ dish.

3. Mother believed that the _____ had been invented for her.

4. Father surprised Mother when he made no fuss about a (an) _____.

5. Mother went with friends to _____.

6. Clarence disapproved of his _____ Bible.

7. Father often opened _____ mail.

8. Father gave Clarence one hundred dollars to go to _____.

9. Father's old _____ gave Clarence a guilty conscience.

10. Father swore when he came home during the _____.

11. Despite his conservative habits, Father liked colored _____.

12. Mother always had problems keeping her _____ orderly.

13. A dinner was spoiled by the clumsiness of _____.

14. Father and his sons all had _____ hair.

charge account
Clarence's
Egypt
room
red
Chicago
trousers
musicale
yelled
Mother's
rug
socks
dance recital
hat
slept
grandfather's clock
French
steak
Bridget
London
chicken
black
Margaret

15. Every fall, Father loosed a barrage about his _____.

Answers

1-yelled, 2-chicken, 3-charge account, 4-grandfather's clock, 5-Egypt, 6-French, 7-Clarence's, 8-Chicago, 9-trousers, 10-musicale, 11-socks, 12-room, 13-Bridget, 14-red, 15-rug

III. *Ideas for Written or Oral Book Reports or Class Discussions*

1. The series of anecdotes about Father was, of course, written from the point of view of his son Clarence. In what ways is the description of a person likely to be distorted if it represents "one man's opinion"? How might the story have been different if it had been written by Mother, George, one of the other children, an employee, or a tradesman? In any case, what evidence is there that Clarence was basically very fond of Father? What aspects of Father's personality did his son find objectionable? To what extent would a similar relationship between a father and a son be possible today, in view of the frequent references to the so-called generation gap?

2. To analyze Father's character properly, the reader must think of him in terms of the period during which he held sway (approximately 1880–1920), at a time when respectability and conformity were very important to well-to-do people. In this connection, why can it be said that Father was very much a product of his times? What examples can you give to illustrate that Father, like most men in his class, was inclined to be snobbish, superstitious, prejudiced, and often insensitive to the feelings of persons in less fortunate circumstances? Even in these areas, however, what prevented the reader from feeling that Father's behavior was sometimes downright offensive? What other traits did Father reveal that would not be acceptable today? On the other hand, what was there commendable about Father's zest for living and his attitude toward his

responsibilities, his family—especially his wife—and his dealings with other people? Why might it be said that, despite his frequent blasphemous outbursts, Father was a deeply religious man? To what extent could Father be looked upon as a symbol of a vanished breed?

3. Very often a writer of fiction will create someone who acts as a "foil" for another character; that is, the foil is so different that the important characteristics of the opposite individual are thereby sharply accentuated. Naturally, in a biography one doesn't expect to meet fictional characters, but certainly Mother would have qualified as the perfect foil for Father. Why was Father secretly pleased that Mother was less practical than he was, more outgoing, more sociable, more resistant actually than other people he could easily browbeat? Who was the real "boss" of the household? Give reasons for your choice. What would you point to to prove that Mr. and Mrs. Day were happily married and quite devoted to each other?

4. On several occasions, Clarence spent some time in the houses of friends. Why did he feel vaguely uncomfortable in one house where everyone was overly polite and in another where anger resulted in silence rather than in an explosion? What did Clarence's reactions to other families tell about his attitude toward his own home life? With so much noise and excitement going on in the Day house, why did the children still seem to love their parents and enjoy their daily existence? Might the same sort of mutual respect, lack of inhibitions, and obvious affection be possible in a home where the family income was just enough to survive? How? Judging from your analysis of *Life with Father,* what are the main ingredients of a happy home life?

5. At times, it seemed that the author did not accept the cult of respectability as wholeheartedly as his father did. As a child, Clarence dreamed of becoming a tramp (p. 2M). As a young man, he could not understand what difference it made to Father that a fellow passenger on the horse-car had his vest unbuttoned (p. 144M). To what extent was the son actually in rebellion against the customs and standards of his time? Nevertheless, what indications

were there to suggest that Clarence, too, conformed in the important areas, except for the few occasions mentioned? In general, what is the likelihood that the son grew up to be practically a carbon copy of his father? Support your conclusion with references to the text.

6. Father had periodic run-ins with tradesmen, especially the ice dealers (pp. 19–26). He hired Margaret the cook under rather extraordinary circumstances (pp. 36–38), and he bullied doctors throughout the story. How much of Father's behavior in these episodes could be attributed to his basic snobbishness and how much to his own sense of integrity and confidence in his knowledge of people? Explain. What would happen these days if someone approached service personnel, businessmen, and professionals in the manner in which Father did in his time? To what extent have relationships improved between those who buy and those who sell services, appliances, and professional advice?

7. Modern psychologists, as Clarence Day well understood, heavily stress the role of the father image in a person's psychological development. Even adults sometimes prefer political leaders to whom they can relate almost as children to a parent; the leader embodying the father image makes people feel that he will show them what to do when they are bewildered, and he will somehow take care of their interests when the challenges of their lives are altogether too difficult for them to master. The importance of the father image to people in general is one of the reasons for the sensational success of *Life with Father*. But Father Day was occasionally incompetent or ridiculous. He complained absurdly of being "poisoned" by the Japanese cook (p. 40M). When he tried to sew on a button he succeeded only in skewering his finger with the needle (p. 128B). He was entirely outmaneuvered by Mother Day in the matter of his library rug (p. 159M). To what extent did these weaknesses tarnish the father image? Actually, in what respects did Father's occasional defeats make him an even more appealing force in the household?

8. " 'Will you be back, Mr. Day?' the cashier asked respectfully, but eagerly too. On days when Father said yes,

all the clerks looked disappointed" (p. 4B). What did this exchange tell you about Father's employees? What, if anything, has changed in similar situations through the years? From what you learned of Father, how do you think he treated his employees? Estimate what Father's behavior must have been in his dealings with his own clients and business associates. How would you like to work for someone like Father?

9. Clarence Day mentioned many things that were typical of New York City during the 1890s or thereabouts. If you live in New York, describe some of the great changes that have taken place in the last seventy-five years. Even if you have never visited New York City, what reliable guesses can you make about changes that have taken place in regard to dress, transportation, entertainment, household conveniences, and general life-styles? What names, and places were mentioned that are familiar to you? Tell what you know about them. People sometimes speak of the good old days. What might have been good about those old days? What were a few of the bad things about the old days, whether or not mentioned in the book? Suppose someone gave you the choice of going back to live your life during the 1890s. How likely would it be that you would accept the invitation? Give reasons.

10. *Life with Father* does not adhere to a strictly chronological order. Incidents have been selected seemingly at random. Father's age varies as episodes develop. Why was the author selective in his reminiscences? What structural plan for the book do you think he had in mind?

Why did he keep his style as simple as possible? What effect did he try to create in his abundant use of short sentences like "He was right, perhaps"—"He went to the piano"—"He laughed" (pp. 45B–46M)?

The author created the delightful humor in his book through language use, situation, and dialogue. Note the following examples:

Language use: In referring to the ice man, "Father said he'd have to be neighborly in a hurry" (p. 23T). In re-

---

ferring to the music teacher, "He had a queer pickled smell" (p. 50M).

Situation: Father and Rob Roy (p. 9M); Father and the cook (p. 38).

Dialogue: Father and the coffeepot (pp. 68M–70T).

Find other examples of humorous touches. What other style techniques did you enjoy? Describe them and give examples.

IV. *Vocabulary Study*

Diagnostic Test

5M	apex	top point	bottom	butt
6B	gusto	distaste	keen enjoyment	wind
11M	malingering	dwelling	pretending illness	ordering
11B	expansive	narrow	costly	demonstrative
16M	tractable	manageable	stubborn	tillable
19M	tundra	forest	fish	treeless plain
24M	gumption	folly	boldness	vow
32B	impregnability	violence	weakness	firmness
33T	unimpaired	loosened	undamaged	fixed
34T	phlegmatic	sluggish	active	daring
38B	indomitable	fearful	unconquerable	subjugated
48T	thwarted	acceded	frustrated	touched
50T	uncanny	weird	soft	closed
54M	dingy	bright	blue	grimy
57M	eerie	homely	frightening	reassuring
58T	tautness	flabbiness	tightness	richness
66B	daunted	intimidated	overpowered	routed
70B	avaricious	generous	helpful	greedy
71M	idiosyncrasies	thoughts	dreams	peculiarities
73B	pertinacious	careless	persistent	heavy
75M	voluminous	rolled	small	bulky
80T	dirge	lyric	funeral hymn	sweep
80M	admonish	add	allow	warn
81M	dawdling	catching	wasting time	sketching
87T	sardonic	sweet	marble	sarcastic
88M	snivelling	crying	boasting	laughing

91B	astute	dull	sharp	full
92T	denunciation	praise	story	condemnation
101M	preoccupied	alert	moody	witty
102B	imprudent	wise	lofty	rash
104T	recur	end	repeat	hover
104M	surreptitiously	secretly	openly	gladly
120B	impresario	performer	manager	teacher
121M	paragon	scoundrel	model	protégé
128M	tousled	combed	flattened	rumpled
128M	apoplexy	bone break	paralytic stroke	indigestion
130M	morose	gay	light	gloomy
134M	impromptu	prepared	offhand	stifling
134M	sumptuous	thrifty	sudden	lavish
134B	suavely	rudely	roughly	smoothly
144T	imperious	humble	overbearing	soggy
144T	slatternly	sloppily	neatly	widely
151M	inveigling	deceiving	proving	covering
152T	placid	noisy	calm	stuffy
154T	taciturn	silent	talkative	sudden
155T	imperceptibly	obvious	unnoticeably	penetratingly
155T	expostulated	remonstrated	foiled	terminated
163B	wizened	lively	robust	dried up
165T	whim	effort	sudden fancy	rejection
167T	incensed	angry	calmed	agreeable

Answers

apex-top point, *gusto*-keen enjoyment, *malingering*-pretending illness, *expansive*-demonstrative, *tractable*-manageable, *tundra*-treeless plain, *gumption*-boldness, *impregnability*-firmness, *unimpaired*-undamaged, *phlegmatic*-sluggish, *indomitable*-unconquerable, *thwarted*-frustrated, *uncanny*-weird, *dingy*-grimy, *eerie*-frightening, *tautness*-tightness, *daunted*-intimidated, *avaricious*-greedy, *idiosyncrasies*-peculiarities, *pertinacious*-persistent, *voluminous*-bulky, *dirge*-funeral hymn, *admonish*-warn, *dawdling*-wasting time, *sardonic*-sarcastic, *snivelling*-crying, *astute*-sharp, *denunciation*-condemnation, *preoccupied*-moody, *imprudent*-rash, *recur*-repeat, *surreptitiously*-secretly, *impresario*-manager, *paragon*-model, *tousled*-rumpled, *apoplexy*-paralytic stroke, *morose*-gloomy, *impromptu*-offhand, *sumptuous*-lavish, *suavely*-smoothly, *imperious*-overbearing, *slatternly*-sloppily, *inveigling*-deceiving, *placid*-calm, *taciturn*-silent, *imperceptibly*-unnoticeably, *expostulated*-remonstrated, *wizened*-dried up, *whim*-sudden fancy, *incensed*-angry

Teaching Aids

for

THE LITTLE WORLD OF DON CAMILLO

In this book, Giovanni Guareschi tells the story of a remarkable priest in a small Italian village. Father Camillo periodically checks his plans and recent behavior in emotional conversations with the Lord, simultaneously revealing a certain delightful irreverence and a basic Christian humility. He wages ceaseless war on the local Leftists, particularly their leader, Mayor Peppone. Although the good father must occasionally resort to a well-aimed kick or a thunderous right cross to maintain strict adherence to proper religious and humanitarian principles, he keeps his congregation unified despite political differences. He has, as the author puts it, "a constitutional preference for calling a spade a spade."

I. *Objective Test*

In the space provided at the left, insert the *letter* of the correct choice from among those offered; for example:

....b....   The author of his book is (a) Pedro (b) Guareschi (c) Twain

.... 1. The author said that the voice of Christ in the book was the voice of his (a) physical adviser (b) conscience (c) only friend

.... 2. At the end of the book, Don Camillo implied that he considered Peppone (a) evil (b) spiritual (c) foolish

.... 3. The bishop reacted to the villagers with (a) anger (b) impatience (c) amusement

.... 4. The author's mother had been a (a) teacher (b) musician (c) writer

.... 5. Don Camillo seemed to be fond of (a) liquor (b) baseball (c) firearms

.... 6. At the end of the book, Peppone implied that he considered Don Camillo (a) perfect (b) unholy (c) stubborn

.... 7. Don Camillo feared being seen incompletely dressed more than he feared (a) evil (b) mines (c) floods

.... 8. Don Camillo finally decided that a camp for children was more important than a new (a) church (b) bell (c) steeple

.... 9. We get the impression that the source of Signora Carolina's wealth was (a) mining (b) blackmail (c) usury

.... 10. Much of Peppone's communistic feeling seemed to be a (a) political pose (b) desire for vengeance (c) hatred of religion

.... 11. Don Camillo felt that he had Christ's approval for (a) kicking Peppone (b) excommunicating Peppone (c) hitting Peppone with a candle

.... 12. After having a fist fight with Peppone, Don Camillo (a) broke the eggs (b) baptized the baby (c) stole Peppone's horse

.... 13. Don Camillo managed to get a portion of the stolen treasure for a (a) new bell (b) recreation center (c) home for old people

.... 14. The author said that he had spent much time during the war in (a) concentration camps (b) England (c) Russia

.... 15. Peppone's occasional religious gestures were probably caused by his (a) early training (b) war experiences (c) communist beliefs

.... 16. Signora Carolina's donation was used for a (a)

new bell (b) recreation center (c) children's camp

.... 17. Pizzi's murderer was (a) Peppone (b) Smilzo (c) unknown to us

.... 18. During the election campaign, Don Camillo had (a) spoken against Peppone (b) spoken for Peppone (c) taken no part

.... 19. The most surprising actions of Don Camillo involved his use of (a) inspiring words (b) underhanded slander (c) physical force

.... 20. The author's drawings add to the book's (a) realism (b) humor (c) spiritual appeal

.... 21. The final scene between Don Camillo and Peppone leaves us with a feeling of (a) unexplained mystery (b) affectionate understanding (c) violent opposition

.... 22. We gather that Don Camillo had many (a) relatives (b) influential friends (c) guns

.... 23. Don Camillo could not bear to punish Straziami and his son because they were so (a) thin (b) polite (c) penitent

.... 24. Before the soccer game, Don Camillo had tried to (a) drug the opposing team (b) bribe the referee (c) teach his team improper tactics

.... 25. The "representative of a foreign power" whose visit Peppone deplored in advance was (a) the bishop (b) President Truman (c) the representative of the Liberal party

Answers

1-b, 2-c, 3-c, 4-a, 5-c, 6-c, 7-b, 8-b, 9-c, 10-a, 11-a, 12-b, 13-b, 14-a, 15-a, 16-c, 17-c, 18-a, 19-c, 20-b, 21-b, 22-c, 23-a, 24-b, 25-a

II. *Alternate Objective Tests*

A. Matching

Before each number in the column on the left, write the *letter* of the item in the column on the right that matches:

....	1. the missing bell	a. Straziami
....	2. locale of the story	b. World War I
....	3. an expert mechanic	c. Pizzi
....	4. the missile that hit the Liberal	d. Spain
....	5. Don Camillo's physical asset	e. Gertrude
....	6. scene of Don Camillo's embarrassment	f. Peppone
....	7. the war in which Peppone fought	g. Italy
....	8. he stole Peppone's gun	h. World War II
....	9. he died of a gunshot wound	i. Maria
......	10. gift from Peppone to Don Camillo	j. strength
		k. beauty
		l. the river
		m. a rabbit
		n. Don Camillo
		o. a tomato

Answers

1-e, 2-g, 3-f, 4-o, 5-j, 6-l, 7-h, 8-n, 9-c, 10-m

B. Fill-ins

From the column on the right, select the item that best completes each statement below, and write it in the space provided:

1. Peppone wanted to name his son after _____ .

2. In the soccer match, Peppone's team _____ .

3. The largest church bell had been carried away by the _____ .

4. The bearded man who leaped into the boxing ring was _____ .

5. The crucifix was carried in procession in order to bless the _____ .

6. Don Camillo was returned to his parish because of the request of _____ .

Liberal
drowned
buried
Stalin
Don Camillo
Lenin
lost
Kennedy
church
won
Germans
river

7. Don Camillo demonstrated that he believed Pizzi had been _____.
8. The powerful Peppone could make _____ repairs.
9. The abandoned loot was concealed by Peppone in a (an) _____.
10. The United States president at the time of the story was _____.
11. Peppone and Don Camillo worked together to save the _____.
12. At the end of the book, Peppone helped Don Camillo by _____.
13. The People's Palace contained a large portrait of _____.
14. In another town, Don Camillo saw a man he thought he had _____.
15. Peppone and Don Camillo clashed over taking the _____ to lunch.

Peppone
cows
horses
British
delicate
Truman
coffin
plowing
murdered
Bishop
painting

Answers

1-Lenin, 2-won, 3-Germans, 4-Don Camillo, 5-river, 6-Peppone, 7-murdered, 8-delicate, 9-coffin, 10-Truman, 11-cows, 12-painting, 13-Stalin, 14-buried, 15-Liberal

III. *Ideas for Written or Oral Book Reports or Class Discussions*

1. Prepare a character sketch of Don Camillo, giving examples from the book to illustrate each of the traits you mention. Include in your character sketch detailed coverage of these topics:

   a. Why you believe that Don Camillo is or is not a typical priest
   b. How you compare or contrast Don Camillo with a clergyman you have known
   c. How some of Don Camillo's attitudes and actions may be partially explained by the author's com-

ment (p. 5B): "The war destroyed a lot of things we had within us. We have seen too many dead and too many living."

2. *The Little World of Don Camillo* is known as a predominantly humorous book. *Humor* is often defined thusly: "That quality in an event, situation, or expression of ideas that appeals to the sense of the ludicrous or absurdly incongruous." Giving at least two examples for each, analyze the elements of humor involved in the following relationships:

a. Don Camillo and his personal Christ
b. Don Camillo and Peppone
c. The townsfolk and Don Camillo
d. The townsfolk and Peppone
e. The bishop and the townsfolk.

In a concluding paragraph, explain your reasons for considering the people and actions of the book true to life or merely inventions of the author contrived for the sake of humor.

3. Early in the book (p. 7M), the author offers the following apology: "But if there is anyone who is offended by the conversations of Christ, I can't help it; for the one who speaks in this story is not Christ but my Christ—that is, the voice of my conscience."

In a well-developed composition, discuss the following topics, each illustrated by examples from the book:

a. The relationship between Don Camillo and his personal Christ
b. Your reasons for believing that the Christ in the story is or is not the voice of Don Camillo's conscience
c. Your analysis of whether or not the conversations of Christ seem to you offensive or sacrilegious.

4. One of the elements of humor in the book is the changing relationship between Don Camillo and Mayor Peppone. Sometimes they seem to be bitter enemies; at

other times, they are staunch allies, each having great respect for the other. In an analysis of the changing relationship between the two, show the varying attitudes each had toward the other in *five* of the following episodes:

 a. The baptism of Peppone's baby
 b. The repair of the church tower
 c. Hunting on Baron Stocco's private preserve
 d. Financing the Recreation Center
 e. The strength-testing machine
 f. Don Camillo's transfer and return to the parish
 g. The boxing match
 h. The strike at La Grande
 i. The religious procession to the river
 j. The shot intended for Don Camillo.

5. Prepare an analytical character sketch of Peppone. Be sure to stress his qualities as a father, a workman, a parishioner, a member of the community, a political leader, and a friend. Just how do you suppose he became a communist? Explain by means of examples how sincere a communist you think he was. In what ways does the author seem to be poking fun at Italian communists by his treatment of Peppone and his followers? What conflicts do you see between Peppone's political and religious beliefs? Try to analyze his varying feelings toward Don Camillo.

6. On the last page of the book, we find Don Camillo and Peppone quietly working together painting the figures for the crèche. Using illustrations from the various episodes in the book, explain why you think the author selected this scene as his conclusion, why Don Camillo compared Peppone to an ass, why Peppone compared Don Camillo to an ox, and what light this final scene throws on the real relationship between the two men.

7. It seems evident that the request of Peppone and his followers induced the bishop first to transfer Don Camillo away from his parish and later to arrange for his return. Explain in detail the reasons why Peppone wanted Don Camillo removed and the reasons why Peppone petitioned for Don Camillo's return. In what ways do the events of

Don Camillo's train journey reveal the true feelings of the villagers toward him and toward Peppone? How did Peppone reveal his own feelings during Don Camillo's train trip and upon his return? Explain (a) why you think Don Camillo tore the deck of cards in half (p. 61T) and (b) what effect that action had on Peppone.

8. The author never explains overtly either the killing of Pizzi or the shooting at Don Camillo in the church. Using the details as given in the story, demonstrate your ability as a detective by proving the identity and motives of the gunman or gunmen who fired the shots. In accordance with your version of the shootings, explain the attitudes of Pizzi's widow, Pizzi's son, Peppone, Don Camillo, the police sergeant, and the other villagers.

9. Analyze the bishop as an understanding character, and explain what humor his words and actions add to the book. What do you believe he really thought of Don Camillo and Peppone? Why do you think he so readily agreed to transfer Don Camillo and later to restore him to the parish? Assess the wisdom of his choice of a priest to succeed Don Camillo in the village. Finally, explain his possible reasons for deciding to visit the village, the effects of his visit, and the probable impressions he took away with him.

10. The author explains (p. 6B) that "in the Little World between the river and the mountains, many things can happen that cannot happen anywhere else." Taking the author at his word, list five events in the book that you believe could not have happened anywhere else, and explain why you do or do not think that the author has made these five events believable in the context of the story. Why do you believe that a priest like Don Camillo could or could not have existed anywhere else? In a final paragraph, compare life in Don Camillo's village with life in your own town or city, and explain why you think you might prefer one or the other.

IV. *Vocabulary Study*

Diagnostic Test

4B	malign	praise	slander	make sick
9T	explicit	inferred	clearly stated	outworn
11T	incarnate	jailed	in the spirit	in the flesh
14T	melodramatic	impure	unemotional	sensational
18B	sacrilegious	profane	priestly	reverent
22B	deference	contrast	respect	discourtesy
27B	retaliate	reward	sell	repay in kind
29M	innocuous	harmless	not happy	poisonous
35M	simultaneously	earlier	later	at the same time
36B	villa	apartment	town house	suburban residence
37T	complacently	fully	contentedly	enviously
41M	restive	calm	obedient	unmanageable
42T	ambiguous	uncertain	capable	definite
46T	formidable	pleasing	antlike	causing dread
46B	skeptical	unwieldy	doubtful	positive
48B	implacably	relentlessly	amicably	impatiently
48B	inexorable	inexpert	unyielding	unspoken
50M	seething	biting	boiling	cooling off
56B	incumbent	ungracious	officeholder	loser in election
60T	coercion	pleading	persuasion	forcible compulsion
63T	embryonic	untried	undeveloped	fully grown
63M	strata	layers	multitudes	molten masses
63B	uncouth	unrefined	cultured	not related
66M	impregnable	easily won	unconquerable	not transparent
71M	prestige	renown	bravado	disgrace
72M	bravo	warrior	Excellent!	Shame on you!
73B	innate	inborn	prisoner	unnatural
75M	parried	evaded	traded	attacked
80M	absolution	cleanliness	accusation	forgiveness of sin
90B	candor	warmth	frankness	stealthiness
98M	brigands	robbers	donors	messengers
98M	atheist	minister	philosopher	disbeliever in God

100T	provocation	announcement	peace effort	intentional irritation
103T	disconcerted	calmed	perturbed	struck
107M	blatantly	openly	sheeplike	quietly
107M	thicket	clearing	storm	dense growth of shrubs
110M	sinister	threatening	crooked	soothing
116T	alleging	asserting	denying	hinting
116M	categorically	ably	questioningly	unconditionally
116M	exhort	drag out	plead against	urge strongly
120T	precarious	certain	insecure	precious
121T	manifesto	secret talk	ship's list	public declaration
126M	usurer	envier	benefactor	money lender
126B	contingencies	chance events	close kin	certainties
127M	emaciated	sharp	very thin	fleshy
136B	bigots	pacifiers	giants	intolerant ones
139M	obituary	death notice	observation	birth notice
143M	staccato	tall	jerky	smooth
144B	senile	old	young	middle-aged
153M	ominous	threatening	important	presaging success

Answers

malign-slander, *explicit*-clearly stated, *incarnate*-in the flesh, *melodramatic*-sensational, *sacrilegious*-profane, *deference*-respect, *retaliate*-repay in kind, *innocuous*-harmless, *simultaneously*-at the same time, *villa*-suburban residence, *complacently*-contentedly, *restive*-unmanageable, *ambiguous*-uncertain, *formidable*-causing dread, *skeptical*-doubtful, *implacably*-relentlessly, *inexorable*-unyielding, *seething*-boiling, *incumbent*-officeholder, *coercion*-forcible compulsion, *embryonic*-undeveloped, *strata* -layers, *uncouth*-unrefined, *impregnable*-unconquerable, *prestige*-renown, *bravo*-Excellent! *innate*-inborn, *parried*-evaded, *absolution*-forgiveness of sin, *candor*-frankness, *brigands*-robbers, *atheist*-disbeliever in God, *provocation*-intentional irritation, *disconcerted*-perturbed, *blatantly*-openly, *thicket*-dense growth of shrubs, *sinister*-threatening, *alleging*-asserting, *categorically*-unconditionally, *exhort*-urge strongly, *precarious*-insecure, *manifesto*-public declaration, *usurer*-money lender, *contingencies*-chance events, *emaciated*-very thin, *bigots*-intolerant ones, *obituary*-death notice, *staccato*-jerky, *senile*-old, *ominous*-threatening

Teaching Aids

for

LOST HORIZON

This is the story of four people brought against their will to mysterious Shangri-La, set in the hidden mountains of the Blue Moon, a place where no one grows old. Most of all, it is the story of one man—Hugh Conway—who was trapped by the fascination of eternal life. One of the most beloved of modern novels, *Lost Horizon* enthralls readers with its haunting, timeless tale. It was awarded the Hawthornden prize, the English equivalent of the Pulitzer prize, and has been adapted as a motion picture several times. Its basic appeal rests on its contribution to mankind's recurrent dream of the ideal society, the perfect human being.

I. *Objective Test*

In the space provided at the left, insert the *letter* of the correct choice from among those offered; for example:

....c....   The author of this book is (a) Eliot (b) London (c) Hilton (d) Wells

.... 1. In the Prologue, the narrator meets Rutherford in Tempelhof (a) at a class reunion (b) at a soccer game (c) in a hotel room (d) in an airplane

.... 2. Conway is nicknamed "Glory" at school because (a) he is very patriotic (b) he is quite religious (c) he is extremely ambitious (d) his exploits are "glorious"

.... 3. In China, Conway greets Rutherford with (a) joy (b) indifference (c) fear (d) amazement

.... 4. On board ship, Sieveking is impressed with Conway's piano playing because the (a) compositions are original (b) selections are unknown Chopin pieces (c) pieces are known only to Sieveking (d) skill is extraordinary for a beginner

.... 5. During the plane ride, Miss Brinklow is (a) calm and quiet (b) nearly hysterical (c) gay and talkative (d) obviously unconcerned

.... 6. Even after he sees the plane is off course, Conway ignores Mallinson's pleas to try to stop the pilot because he (a) doesn't see anything wrong (b) is basically a coward (c) doesn't think he can do anything (d) is too absorbed in his thoughts to bother or care

.... 7. Just before he dies, the pilot helps his passengers by (a) introducing them to Chang (b) starting them on their way to Shangri-La (c) supplying them with food and extra clothing (d) telling them of the nearby lamasery

.... 8. Chang's responses to the visitors' questions are (a) polite but limited (b) unnecessarily abrupt (c) friendly and gossipy (d) deceptive and false

.... 9. Mallinson's major preoccupation at Shangri-La is (a) carousing in the village (b) talking with Lo-Tsen (c) making plans to leave (d) solving the mysteries of the lamasery

.... 10. At first, Miss Brinklow believes that life in Shangri-La will be (a) spiritually rewarding (b) like doing nothing at all (c) dangerously vain (d) clearly immoral

.... 11. There is little crime in Shangri-La because (a) there is a large police force (b) the punishment is usually severe (c) no one has ever thought of doing anything wrong (d) the inhabitants usually follow the principle of moderation

.... 12. Barnard says, in defense of his swindling, (a) "You would have done the same thing in my place" (b) "I got tired of playing by the rules" (c) "The whole game's going to pieces" (d) "I didn't do anything wrong"

.... 13. Father Perrault believes that he did not die at one hundred eight because he (a) had a vision to fulfill (b) had not prepared his soul for death (c) had to reconvert the villagers to Christianity (d) was destined to live forever

.... 14. Both Chang and Perrault admire Conway for his (a) liberal education (b) patience and wisdom (c) cynicism toward the world (d) spirit and courage

.... 15. Barnard responds to Mallinson's periodic attacks with (a) his characteristic good humor (b) increasing impatience (c) his attitude of American superiority (d) an understandable self-consciousness

.... 16. One provision placed on all the people who come to Shangri-La is that they (a) must eventually become lamas (b) can never leave (c) must subdue all passion (d) must promise never to reveal Shangri-La's location

.... 17. Conway's attitude toward Western women in general is (a) admiring (b) malicious (c) scornful (d) laudatory

.... 18. Miss Brinklow decides to stay in Shangri-La because she (a) has fallen in love (b) has unconsciously accepted the morals she formerly abhorred (c) plans to start a mission there (d) has been asked to teach Tibetan in the school

.... 19. In his last meeting with Perrault, Conway learns that he (a) will be allowed to leave Shangri-La (b) can marry Lo-Tsen (c) can mine for gold in the valley (d) is the new leader of Shangri-La

.... 20. At the end of the story, Conway is surprised by Mallinson's (a) influence over Lo-Tsen (b) calmness and rationality (c) dedication to him (d) dislike for Shangri-La

.... 21. After Conway tells him the whole story of Shangri-La, Mallinson (a) becomes more understanding (b) thinks Conway is insane (c) leaves without a word (d) seriously reconsiders staying there

.... 22. The thought of leaving Shangri-La makes Conway feel (a) pleased and relieved (b) indifferent and unconcerned (c) enraged and resentful (d) confused and saddened

.... 23. When Conway first sees Lo-Tsen after he leaves Shangri-La, he realizes that (a) she loves him (b) he shouldn't have left Shangri-La (c) Mallinson has tricked him (d) she loves Mallinson

.... 24. Rutherford's final investigation of Conway and Shangri-La (a) convinces him that Conway must have been mad (b) finally solves the mystery (c) yields only inconclusive evidence (d) inspires him to give up everything and go looking for Shangri-La

.... 25. If the old woman at the Chinese mission is Lo-Tsen, we can conclude that (a) beauty exists only in Shangri-La (b) no one can stay young long in the outside world (c) Lo-Tsen was almost ready to die when she left Shangri-La (d) many years have gone by since she left Shangri-La

Answers

1-a, 2-d, 3-b, 4-b, 5-a, 6-c, 7-d, 8-a, 9-c, 10-b, 11-d, 12-c, 13-a, 14-b, 15-a, 16-b, 17-c, 18-c, 19-d, 20-a, 21-b, 22-d, 23-d, 24-c, 25-b

II. *Alternate Objective Tests*

A. Matching

Before each number in the column on the left, write the *letter* of the item in the column on the right that matches:

.... 1. Briac
.... 2. Rutherford
.... 3. Conway
.... 4. Perrault
.... 5. Barnard
.... 6. Lo-Tsen
.... 7. Karakal
.... 8. Baskul
.... 9. Shangri-La
...... 10. Miss Brinklow

a. rebellion
b. missionary
c. hot-tempered
d. harpsichord player
e. High Lama
f. policeman
g. novelist
h. Milan
i. consul
j. Chopin student
k. "mountain pass"
l. American
m. "Blue Moon"

Answers

1-j, 2-g, 3-i, 4-e, 5-l, 6-d, 7-m, 8-a, 9-k, 10-b

B. Fill-ins

From the column on the right, select the item that best completes each statement below, and write it in the space provided:

1. The Baskul plane incident causes the British government _____.
2. The stolen plane stops once for _____.
3. Most people think Conway is a (an) _____.

Talu
speak English
cynicism
ease
embarrassment
fly a plane

4. Barnard adjusts to Shangri-La with _____.

5. Father Perrault believes in a _____ life.

6. The name of the pilot of the stolen plane is _____.

7. According to Chang, Lo-Tsen wants to become a (an) _____.

8. Conway's general attitude toward the outside world is one of _____.

9. Like Mallinson, Lo-Tsen is a creature of _____.

10. Miss Brinklow doesn't think the lamas' activities are very _____.

11. Chang says that the rough terrain near Shangri-La makes _____ very difficult.

12. To Conway, Lo-Tsen resembles a lovely _____.

13. Chang surprises Conway at first by being able to _____.

14. Conway is _____ with life at Shangri-La.

15. Mallinson refuses to believe that Lo-Tsen is very _____.

passion
practical
old
repairs
delighted
refueling
missionary
weakling
hero
lama
Barnard
vase
escape
meditative
bored

Answers

1-embarrassment, 2-refueling, 3-hero, 4-ease, 5-meditative, 6-Talu, 7-lama, 8-cynicism, 9-passion, 10-practical, 11-escape, 12-vase, 13-speak English, 14-delighted, 15-old

III. *Ideas for Written or Oral Book Reports or Class Discussions*

1. From biblical times to the present, mankind has dreamed of an ideal society where peace and social harmony prevail. There have even been experiments in group living in an attempt to achieve these goals. In this country,

famous writers and thinkers like Hawthorne and Emerson were associated with Brook Farm in Massachusetts from 1841 to 1847, where a sort of cooperative was established. In recent years, some young people have formed communes modeled after earlier attempts to seek identity and happiness in a rural setting. Why does the dream of utopia continue to fascinate us? What does the persistence of the dream say about society at any given time? What needs, *other than food and shelter,* would have to be satisfied to make us sufficiently content to reduce the frequency of dreams of ideal societies? On the other hand, why could one argue that our basic characteristics as human beings make it unlikely that we could ever be satisfied with our lot? Is this good or bad? Explain.

2. Although the novel contains few direct references to world conditions at the time it was published, it is important to consider these in analyzing the enormous popularity the book achieved within a year after it first went on sale in 1933. What political events were shaping up to make people fearful of the possible outbreak of another war? What economic problems had arisen to cause great concern about the quality of life? What scientific experiments had already begun that threatened to produce the power to destroy the earth? Why would all these challenges to peace and security influence people to turn to a book that introduced a new word, *Shangri-La,* into the language —and perhaps new hope? To what extent has *Lost Horizon* retained its appeal and relevance to modern readers?

3. Consider Shangri-La as Conway and his party found it. Before they even reached the community, what evidence did the four strangers have that it was well civilized? What further proof did they discover when they arrived? What objects and customs at the lamasery led Barnard to observe that Shangri-La had preserved the best of the two worlds—the East and the West? Explain whether or not you agree with this assessment? What was Shangri-La's guiding principle? How did that principle affect the view of the inhabitants toward age, religion, politics, material rewards, virtue, crime, excitement, distinctions of sex? To what extent do you find the principle wise and reasonable?

In what areas might the principle fail to apply satisfactorily? How content would you have been as an inhabitant of Shangri-La?

4. Though it may be impossible for us to accept the fact that Perrault lived for about two hundred fifty years, what in his way of life does make it seem plausible that he might well have lived a very long time? What in the general character and atmosphere of Shangri-La encouraged long life? What did the lamas, and specifically Perrault, give up for this longevity? What one provision did the High Lama make for everyone who visited Shangri-La? Why do you suppose he did this? How justified was he in imposing on people in this way? Explain whether you think the provision was selfish and narrow or broad-minded and reasonable. What sacrifices would you be prepared to make—and which would you not want to make—in order to achieve better than average longevity?

5. During the flight of the stolen plane, you had your first opportunity to make a preliminary analysis of the general character of each of the four kidnaped passengers. What did they reveal about themselves in their reactions to their predicament and the possibility of a crash? To what extent were your preliminary estimates of the characters' traits borne out in the reactions of each passenger to Shangri-La?

For example, why could you have predicted Miss Brinklow's attitude toward the morals and religion of the inhabitants? Why was she impelled to try to institute changes? Why did she decide to stay?

Again, why weren't you surprised at Mallinson's attitude toward Shangri-La in general? Why couldn't he ever come to enjoy the place? How consistent with his character were his spirited outbursts from time to time?

What obvious reason did you already know for Barnard's desire to stay in Shangri-La? Without that reason, why else might he have wanted to stay? How long do you think he would be happy there?

What had you learned about Conway's character to account for his thorough delight with Shangri-La? How important had his World War I experiences been in developing his attitude?

6. To bring the divergent views of Mallinson and Conway toward Shangri-La into sharper focus, review the conversation between the two (pp. 206–217). What was Mallinson's attitude toward Shangri-La throughout his talk with Conway? Why did he feel this way? What specific points did he mention that seemed to be valid criticisms of the lamasery? Compare Mallinson's attack on Shangri-La with Conway's defense of it. Which was more rational? Why? Why did Conway defend the community so faithfully? Why didn't he respond to Mallinson's logical arguments? In what way was Conway no longer objective? What did Mallinson say about Lo-Tsen that persuaded Conway to leave? Why was this one fact so important? What did it tell Conway about Shangri-La? With whom did you side in the discussion? Why?

7. We saw Conway in many different lights, and we were conscious of great contrasts between the way he regarded himself and the way he appeared to the world. What were the major contrasts? Considering Conway's personality, great physical and mental capabilities, varied achievements, and capacity for hard work, how can you account for his apparent lack of ambition and his preference for a quiet life? How would this explain his initial willingness to stay in Shangri-La? With so many people to choose from, why did the High Lama select Conway to succeed him? What might have made Rutherford, who had known Conway only slightly, so willing to spend time and effort to trace him? Assuming that there was such a place as Shangri-La, what are the chances that Conway did indeed one day return?

8. The lamas of Shangri-La sought neither eternal life nor eternal youth. The High Lama told Conway that a person was too young in the first twenty-five years of life and too old in the last twenty-five years (p. 154T), and that it was the portion of life between these two extremes that would be prolonged in Shangri-La. To what extent do you agree with this philosophy? What advantages would come of extending the middle years of life? What disad-

vantages might accrue? If you had a choice, what segment of your life would you wish to extend? Why?

9. Several aspects of Hilton's writing style are worthy of consideration. What advantages, if any, did the *structure* of the novel gain by its arrangement into a Prologue, main story, and Epilogue? How did the use of the *flashback* technique in the Prologue introduce the elements of *suspense* and *mystery?* How were these elements maintained? Why didn't the author present the complete solution to the mystery involving the central characters; that is, the ultimate fate of Conway and the three other passengers in the plane? How did Hilton create further suspense through his use of *foreshadowing,* as he did in his references to the difficulty of recognizing a pilot in flying gear and Sanders' reply that he had been at Baskul (p. 2)? What other examples of foreshadowing can you mention? Look at several of Hilton's descriptive passages (pp. 24B–25T, 37T, 42M, 46M, 50M, 80B, 94M, 99B, 106B, 130M, 173M, 203M). What specific words or phrases convey an atmosphere or depict a place in a unique way? Which words are particularly effective because they are unusual in that context? What details did the author choose in order to describe an entire scene in a short passage? How might this device account for the fact that so much atmosphere and suspense are created in the relatively few pages of the novel? Note, too, Hilton's use of analogies to everyday life (pp. 25M, 42M, 58M, 61M, 130M, 219T). How did these *similes* and *metaphors* sharpen the descriptions? Finally, how well did the author use *dialogue* to create reality in character and episode? Choose several passages of dialogue that could also have been written in narrative form, and show why the former approach was more effective as a stylistic technique.

10. Throughout your reading of *Lost Horizon,* you were confronted with the advantages and disadvantages of life at Shangri-La. You should have some definite opinions about what was good and bad about Hilton's mountain paradise, what was well planned, and what would simply not work in society as you know it. Using Shangri-La as your point of departure, present *your* idea of an ideal community.

Where should your earthly paradise be located? What about its climate, terrain, resources, isolation from the rest of the world, border protection? Who should live there? What modern conveniences would you want retained? What principles of government should be established? What rights and responsibilities should each individual have? How would you deal with crime or persistent refusal to live within the established code of behavior? What provisions would you make for work assignments, leisure time, social relationships, personal relationships like marriage and families? Judging from your estimate of man's (woman's) basic nature, what are the odds that any such community could ever succeed for any length of time? Explain.

IV. *Vocabulary Study*

Diagnostic Test

1M	precocious	late	silly	developed early
2M	hiatus	depth	gap	top
7B	effervescent	bubbling	serene	frigid
9T	amnesia	recall	loss of memory	disease
10M	phenomenon	outrage	clarity	remarkable thing
15T	amiably	harshly	timidly	agreeably
16B	repertoire	solo	criticism	list of presentations
19M	diffident	various	retiring	bold
22T	luxurious	tawdry	intricate	elegant
22T	indulgently	leniently	stiffly	bravely
26T	colloquy	letter	conversation	friend
27T	incredulity	faith	abandonment	disbelief
30B	equanimity	calmness	equality	anger
36T	laconic	lazy	lengthy	brief
37M	garish	plain	gaudy	heavy
59T	truculent	pleasing	belligerent	loaded
61B	fastidious	hard to please	boorish	quick
67M	cataclysm	repetition	violent change	fit
68T	impervious	haughty	open	impenetrable
72B	deprecation	praise	claim	disapproval

74B	prevalent	rare	widespread	famous
82T	cajoled	argued	hunted	coaxed
83B	dilatory	tardy	open	prompt
85B	prevarication	untruth	variety	sincerity
101B	inscrutable	clear	incomprehensible	tight
107T	profusion	loss	scarcity	abundance
109B	mellifluous	smoothly flowing	grinding	halting
114T	autocracy	liberalism	one-man rule	selfishness
115T	acrimoniously	bitterly	sweetly	grandly
116T	simulated	copied	pretended	designed
127T	arduous	simple	loving	difficult
127B	aversion	refusal	dislike	return
131M	corporeal	obese	of the body	official
131M	emaciated	wasted away	hearty	eager
133T	candid	gruff	frank	false
135M	surveillance	neglect	measurement	watching over
136T	inveigh	talk violently	test	remain silent
142M	vicissitudes	crimes	changes	duplicates
151T	charlatan	dancer	expert	quack
151M	inured	introduced	accustomed	rejected
157T	cynicism	distrust	acceptance	probe
174M	clairvoyant	bright	dull	perceptive
177M	sumptuous	cheap	lavish	coarse
186B	mundane	unusual	foreign	routine
195T	solace	comfort	pain	truth
197B	inexorable	unalterable	possible	deplorable
202T	irascibility	charm	irritability	cruelty
209T	elixir	deadly medicine	life-prolonging substance	mineral extract
211B	wizened	dried up	flourishing	savage
224T	longevity	deep breath	long life	calamity

Answers

precocious-developed early, *hiatus*-gap, *effervescent*-bubbling, *amnesia*-loss of memory, *phenomenon*-remarkable thing, *amiably*-agreeably, *repertoire*-list of presentations, *diffident*-retiring, *luxurious*-elegant, *indulgently*-leniently, *colloquy*-conversation, *incredulity*-disbelief, *equanimity*-calmness, *laconic*-brief, *garish*-gaudy, *truculent*-belligerent, *fastidious*-hard to please, *cataclysm*-violent change, *impervious*-impenetrable, *deprecation*-disapproval, *prevalent*-widespread, *cajoled*-coaxed, *dilatory*-tardy, *prevarication*-untruth, *inscrutable*-incomprehensible, *profusion*-abundance, *mellif-luous*-smoothly flowing, *autocracy*-one-man rule, *acrimoniously*-bitterly, *simulated*-pretended, *arduous*-difficult, *aversion*-dislike, *corporeal*-of the body, *emaciated*-wasted away, *candid*-frank, *sur-veillance*-watching over, *inveigh*-talk violently, *vicissitudes*-changes, *charlatan*-quack, *inured*-accustomed, *cynicism*-distrust, *clairvoyant*-perceptive, *sumptuous*-lavish, *mundane*-routine, *solace*-comfort, *inexorable*-unalterable, *irascibility*-irritability, *elixir*-life-prolonging substance, *wizened*-dried up, *longevity*-long life

Teaching Aids

for

LUST FOR LIFE

In an age when a single original by Vincent Van Gogh can bring more than eighty thousand dollars in a gallery auction, it is especially ironic to note that during his lifetime the great artist managed to sell only one of the nearly eight hundred paintings he produced. His struggles with poverty, his dependence on a devoted brother, his fierce dedication to a style dictated by an inner fire, his tragic emotional conflicts—all these impacts on a tortured soul are brilliantly revealed in this biographical novel that has become a classic of its kind.

I. *Objective Test*

In the space provided at the left, insert the *letter* of the correct choice from among those offered; for example:

....c....　The author of this book is (a) Van Gogh (b) Dickens (c) Stone

....　1. Vincent was employed at the beginning of the book as (a) an evangelical minister (b) an artist (c) a salesman

....　2. Vincent's father had hoped that Vincent would (a) follow in his footsteps (b) study medicine (c) find out his one natural interest in life

....　3. Vincent went to Amsterdam to stay at his uncle's home to (a) forget his keen disappointment (b) study for the ministry (c) find a suitable new position

250

.... 4. Vincent felt he was a part of the society of the Borinage for the first time (a) immediately on his arrival (b) after he had preached his first sermon (c) after he had gone down into a mine shaft and begrimed his face

.... 5. Vincent lost faith in his religious mission to the miners when (a) they failed to attend his sermons (b) he felt religious consolation could not relieve their abject misery (c) the miners accused Vincent of hypocrisy

.... 6. When Vincent fell ill in the Borinage, the fundamental cause was (a) an epidemic (b) malnutrition (c) exposure to the storm

.... 7. Vincent's cousin Mauve disapproved most strongly of Van Gogh's (a) having a mistress (b) despising Mauve's painting (c) copying Mauve's style

.... 8. While in The Hague, Vincent had to raise some money to (a) bail Christine out of jail (b) pay a fine for having been convicted of disorderly conduct (c) pay for the delivery of Christine's baby

.... 9. In The Hague, Vincent chose as his favorite subjects (a) the poor and depressed (b) sailors (c) dance-hall girls

.... 10. When Vincent left Christine and The Hague, he went straight (a) to his Paris quarters (b) back to London (c) home to his father's house

.... 11. While oil painting in the fields around Nuenen, Vincent discovered (a) his finest technique for mixing colors (b) he was being followed (c) he had no interest at all in painting landscapes

.... 12. Margot made Vincent the present of a book on the occasion of (a) his birthday (b) the anniversary of their wedding (c) her birthday

.... 13. Margot's family greeted the prospect that she and Vincent were to marry with (a) enthusiastic approval (b) solid opposition (c) indifference

.... 14. Margot reacted to her imminent separation from Vincent by (a) flirting with other men (b) accusing him of having betrayed her (c) taking poison

.... 15. Theo was eager to get the opportunity to show and sell the work of a group of painters known as the (a) Impressionists (b) Surrealists (c) Cubists

.... 16. The De Groots, a family that included a young daughter with whom Van Gogh was mistakenly supposed to have "become involved," were (a) potato eaters (b) coal miners (c) humble fisher folk

.... 17. After Van Gogh had been in Paris for a time, Theo expressed serious dissatisfaction because Vincent (a) stayed up too late (b) did very little painting (c) seemed to be copying the styles of the artists around him

.... 18. Van Gogh's first reaction to the paintings of the new artists whom Theo had praised (a) shocked Theo tremendously (b) pleased him immediately (c) impressed him because of the soundness of the criticism

.... 19. Henri Toulouse-Lautrec told Vincent that all great art springs from (a) conviction (b) dedication (c) hatred

.... 20. Theo's life, once his brother came to Paris to live with him, was (a) orderly and calm (b) stormy and sleepless (c) unchanged

.... 21. When Theo and Vincent went to the party given by Henri Rousseau, they observed the painter (a) being patronized and insulted (b) giving a piano lesson (c) creating one of his primitive paintings

.... 22. When Van Gogh felt he had had enough of the society of other painters, he set out from Paris for (a) Tahiti (b) the Holland he knew and loved (c) the south of France

.... 23. Arles had once been (a) an important stage-

coach stop (b) an old Roman settlement (c) a
well-known seaport town

.... 24. Van Gogh made friends with the postman at
Arles and his family, named (a) Roulin (b)
Montmartre (c) Decrucq

.... 25. While in the sun-drenched fields around Arles,
Van Gogh had a vision of a woman named
(a) Margot (b) Christine (c) Maya

Answers

1-c, 2-a, 3-b, 4-c, 5-b, 6-b, 7-a, 8-c, 9-a, 10-c, 11-b, 12-c, 13-b,
14-c, 15-a, 16-a, 17-c, 18-a, 19-c, 20-b, 21-a, 22-c, 23-b, 24-a, 25-c

II. *Alternate Objective Tests*

A. Matching

Before each number in the column on the left, write the
letter of the item in the column on the right that matches:

.... 1. Ursula Loyer   a. insisted Van Gogh had no talent

.... 2. Jacques Verney   b. believed his method, pointillism, was the perfect way to paint

.... 3. Postman Roulin   c. a writer acquaintance of Theo's

.... 4. Dr. Gachet   d. accused Vincent of bad faith in not living up to their bargain

.... 5. Rachel   e. helped Vincent and his friends try to sell their paintings

.... 6. Paul Gauguin   f. Vincent's best friend among the miners

.... 7. Theo Van Gogh   g. befriended Vincent in Arles

.... 8. Émile Zola   h. teased Vincent about giving her his ears

.... 9. Kay Vos   i. helped Vincent when no one else would

...... 10. Seurat   j. delivered Vincent's only eulogy

   k. Van Gogh's best friend among the Paris painters

l. the girl Vincent loved first

m. hired Vincent when he needed help desperately

n. the cousin whom Vincent loved

Answers

1-l, 2-f, 3-g, 4-j, 5-h, 6-k, 7-i, 8-c, 9-n, 10-b

B. Fill-ins

From the column on the right, select the item that best completes each statement below, and write it in the space provided:

1. _____ appeared to Vincent in his seizures of madness.
2. The scene of Vincent's maiming himself was the _____.
3. Vincent's model in Arles was _____, the postman.
4. The woman whom Vincent loved in London was _____.
5. _____ was the girl Vincent saw most often in Arles.
6. _____ tried to commit suicide because her love for Vincent was hopeless.
7. Vincent's uncle in Amsterdam was a (an) _____.
8. Vincent's second job in England was as a (an) _____.
9. Vincent was helped in his study of Latin and Greek by _____.
10. The first one to comment on Vincent's inclination to associate ideas expressed in literature with paintings was _____.

Rachel
teacher
Ursula Loyer
Rousseau
yellow house
Jacques Verney
Émile Zola
Victor Hugo
Christine
blackbirds
admiral
salesman
coal mines
Margot
Kay
Toulouse-Lautrec
Mendes da Costa
Roulin

11. The painter who gave violin lessons was _____.

12. The painter who was a cripple was _____.

13. The owner of the house where Vincent stayed first in Petit Wasmes was _____.

14. A writer whom Vincent met in Paris was _____.

15. _____ was the woman whose baby's delivery was paid for by Vincent.

Answers

1-blackbirds, 2-yellow house, 3-Roulin, 4-Ursula Loyer, 5-Rachel, 6-Margot, 7-admiral, 8-teacher, 9-Mendes da Costa, 10-Kay, 11-Rousseau, 12-Toulouse-Lautrec, 13-Jacques Verney, 14-Émile Zola, 15-Christine

III. *Ideas for Written or Oral Book Reports or Class Discussions*

1. People generally agree that they are willing to make certain sacrifices to achieve success or happiness, or both. Disagreements flare and often reach white heat, however, over definitions of either success or happiness that can be universally agreed upon. To what extent was the kind of life selected by Theo, Vincent's brother, a satisfying approach to either of these ideal goals? How correct was Mendes da Costa in his statement that the chief value of art lies in the expression it provides for the artist—irrespective of its merit or lack of it? How rewarding to you would be a life dedicated to trying to express yourself adequately (pp. 33B–34M)? How convinced are you that the sincere, quiet dedication of Vincent's father to his career and family seems to be the best way to seek satisfaction? How would you defend Vincent's life as a success or condemn it as a total failure? What ideas about

the way you might want to plan your future or live your life are suggested by reading this book?

2. Letters from and to Vincent were a major source of the material for this book. Use your imagination to reconstruct another common source of biographical information and ideas, a diary. Construct at least ten detailed diary entries that Vincent might have written concerning a substantial segment of the events described in the book. Remember, your task is not to report objectively on events, but to convey the feelings Van Gogh himself might have had as he lived the experiences mentioned. You might wish to include any or all of the following occurrences in your personal "Vincent Van Gogh diary":

a. Ursula's rejection of Vincent's proposal (pp. 8T–9B, 17M–18T)
b. Vincent's disappointment over the outcome of the interview with the mine owners when he tried to intercede on behalf of the striking miners (pp. 78T–79T)
c. Vincent's feelings after his talk with Reverend Pietersen about further evangelical work and painting (pp. 88T–91B)
d. Vincent's realization that he was actually loved by Margot (pp. 236B–238M)
e. Vincent's feelings on the eve of his departure for Arles (pp. 340T–341B).

3. In accordance with the evolution of new theories in fields such as geopolitics, speculations have been voiced as to the effect a person's surroundings may have in determining the kind of individual he finally becomes. Some opposing theorists contend that a person will develop essentially in his unique way regardless of external circumstances of environment. To what extent would Vincent have been significantly different had he not originally come from Holland? How did the environment of Paris, with its artistic and intellectual ferment, contribute to the developing personality of Vincent Van Gogh? Comment on whether or not madness would have overtaken Vincent

in some place other than the blast-furnace environment of Arles? If Vincent had been more "fortunate" in his first assignment as an evangelical minister, what possibility was there that he would have spent his life as a relatively successful preacher? Mendes da Costa indicated that every individual eventually seeks out and fulfills his own essential integrity (pp. 34B–35B). Obviously, this concept is in direct contrast to the idea that the environment shapes the individual. Explain why you agree with one concept or the other, and support your opinion by giving evidence derived from *Lust for Life*.

4. Virtually all novelists make use of certain literary devices that are intended to enrich the experience of their readers. Some of the standard techniques employed in *Lust for Life* include *foreshadowing, symbols,* and *point of view.* Indicate four specific instances of foreshadowing (events in the book that clearly suggest other occurrences that inevitably follow them); for example, the conversation with the journalist about the effect of Arles's climate on people (pp. 344B–346B). Discuss the effectiveness of at least four symbols. These might include Maya (pp. 367B–374M), the slicing off of Vincent's ear, the appearance of the blackbirds (p. 400T), the necessity for Vincent to get grime on his face before the people of the Borinage could accept him. Analyze the point of view adopted by Stone. Is the story told as only Vincent could have seen it? Is there a narrator who plays a part in the action, but not the major part? Does the author assume an omniscient (all-knowing) point of view? Prove by specific examples which approach is used. Indicate whether or not you think it is effective.

5. To an ever-increasing extent, society is impinging on the lives of individuals. This influence is felt through mass media such as television and the movies. Resistance to pressures to conform in every way is reflected in such occurrences as extremes in dress and personal appearance, especially on the part of young people, and "free speech" and "free behavior" protests on college campuses. The fact that the rebellions are developing indicates that while most people seek economic security, many react unfavorably

to increased limitations on their individual freedoms. In your opinion, how well could a Vincent Van Gogh have developed in a completely conformist society? How much freedom can a society permit its deviationists without seriously endangering its continued existence? Should every individual have the right to do as he wishes? Using characters from *Lust for Life* as evidence and examples, develop your ideas about the ideal balance between individual freedom and government concern in the lives of people.

6. One of the rewards we might legitimately expect from a biographical novel is an insight into some of the peculiar features of the personality and character of its subject. Thus, in reading this book, we might seek answers to the questions: "What was Vincent really like?" "How was he like most other people?" "In what significant ways was he different from most other people you have met or read about?" Write a concise summary of the traits ascribed to Van Gogh in the book. Comment on why you do or do not believe he was destined to be rebuffed by Ursula and Kay. What were the reasons for his failure as a salesman, a divinity student, an evangelist? Why was it natural for Vincent to love Christine but to be unable to love Margot, the one woman to whom he meant so much? What is your opinion of the statement made by Doctor Gachet (p. 434T) that "All artists are crazy"? Indicate whether you agree or disagree with ". . . there is no room for moral judgments in art" (pp. 310B–311T). Does the concept that art is amoral extend also to the artists who produce it? Use the ideas, events, and characters in *Lust for Life* to support what you have to say in each instance about the book's protagonist.

7. Society has established codes of behavior by which individuals are expected to abide. These may dictate practices in professions, standards of morality, the role a person is expected to play in a given situation. Vincent violates several of the most supposedly inviolable patterns of accepted behavior. Discuss at least six ways in which he departs from conventional behavior. Go into some detail when you describe examples from the book to indicate exactly which "social commandments" he transgresses. In-

dicate why Van Gogh violates the code in each instance and whether you feel he was justified in so doing. As possible sources of ideas, you might consider Vincent's relations with Theo, the chapters that deal with his efforts as an evangelist, the events that occur during his liaison with Christine, the work Vincent does as a painter, the events surrounding his stay in Arles, and his life after that.

8. Science-fiction writers, and those who have tried to visualize what might be left of the world after a super-weapon holocaust, have inspired speculations about the individuals it might be best to preserve if only a few could be saved from almost universal destruction. If the individuals who might be protected from general annihilation included people such as Émile Zola (pp. 307T–311B), Theo Van Gogh, Vincent, Ursula (pp. 7T–9B), the Reverends de Jong and Pietersen (pp. 37M–41B), Decrucq (pp. 46T–48T, 60B–61B), De Bock (pp. 181T–182T), Gauguin, Rousseau (pp. 297M–301B), Margot (pp. 233M–254M), and Mendes da Costa (pp. 33T–35B), indicate which five you would nominate to be preserved, and give detailed reasons why you selected them in preference to the others. Which of these individuals would contribute most to the rebuilding of a new and perhaps better world? Why?

9. No matter what his ability or station, every person is faced with problems during the course of his life. In general, we feel that certain institutions, practices, or individuals may help us to overcome our difficulties. Among the widely accepted sources of assistance and solace to the individual are his family, religion, training, experience, and strengths either inherited or developed early in life. Irving Stone implies certain things about how much help religion may be in his accounts of Vincent's experiences and in the comments made by Toulouse-Lautrec (p. 311M) and Émile Zola (pp. 310B–311B). Stone reflects on the role of the family in the lives of Georges Seurat and Vincent. Training and experience as aids in solving serious problems are commented upon in the accounts of Vincent's various efforts to find a career; the character of Vincent is alternately a trial and a tower of strength. Describe in

some detail Stone's ideas about the usefulness of each of these aspects of life in helping the struggling individual strive for success. Indicate whether or not you agree with the author's ideas.

10. *Lust for Life* shows us something of the life lived by people of various classes during the last decade of the nineteenth century. Citing specific evidence from the book, describe some of the conditions of life for middle-class people in and around London. What was life like for the miners in the Borinage? How did the life of artists in Paris differ from that of businessmen such as Theo? Indicate whether or not significant differences are described between the situations reflected in the book and life in our own times. In what important ways have things remained unaltered in spite of the differences in location and time between *Lust for Life* and our own world? How true is it still, for example, that "Whether our rulers be kings or ministers, we poor people have just as little as before" (pp. 358B)? To what extent do you accept the idea that economic or other forces determine the lives most of us live in spite of any efforts we may make to change them (p. 78M)? In what ways is life preferable today? How might things have been better then, and for whom?

IV. *Vocabulary Study*

Diagnostic Test

2T	piquant	bland	lively	angry
12B	indefatigable	tireless	unusual	interrupted
13B	vestige	apparel	duplication	trace
16M	peremptorily	pleadingly	temporarily	arbitrarily
20T	satiety	deprived	dizziness	overfullness
25B	immutably	varying	impossibly	permanently
34T	gratuitous	uncalled for	polite	essential
55T	redolent	scarlet	fragrant	malodorous
56B	abysmal	exalted	bottomless	small amount
101B	incredulity	gullibleness	strangeness	disbelief
118M	extricated	instilled	released	exaggerated
160T	viscera	internal organs	skin	eyelids

161B	coveted	desired	despised	changed
163M	lacerate	mangle	cure	build
170T	licentiously	conventionally	curiously	immorally
175M	sporadically	occasionally	continually	efficiently
175B	reproving	blaming	verifying	forgiving
178M	unabashed	blustering	unashamed	embarrassed
179T	improvident	unthrifty	frugal	unusual
181M	doldrums	enthusiasm	storminess	dullness
206B	obliterated	succeeded	erased	installed
206B	aura	downpour	atmosphere	instinct
215B	menial	minor	aristocratic	lowly
217M	insidious	deceitful	encouraging	sincere
248B	viragoes	shrews	pleasant women	noblewomen
249T	tirades	brief comments	complaints	fiery speeches
253T	gloaming	daybreak	midday	twilight
258T	banalities	innovations	witticisms	commonplaces
270B	palpitant	lifeless	made of paper	pulsating
271M	replete	unfinished	questing	stuffed
294T	assimilate	expel	absorb	resemble
294M	affable	repulsive	antagonistic	friendly
299T	vociferously	resignedly	noisily	uninterestedly
322M	spleen	peevish temper	joining	charity
337B	meticulous	careless	incomplete	very particular
345B	imminent	important	delayed	impending
346M	volatile	unvarying	changeable	willing
352T	naïveté	artlessness	sincerity	cynicism
374M	undulations	dashes	waves	digressions
380B	anathema	idol	faith	damned
383B	vindicated	released	accused	justified
387T	plethoric	unusual	empty	overfull
387M	cajoled	unwanted	commanded	coaxed
397B	lethargic	energetic	dull	sleepless
409M	moribund	dying	vital	loyal
418B	vertigo	self-command	dizziness	form
421B	ingenuously	calmly	cleverly	openly
428B	macabre	ordinary	gruesome	colorful
440T	verdancy	greenness	coarseness	interest
448T	mendicant	doctor	millionaire	beggar

Answers

piquant-lively, *indefatigable*-tireless, *vestige*-trace, *peremptorily*-arbitrarily, *satiety*-overfullness, *immutably*-permanently, *gratui-*

tous-uncalled for, *redolent*-fragrant, *abysmal*-bottomless, *incredulity*-disbelief, *extricated*-released, *viscera*-internal organs, *coveted*-desired, *lacerate*-mangle, *licentiously*-immorally, *sporadically*-occasionally, *reproving*-blaming, *unabashed*-unashamed, *improvident*-unthrifty, *doldrums*-dullness, *obliterated*-erased, *aura*-atmosphere, *menial*-lowly, *insidious*-deceitful, *viragoes*-shrews, *tirades*-fiery speeches, *gloaming*-twilight, *banalities*-commonplaces, *palpitant*-pulsating, *replete*-stuffed, *assimilate*-absorb, *affable*-friendly, *vociferously*-noisily, *spleen*-peevish temper, *meticulous*-very particular, *imminent*-impending, *volatile*-changeable, *naïveté*-artlessness, *undulations*-waves, *anathema*-damned, *vindicated*-justified, *plethoric*-overfull, *cajoled*-coaxed, *lethargic*-dull, *moribund*-dying, *vertigo*-dizziness, *ingenuously*-openly, *macabre*-gruesome, *verdancy*-greenness, *mendicant*-beggar

Teaching Aids

for

THE MAYOR OF CASTERBRIDGE

Michael Henchard, an itinerant laborer, in a moment of drunken despair, sells his wife to the highest bidder in a refreshment tent on the village fairgrounds. After Henchard has become prosperous, his act of inhumanity comes back to haunt him, and finally to destroy him. This record of an anguished soul, as it struggles hopelessly against a relentless, fatal retribution, makes one of the great novels of the English language.

I. *Objective Test*

In the space provided at the left, insert the *letter* of the correct choice from among those offered; for example:

....c.... The author of this book is (a) Melville (b) Hawthorne (c) Hardy (d) Dickens

.... 1. Awakening from his drunken sleep, Henchard realized he had sold his wife when he found the (a) bill of sale (b) money in his pocket (c) ring on the floor (d) note from his wife

.... 2. Henchard's first impulse, after the loss of Susan, was to (a) thank his lucky stars (b) go to the police (c) try to find his wife (d) leave in an angry mood

.... 3. Susan believed that Newsom had (a) drowned at sea (b) abandoned her (c) died of a fever (d) committed suicide

.... 4. Susan first saw Henchard in Casterbridge at (a) a grain auction (b) a warehouse (c) the city hall (d) a public dinner

.... 5. In his first note to Henchard, Farfrae stated that he could (a) be a good manager (b) design a reaping machine (c) cure bad wheat (d) raise larger crops

.... 6. During their stay at the Three Mariners, Elizabeth-Jane disturbed her mother by (a) singing several songs (b) serving dinner to Farfrae (c) offering to make beds (d) being insolent to the innkeeper

.... 7. Abel Whittle was punished at work for (a) arriving late (b) refusing orders (c) quitting early (d) stealing money

.... 8. Henchard's project at the fair was spoiled by (a) lack of interest (b) lack of proper equipment (c) excessive heat (d) foul weather

.... 9. Susan created an embarrassment for Elizabeth-Jane and Farfrae at Durnover Hill by (a) publicly scolding her daughter (b) upbraiding Farfrae (c) sending an anonymous letter (d) telling Henchard about the secret date

.... 10. Elizabeth-Jane offended Henchard at the Walk by (a) refusing to dance (b) dancing with Farfrae (c) talking against her father (d) leaving too early

.... 11. Elizabeth-Jane first saw Lucetta at (a) Susan's grave (b) the fair (c) High Place Hall (d) the reception given by Henchard

.... 12. When Henchard read Susan's deathbed letter, he learned that he was (a) the cause of her death (b) Elizabeth-Jane's real father (c) *not* Elizabeth-Jane's real father (d) the sole inheritor of Susan's estate

.... 13. After her mother's death, Elizabeth-Jane was often reprimanded by Henchard because she (a) refused to take his name (b) became too independent (c) sometimes spoke in dialect (d) continued to see Farfrae

.... 14. One reason Lucetta hired Elizabeth-Jane was to (a) give Henchard an excuse to visit (b) get even with Henchard (c) show how rich she was (d) teach Elizabeth-Jane better manners

.... 15. When Farfrae first went to Lucetta's house, his purpose was to (a) welcome the new owner (b) borrow money (c) arrange for courtship (d) see Elizabeth-Jane

.... 16. Elizabeth-Jane was greatly disturbed to learn that Farfrae (a) had plotted against her father (b) had been married before (c) was planning to leave the town (d) was interested in Lucetta

.... 17. Henchard's bankruptcy was caused by (a) Farfrae's secret deals (b) crop failure (c) gambling in grain (d) Lucetta's refusal to lend money

.... 18. Henchard forced Lucetta to promise to marry him by threatening to (a) reveal their past together (b) ruin Farfrae's business (c) tell that she had come from Jersey (d) use his powers as a magistrate

.... 19. Elizabeth-Jane and Lucetta were saved by Henchard from (a) drowning in the pond (b) being gored by a bull (c) being run down by a wagon (d) falling down a ravine

.... 20. After twenty-one years, Henchard broke his vow never to (a) leave Casterbridge (b) take a drink of liquor (c) work for another man (d) marry again

.... 21. During the visit of royalty to Casterbridge, Henchard (a) greeted the queen (b) stayed in his house (c) was allowed to be master of ceremonies (d) was roughly dragged from the scene by Farfrae

.... 22. Jopp revealed the contents of Lucetta's letters because (a) he hated Farfrae (b) Henchard ordered him to do so (c) Lucetta had refused to help him (d) he wanted revenge on Henchard

.... 23. Henchard failed to get Lucetta's husband to go
        back home after her fit because (a) Henchard
        could not catch up (b) Farfrae had gone by
        another route (c) Jopp blocked the road (d)
        Farfrae did not believe Henchard's story

.... 24. When Newsom arrived unexpectedly in Caster-
        bridge, (a) Henchard refused to see him (b)
        Elizabeth-Jane greeted him warmly (c) Hen-
        chard said Elizabeth-Jane was dead (d) the
        townspeople drove him off

.... 25. Henchard's will revealed that he wanted (a)
        no notice taken of his death (b) Farfrae to
        make a public funeral (c) Elizabeth-Jane to
        acknowledge him as her father (d) Abel Whit-
        tle to inherit the estate

Answers

1-b, 2-c, 3-a, 4-d, 5-c, 6-b, 7-a, 8-d, 9-c, 10-b, 11-a, 12-c, 13-c, 14-a,
15-d, 16-d, 17-c, 18-a, 19-b, 20-b, 21-d, 22-c, 23-d, 24-c, 25-a

II. *Alternate Objective Tests*

A. Matching

Before each number in the column on the left, write the
letter of the item in the column on the right that matches:

.... 1. furmity woman		a. skimmity-ride
.... 2. hay trusser		b. Mrs. Judd
.... 3. loser in wrestling		c. companion-house-
match		keeper
.... 4. Lucetta's collapse		d. Henchard's secret
.... 5. Henchard's excuse		e. Farfrae
.... 6. Susan's secret		f. Henchard
.... 7. Lucetta's house		g. Three Mariners
.... 8. Elizabeth-Jane's job		h. drunkenness
.... 9. Miss Templeman		i. High Place Hall
...... 10. Jopp		j. governess
		k. Lucetta

l. Henchard's fore-
man
m. poverty
n. Elizabeth-Jane's
father

Answers

1-d, 2-f, 3-e, 4-a, 5-h, 6-n, 7-i, 8-c, 9-k, 10-l

B. Fill-ins

From the column on the right, select the item that best completes each statement below, and write it in the space provided:

1. Farfrae first attracted attention because of his _____.
2. Lucetta became rich from _____.
3. Lucetta offered to lend money to _____.
4. Henchard's own daughter _____ as a child.
5. While Susan thought Newsom dead, he was really in _____.
6. Henchard punished Whittle by making him work without his _____.
7. Lucetta did not want people to know she had come from _____.
8. The plan for the _____ was hatched at Peter's Finger.
9. Elizabeth-Jane was witness to _____ promise to marry Henchard.
10. Whittle was grateful because Henchard had been good to his _____.
11. Henchard learned about Newsom's child in _____ letter.
12. Henchard's wedding gift to Elizabeth-Jane was a (an) _____.

Farfrae
lie
trial
singing
bird
skimmity-ride
Susan's
wife
mother
a grain deal
Henchard
was abandoned
Newfoundland
Jersey
Lucetta's
pants
furmity woman
an inheritance
died
boots
jewelry
shawl
insult

13. The sale of Henchard's wife was re-   town clerk
    vealed at a trial by the _____.
14. Farfrae's early gifts to Elizabeth-Jane
    consisted of _____.
15. Elizabeth-Jane finally turned against
    Henchard because of his _____
    to Newsom.

Answers

1-singing, 2-an inheritance, 3-Henchard, 4-died, 5-Newfoundland, 6-pants, 7-Jersey, 8-skimmity-ride, 9-Lucetta's, 10-mother, 11-Susan's, 12-bird, 13-furmity woman, 14-books, 15-lie

III. *Ideas for Written or Oral Book Reports or Class Discussions*

1. The subtitle of the book refers to Henchard as "A Man of Character." The question is: What kind of character? Evaluate his actions, attitudes, and decisions in the following crucial episodes in his life:

   a. The sale of Susan, the subsequent remarriage, the violation of a deathbed request
   b. The reactions to Elizabeth-Jane, both before he knew the identity of her real father, directly thereafter, and later
   c. The relationship with Farfrae; again early, middle, and late
   d. The reappearance of Lucetta, her marriage, her death
   e. The deception of Newsom
   f. The varying financial status, from hay trusser to mayor to hay trusser.

Point out instances where he exhibited strength of character. In what way did he succumb to certain character weaknesses? On balance, how would you rate the character of Henchard?

2. Susan Henchard (Newsom) represents quite a de-

parture from some of the women Hardy has portrayed in other books; for instance, the fiery, passionate Eustacia Vye in *The Return of the Native*. What was revealed about Susan's general nature at the very beginning when (even though she was ignorant of the illegality of her husband's sale) she meekly went along with Newsom? What prompted her many years later to return to the Wessex area to look for Henchard? At what moments did she reveal surprising strength and perseverance? What kind of mother was she to Elizabeth-Jane? Why do you suppose Hardy developed her character as he did? How accurate was the description of Susan by Newsom (p. 289)?

3. In what respects did Elizabeth-Jane resemble her mother? Why was Henchard disappointed in her from time to time? What did this disappointment reveal about her character and his? Why might it be said that she represented one of the few stable elements in the novel? Why did she marry Farfrae after all that had happened with Lucetta? How do you evaluate Elizabeth-Jane's behavior in getting a job with Lucetta, after Henchard's bankruptcy, during Farfrae's affair with Lucetta, after discovering Henchard's lie to Newsom, and in the final chapters?

4. Farfrae has puzzled some readers, who find it difficult to label him either hero or villain. In the early chapters, how did he reveal independence, intelligence, a feeling for the common man, a willingness to forget (p. 156), and a marked sociability? In what ways might he have been unfair to Henchard? To what extent were his activities responsible for Henchard's financial and emotional failures? When he married Lucetta, gave Henchard a menial job, exposed the former mayor to ridicule during the royal visit—how reasonable was Henchard's view that these were acts of reprisal? What subconscious motivation, if any, might have driven him to marry Elizabeth-Jane toward the end? How did you see Farfrae—hero or villain? Offer reasons for your final judgment.

5. What might have led you to suspect that Hardy showed more interest in developing the character of Lucetta than he did with the other women in the story? Why were her actions both helpful and harmful in her relations

with Elizabeth-Jane? How reasonable was her desire to sever relations with Henchard and become involved with Farfrae? How do you account for the fact that she broke her promise to marry Henchard? Why didn't she tell Farfrae all about the letters to Henchard before they brought about her destruction? To what extent were her reasons valid, considering the nature of the times, her belief that her secret would be kept, and Henchard's continuing presence on the scene? Why did Farfrae seem to recover from her death so quickly?

6. Some critics suggest that Hardy's strength in character portrayal lies in the way he handled his minor characters. Why is it that in this book, as in others, the only humorous moments occur when the villagers are on the scene? Give examples of the few light spots in the novel. Apart from their roles in the plot, what did each of the following contribute to local color: the furmity woman, Abel Whittle, Jopp, and the villagers who appeared at Peter's Finger? What was the point in Henchard's visit to the weather prophet or the reference to the waxen image (p. 189T)? Why might Hardy have been freer in his prose, less analytical, indeed, less architectural and more entertaining in his development of the minor characters?

7. The constant interactions between Henchard and Farfrae provide an interesting base for comparison with questions that are very relevant today. In what respects could one say that the conflict between the two men symbolizes typical problems that arise from the generation gap, as we refer to it these days? Describe situations in which understandable jealousies arose, differences of opinion developed over methods of handling crops or men, efforts to "show up" each other created hostility, and even rivalry in love focused on the unequal appeal of youth and age? How can the same point be made in the matter of Farfrae's choice of the older, sophisticated Lucetta over young, relatively simple Elizabeth-Jane?

8. An analysis of Hardy's style of writing reveals many of the literary devices used by great classic writers to advance the narrative and develop the characters. Here are some of the techniques he used. Examine each example,

find others, and then, in summary, explain how the devices contributed to the richness of his prose.

a. *Understatement:* Hardy rarely elaborates on important scenes; rather he lets the situation speak for itself. Note, for example, how little we are told of Susan's feelings after she is sold and how fragmentary are the details we get of Lucetta's confession to Farfrae the night of her death.

b. *Foreshadowing:* The author uses foreshadowing frequently to heighten suspense. Observe that the strength of the friendship between Henchard and Farfrae is described (p. 94B) and immediately thereafter comes the hint that the friendship will soon be ended (p. 95T). Later, after a quarrel and reconciliation, Henchard constantly thinks of Farfrae "with a dim dread" (p. 100M). At the fair, the townsfolk do not think Farfrae will be in the employ of Henchard very long (p. 105M).

c. *Descriptive power:* The opening pages of the novel provide ample evidence of Hardy's ability to describe people and places with striking accuracy. To add to the poetic quality of his direct descriptions, he uses *comparison* (simile): Casterbridge—"It was compact as a box of dominoes" (p. 26M) or it stood clean-cut and distinct "like a chess-board on a green tablecloth" (p. 89B). Also, there is *parallel structure,* as in the comment of the weather prophet "that men could profess so little and believe so much at his house, when at church they professed so much and believed so little" (p. 184M).

d. *Symbols:* With this technique, the writer uses a thing or person to represent a concept much broader in scope than the original. For instance, what was the purpose of introducing the flight of the swallow (p. 8T) during the sale? What beyond the surface was being suggested by the dead bird in the cage (p. 326T)?

e. *Humor:* Hardy does not use humor very often, but when he does, it seems to appear in scenes involving villagers; for example, the trial scene (p. 198). Why with Abel Whittle or the people in Peter's Finger and not with Henchard or the other major characters?

9. Critics have charged Hardy with excessive use of coincidence in developing his plots and with injecting his architectural training in manipulating and designing events to effect a perfect fit of the narrative sequence. The furmity woman seems to reappear whenever she is needed to advance the plot, first telling Susan where to find Henchard, later showing up at the trial to expose Henchard. Similarly, Newsom is present, gets lost, comes back, goes away, comes back again. Moreover, some have said that improbabilities becloud reality. What woman other than Susan would have accepted the sale so meekly? What are the odds that a man (Newsom) seeking his daughter would accept news of her death just on the word of someone whom he had had reason to doubt earlier? How do you answer these charges? To what extent do you agree with the critics?

10. In Hardy's philosophy of life, as expressed in his novels, mankind's existence is marked by a constant struggle against fate, with the odds heavily weighted in favor of disappointment, tragedy, and hopelessness. Note how he speaks through his characters (p. 240B) and closes the book with a sort of summary statement (p. 332). How well did he advance his theory of existence in *The Mayor of Casterbridge?* How, for example, might an act of will have changed Susan's life at the very beginning of the story? Why didn't Henchard make a partner of Farfrae rather than permit him to set up a rival concern? Why would an experienced businessman like Henchard gamble in grain futures? In short, to decide whether or not Hardy has made a good case of fate's mastery over one's life, you must analyze each crucial turn in the action, determine whether or not an exercise of will power would have made a difference, and evaluate the extent to which character failure rather than fate determined the outcomes. After you have done this with at least the major characters, explain your acceptance or rejection of Hardy's philosophy of life.

IV. *Vocabulary Study*

Diagnostic Test

1B	fustian	fine silk	rayon	cotton cloth
1B	reciprocity	independence	revenge	cooperation
2B	nimbus	cloud	speed	sun
5M	deterrent	joyful	discouraging	encouraging
12M	intermittent	periodic	steady	warm
17B	dingy	bright	shabby	nautical
31T	revelation	darkening	disclosure	excitement
37B	grimace	big grin	stare	wry look
42M	taciturn	voluble	not talkative	angry
50B	slatterns	untidy women	bed posts	prima donnas
53B	ambiguities	facts	uncertainties	perfumes
60M	chicanery	fairness	neatness	trickery
77M	philandering	flirting	ignoring	adoring
78T	reverie	discovery	daydream	plan
81M	castigate	pamper	compliment	punish
85M	paraphrase	reword	quote	define
90T	purlieu	distance	theft	neighborhood
109M	calligraphy	heat measure	penmanship	scrawl
114T	inadvertently	pointedly	loudly	unintentionally
124T	genealogical	artificial	inherited	raucous
124M	ironical	contradictory	presumed	logical
125M	lugubrious	lively	mournful	oily
131T	contiguous	apart	repeated	touching
141M	apotheosis	degradation	glorification	drug
147M	upbraid	scold	clip	praise
153M	stultified	made foolish	made wise	made sick
154M	equivocal	definite	uncertain	equal
156T	hyperborean	southern	heavenly	northern
156T	stringency	leniency	severity	connection
163M	undulated	rose and fell	collapsed	oiled
172T	trepidation	delight	bravery	fear
183M	copse	desert	hill	thicket
190M	extricated	released	bound	added
192M	capricious	regulated	unpredictable	sprightly
218M	straitened	limited	loosened	pointed
223M	chattel	property	farm	yearning
229B	rantipole	praying	romping	climbing
238B	counter-manded	approved	canceled	marched

242M	sardonic	sneering	smiling	drunken
251M	tyro	veteran	mechanic	beginner
270M	adroitly	clumsily	skillfully	secretly
283M	unscrupulous	moral	easy going	unprincipled
294T	fugue	fog	musical form	drama
304M	noxious	balmy	poisonous	fragrant
317M	amelioration	improvement	deterioration	maturity
321M	satirize	compliment	corrupt	ridicule
322T	emolliated	softened	hardened	greased
322M	gyrations	slidings	liftings	spinnings
331B	equable	stormy	tranquil	uneven
332M	effusiveness	gushiness	silence	restraint

Answers

fustian-cotton cloth, *reciprocity*-cooperation, *nimbus*-cloud, *deterrent*-discouraging, *intermittent*-periodic, *dingy*-shabby, *revelation*-disclosure, *grimace*-wry look, *taciturn*-not talkative, *slatterns*-untidy women, *ambiguities*-uncertainties, *chicanery*-trickery, *philandering*-flirting, *reverie*-daydream, *castigate*-punish, *paraphrase*-reword, *purlieu*-neighborhood, *calligraphy*-penmanship, *inadvertently*-unintentionally, *genealogical*-inherited, *ironical*-contradictory, *lugubrious*-mournful, *contiguous*-touching, *apotheosis*-glorification, *upbraid*-scold, *stultified*-made foolish, *equivocal*-uncertain, *hyperborean*-northern, *stringency*-severity, *undulated*-rose and fell, *trepidation*-fear, *copse*-thicket, *extricated*-released, *capricious*-unpredictable, *straitened*-limited, *chattel*-property, *rantipole*-romping, *countermanded*-canceled, *sardonic*-sneering, *tyro*-beginner, *adroitly*-skillfully, *unscrupulous*-unprincipled, *fugue*-musical form, *noxious*-poisonous, *amelioration*-improvement, *satirize*-ridicule, *emolliated*-softened, *gyrations*-spinnings, *equable*-tranquil, *effusiveness*-gushiness

Teaching Aids

for

MOBY DICK

Herman Melville's novel has been variously described as a powerful story of the sea, a poetic epic, an adventure in mythology, a tour de force in symbolism, and a deeply spiritual allegory. It is all of these. It is certainly epic in its sweep, poetic in its images, almost photographic in its realism, and extraordinarily rich in its symbolic and allegorical implications. Ishmael's account of Captain Ahab's compulsive quest of the Great White Whale is a gripping narrative of swift-moving action—violent and taut with suspense. Yet beyond the excitement of the story, the reader inevitably becomes aware of a brooding intellect that raises disturbing questions about good and evil, faith and rebellion, and man's eternal efforts to penetrate the mysteries that control his destiny.

I. *Objective Test*

In the space provided at the left, insert the *letter* of the correct choice from among those offered; for example:

....b....   The author of this book is (a) Hawthorne (b) Melville (c) Poe (d) Dickens

.... 1. Ishmael goes to sea as a common sailor on a whaling vessel mainly to (a) learn sail rigging (b) study to become a captain (c) experience the great whale (d) meet the fabled Ahab

.... 2. Queequeg comes late to the Spouter Inn because he is busy (a) selling a human head (b) looking for a ship (c) fixing his tomahawk (d) looking for his idol

.... 3. During breakfast at the inn, Ishmael is amazed to see Queequeg (a) drinking gallons of coffee (b) consuming numerous rolls (c) sitting shyly at the foot of the table (d) spearing steaks with his harpoon

.... 4. At New Bedford's Whaleman's Chapel, Father Mapple reaches his pulpit by a (a) secret rear door (b) perpendicular side ladder (c) flight of wooden steps (d) gently rising ramp

.... 5. En route to Nantucket, Queequeg (a) insults the captain (b) falls overboard (c) saves a jeering bumpkin's life (d) sights a whale

.... 6. Aboard the *Pequod,* Captains Peleg and Bildad have violent words over (a) Ishmael's share, or "lay" (b) Queequeg's skill as a harpoonist (c) the ship's stores (d) the size of the crew

.... 7. Shortly after an argument with Captain Ahab, Stubb dreams of (a) visiting a tropical island (b) kicking a pyramid (c) tossing a pipe in the sea (d) rescuing Flask

.... 8. Starbuck says he came along to hunt whales, not (a) "this Spanish ounce of gold" (b) "his crooked jaw" (c) "a dumb thing" (d) "my commander's vengeance"

.... 9. Melville gets *inside* a character occasionally by having him (a) deliver a soliloquy, as in a play (b) pray in the chapel (c) write confessions (d) speak secretly to Ishmael

.... 10. During a wild revelry in the crew's quarters, Pip (a) gets hopelessly drunk (b) fights with a Belfast sailor (c) voices his fears (d) sings with St. Jago's sailor

.... 11. In thinking about the Great White Whale, Ishmael wonders about (a) its huge size (b) its storied ferocity (c) the wrinkled forehead (d) the symbolic meaning of whiteness

.... 12. During "The First Lowering," it becomes clear

that Ahab has secretly taken aboard (a) extra rations of rum (b) his own boat crew (c) a Nantucket reporter (d) Fedallah's brothers

.... 13. At the end of the first whale chase, the *Pequod* (a) captures a whale (b) strikes a hidden reef (c) rams Ishmael's boat (d) sights Moby Dick

.... 14. After killing a whale, Stubb complains about (a) a pain in his shoulder (b) the lack of co-operation (c) the sharpness of his harpoon (d) the poor cooking of Fleece

.... 15. While extracting the valuable spermaceti oil from a whale (a) Tashtego falls into the head (b) Daggoo cuts himself (c) Queequeg smashes the forehead (d) Stubb loses the chain

.... 16. The "try-works" refer to (a) the ship's engines (b) a brick kiln for boiling blubber (c) the forecastle (d) the skin-drying mats

.... 17. Captain Boomer of the *Samuel Enderby* reports seeing the White Whale, which (a) simply swam away (b) cost the captain his arm (c) overturned a boat (d) carried no harpoon in his side

.... 18. After leaving the *Samuel Enderby,* Ahab calls the ship's carpenter to (a) build a coin box (b) design a cabinet (c) fashion a new leg (d) send for Prometheus

.... 19. Ahab asks the blacksmith to make him a harpoon point from (a) iron spikes (b) a silver cross (c) a hammer head (d) horseshoe nails

.... 20. Annoyed that his quadrant cannot locate Moby Dick for him, Ahab (a) tramples it under foot (b) heaves it overboard (c) gives it to Fedallah (d) tries it from another angle

.... 21. When thunder "turns the compass" during the typhoon, Ahab (a) decides to follow the sun (b) asks the steersman to take over (c) builds a new compass (d) calls on Starbuck for help

.... 22. Ahab refuses to help Captain Gardiner of the *Rachel* even though (a) money is offered (b)

.... a son is involved (c) Nantucket is mentioned
(d) Stubb returns the watch

.... 23. Captain Ahab spots Moby Dick while (a)
standing at the rail (b) walking the deck (c)
swinging toward the crow's nest (d) peering
through glasses

.... 24. Ahab dies when he is (a) caught by his own
line attached to the whale (b) swept under the
rammed *Pequod* (c) smitten by the huge tail
(d) crushed by Moby Dick's teeth

.... 25. Ishmael, the sole survivor, is picked up by the
Rachel after drifting for a day (a) on a piece
of wreckage (b) in a damaged boat (c) on the
Pequod's mast (d) in Queequeg's coffin

Answers

1-c, 2-a, 3-d, 4-b, 5-c, 6-a, 7-b, 8-d, 9-a, 10-c, 11-d, 12-b, 13-c,
14-d, 15-a, 16-b, 17-b, 18-c, 19-d, 20-a, 21-c, 22-b, 23-c, 24-a, 25-d

II. *Alternate Objective Tests*

A. Matching

Before each number in the column on the left, write the
letter of the item in the column on the right that matches:

.... 1. Heidelburgh tun
.... 2. he thought of shooting
Ahab
.... 3. impaled on the mast tip
.... 4. Bildad's sister
.... 5. leviathan
.... 6. a Polynesian prince
.... 7. *Pequod*'s part owner
.... 8. an idol
.... 9. Ramadan
...... 10. Parsee

a. Queequeg
b. sky-hawk
c. Yojo
d. Fedallah
e. fasting period
f. sperm whale's fore-
head
g. whale
h. Starbuck
i. German town
j. Peleg
k. Stubb
l. Aunt Charity

Answers

1-f, 2-h, 3-b, 4-l, 5-g, 6-a, 7-j, 8-c, 9-e, 10-d

B. Fill-ins

From the column on the right, select the item that best completes each statement below, and write it in the space provided:

1. Despite his principles, _____ joins in worshiping Queequeg's idol.
2. Father Mapple's sermon is based on the first book of _____.
3. Captain Peleg pronounces Queequeg's name as _____.
4. Ishmael is warned about sailing with Ahab by _____.
5. Captain Ahab's white leg is made of _____.
6. Ishmael first sees _____ several days after the voyage begins.
7. Ahab nails the gold piece reward to the _____.
8. Ishmael refers to Moby Dick as a (an) _____ whale.
9. A pleasant exchange between ships that meet at sea is called a (an) _____.
10. The most difficult whale to capture is the _____.
11. Perth, the blacksmith, has been ruined by _____.
12. A dying whale faces the _____.
13. The second hearse of Fedallah's prophecy turns out to be the _____.
14. Ahab displays a brief moment of pity when _____ goes mad.

whale ivory
Albino
masthead
Fin-Back
Quigmig
northern lights
gam
Pequod
Jonah
alcohol
Pip
Devil
Delight
mahogany
setting sun
Ishmael
cabin door
Elijah
Quohog
Captain Ahab
gambling

15. Five men of the —————— are lost
in an encounter with the Great White
Whale.

Answers

1-Ishmael, 2-Jonah, 3-Quohog, 4-Elijah, 5-whale ivory, 6-Captain
Ahab, 7-masthead, 8-Albino, 9-gam, 10-Fin-Back, 11-alcohol, 12-
setting sun, 13-*Pequod,* 14-Pip, 15-*Delight*

III. *Ideas for Written or Oral Book Reports or Class Discussions*

1. Most readers will find in *Moby Dick* an extended
allegory, a term that suggests that there is a meaning above
and beyond the details of the story. A book written in this
fashion can be read on several levels, as can *Gulliver's
Travels,* which has appeal both as an imaginative adventure story about strange people and as a vehicle for
Jonathan Swift's violent attacks upon the pettiness and
corruption of man and his institutions. To arrive at your
own interpretation of the allegorical implications of *Moby
Dick,* you should consider certain elements introduced by
Melville. Note his frequent use of *symbols;* that is, names,
places, and events that represent meanings much broader
than their literal sense. For example, what is significant
about the fact that Ishmael stops at the Spouter Inn,
owned by Peter Coffin (p. 10T)? What is suggested by the
name Ahab for the central character, or Ishmael for the
narrator, or the international composition of the crew?
What about Stubb's dream (p. 129)? Why is it a white
whale (pp. 153–163)? What does the very quest for it
signify? What is your reaction to the critic who reads
Pequod as "pique-at-God"? What other names, objects,
and events contribute to structuring the allegory, which
has been variously described as man's struggle against evil,
a man's quarrel with God, or a futile attempt to cope with
the mysteries of religion and a supreme being? Finally,

what is your own reading of the hidden significance of the story?

2. The critic Raymond Weaver said of the book: "For such is the breadth, the vitality, the solid substance out of which Melville's allegory is fashioned that . . . the account of Ahab's hunt of the abhorred whale can be read in all but perfect innocence of Melville's dark intent." What does Weaver mean by "dark intent"? What hints did you find in the story of this feature? Why do you suppose the author wrote to his friend Nathaniel Hawthorne that it was a "wicked book"? Why did Weaver also call the book "indisputably the greatest whaling novel, and a hideous and intolerable allegory"? How did Melville try to hide the allegory that was "hideous and intolerable" to himself and the public? If he wanted to keep his intent "dark," why did he reveal it at all? What dimension and effect do the existence and nature of the intent add to *Moby Dick?*

3. The names of Ahab and Ishmael come, of course, from the Bible. Father Mapple's sermon is another of many examples of the biblical influence on this vast work. William Simpson (*The Jonah Legend,* 1899) characterizes the account of Jonah and the whale as the initiation of a young man who at first rebels against submission to the Divine Will and, after a symbolic death, emerges into the priesthood of God. What relevance does this biblical tale have to the adventures that befall not only Ahab and Ishmael but also the harpooners, Tashtego and Queequeg, and the mad cabin boy, Pip? Find other examples (the Book of Job and the discussion of vanity in Ecclesiastes are but two) of biblical material in the novel. How did Melville's choice of the Bible for so many of his references affect the meaning and power of *Moby Dick?* How is Christianity compared and contrasted in the characters of Ishmael and Queequeg? How relevant is Father Mapple's "top-gallant delight" in Christianity to the world on the waves, the microcosm of the whaling ship? To what extent is Melville's book an acceptance, to what extent a rejection, of the hardrock Calvinism in which the author was brought up?

4. Ahab sees the white whale not as God but as a sym-

bol of "the intangible malignity which has been from the beginning" and on the whale he heaps "all the subtle demonisms of life and thought." What is there in Ahab's character that causes him to do this, in his experience that convinces him that to do so is right? What does his pursuit of the whale mean to Captain Ahab? How does this affect what the book should mean to the reader? To Ishmael, the meaning of the whale is different; it represents a cosmic nothingness in its white "colorless all-color of atheism." Find passages in *Moby Dick* in which Ishmael's interpretation of the white whale is made clear. What is suggested about the nature of the whale by Ahab's final experience with it and by Ishmael's conviction that it (and the God that made it) are at the last unknowable? How does the whale tell us of God's power without revealing God's essence? What moral are we to derive from the end of *Moby Dick?*

5. For Ahab, in this book full of imagery, God's message is "woven into the shrouds and cordage" of the *Pequod.* For Ishmael, in contrast, the problem is not to know the Unknowable but to live in harmony with nature, aware of one's true and immutable place in the scheme of things. Point out passages in *Moby Dick* that illustrate that Ahab believes he can plumb the depths of God's mystery, while Ishmael strives to accept. How does Queequeg, whose god is the idol Yojo, help Ishmael to avoid being an "isolate" like Ahab and bring him to fuller knowledge than Ahab's "blindness" will permit the captain? To what is Ishmael "married" (symbolized in Queequeg, the heathen, whose origin is "not down on any map; true places never are")? How does this concept save Ishmael, encourage him to live without the desperation and the destiny of Ahab, who thinks that the world is all wrong and God made it so? Indicate the stages in the damnation of Ahab and the salvation of Ishmael. When are the stages presented explicitly, when expressed in symbols (such as the "keystone sun," the doubloon)?

6. R. S. Crane, in an essay on the concept of plot, states:

. . . the plot of any novel or drama is the particular
temporary synthesis effected by the writer of the elements of action, character, and thought that constitute
the matter of his invention. It is impossible, therefore,
to state adequately what any plot is unless we include
in our formula all three of the elements or causes of
which the plot is the synthesis; and it follows also that
plots will differ in structure as one or another of the
three causal ingredients is employed in the synthesiz-
ing principle. There are, thus, plots of action, plots of
character, and plots of thought. In the first, the syn-
thesizing principle is a completed change, gradual or
sudden, in the situation of the protagonist, determined
and affected by character and thought . . . ; in the second, the principle is a completed process of change in
the moral character of the protagonist, precipitated or
molded by action, and made manifest both in it and in
thought and feeling . . . ; in the third, the principle is
a completed process of change in the thought of the
protagonist and consequently in his feelings, condi-
tioned and directed by character and action. . . .

We see that plot cannot be limited to action alone. In
Moby Dick, who is the protagonist (chief character) and
what is his *agon* (conflict, struggle)? Is the emphasis of
the plot on "a completed process of change" in his situation (action), in his moral character (character), or in his
ideas (thought)—or in a synthesis involving all three
elements? Defend your answer with specific references to
the structure of the plot in terms of relevant incidents,
character development, and ideas.

7. The writer of fiction must choose a *focus of narration,* or *point of view,* terms that refer to how the narrative will be told. A character may be chosen to tell the
story in the first person. What are the advantages or disadvantages of this approach? How does it differ from that
of having the story told in the third person, from the point
of view of a single character? How do both techniques differ from that used by an omniscient author in which the
writer can be everywhere, get inside his characters, and

even add his own analysis of characters, motivation, and outcomes? In *Moby Dick,* from what point of view is the major part of the story told? Offer evidence. Where does Melville depart occasionally from the basic design (for example, pp. 140–153)? What other examples can you cite? What reasons might Melville have had for using the techniques of a dramatist when he did change his approach?

8. Apart from its allegorical aspects, *Moby Dick* is certainly a superb adventure of the sea told by an expert in sea lore. What evidence is there that Melville had a good knowledge of life aboard a sailing vessel, the characteristics of whales, and the procedures for converting whales into commercial use? What information did you acquire in these areas? How did the author create *suspense* to maintain excitement in his narrative? In this connection, indicate how *foreshadowing* (hints of the future) contributed to the suspense, referring to examples in addition to the "marble tablets" (p. 41B), Elijah (p. 107B), "God help us all" (p. 137M), and statements by Starbuck (p. 142T) and Fedallah (p. 312T). Consider, too, how Melville used the qualities of the *myth* in adding another dimension to his tale. In what respects does the very quest for the whale remind you of some of the great myths you have read? Point out the mythical aspects of the Great White Whale, Ahab's raging at the sun (p. 314T), Fedallah's role in the chase (especially toward the end). What other elements of the narrative contribute to the feeling that "you are there" as the action builds to a climax? How deserved is the reputation of *Moby Dick* as ranking with the very best sea adventures ever written?

9. Evert A. Duyckinck, reviewing *Moby Dick* in the New York *Literary World* (November 22, 1851), complained of Ishmael and the "painful contradictions of this self-dependent, self-torturing agency of a mind driven hither and thither as a flame in a whirlwind is," saying that he had not "much admiration for the result." Where do you find inconsistencies in Ishmael? In Ahab? In the "whirlwind" of the story? To what can they be attributed? Richard Chase, in *The American Novel and Its Tradition*

(1957), points out other inconsistencies: the *Pequod* seems to be heading for Cape Horn and then rounds the Cape of Good Hope; sometimes the ship seems to have a wheel, sometimes a rudder (significantly of whalebone); Stubbs is called both third mate and second mate; Queequeg is at first an important figure and later merely another harpooner; Ishmael grows less central as the story proceeds; Ahab seems to begin as a tyrannical villain and grows into "a great, doomed hero." Find other inconsistencies in the text, and comment on their importance or lack of it, from details of plot to changes in style. Most of all, what was Melville's purpose and what did he achieve in altering the tone of the novel and the nature of its central figures so that *Moby Dick* "evolved from a travelogue" and sea story into the work of genius it is?

10. Although several characteristics of Melville's style have already been considered—notably symbolism, biblical and mythical references, foreshadowing, and authentic background detail—the novel is so rich in writing techniques that much more remains to be analyzed. In each of the following style elements, note the device, study the examples given, and then find other examples for each device.

a. *Unusual word use:* Melville uses language like an inventor, sometimes creating startling images—"snow-howdahed Andes" (p. 161T), "ocean's skin" (p. 305T)—and at other times taking liberties with parts of speech, converting words into unfamiliar usages—Captain Ahab's reference to Moby Dick, "He *tasks* me; he *heaps* me," or, in disciplining a seaman, "Down dog and *kennel,*" or, in describing Stubb's manner of rowing, "he *loungingly* managed his steering oar" (p. 172M).

b. *Descriptive power:* Note how the author uses imaginative phrases and words that appeal to all the senses to heighten the effects of description—"It was a sight full of quick wonder . . ." (p. 178M); how he builds detail upon detail—the *Pequod,* pp. 78B–79; Captain Ahab, p. 121B; the typhoon and lightning, pp. 318B–322.

c. *Poetic qualities:* Like a poet, Melville uses the *apostrophe* often (turning from one's audience to address someone or something not present), as in "The Dying Whale" (p. 310) and "The Candles" (p. 321). It is hard to believe that the passages (pp. 124T, 189B, 360B–362T) are prose, because they have all the characteristics of poetry. Observe the frequent use of *similes* and *metaphors* (direct or implied comparisons) and *alliteration* (duplication of sound in language): "like a quiet ghost" (p. 183B), "like tin kettles" (p. 235T), "ivory-tusked *Pequod* . . . gored the dark waves" (p. 189B), "interblending bubbles" and "begrimed, blistered old blacksmith" (p. 297B).

d. *Humor:* Despite the general gloom, Melville inserts humor repeatedly: Queequeg's use of a human as a cushion, "Tic-Dolly-Row" (p. 127T), old Fleece preaching to the sharks (p. 229M), the honey hunter (p. 229M), and the entire sequence with Queequeg in the Spouter Inn (Chapters III–V).

IV. *Vocabulary Study*

Diagnostic Test

1B	circumambulate	walk through	walk around	baby carriage
6B	cajoling	wheedling	refusing	tricking
10M	zephyr	harp	breeze	tornado
12M	chaos	utter confusion	strict order	troika
13M	weltering	smoothing	wallowing	giving birth
20M	farrago	jumble	consternation	unity
28M	comely	hideous	handsome	prompt
37T	felled	dropped	chopped down	erected
48B	parricide	poison	murder of father	fencing move
58T	dyspeptic	crying	near-sighted	suffering indigestion
67T	punctilious	pointed	careless	precise
78T	acquiesce	agree	watery	reject
84T	anomalously	normally	abnormally	namely
94B	apoplexy	revaluation	stroke	relaxation

103M	heterogeneously	variedly	clearly	similarly
117T	lay	Hawaiian garland	ballad	music
124M	redundant	succinct	repetitious	loud
133M	countenance	body	emotion	face
147B	pagoda	Chinese temple	Venetian boat	South Sea island
154T	magniloquent	taciturn	extraordinary	pompous
164T	corporeal	spiritual	bodily	lower
165T	evanescent	fleeting	permanent	perfume
174B	descried	ignored	discerned	cried out
187T	mundane	workaday	worldly	heavenly
199M	denizens	numbers	inhabitants	corpses
209T	argosy	large ship	canoe	false doctrine
219M	unctuous	solitary	greasy	dry
224B	dexterously	deftly	awkwardly	unsinister
234M	spasmodically	calmly	intermittently	sarcastically
240M	ponderosity	weightiness	thoughtfulness	lightness
242M	armada	war fleet	ship	rodent
257T	embonpoint	leanness	plumpness	place of departure
261T	investiture	rigidity	throwing off	conferring of office
263T	misanthrope	benefactor	hater of mankind	seer
265M	contingency	possibility	end	doubt
272T	facetious	serious	joking	untrue
276M	primogeniture	first-rate	inheritance	law of first born
280T	stolidity	impassivity	hysteria	gaiety
296M	somnambulism	sleepwalking	perceptiveness	navigation
305B	vernal	of summer	of winter	of spring
317B	doxology	pharmacy	whaling lore	hymn
328M	vicissitude	sudden change	principle	quietness
340T	bodings	warnings	assurances	lodgings
343B	arrant	good	evil	guarantee
356M	incommodiously	crampedly	roomily	happily
367T	pennons	flags	tools	feathers
379M	billows	fans	bolsters	waves
383B	immutably	permanently	dumbly	changeably
391M	pinioned	feathered	freed	bound
397M	vortex	whirlpool	keel	supreme crisis

Answers

circumambulate-walk around, *cajoling*-wheedling, *zephyr*-breeze, *chaos*-utter confusion, *weltering*-wallowing, *farrago*-jumble, *comely*-handsome, *felled*-chopped down, *parricide*-murder of father, *dyspeptic*-suffering indigestion, *punctilious*-precise, *acquiesce*-agree, *anomalously*-abnormally, *apoplexy*-stroke, *heterogeneously*-variedly, *lay*-ballad, *redundant*-repetitious, *countenance*-face, *pagoda*-Chinese temple, *magniloquent*-pompous, *corporeal*-bodily, *evanescent*-fleeting, *descried*-discerned, *mundane*-workaday, *denizens*-inhabitants, *argosy*-large ship, *unctuous*-greasy, *dexterously*-deftly, *spasmodically*-intermittently, *ponderosity*-weightiness, *armada*-war fleet, *embonpoint*-plumpness, *investiture*-conferring of office, *misanthrope*-hater of mankind, *contingency*-possibility, *facetious*-joking, *primogeniture*-law of first born, *stolidity*-impassiveness, *somnambulism*-sleepwalking, *vernal*-of spring, *doxology*-hymn, *vicissitude*-sudden change, *bodings*-warnings, *arrant*-evil, *incommodiously*-crampedly, *pennons*-flags, *billows*-waves, *immutably*-permanently, *pinioned*-bound, *vortex*-whirlpool

Teaching Aids

for

MUTINY ON THE BOUNTY

A novel of adventure and excitement, of the clash of personalities in tense circumstances that led to perhaps the most famous mutiny in the history of the sea, this perennial best-seller has become a classic. The story of Captain Bligh has reached many millions in various motion picture versions, but is nowhere told better than in the gripping pages of this novel of romance and danger, justice and revenge. Important moral issues and great insight into human motivations enhance a rousing yarn of exotic and stirring action involving men caught in the whirlwind of conflict between loyalty and freedom from oppression.

I. *Objective Test*

In the space provided at the left, insert the *letter* of the correct choice from among those offered; for example:

....b....　　The authors of *Mutiny on the Bounty* are (a) Lewis and Clark (b) Nordhoff and Hall (c) Gilbert and Sullivan (d) Ashley and Aron

.... 1. The story is told by (a) Captain Bligh (b) Nordhoff and Hall in the third person (c) a retired sailor named Byam (d) the documents of a court-martial

.... 2. Captain Bligh is invited to dinner at the Byams to talk about his (a) retirement from the Navy

(b) appointment as admiral (c) court-martial
(d) adventures with Captain Cook

.... 3. Captain Bligh is recalled to active service to
(a) command a breadfruit-gathering expedition
to Tahiti (b) join Captain Cook on a voyage
(c) command the merchant ship *Britannia* (d)
replace Sir Joseph Banks

.... 4. Roger Byam is invited to join Captain Bligh because the young man (a) has experience at sea
(b) is an expert botanist (c) is rich (d) knows
languages

.... 5. Captain Bligh accuses the crew of stealing two
cheeses that had been (a) lost at sea (b) delivered to Bligh's own house (c) devoured by
rats (d) left on the dock

.... 6. Fletcher Christian is (a) young and handsome
(b) old and very experienced (c) a midship-
man (d) a ship's surgeon who drinks

.... 7. The punishment for striking an officer in His
Majesty's Navy is (a) dismissal from the service (b) death by hanging (c) two dozen
lashes (d) solitary confinement

.... 8. Midshipmen are (a) the lowest-ranking seamen
(b) apprentice officers (c) the men who work
only below decks (d) in charge of the breadfruit trees

.... 9. The food on the *Bounty* is (a) plain but plenti-
ful (b) the reason most men signed up (c) as
bad as anywhere else in the navy (d) worse
than elsewhere

.... 10. "Our seamen understand kindness as well as
they understand Greek" is the opinion of (a)
Old Bacchus, the surgeon (b) Roger Byam, the
midshipman (c) Captain Bligh (d) Thomas
Burkitt, able seaman

.... 11. After repeated insults, Fryer and Christian (a)
refuse to talk to Bligh (b) decide to plot revenge (c) ask Bligh to relent (d) quit the
captain's mess

.... 12. Purcell the carpenter is put in irons for (a) arguing with Captain Bligh (b) cutting down trees that are too large for use (c) stealing food (d) drinking

.... 13. At Tahiti, the *Bounty* is greeted with (a) resistance by savages (b) a plague of scurvy (c) friendly natives (d) a Spanish ship from Peru

.... 14. Hitihiti is (a) a local taboo (b) the Tahitian king (c) the man who murdered Captain Cook (d) lied to by Captain Bligh

.... 15. Breadfruit trees have to be taken aboard because (a) they cannot be propagated by seeds (b) Captain Bligh orders it (c) the natives threaten to destroy them (d) they have already been uprooted

.... 16. The *Bounty* is nearly wrecked by (a) Tehani, a dancing girl (b) Hayward's friend Moana (c) Hitihiti's guards (d) Christian's beloved Maimiti

.... 17. The Friendly Islands had been named by (a) Bligh on a previous voyage (b) Byam, translating the native words (c) Captain Cook (d) the natives

.... 18. Captain Bligh reduces consumption of water on the *Bounty* by (a) throwing some plants overboard (b) selling it for several coconuts (c) making it unpalatable with quinine (d) making men climb to the main top to get it

.... 19. Byam first learns of the mutiny when (a) he is asked by Christian to join (b) he is asked by Quintal for advice (c) Tinkler reveals the plan (d) he is awakened to find it in progress

.... 20. The nineteen men shoved off in a launch by the mutineers (a) are handpicked by Bligh (b) are given guns to defend themselves (c) include Churchill and William Brown (d) are given some food but no hopes for safety

.... 21. "Had Bligh not goaded his junior officer beyond endurance, no other man on the ship would have raised the cry of mutiny" is (a)

Churchill's theory (b) Byam's explanation (c) the finding of the court-martial (d) the final confession of Fletcher Christian

.... 22. Byam is happy with Tehani, but is (a) forced to leave to defend Bligh (b) arrested by Captain Edwards of H.M.S. *Pandora* (c) tracked down by Sir Joseph Banks (d) captured by Norton and Nelson

.... 23. Aboard the *Gorgon,* Byam learns that (a) Fletcher Christian has been located (b) Captain Bligh has not accused him (c) Bligh has written an accusing letter (d) Tinkler wants to testify

.... 24. Byam thinks that Hayward's testimony at the trial is (a) totally irrelevant (b) incomplete but fair (c) relatively unimportant (d) deliberately malicious

.... 25. Byam is (a) found innocent and retired from the navy (b) found guilty and hanged (c) found guilty but escapes (d) saved by further evidence in his behalf

Answers

1-c, 2-d, 3-a, 4-d, 5-b, 6-a, 7-c, 8-b, 9-d, 10-c, 11-d, 12-a, 13-c, 14-d, 15-a, 16-b, 17-c, 18-d, 19-d, 20-d, 21-b, 22-b, 23-c, 24-d, 25-a.

II. *Alternate Objective Tests*

A. Matching

Before each number in the column on the left, write the *letter* of the item in the column on the right that matches:

.... 1. coconuts and insults   a. the ship's surgeon
.... 2. Old Bacchus   b. Captain Edwards
.... 3. Churchill   c. William Purcell
.... 4. account book signature   d. in the launch with Bligh

.... 5. the *Gorgon*   e. Captain Montague
.... 6. the *Pandora*   f. Tehani's uncle
.... 7. Peckover   g. in on the mutiny
.... 8. Lord Hood   h. Dr. Hamilton
.... 9. Sir Joseph Banks   i. Tinkler's theory
...... 10. Tuahu   j. Fryer
                                        k. all condemned to
                                           death
                                        l. presiding at the court-
                                           martial
                                        m. "man of science"
                                        n. breadfruit idea origi-
                                           nally his

Answers

1-i, 2-a, 3-g, 4-j, 5-e, 6-b, 7-d, 8-l, 9-n, 10-f

B. Fill-ins

From the column on the right, select the item that best completes each statement below, and write it in the space provided:

1. During his visit to Captain Courtney, Bligh witnesses a (an) _____.

2. Mills throws shark meat into the face of _____.

3. Hitihiti knows a little English because he had sailed with _____.

4. Christian's beloved is _____.

5. The reaction by _____ to Christian's mutiny is that it "means the ruin of everything."

6. On the appeal of _____, Muspratt receives a pardon.

7. Byam and _____ are too late to board the launch.

Maimiti
his daughter
Morrison
court-martial
John Fryer
Tautira
flogging
Sir Joseph
  Banks
Thompson
Captain Cook
One Tree Hill
Lord Hood
Samuel

8. Vehiatua approves the marriage of Tehani, provided she stays in _____.
9. Churchill is murdered by _____.
10. The lookout near Hitihiti's house is called _____.
11. Byam asserts that _____ "can corroborate every word of my testimony."
12. Stewart's wife is a native girl called _____.
13. Byam mistakenly thinks that the place to look for Christian and the mutineers is _____.
14. Byam finds peace of mind at the ancestral estate in _____.
15. At the end, Byam decides not to reveal his identity to _____.

Withycombe
Peggy
Tuahu
Captain Bligh
Pitcairn
Rarotonga
Tinkler

Answers

1-flogging, 2-Samuel, 3-Captain Cook, 4-Maimiti, 5-John Fryer, 6-Lord Hood, 7-Morrison, 8-Tautira, 9-Thompson, 10-One Tree Hill, 11-Tinkler, 12-Peggy, 13-Rarotonga, 14-Withycombe, 15-his daughter

III. *Ideas for Written or Oral Book Reports or Class Discussions*

1. Two important structural techniques are *point of view* and *narrative sequence*, terms that apply to the way in which the reader is presented with the materials of a story. In an historical novel, such as *Mutiny on the Bounty*, the easiest way to tell the story is chronologically. But *Mutiny on the Bounty* does not begin with the sailing of the ship for Tahiti or even with Captain Bligh's being appointed to command the expedition. It begins with Roger Byam in old age. What is gained by having Roger at "three-and-seventy years" look back on his forty years at sea and philosophize about "the British" before he arrives

at Sir Joseph Banks's letter and Bligh's appearance all those years ago? What do we know of both Byam and Bligh as they were before they first met? What does this add to the story? Why are certain periods of time passed over in the story? What is the purpose of attaching an Epilogue? Most important, why is the story told from the perspective of Roger Byam? He is not really an historical character; the *Bounty* actually had only two midshipmen (Thomas Hayward and John Hallett) and three acting midshipmen (George Stewart, Peter Haywood, and Edward Young), young boys whose families Bligh knew and whom he was persuaded to take along. Why did Nordhoff and Hall invent the character of Roger Byam (based upon Peter Haywood, who is therefore omitted)? What does his presence as narrator add to the book? What limitations are involved in telling the story through him, rather than from the more impersonal, omniscient, third-person point of view?

2. Another common and useful technique in narration is *foreshadowing,* a device by which the authors hint at coming events and their outcomes. Chapter One ends with Byam's hearing from Sir Joseph Banks that "Discipline's the thing!" (p. 13T) and adding, "I was destined to ponder over them deeply, and sometimes bitterly, before we met again." To what extent does Banks's advice prepare us for what is to follow? To what extent is discipline the key to all that goes on? In Chapter Two ("Sea Law"), for instance, what events and reactions from Captain Bligh foreshadow his later actions? Why is it useful for the authors to plant expectations in the mind of the reader? How do they do it? Find other examples of foreshadowing throughout the story. To what extent are we prepared for the mutiny? for Christian's subsequent actions? for Bligh's survival of the terrible 3600-mile ordeal in the small boat? for Byam's eventual trial with other "mutineers"? for the outcome of the trial? for Chapter Twenty-Five ("Tinkler")? and for the conclusion of the story in the Epilogue?

3. Of course, the key to all the action is the character of Captain Bligh, who in real life had other troubles at sea

and in New South Wales (of which he was appointed governor) and other court-martials of his own. Before he died of cancer at the age of sixty-three, William Bligh survived not only the mutiny on the *Bounty* (which stuck him thereafter with the nickname of "Old Breadfruit") but other arguments and setbacks, although he eventually became a Rear-Admiral. When we first meet him, he is Lieutenant Bligh, but deep within him are the seeds of his tragedy. Where, early in the story, do you see evidences of the character traits that are to precipitate his troubles? How, later on, do circumstances act upon these traits to produce trouble? To what extent is he the victim of other people? of himself? Cite references to the text as evidence for your conclusions. What are some of the theories about the causes of the mutiny expressed by the characters in the book? How much blame is to be placed upon the demands of Bligh's command, the naval regulations of his time, the tensions created by crew and circumstances? What are Captain Bligh's major mistakes? If you court-martialed Bligh, what is your case for the Crown? your case for the defense? Arrive at a verdict, and defend your position on the question of whether or not Captain Bligh's own weaknesses and errors led to the mutiny on the *Bounty*.

4. The ancient Greeks used to speak of the *agon* (struggle, akin to our word *agony*) between the conflicting characters in a tragedy, the *protagonist* and the *antagonist*. In our story, the protagonist (main character) is Bligh. The antagonist opposed to him turns out to be Fletcher Christian. Look at Tinkler's speeches (p. 354) about how the mutiny occurred. To what extent do you accept his explanations? If Christian had not been "goaded . . . to desperation" would anyone else have led a mutiny on the *Bounty* over coconuts or anything else? What other possible justifications for a mutiny existed? Why should no one but Christian have made the fatal step? To what extent did character and circumstance combine to motivate him? What actions of Bligh or Christian might have avoided the confrontation? Why could neither of them escape it? What special power is added to the story by a pervading sense of inevitability? To what extent are both Bligh and Christian

more surprised at the mutiny than the reader, who is being led along by Byam and benefiting from the insights of the authors? What does this tell you about Bligh and Christian and about the roots of tragedy? How are other characters in the events drawn more or less willingly and consciously into the tragedy? How culpable, how much to blame, are they? Why do we admire Christian more than some of the others? *Mutiny on the Bounty* is part of a trilogy, though fully complete in itself. In *Pitcairn's Island* the authors go deep into the fate of Christian and his mutineers as they hide away on a remote island, fearful of the wrath of Bligh and the whole Establishment behind him. From what you know of Christian's character and that of his fellows, as seen in *Mutiny on the Bounty,* what would you guess their life would be like under Christian's leadership on Pitcairn's Island?

5. The idyllic life on the easy-going South Sea islands stands in sharp contrast to the hard life of sailors at sea (especially under the tyrant Bligh). How does the sojourn on Tahiti, while the ship is loaded with breadfruit trees, not only contrast with early and later episodes at sea but also help to explain the subsequent tensions that erupt into mutiny? What other South Sea episodes exist in the book? What purpose do they have other than chronicling events that we must know? What do they add to the exotic appeal of *Mutiny on the Bounty?* Both authors themselves lived in Tahiti, escaping the unpleasantness of the modern world after active, even heroic, careers during World War I, and they wrote about it in other works as a paradise. Where in *Mutiny on the Bounty,* especially in the life of the fictional character Byam, with whom both authors identify to a limited extent, do the love of Nordhoff and Hall for this kind of life and their respect for the peoples of such distant islands come shining through?

6. Even exotic settings (combined with detailed knowledge of life at sea in the age of sailing ships), even a clash between two such colorful characters as Bligh and Christian, cannot make a whole book. The settings and the ships must be populated with more or less minor characters who influence the lives of the central characters, in turn are in-

fluenced by them, and create the world in which the whole narrative moves. Select a few of the "good guys" and compare and contrast them with an equal number of "bad guys." Compare and contrast selected Englishmen and women with native characters. Which do you think come off better in the comparison? How have the authors achieved this? Why do they attempt it? What does it add to the book? Which characters other than Bligh and Christian remain most vivid? Why? What techniques do the authors use to make you see and sympathize with people who have only a lesser part to play in the action? If you have seen one of the film versions of *Mutiny on the Bounty,* discuss how close the casting directors came to realizing your own ideas about the appearances of some minor characters. If you have not seen a film version, suppose that you are casting for one among well-known actors. Whom would you choose for which parts—and why?

7. *Mutiny on the Bounty* became a best-seller and then a classic because it added serious undertones and significant insights into human behavior to entertainment and undeniable box-office appeal, not just at a distant time and in distant places but here and now. The authors brought history to life and then went a step farther to make it meaningful and accessible to all sorts of modern readers. Their deep understanding of human nature flashes out everywhere in the book. The reader says, even of characters he has just met or only glimpsed, "Yes, that's what they would do." The characters are credible, alive. This comes from being able to explain their natures, their motivations, to go beyond sketching the surfaces. Take Roger Byam, for example. By the time you finish the book, you feel you know him well. How do the authors create this effect? You even understand the thinking of natives of Tahiti and other unfamiliar cultures. Explain how we are given insights into their value systems, their ways of looking at things, their views of life. If you had been Byam and, after many years, had finally met your daughter and granddaughter, what would you have done about the problem of identifying yourself? Explain.

8. Critics tend to give best-selling novelists, especially

historical novelists, a hard time when it comes to discussion of literary style. Still, the worst that any of them said of Nordhoff and Hall was that they were workmanlike in their writing—if not inspired, at least entertaining, straightforward, and readable. To what extent is the style of the book affected by the fact that it is presented through Roger Byam, an old man walking through a "graveyard of memories" (p. 372M)? Cite examples of how this old sailor peppers his talk with nautical language. Where do you see evidence throughout the book of his educational background, his interest in philosophy, his fascination with languages? Why do the authors attempt to "localize" the story by affecting an eighteenth-century diction or rhetoric? (Find words and phrases that sound old-fashioned.) Where do the authors produce the most striking examples of descriptions of physical settings? of descriptions of people's personalities? Choose a particularly exciting scene, and show how it attains its effect through the pace of description, through the use of dialogue, or through some other striking means.

9. Every popular novel—or almost every one—has got to have romance, which means to most people one or more love affairs. How are certain characters given another dimension by reference to the women they leave behind as they go on this voyage? How effectively do the authors handle those characters who find love in the romantic atmosphere of the South Seas? Which love story do you think adds most to the appeal of this novel? Why? Comment on the extent to which you think the way romance is handled seems dated to the modern reader.

10. Critics say that novels are of two principal kinds: Either they are purely imaginative works that entertain with verisimilitude (lifelike qualities) and human interest, imitating life *(mimetic)* but not really commenting on it— or they are designed to teach us something theoretical or practical (that is, they are *didactic*) or to convey a message or preach a moral. Explain whether *Mutiny on the Bounty* is mimetic, didactic, or a combination of them both. If it does teach us something about human nature, rather than merely portraying it, by what means does it

convey a philosophy of life, give us a moral, or instruct us in ways that will alter our values and increase our judgment? In your reply, make specific references to Bligh (before the mutiny and later, pp. 366–367), Christian (before and after the mutiny), Byam, and the natives.

IV. *Vocabulary Study*

Diagnostic Test

1M	averse	opposed	poetic	agreeing
3B	enigmatical	clear	puzzling	dark
11T	florid	pale	flowery	ruddy
14B	pandemonium	calm	wild disorder	apathy
17M	equine	horselike	even	steep
28M	taciturn	wordy	of few words	loud
33M	onerous	light	single	burdensome
39M	obsequiously	gruffly	fawningly	forcibly
43T	fastidiously	daintily	roughly	carelessly
50M	mollify	annoy	coddle	pacify
56B	arbitrary	gentle	despotic	judicious
60B	labyrinth	maze	path	temple
67B	carousing	circling	drifting	partying
73M	deferentially	curtly	respectfully	delayingly
79T	meticulous	precise	sloppy	argumentative
90M	reticent	pushy	careful	shy
104M	congenial	nasty	related	pleasant
113B	malicious	cooperative	spiteful	ill
123B	incredulity	applause	inquiry	disbelief
135M	imprecations	prayers	curses	questions
145M	turbulent	disorderly	patterned	muddy
152T	formidable	handsome	threatening	smiling
161M	progeny	miracle	offspring	progress
166M	extenuate	excuse	sting	invent
175M	prodigious	tiny	huge	tight
181B	desecration	sanctification	defilement	release
193M	avarice	generosity	stupidity	greed
213M	implicated	refused	involved	delivered
224M	connivance	passive consent	open defiance	refusal
230M	manacles	pygmies	handcuffs	fish
237M	squalls	calms	birds	storms
243M	tortuous	straight	twisting	punishing

252B allay	inflame	mix	soothe
261M respite	hate	pressure	relief
271B deposition	formal statement	passing remark	joke
281B lethargy	spirit	sluggishness	glove
285B refuted	disproved	corroborated	defended
303T intercession	accusation	plea for	vacation
313M scrupulously	clumsily	vengefully	conscientiously
317B thwarted	aided	prevented	bullied
326T clemency	mercy	ferocity	sternness
326B perceptibly	dully	noticeably	covertly
335T irrevocable	changeable	rude	unalterable
335T recompense	rejection	repayment	money
335T acquiescence	agreement	argument	secret
336M reprieve	sentence	pardon	execution
343T diversion	attraction	distraction	subtraction
353M unimpaired	weakened	fixed	undamaged
363M portico	official	covered walk	window
369M apathetically	indifferently	keenly	sadly

Answers

averse-opposed, *enigmatical*-puzzling, *florid*-ruddy, *pandemonium*-wild disorder, *equine*-horselike, *taciturn*-of few words, *onerous*-burdensome, *obsequiously*-fawningly, *fastidiously*-daintily, *mollify*-pacify, *arbitrary*-despotic, *labyrinth*-maze, *carousing*-partying, *deferentially*-respectfully, *meticulous*-precise, *reticent*-shy, *congenial*-pleasant, *malicious*-spiteful, *incredulity*-disbelief, *imprecations*-curses, *turbulent*-disorderly, *formidable*-threatening, *progeny*-offspring, *extenuate*-excuse, *prodigious*-huge, *desecration*-defilement, *avarice*-greed, *implicated*-involved, *connivance*-passive consent, *manacles*-handcuffs, *squalls*-storms, *tortuous*-twisting, *allay*-soothe, *respite*-relief, *deposition*-formal statement, *lethargy*-sluggishness, *refuted*-disproved, *intercession*-plea for, *scrupulously*-conscientiously, *thwarted*-prevented, *clemency*-mercy, *perceptibly*-noticeably, *irrevocable*-unalterable, *recompense*-repayment, *acquiescence*-agreement, *reprieve*-pardon, *diversion*-distraction, *unimpaired*-undamaged, *portico*-covered walk, *apathetically*-indifferently

Teaching Aids

for

OEDIPUS THE KING

Of the hundred or so plays written by Sophocles, *Oedipus the King* is considered his masterpiece. It has been universally praised for its ingeniously constructed plot and extraordinary insight into human motive and circumstance. In *The Interpretation of Dreams,* Sigmund Freud summarized the psychological implications: "As the poet brings the guilt of Oedipus to light by his investigation, he forces us to become aware of our own inner selves, in which the same impulses are still extant, even though they are suppressed. . . ." After more than two thousand years, the basic questions about human behavior raised in this drama are still being vigorously debated.

I. *Objective Test*

In the space provided at the left, insert the *letter* of the correct choice from among those offered; for example:

....c....   The author's name is (a) Socrates (b) Plato (c) Sophocles (d) Shakespeare

.... 1. "We sit here," the priest told Oedipus, "in (a) adoration (b) supplication (c) meditation (d) resentment"

.... 2. "I have already," Oedipus told the priest, "sent Creon to consult the (a) oracle (b) queen of Corinth (c) god of war (d) astrologers"

.... 3. Anyone who shielded the murderer, said Oedipus, would suffer (a) only exile (b) banishment and ostracism (c) banishment, ostracism, and excommunication (d) imprisonment

.... 4. When he heard what Oedipus wanted, Tiresias at first asked (a) to be sent home (b) permission to consult Creon (c) to see Jocasta (d) how the birds were flying

.... 5. Oedipus suspected that one of the conspirators in the murder of Laius was (a) Apollo (b) Tiresias (c) Antigone (d) Polynices

.... 6. Oedipus gloated that Tiresias was unable to solve the riddle of (a) the stars (b) the oracle (c) the Sphinx (d) life

.... 7. The chorus pointed out that in the Oedipus-Tiresias quarrel, "words have been spoken in anger" by (a) Tiresias (b) Oedipus (c) neither (d) both

.... 8. Creon said his innocence was obvious because (a) he had been out of the country (b) he already had power without responsibility (c) his low birth barred him from kingship (d) he could not gain popular support

.... 9. Creon hinted that a king could stay in power only if (a) he ruled well (b) he silenced all opposition (c) Tiresias agreed (d) he begot heirs

.... 10. Jocasta scolded (a) the chorus for interfering in a family quarrel (b) Tiresias (c) her brother for starting a fight (d) Oedipus and Creon for having no sense of shame

.... 11. Oedipus let Creon go free on the urging of (a) Creon (b) the chorus (c) Jocasta (d) Tiresias

.... 12. Jocasta said she could rid Oedipus' mind of fear by proving to him that (a) Laius died a natural death (b) prophets are infallible (c) prophets can be wrong (d) Laius' murderer was dead

.... 13. In telling Oedipus of how Laius died, Jocasta (a) put her husband's mind at ease (b) unwittingly disturbed him with new fears (c)

broke down (d) said Oedipus should suspect himself

.... 14. Oedipus recalled a violent encounter at a crossroads with (a) an imperious man with attendants (b) sirens (c) armed Corinthians (d) an armed king traveling alone

.... 15. If the prophecies did not come true, the chorus said, the gods would (a) punish the prophets (b) themselves be defeated (c) punish mankind (d) retract the prophecy

.... 16. Jocasta's first reaction to the news from Corinth was that it (a) verified the prophecy (b) was based on vicious rumor (c) proved prophecies are nonsense (d) vindicated her boy

.... 17. "Many a man before you," Jocasta told Oedipus, "has dreamed of (a) death on the rack (b) struggle at the crossroads (c) birds screaming (d) marriage with his mother"

.... 18. Evidence of his exposure as an infant was Oedipus' (a) thick ankles (b) branded shoulders (c) swollen wrist (d) rheumy eyes

.... 19. Intending to release Oedipus from fear that he would marry Merope, the Corinthian messenger told him (a) Merope was dead (b) Polybus was not his father (c) Merope was not nubile (d) Polybus told all

.... 20. Jocasta begged Oedipus to quit the search because (a) it was hopeless (b) his main fear was allayed (c) without saying so, she could foresee the outcome of the confrontation with the local shepherd (d) festival time was near

.... 21. Oedipus attributed Jocasta's rushing away in wild grief to her (a) shame over his mean origin (b) annoyance at being disobeyed (c) fear of being unveiled as the shepherd's mother (d) choleric nature

.... 22. To make the shepherd talk, Oedipus resorted to (a) bribery (b) threats of exile (c) torture (d) flattery

.... 23. "Let this be the last time I see you," Oedipus

said to (a) the shepherd (b) light (c) the messenger (d) Jocasta

.... 24. Oedipus found Jocasta as surely as if led by (a) a supernatural being (b) her maid (c) the scent of her perfume (d) a wild surmise

.... 25. In lines that may not be Sophocles', the chorus says we must count no man happy until he is (a) back from the war (b) married (c) blessed with children (d) dead

Answers

1-b, 2-a, 3-c, 4-a, 5-b, 6-c, 7-d, 8-b, 9-a, 10-d, 11-b, 12-c, 13-b, 14-a, 15-b, 16-c, 17-d, 18-a, 19-b, 20-c, 21-a, 22-c, 23-b, 24-a, 25-d

II. *Alternate Objective Tests*

A. Matching

Before each number in the column on the left, write the *letter* of the item in the column on the right that matches:

.... 1. olive branches
.... 2. oracle
.... 3. two-pronged goad
.... 4. riddling songs
.... 5. boy-guide
.... 6. old men
.... 7. "on equal basis"
.... 8. "child of violent pride"
.... 9. grazing land
...... 10. noose

a. Oedipus
b. Cithaeron
c. Sphinx
d. Tiresias
e. Jocasta
f. procession
g. Antigone
h. despot
i. Creon
j. Delphi
k. Laius
l. Zeus
m. chorus

Answers

1-f, 2-j, 3-k, 4-c, 5-d, 6-m, 7-i, 8-h, 9-b, 10-e

B. Fill-ins

From the column on the right, select the item that best completes each statement below, and write it in the space provided:

1. Oedipus, said the priest, must take thought for his _____.
2. Hesitating, Creon suggested he might make his report _____.
3. Oedipus wanted to hear Creon's news _____.
4. The oracle said Thebes was _____ by a murderer.
5. The chorus consisted of fifteen _____.
6. Tiresias was _____ into telling the truth.
7. An important event occurred where _____ highways meet.
8. There were _____ men in Laius' party.
9. According to a survivor, the king was killed by a group of _____.
10. Oedipus would feel cleared of responsibility if there were _____ killers.
11. The Corinthian messenger expected to be _____.
12. Oedipus referred to the condition of his _____ as "that old affliction."
13. Oedipus felt compelled to learn the truth about his _____.
14. The chorus speculated that perhaps Oedipus was born to one of the mountain _____.
15. The sherpherd was _____ into telling the truth.

tortured
defiled
three
robbers
several
rewarded
reputation
angered
five
inside
shepherds
affliction
publicly
origin
nymphs
dancers
tomorrow
tree-lined
ankles

Answers

1-reputation, 2-inside, 3-publicly, 4-defiled, 5-dancers, 6-angered, 7-three, 8-five, 9-robbers, 10-several, 11-rewarded, 12-ankles, 13-origin, 14-nymphs, 15-tortured

III. *Ideas for Written or Oral Book Reports or Class Discussions*

1. In Homer's *Odyssey,* the hero says:

> A "blameless king . . . upholds righteousness . . . the earth yields its wheat and barley, the trees are loaded with fruit, the ewes bring forth lambs, and the sea abounds with fish *by reason of his virtues,* and his people do good deeds under him."

Make a detailed comparison of this passage—which was well known to all Athenians—with the priest's speech to Oedipus (pp. 2M–3T) and the chorus's description of Thebes (pp. 11B–13B). If the typical Greek believed that Homer was right, then what hidden message is there in the long speeches cited? Do you think Oedipus gets the message? What aspects of his behavior become more explicable in light of this popular belief? In what sense could one make (or not make) such claims for a democratic regime as Homer does for a monarchy?

2. The Canadian scholar S. M. Adams says that the concluding verses of *Oedipus* (p. 108M) "are perhaps the addition of an actor or a *choregus* who felt the need of something for the chorus to chant as they filed out of the orchestra." Note that Dr. Knox, translator of the version we are studying, takes much the same view (p. 108T). But Adams goes on to say that "the lines are not unwelcome, for they express the fall of transient greatness and the familiar theme of life's uncertainty. Nothing could illustrate these better than the fate of Oedipus. . . ." Reread the end of the play, first with this final "Citizens" chorus, then

without it. What advantages and disadvantages do you see in ending the play with Creon's speech (p. 107B)? What advantages would there be in having the chorus file out in silence? If you were going to produce the Knox version, what reasons would influence your decision about whether to include or exclude the disputed chorus?

3. Even among psychoanalysts, the so-called Oedipus complex is a controversial question. It might be valuable here, in connection with the play that gave the "complex" its name, to review three hypotheses about the nature of the "Oedipal situation."

Here is a summary of Freud's position as given in a standard text, *Childhood and Adolescence,* by L. J. Stone and Joseph Church:

> The term "Oedipus complex" comes from the Greek myth of King Oedipus, who unwittingly, but in fulfillment of an old prophecy, killed his father and married his mother. Analogously, the small boy is seen as falling in love with his mother and turning against his father as a rival for her affections. Naturally, these strivings are opposed by the realities of the situation, by the child's sense of danger in competing with an all-powerful father, and by contradictory impulses of affection for the father and resentment (as when she disciplines him) against the mother. The normal outcome of this (in Freud's view) universal *conflict* of opposing forces is to align and identify oneself with the father, submerging (i.e., *repressing*) the unacceptable wishes. . . . In regard to turning against the parents, although adults were long loath to accept the fact, children are *ambivalent* about their parents; that is, they blend or alternate hostility with affection. It likewise seems to be true, as Freud proposed, that children feel guilty about their anger and conceal or deny it.

Erich Fromm, regarded as one of our foremost living psychoanalysts, claims that the Oedipus "myth has to be understood not as a symbol of the incestuous tie between mother and son, but as the rebellion of the son against the authority of the father in the patriarchal family; and that the marriage of Oedipus and Jocasta is only a secondary element, only one of the symbols of the son's victory, who takes over his father's place and with it all his privileges."

Another distinguished psychoanalyst, Harry Stack Sullivan, also sees the Oedipal situation differently from Freud. According to Patrick Mullahy, in his *Oedipus: Myth and Complex:*

> Sullivan attaches fundamental importance to the role of the parents, especially the mother or her surrogate in infancy and childhood. But this role is not a sexual one, even in the wide sense in which Freud conceives sexuality. The feeling of familiarity which a parent has toward his or her child of the same sex is said to lead to an authoritarian attitude, which, of course, produces resentment and hostility in the child. On the other hand, because of the difference in sex, leading to a sense of strangeness, the parent treats his or her child of the opposite sex with more consideration. Why? In the first case, the parent thinks that he is justified in dictating to someone who seems to be like himself, while in the latter case the feeling of strangeness deprives him of the notion that he is peculiarly fitted to run the child's life. Hence parents tend to treat their children of the opposite sex, so to speak, "with kid gloves." In this case, the freedom or relative freedom from pressure by the parent of the other sex results, at least often, in a feeling of greater affection and attraction by the child for him.

Apply each of these explanations of conflict between generations to *Oedipus the King*. Explain in detail which seems most natural to you as a description of what might have happened between Oedipus and the father- and mother-figures in his life. From your own observation of parent-child relations, which theory—Freud's, Fromm's, or Sullivan's—seems most accurate? Why? Can you see—and describe—some combination of these that would make better sense to you?

4. Review your impressions of the women in the play: (a) consider first the passages about goddesses, pp. 12T, 12B, 13M, 80T; (b) then read between the lines to see what images you can conjure up of Antigone and Ismene, pp. 103M–105B; (c) study carefully what Oedipus has to say about Merope, pp. 55B–56M, 67M–69M; (d) and finally consolidate your impression of Jocasta, rereading especially pp. 16T, 39M–39B, 43B–45T, 47M–55M, 58M–59B, 62T, 63T–68M, 76B–79M, 87B–88B, 92M–93B, 100T, 103T.

Now why, do you imagine, was the person who solved the riddle of the Sphinx offered the crown *and the hand of the dowager-queen?* Why is it that when Oedipus says (p. 10B), "Summon the people of Thebes here," only men appear? How do you reconcile this with your conclusions about queens and goddesses? about the daughters compared with the sons (p. 103M)?

Formulate an overall statement that sums up "the position of women in ancient Greek society as seen by Sophocles."

5. Poets use comparisons and analogies to enhance their descriptions. For example, Oedipus calls Tiresias "our shield" (p. 19M). Tiresias is not *literally,* of course, a shield, but is being likened to a shield, which one can place in front of one as a protection. By speaking *figuratively,* Oedipus is expressing his feelings more effectively than if he had said, "You are our protector." A figure of speech is more arresting; it forces us to think out the description in our own way, with our own emotional as well as intellectual cues.

Here is a partial list of figures of speech that Sophocles uses in *Oedipus.*

the city is like a ship (p. 2B)
a ship abandoned (p. 4T)
sword of thought (p. 12M)
people like winged birds (p. 12M)

our shield (p. 19M)
despot is . . . child (p. 60M)
like passengers (p. 62M)
like a towered wall (p. 90T)
harbor sheltered (p. 90B)
sea of dreadful trouble (p. 108M).

In each case, restate the idea *literally* according to the way it is developed in context; then spell out the comparison (why, for example, the despot is called the *child* of pride); describe the image that is conjured up; then describe the emotion that the poet is attempting to transfer.

Notice that most of the images are drawn from seamanship. Why is this such an apt source of figures for Sophocles? Show how sea analogies, used in different scenes, help establish connections between those scenes.

6. To whom is the chorus referring when they ask Zeus to "destroy him" (p. 13M) and Dionysus to "fight the god who is without honor among all other gods" (p. 13B)? How can you explain the fact that a pious Greek chorus, in a play performed as a religious ceremony, could make such a statement? What does it say about the Athenian character that this particular deity was freely disparaged by writers, while in Sparta he was especially honored?

7. In his *Poetics,* Aristotle says: "Reversal of the situation is a change by which the action veers around to its opposite, subject always to our rule of probability or necessity. Thus in *Oedipus* the messenger comes to cheer Oedipus and free him from alarms about his mother, but by revealing who Oedipus is, he produces the opposite effect." Find in *Oedipus* another example of reversal. Show how this example fits Aristotle's specifications. Demonstrate the relationship between reversal and irony.

8. Jocasta says (p. 67B) that ". . . life is governed by the operations of chance. Nothing can be clearly foreseen. The best way to live is by hit and miss. . . ." She was, of course, trying to free Oedipus from his fears of oracles and prophecies. Nowadays modern religions do not advocate

prophecy. Explain whether (and why) this doctrine of chance would be acceptable or unacceptable to a *religious* thinker today? Explain how a doctrine of chance can or cannot be reconciled with a *scientific* outlook.

9. St. Augustine said: ". . . the question that torments the greater part of mankind [is] how these two things can fail to be contrary and opposed, that God should have foreknowledge of all things to come and that we should sin, not by necessity, but by our own free will." Explain the torment and the mystery of *Oedipus* in light of this paradox. Explain whether (and why), in your opinion, divine foreknowledge and human free will can coexist.

10. Given the character of Oedipus, as you know him, consider fully (and explain in detail) the psychological possibilities in his adopting a plan of action something like this:

a. *It is predicted that I will kill my father; if I stay out of all fights, I am safe.*

b. *It is predicted that I will marry my mother; therefore, I shall never marry anyone except someone born after I was born.*

IV. *Vocabulary Study*

Diagnostic Test

1B supplication	entreaty	silence	defiance
2M resignation	delight	loss	passive acceptance
2B prophetic	revealing	concealing	pushing
2B blight	construction	destruction	instruction
3M tribute	official	gift	forced payment
4B oracle	divine pronouncement	relief	prayer
5M laurel	praise	annual	evergreen foliage
7T atone	hurt anew	make amends	let down
7T rites	ceremonies	liberties	amendments

10M	solicitude	contempt	judgment	concern
11M	unison	discord	harmony	solo
14M	indictment	accusation	exoneration	interdiction
15T	communion	conflict	sharing	breakfast
21B	scoundrel	peddler	musician	rascal
23M	defilement	petition	nutrition	pollution
25M	impunity	punishment	safety	liability
25B	reproaches	rebukes	departures	praises
26B	intriguing	strange	plotting	helpful
26B	quack	expert	feather	faker
27M	witch-hunting	broomstick	divining	seeking scapegoats
28B	equate	divide	make equal	subtract
30T	obscurities	revelations	mysteries	clarifications
31T	proclamations	orders	songs	public announcements
31M	revelation	concealment	disclosure	upheaval
41T	conspired	schemed	hoped	showed
41M	fancy	decision	whim	intricacy
41B	counterplot	table	rival scheme	confession
45M	concession	goblet	yielding	refusal
45M	stature	infamy	length	standing
46T	hearsay	rumor	fact	speech
46B	compassion	sympathy	violence	hatred
50T	endowed	cursed	gifted	lowered
56M	calamitous	salutary	valuable	disastrous
56M	beget	give birth to	send away	take hold
56B	herald	ruler	messenger	soldier
57T	goad	animal	prod	rope
60M	despot	tinker	tyrant	legislator
61T	overbearing	bullying	humble	true
62T	distracted	confused	focused	oriented
74M	affliction	loss	disease	desire
79M	lineage	drawing	march	ancestry
90T	riddling	puzzling	driving	lending
90B	furrows	grooves	farms	caves
91M	involuntary	forthcoming	deliberate	unintentional
92B	monstrous	hideous	comely	elongated
93T	supernatural	ordinary	miraculous	puzzling
99T	impious	devout	tricky	not devout
99M	isolated	early	cut off	attended
100T	incestuous	inbred	pure	open
104B	intervened	sang	interfered	removed

Answers

supplication-entreaty, *resignation*-passive acceptance, *prophetic*-revealing, *blight*-destruction, *tribute*-forced payment, *oracle*-divine pronouncement, *laurel*-evergreen foliage, *atone*-make amends, *rites*-ceremonies, *solicitude*-concern, *unison*-harmony, *indictment*-accusation, *communion*-sharing, *scoundrel*-rascal, *defilement*-pollution, *impunity*-safety, *reproaches*-rebukes, *intriguing*-plotting, *quack*-faker, *witch-hunting*-seeking scapegoats, *equate*-make equal, *obscurities*-mysteries, *proclamations*-public announcements, *revelation*-disclosure, *conspired*-schemed, *fancy*-whim, *counterplot*-rival scheme, *concession-yielding*, *stature*-standings, *hearsay*-rumor, *compassion*-sympathy, *endowed*-gifted, *calamitous*-disastrous, *beget*-give birth to, *herald*-messenger, *goad*-prod, *despot*-tyrant, *overbearing*-bullying, *distracted*-confused, *affliction*-disease, *lineage*-ancestry, *riddling*-puzzling, *furrows*-grooves, *involuntary*-unintentional, *monstrous*-hideous, *supernatural*-miraculous, *impious*-not devout, *isolated*-cut off, *incestuous*-inbred, *intervened*-interfered

Teaching Aids

for

OF HUMAN BONDAGE

She used him . . . she rejected and despised him . . . and still he came back for more! Mildred was his woman, and when she needed him, Philip was there, even while hating himself for his weakness. This is the story of a sensitive young man who was a slave to an unreasoning passion. Written by a master storyteller at the peak of his powers, the novel has become a classic of modern literature. As the critic Godfrey Winn said, *"Of Human Bondage* is not only Somerset Maugham's best work but also one of the few books written during the present century to which the epithet *great* can be truly applied."

I. *Objective Test*

In the space provided at the left, insert the *letter* of the correct choice from among those offered; for example:

....b....   The author of this book is (a) Shaw (b) Maugham (c) Conrad

.... 1. Philip Carey's father had been a (a) lawyer (b) physician (c) painter

.... 2. William Carey, with whom Philip went to live after his mother's death, was his (a) grandfather (b) mother's brother (c) father's brother

.... 3. Aunt Louisa's attitude toward Philip may best be designated as one of (a) affection (b) hatred (c) indifference

.... 4. At King's School in Tercanbury, Philip distinguished himself most (a) in the school's social affairs (b) as an athlete (c) as a student

.... 5. Young Philip was affected very deeply when his earnest prayers to God did not (a) free him from the control of William Carey (b) release him from school at Tercanbury (c) cure him of his clubfoot

.... 6. William Carey had hoped that Philip would enter Oxford to study (a) for the ministry (b) medicine (c) art

.... 7. Philip decided to (a) quit Tercanbury before graduating and enter an accountant's office (b) finish his courses at school and then go on to Oxford (c) finish his courses at school and then go to Germany

.... 8. Philip was attracted by Hayward's (a) fascinating conversation (b) record of accomplishments (c) bold behavior with the ladies

.... 9. Emily Wilkinson impressed Philip with her (a) remarkable beauty (b) hunger for a man's love (c) profound learning

.... 10. Articled as a clerk in an accountant's office, Philip soon found that (a) he hated the work (b) the work was exactly what he had been seeking (c) he could function comfortably as a businessman and after hours attend to his real interests

.... 11. At the studio in Paris where he was studying painting, Philip discovered (a) what a vast number of people are gifted with artistic talent (b) how the sympathetic comment of a critic can help a student achieve artistic stature (c) how frustrating, even tragic, it could be for people without talent to insist on becoming creative artists

.... 12. Philip was profoundly moved by Fanny Price's (a) love for him (b) artistic genius (c) suicide

.... 13. Philip decided to abandon the career of painter

because (a) his aunt Louisa died suddenly
(b) Foinet told him frankly how meager his
talent was (c) he was depressed by the life
among the artists of the Latin Quarter

.... 14. When Philip finally decided to study medicine,
he registered at (a) Oxford University (b) St.
Luke's Hospital (c) the University of Heidelberg

.... 15. When Philip first met Mildred Rogers, she was
a (a) waitress (b) model (c) singer

.... 16. Upon first becoming acquainted with Mildred,
Philip found her (a) extraordinarily beautiful
(b) physically unattractive (c) full of grace
and charm

.... 17. Mildred Rogers was (a) highly cultured (b) a
witty and brilliant conversationalist (c) an ignorant and vulgar woman

.... 18. Philip's love for Mildred (a) persisted despite
her lack of consideration (b) was deepened by
her strong affection (c) was aided by the
friendly interest of Miller

.... 19. The father of Mildred's child was (a) Miller
(b) Griffiths (c) Philip

.... 20. Thorpe Athelny's outstanding characteristic was
his (a) cruelty (b) pessimism (c) vitality

.... 21. During one longish separation from Mildred,
Philip developed a very strong affection for (a)
Emily Wilkinson (b) Norah Nesbit (c) Ruth
Chalice

.... 22. Philip was convinced at last that he would do
well as a doctor when he (a) received his
medical degree with honors (b) satisfied the
cantankerous Dr. South (c) cured Athelny's
jaundice

.... 23. Philip became financially desperate when he
(a) lost almost all his money on the stock
market (b) gave away most of his money to
Mildred (c) finally had to pay for all his medical courses

.... 24. The Athelnys used to spend their summers (a)

sailing on their yacht (b) picking hops in the country (c) visiting a different foreign country each year

.... 25. Philip finally married (a) Norah Nesbit (b) Mildred Rogers (c) Sally Athelny

Answers

1-b, 2-c, 3-a, 4-c, 5-c, 6-a, 7-c, 8-a, 9-b, 10-a, 11-c, 12-c, 13-b, 14-b, 15-a, 16-b, 17-c, 18-a, 19-a, 20-c, 21-b, 22-b, 23-a, 24-b, 25-c

II. *Alternate Objective Tests*

A. Matching

Before each number in the column on the left, write the *letter* of the item in the column on the right that matches:

.... 1. completely self-denying
.... 2. author of cheap romantic novels
.... 3. disillusioned painter, caustic critic
.... 4. ready to retire
.... 5. ignorant waitress
.... 6. only outwardly religious
.... 7. dominated by a clubfoot
.... 8. suicide
.... 9. irrepressible conversation-alist
...... 10. enthusiastic educator

a. Philip
b. William Carey
c. Louisa Carey
d. Mr. Perkins
e. Fanny Price
f. Thorpe Athelny
g. Foinet
h. Norah Nesbit
i. Mildred Rogers
j. Dr. South
k. Emily Wilkinson
l. Josiah Graves

Answers

1-c, 2-h, 3-g, 4-j, 5-i, 6-b, 7-a, 8-e, 9-f, 10-d

B. Fill-ins

From the column on the right, select the item that best completes each statement below, and write it in the space provided:

1. The faculty member at Tercanbury Philip admired most was _____.
2. Philip found it easier to support himself in Paris because of a gift of her life savings by _____.
3. Philip tortured himself by giving Mildred enough money to go on a trip with _____.
4. Though he really didn't love her, Philip lived with _____ as affectionately as though he were married to her.
5. Only after he died did people suddenly say that _____ had never really lived.
6. The hospital patient who had the greatest impact on Philip's life was _____.
7. With Mr. Goodworthy, the managing clerk at the accountant's office, Philip took his first look at _____.
8. The first person Philip actually made love to was _____.
9. The only one of Philip's fellow art students at Paris who actually did become an artist was _____.
10. Philip was introduced to Mildred by _____.
11. Griffiths once acted as a combination doctor, mother, and nurse when _____ was very ill.
12. Because he already had a wife and three children, _____ did not

Lawson
Griffiths
Paris
Macalister
Sally
Hayward
Mr. Perkins
Spain
Dunsford
India
Philip
Emily Wilkinson
Miller
Athelny
Mr. Turner
Rome
Norah Nesbit
Dr. South
Louisa Carey
Mildred Rogers

marry Mildred, although he had promised to.
13. Philip was induced to speculate in
stocks by _____.
14. Philip was astonished and flattered to
be offered a partnership by _____.
15. Before Philip and Sally decided to be
married, he had dreamed of traveling
through _____.

Answers

1-Mr. Perkins, 2-Louisa Carey, 3-Griffiths, 4-Norah Nesbit, 5-
Hayward, 6-Athelny, 7-Paris, 8-Emily Wilkinson, 9-Lawson, 10-
Dunsford, 11-Philip, 12-Miller, 13-Macalister, 14-Dr. South, 15-
Spain

III. Ideas for Written or Oral Book Reports or Class Discussions

1. What seems to have been Maugham's purpose in
giving Philip a clubfoot? Which aspect—if any—of Philip's
character was Maugham able to penetrate more deeply because of Philip's limp? What symbolic use does Maugham
make of the clubfoot? Which idea or concept is he
able or anxious, through the symbol of the limp, to get his
readers to understand and appreciate? On the other hand,
would you or would you not agree that the limp was incidental rather than essential to the story, and that
Maugham could have achieved all the emotional and psychological effects he did produce by creating a Philip
Carey who was physically normal? Be sure to offer ad-
equate support for your opinions.

2. In writing about the art of the novel, Maugham said
that "the creatures of the novelist's invention should be
observed with individuality, and their actions should proceed from their characters." Choose five characters from
Of Human Bondage—William Carey, Hayward, Fanny
Price, Emily Wilkinson, Griffiths, or any others that you

wish—and show that Maugham has either obeyed his own injunction and that "their actions . . . proceed from their characters," or that Maugham has strayed from his own standards and that the actions of his characters are not those that we should expect of them.

3. In the course of his development toward maturity, Philip becomes emotionally involved with a number of women—Emily Wilkinson, Norah Nesbit, Mildred Rogers, and Sally Athelny.

Justify Emily Wilkinson's inclusion in this group, or explain why you would exclude her.

Analyze the difference between Philip's feelings for Mildred and those he had for Norah and Sally.

Why would you agree or disagree with the remark that because they caused him tremendous emotional upheavals his feelings for Mildred must have been much deeper than those for Norah and Sally?

Because his relationships with Norah and Sally were generally of a serene and peaceful nature, indicate why you think his feelings for Sally were similar to—or different from—those for Norah.

4. In the middle of p. 21, Maugham says, "The feeling of apartness from others comes to most with puberty, but it is not always developed to such a degree as to make the difference between the individual and his fellows noticeable to the individual. It is such as he, as little conscious of himself as the bee in a hive, who are the lucky in life, for they have the best chance of happiness: their activities are shared by all, and their pleasures are only pleasures because they are enjoyed in common. . . ." Maugham seems to be saying in this passage that those people who most closely resemble their fellowmen and conform to the tastes and aspirations of those around them are most likely to be happy and successful in this world. What evidence does Maugham furnish in *Of Human Bondage* that this is true of his characters? What evidence do you find in *Of Human Bondage* that some, at least, of Maugham's characters actually contradict his theories: Some are happy despite their personal peculiarities, their differences from most of their fellowmen, and others are unhappy, even

though they are thorough conformists in every aspect of life? Why do you agree or disagree with Maugham about people in general? Indicate in detail whether you think the individualists or the conformists have the best chance in this world of achieving true happiness.

5. What means does Maugham employ to make us believe that the love of Philip for the worthless Mildred is credible? The answer involves not only a consideration of the skills by which an author ensnares his readers, but also a good deal of thinking about the psychology of Philip, the ways in which his mind and his emotions respond to people in general and to Mildred in particular. Quite possibly, you may be of the opinion that Philip's love for Mildred has not been made credible by Maugham. If that is so, explain your point of view in detail.

6. During nearly all of our acquaintanceship with Philip, he is going through one phase or another of his education —at Tercanbury, in Heidelberg, at the art school in Paris, at medical school, and at the hospital, not to mention what he learns from his business experiences in two different London firms, from wandering through the streets of London starving and desperate, and from his experiences as an assistant to Dr. South in Dorsetshire. In a paragraph devoted to each of these phases—the informal ones as well as the formal ones—explain how each contributed to Philip's education and maturity.

How would you criticize his formal schooling? Explain why you think he would have received a better or a worse education in the schools of today.

7. How would you explain Philip's tolerance of and affection for people at the end of the story? Is it that he has grown more sympathetic toward mankind? Or can it be that his attitude and behavior are reactions to the affection and sympathy of Thorpe and Betty and Sally Athelny for him? In what manner did Philip's experiences—his education, his jobs, his contacts with various men and women, his sojourns in Heidelberg and in Paris, his life in London, his humiliations, his sufferings—contribute to his mellowness, his ability to develop an affection for other people as well as inspire affection in them?

8. Many readers of *Of Human Bondage* are impressed with the gradual growth in maturity of Philip Carey. Do some of the other characters in the novel also grow mentally and emotionally—in any way at all? Choose any five of the principal characters in *Of Human Bondage*—the vicar, his wife, Hayward, Mildred, Norah, Griffiths, Sally, Thorpe, or any others—and prove by citing specific evidence from the book that each one did or did not undergo a significant development in maturity. Feel free to point out and prove—if this is your opinion—that certain of the characters in *Of Human Bondage* actually regressed, actually grew less mature as time went on. Your answer will be appreciated more readily if it includes an explanation of your concept of maturity.

9. Is there anything in *Of Human Bondage* that makes you realize that Somerset Maugham is writing about the period from 1885 to about 1905? If he were telling the same story today, what differences would there be in his treatment of such subjects as these:

a. the education of the young
b. the relationship between the older generation and the younger one
c. the position in society of people like Hayward, the dilettante; Thorpe Athelny, the nonconformist; Fanny Price, the failure; Lawson, the "promising" artist
d. the education and training of a doctor
e. the problem of the completely destitute person
f. the role of advertising and the status of the advertising man.

10. We are usually so deeply impressed with the effect on Philip's life of the various women he was involved with that there may be some danger of our losing sight of the men he came to know—William Carey, Perkins, Hayward, Goodworthy, Watson, Thompson, Foinet, Lawson, Miguel Ajuria, Griffiths, Dunsford, Thorpe Athelny, and Dr. South, among others. Of the men in Philip's life, which three had the greatest influence on Philip's intellectual

development? Which three exercised the greatest effect on his emotional life? Support your opinions by making specific references to the contents of the novel.

IV. *Vocabulary Study*

Diagnostic Test

5B	corpulence	gauntness	flippancy	fleshiness
8M	impelled	forced	deterred	surprised
13T	uncouth	urbane	graceful	unrefined
14T	ascetic	offensive	self-denying	indulgent
25T	tremulous	nonchalant	enormous	quivering
26T	resurrection	restoration to life	resignation to death	religious revolution
31T	choleric	diseased	hot-tempered	sedate
33B	flippancy	pertness	gravity	graciousness
35M	aridity	ardor	barrenness	enthusiasm
37M	slovenly	sloppy	imitative	meticulous
40M	vitriolic	kindly	caustic	considerate
46M	demurely	awkwardly	boldly	modestly
50T	archaic	antiquated	fashionable	novel
53M	supercilious	haughty	mysterious	humble
65B	milksop	brute	unmanly man	milkman
81T	ramshackle	tumbledown	picturesque	brand new
94M	bilious	healthful	billowy	sickly
98M	straitened	extended	confined	improved
99B	artifice	adventure	epigram	trick
108T	expostulated	argued	proceeded	agreed
110M	penury	wealth	poverty	imprisonment
113T	subsistence	reputation	respect	livelihood
117M	inept	inappropriate	unlikely	justified
120M	forbearance	patience	anger	strength
125T	rankled	glanced off	sparkled	festered
130B	vivacity	gloom	liveliness	emptiness
141T	obsequious	arrogant	servile	indifferent
156M	blackguard	villain	hero	stranger
160M	remonstrate	protest	show	defend
163M	loquacity	silence	informality	talkativeness
175B	callousness	sensitivity	insensibility	concern
199M	austere	beautiful	stern	generous

204T	querulous	complaining	curious	unpleasant
221B	placidly	fretfully	stupidly	peacefully
226M	philistine	idealist	materialist	fanatic
229T	facetious	humorous	sad	exact
236T	pique	gratitude	favor	resentment
236T	incessantly	occasionally	unceasingly	quietly
239T	invective	statistics	denunciation	praise
239T	opprobrious	shameful	flattering	unusual
240M	jibe (gibe)	compliment	taunt	proposal
255T	edification	judgment	moral improvement	curiosity
255B	decorum	aesthetics	propriety	beauty
259B	florid	ruddy	pale	handsome
262M	musty	wet	fresh	stale
263M	queue	line	crowd	circle
266T	ravenous	satiated	voracious	suspicious
274B	circumvented	avoided	yielded	followed
278T	obtuse	sharp	clever	insensitive
282B	inscrutable	mistaken	clear	incomprehensible

Answers

corpulence-fleshiness, *impelled*-forced, *uncouth*-unrefined, *ascetic*-self-denying, *tremulous*-quivering, *resurrection*-restoration to life, *choleric*-hot-tempered, *flippancy*-pertness, *aridity*-barrenness, *slovenly*-sloppy, *vitriolic*-caustic, *demurely*-modestly, *archaic*-antiquated, *supercilious*-haughty, *milksop*-unmanly man, *ramshackle*-tumbledown, *bilious*-sickly, *straitened*-confined, *artifice*-trick, *expostulated*-argued, *penury*-poverty, *subsistence*-livelihood, *inept*-inappropriate, *forbearance*-patience, *rankled*-festered, *vivacity*-liveliness, *obsequious*-servile, *blackguard*-villain, *remonstrate*-protest, *loquacity*-talkativeness, *callousness*-insensibility, *austere*-stern, *querulous*-complaining, *placidly*-peacefully, *philistine*-materialist, *facetious*-humorous, *pique*-resentment, *incessantly*-unceasingly, *invective*-denunciation, *opprobrious*-shameful, *jibe (gibe)*-taunt, *edification*-moral improvement, *decorum*-propriety, *florid*-ruddy, *musty*-stale, *queue*-line, *ravenous*-voracious, *circumvented*-avoided, *obtuse*-insensitive, *inscrutable*-incomprehensible

Teaching Aids

for

OLIVER TWIST

Glancing back at the nightmare of poverty and neglect, almshouses and debtor's prisons that marked his own childhood, Charles Dickens could write with firsthand awareness of what might happen to a boy born in the workhouse and left to the mercies of public support. The story of how Oliver survives in a world of deceit and corruption—peopled with the likes of Bumble, Fagin, Sikes, Monks—is an exciting tale of dark adventures in obscure slum alleys and rank dungeons. It is also, in the words of the eminent critic Edgar Johnson, "a powerful work of art and a warning. It assaults our hearts like the clamor of a dreadful bell."

I. *Objective Test*

In the space provided at the left, insert the *letter* of the correct choice from among those offered; for example:

....b.... The author of this book is (a) Thackeray (b) Dickens (c) Melville (d) London

.... 1. Soon after Oliver's birth in the workhouse, his mother asked to (a) see the child and die (b) locate his father (c) leave for Liverpool (d) send for Bumble

.... 2. The name "Oliver Twist" was chosen because it was (a) suitable for a boy (b) engraved in a

326

locket (c) chosen by his mother (d) next in Mr. Bumble's list

.... 3. When Oliver was nine, the workhouse board decided that he should be (a) set loose in the streets (b) sent to pick oakum (c) adopted by Mrs. Mann (d) apprenticed as a chimney sweep

.... 4. When Oliver asked for more food, he was (a) praised for his courage (b) given more at once (c) beaten violently (d) placed in solitary confinement

.... 5. Mr. Sowerberry took on Oliver "upon liking," which meant that he (a) liked the boy (b) felt sorry for an orphan (c) had Mr. Gamfield's approval (d) could return the apprentice if found unsuitable

.... 6. Noah received a sound thrashing when he (a) insulted Charlotte (b) pulled Oliver's hair (c) spoke ill of Oliver's mother (d) made Mrs. Sowerberry cry

.... 7. When Oliver first met Fagin, the "old genelman" was busy "sortin' the wipes," which means (a) selecting boys to steal pocketbooks (b) going through his accounts (c) sorting watches (d) checking stolen handkerchiefs

.... 8. On his first meeting with Mr. Brownlow, Oliver was accused of (a) assaulting the old gentleman (b) lying before Mr. Fang (c) picking Mr. Brownlow's pocket (d) running away with Master Bates

.... 9. Sent by his benefactor to deliver some books, Oliver did not return because he (a) disliked Mr. Brownlow (b) did not trust Mr. Grimwig (c) was intercepted by Nancy (d) preferred to stay with Fagin

.... 10. Mr. Brownlow was turned against Oliver by (a) the letter from Bill Sikes (b) Mr. Bumble's report of the boy's past (c) Grimwig's dire prediction (d) the loss of his five pounds

.... 11. During a housebreaking episode, Oliver was

(a) wounded by a gunshot (b) released from Sikes's clutches (c) turned in by Toby Crackit (d) caught and jailed

.... 12. Fagin became even more interested in Oliver because of (a) Nancy's affection for the boy (b) a conversation with Monks (c) a desire for revenge on Sikes (d) a secret revealed by the Artful Dodger

.... 13. Oliver was saved from prosecution for burglary when Dr. Losberne proved that (a) the thief was in Kingston (b) Oliver had been with Mrs. Maylie (c) Giles could not identify Oliver (d) Blathers and Duff had been bribed

.... 14. Oliver could not make up with Mr. Brownlow because (a) Bill Sikes interfered (b) Mr. Brownlow left town (c) Rose refused to co-operate (d) Fagin got there first

.... 15. Rose refused to marry Harry Maylie because she believed (a) his mother would object (b) young Maylie was irresponsible (c) her name was "stained" (d) she was too young

.... 16. At the death of old Sally, the plot took an important turn when Mrs. Corney (a) learned Oliver's true name (b) came into possession of a pawn ticket (c) revealed a secret to Bumble (d) sent for Monks

.... 17. Mr. Bumble married the widow Corney and discovered that she (a) made a fine wife (b) was very rich (c) had a drinking problem (d) dominated him completely

.... 18. Mrs. Bumble redeemed the pawn ticket and (a) came into a fortune (b) refused to part with the kid bag (c) lost the gold locket (d) sold the packet to Monks

.... 19. Before Nancy could give her information to Rose, she had to (a) kill Bill Sikes (b) drug Sikes and escape (c) persuade Fagin to help (d) talk Monks out of his evil plan

.... 20. Rose arranged the reunion of Oliver and Mr. Brownlow after (a) Oliver went to the West

Indies (b) Mr. Grimwig sent for the boy (c) Nancy left Bill Sikes (d) she explained Oliver's story and added Nancy's information

.... 21. Noah Claypole, Oliver's tormenter at the undertaker's, (a) claimed he was Oliver's relative (b) came to London to get rich (c) was murdered by Fagin (d) was poisoned by Charlotte

.... 22. Sikes brutally murdered Nancy because he (a) had tired of her (b) listened to the Artful Dodger (c) found her in the Maylie house (d) thought she had betrayed him

.... 23. Mr. Brownlow learned that Edward Leeford's will was (a) burned by the mother of Monks (b) lost in a storm (c) sold to Fagin (d) stolen by Noah

.... 24. Bill Sikes died when he was (a) shot by the police (b) stabbed by Fagin (c) accidentally hanged in an escape effort (d) thrown from a roof

.... 25. The villainous Monks eventually (a) died in prison in America (b) was exiled to Australia (c) committed suicide (d) reformed and became a merchant

Answers

1-a, 2-d, 3-b, 4-d, 5-d, 6-c, 7-d, 8-c, 9-c, 10-b, 11-a, 12-b, 13-c, 14-b, 15-c, 16-b, 17-d, 18-d, 19-b, 20-d, 21-b, 22-d, 23-a, 24-c, 25-a

II. *Alternate Objective Tests*

A. Matching

Before each number in the column on the left, write the *letter* of the item in the column on the right that matches:

.... 1. Monks   a. a beadle of the parish
.... 2. Sally   b. a housebreaker
.... 3. Sowerberry   c. adopted Oliver

.... 4. Toby Crackit
.... 5. Mr. Brownlow
.... 6. Agnes
.... 7. Artful Dodger
.... 8. Noah Claypole
.... 9. Mr. Fang
...... 10. Edward Leeford

d. spied on Nancy
e. stole a pawn ticket
f. surly magistrate
g. Oliver's father
h. a maker of coffins
i. Oliver's half-brother
j. gold ring
k. Newgate Prison
l. Jack Dawkins

Answers

1-i, 2-e, 3-h, 4-b, 5-c, 6-j, 7-l, 8-d, 9-f, 10-g

B. Fill-ins

From the column on the right, select the item that best completes each statement below, and write it in the space provided:

1. Mr. Bumble was the beadle of the _____.

2. When Oliver spoke up, the magistrate refused to allow him to become a (an) _____.

3. Oliver thrashed Noah but was beaten by _____.

4. Fagin taught Oliver how to remove _____ from stolen goods.

5. After Charley Bates and _____ fled, Oliver was grabbed as a pick-pocket.

6. Mr. Brownlow's friend, _____, was suspicious of Oliver's intentions.

7. Oliver looked remarkably like a young woman in a portrait belonging to _____.

8. The house where Oliver was shot turned out to belong to his _____.

Harry
initials
London Bridge
Fagin
Mr. Grimwig
Folly Ditch
locket and ring
stains
informer
gold coins
workhouse
Charlotte
aunt
Monks
Magistrate's Court
Grazier
Artful Dodger
mother

9. The man most determined to hide the true identity of Oliver was _____.

10. Mrs. Maylie's adopted daughter Rose was courted by _____.

11. Monks threw the _____ into the river.

12. Nancy had a secret meeting at _____.

13. Bill Sikes demanded a rope to reach _____.

14. Mr. Brownlow and Oliver visited _____ in prison.

15. Noah Claypole became a professional _____.

chimney sweep
Mr. Brownlow
pawn ticket
Mr. Fang

Answers

1-workhouse, 2-chimney sweep, 3-Charlotte, 4-initials, 5-Artful Dodger, 6-Mr. Grimwig, 7-Mr. Brownlow, 8-aunt, 9-Monks, 10-Harry, 11-locket and ring, 12-London Bridge, 13-Folly Ditch, 14-Fagin, 15-informer

III. *Ideas for Written or Oral Book Reports or Class Discussions*

1. If you reread the "Biographical Background" of the *Reader's Supplement* to the text, you will note that much of *Oliver Twist* is based on experiences Charles Dickens lived through during the early years of his life. He had firsthand knowledge of the problems created by poverty, insecurity, and the harsh realities of life in the London slums. For example, what connection do you see between the way Dickens felt about working in a blacking factory and Oliver's reaction to being apprenticed to the undertaker Sowerberry (Chapter 5)? What other specific details seem to have been derived from the author's recollections of his own childhood? Note how Dickens, through the use of *ironic humor,* reveals his attitude toward the conditions of the poor and those who ruled their destiny—that is, how he expresses serious criticism in a half-joking manner:

"Oliver cried lustily. If he could have known . . . he would have cried the louder" (p. 4T). Find other examples of the use of this device throughout the story. Why is it effective sometimes to appear to be joking when you are really trying to show your disapproval? If Dickens were alive today, what problems would he still be able to write about as they exist in the treatment of orphans, public education, slums, child psychology, poverty, and youthful offenders?

2. Some critics claim that Dickens relied on *coincidence* too much. They say he manipulated events so that they happened just in time to further his plot. Mr. Brownlow turns out to be a friend of Oliver's father, the thieves break into a house belonging to Oliver's aunt, Fagin traces Oliver's refuge through some clothes, Monks turns out to be Oliver's half-brother, and so forth. Mention other accidental occurrences that help to move the story forward. What is your view of coincidences? How often do they happen in real life? Give examples. (Remember that an unexpected inheritance enabled Dickens' father to get out of debtor's prison!) Review the coincidences and indicate, with reasons why you think so, those that seem perfectly reasonable and those that stretch the imagination a bit. To what extent was the story "spoiled" for you because of too many accidental events? What relationship do you see between Dickens' belief in coincidence and the dreamlike quality of his stories?

3. Few writers can match Dickens in the number of brilliant individual characters he created. To make each one memorably different, he used all the tricks known to storytellers and developed a few of his own, some of which have not been fully appreciated until recently. When it suited his theme, Dickens used what we call the *round* or *three-dimensional character;* that is, one that undergoes change and growth, reveals various sides of personality, and has insight. For instance, Nancy, a neglected child, has been driven into association with criminals (p. 130B). Yet how do we know she isn't satisfied with her lot (pp. 333M, 337T)? Despite everything, why is she grateful (pp. 338B, 387T)? How does she react to Oliver (p.

165)? What are her most serious inner conflicts (pp. 208B, 209M, 374M–375B)? Why might it be said that in death Nancy achieves a tragic nobility? On the other hand, Oliver is more the *ideal character*. Why does Fagin complain that Oliver is "not like other boys in the same circumstance" (p. 214T)? What are the early signs that Oliver would rather die than give up his moral principles? Even when the boy speaks up to the magistrate (p. 23M), laughs with the thieves (p. 150M), or thrashes Noah (p. 46B), why do we continue to look upon him less as a real boy than as a moral force of goodness struggling against the evil around him? In what important respects are there differences in the development of the characters of Nancy and Oliver? Why do you think Dickens chose to develop them as he did? Into which category would you place Rose, Harry, Dr. Losberne, Mr. Grimwig? Tell why.

4. In addition to well-rounded and ideal characters, Dickens also created *types,* usually described as *flat* or *one-dimensional.* Mr. Brownlow, for instance, is a stock Dickens character, a man with sufficient private means to perform miracles. How does his presence help to keep the plot going? Why can we label Mr. Bumble the typical bully, Mrs. Bumble the designing shrew, and Mr. Fang the petty tyrant? What is there at once comical and pathetic about the Dodger, Master Bates, Noah Claypole? How does Dickens, through his static types, make his most telling points about human nature:

a. that people are often polite only because they are frightened (p. 225B)?
b. that the bully is at heart a coward (p. 300T)?
c. that the pious person may secretly be a sneak and a hypocrite (pp. 217B, 222T–223T, 303B)?

What other *types* did you find in the story?

5. Occasionally, for artistic purposes, Dickens chose to draw a *caricature*—deliberately exaggerating a character's dominant trait out of all proportion to reality. This technique is especially evident in the major villains in *Oliver Twist.* Although occasionally a glimmer of humanity ap-

pears in the eyes of Bill Sikes (p. 183T) or even in his heart (pp. 328B, 407B), how does he mostly represent *brute force* lashing out at all opposition? On another level, how does Fagin represent the *power of the mind* turned to destructive purposes? How sharp is he in his awareness of Oliver's usefulness, his analysis of Nancy's state (p. 208B), and his evil control over his "boys"? Why do we perhaps think of the devil when we first meet him, humped over a pot, fork in hand, red hair matted (p. 63B)? In what respects is Monks also a caricature? Why might it have suited Dickens' purposes to exaggerate the characters of his villains just as much as he seemed to over-idealize good people like Oliver and Rose?

6. When *Oliver Twist* became widely read, Jewish readers complained that Dickens had done them a "great wrong" because he had created an anti-Semitic stereotype in Fagin. At first, Dickens replied that, because there were so many wicked Christians in the book, he saw no wrong in there being one wicked Jew. However, in later years, Dickens came to agree that, in situations that foster prejudice, people tend to look upon minority groups differently and unthinkingly judge all by the exceptional few. (See *Our Mutual Friend,* another book by Dickens.) A somewhat similar situation has existed in connection with Mark Twain's use of "nigger" in his famous books, *Tom Sawyer* and *Huckleberry Finn.* How do you react when you read about a character who is identified by race, color, or religion? To what extent do you agree with certain groups that recommend barring such books from the schools? Because both Mark Twain and Dickens were known for their concern about all people and dislike of discrimination of any kind, how can the problem of racial references in acknowledged classics be handled best by both teachers and students?

7. When Nancy is admitted to see Rose (p. 332T), the housemaids are horrified. What does this tell us about them? about Rose? Where, at other places in the novel, is the sense of social caste emphasized? To what extent do the lower classes more rigidly conform to a concept of what is "proper" than the upper classes? How do you ex-

plain this? Even among the thieves and other outcasts there are rules of behavior. What are they, and why do they exist in those lawless groups? How do the culture and what we would today call the counterculture derive and enforce the rules for themselves and others? To what extent is Dickens saying that misapplied concepts of what is proper may lead to lives of deceit and hypocrisy? What characters in the novel pretend to virtues they do not have or disguise the vices they do have? What has Dickens to say about appearances and realities?

8. In Victorian England, a number of surprising changes were made that shook up the Establishment. Entry into the lucrative Indian Civil Service, long the "almost hereditary reward of a few families," was made dependent upon competitive examination. The buying and selling of commissions in the armed services was abolished, also opening the way to promotion on merit. There were many other examples. In his popular novels, Dickens could not but reflect his times. In *Oliver Twist,* what scorn does he show for unmerited position and misplaced privilege? How does he advance an argument for a reward of virtue and merit, and attack the idea that only the high-placed are worthy? Which of his characters seem to be visited by luck as a reward for their goodness or good intentions? To what extent does the novel end with villains getting their "comeuppance" and good people their reward? What moral message can be found in the book?

9. Because Dickens wrote and published *Oliver Twist* in serial form for a public that eagerly awaited each new installment, he had to see to it that every chapter had a dramatic structure of its own so that it seemed to be a separate episode but gave promise of more excitement to come. Thus, he ended chapters with *foreshadowing* (a look toward the future—as on p. 4T), and unanswered questions (p. 15M), or an unresolved situation (p. 24M). He kept several stories going at once and used the "cliff-hanger"—as modern writers would call it—to increase suspense. Oliver is wounded (Chapter 22), but we wait many chapters before we know what has finally happened to him. Point out additional examples of the devices men-

tioned above to maintain interest in installment reading. To what extent do these structural techniques add to or interfere with the enjoyment of the reader who has the entire book available at once?

10. A full appreciation of the genius of Dickens must include an evaluation of his style of writing. Below are some of its outstanding features. *Study the examples, and then find additional ones in the text, explaining why you chose each one:*

a. *Psychological insights:* Dickens was far ahead of other writers of his period in describing what goes on in the mind. Consider the reference to Oliver's "drowsy state" (pp. 65M, 283–284M) or Fagin's mental state during and after his trial (Chapter 52).

b. *Use of realistic detail:* The skillful writer draws pictures with words. Note the description of Fagin's room (p. 215B), the horrible scene of blood and the club (p. 400), and the "dangling heaps of clothes" (p. 447B).

c. *Irony:* Dickens used *verbal irony* frequently—saying one thing and meaning another. Monks and Fagin are "an amiable couple" (p. 216T); the doctor says the criminal does not look ferocious; and, in abandoning Oliver, the Dodger and Master Bates are acting "like good citizens" (p. 74B).

There is also *dramatic irony*—letting the reader know something a character doesn't. Mrs. Mann expresses her real opinion of Bumble before he basks in her fawning attention (pp. 133B–134). Charlotte is delighted that Noah "trusts" her with his "loot" (p. 351B). Of course, details of Oliver's parentage are known to us long before he learns the facts.

d. *Symbolism:* Often a name, place, or event is used to suggest something broader in meaning than the original. Note some of the names: Bumble, Grimwig, the Dodger. Oliver goes from workhouse to coal-cellar to closet—all symbolizing his imprisonment. He is to be apprenticed to a chimney sweep and an undertaker—both symbolizing suffocation and death. Note, too, the references to Mr. Sowerberry's snuffbox (p. 25B), the "stone coffin" (p.

271T), and Sikes in the "Inferno" (p. 407M) when he momentarily forgets his guilt in the purification of the raging fire.

e. *Humor:* In addition to ironic humor so prevalent throughout, Dickens creates funny scenes. Note the Dodger and Master Bates shouting "Stop thief!" (p. 74B), at a moment when we are prompted to laugh at their rascality while pitying poor Oliver. Again, Mr. Fang's treatment of Mr. Brownlow (Chapter 11) is a delightful example of a self-centered tyrant bursting a pompous bubble.

f. *Point of view:* In some of his novels, Dickens chose to tell the story in the first person *(David Copperfield, Great Expectations).* Here we find the omniscient approach, where the author can be everywhere, comment on situations and people, get inside their minds, and so forth. Why was the choice of this point of view best suited to creating maximum sentiment and suspense in *Oliver Twist?*

IV. *Vocabulary Study*

Diagnostic Test

1M	extant	surviving	additional	lost
6T	impertinences	rudenesses	splendors	politenesses
16M	pervade	go through	convince	stay out
23B	stupefied	bewildered	alerted	porchlike
35M	diurnal	nightly	daily	godlike
39T	concurrent	happening together	fast	remote
45B	precursor	forerunner	follower	foul talker
61B	sobriquet	song	sign	nickname
64T	obeisance	insolence	deference	fat
68B	ingenious	cunning	ignorant	motorized
72T	vehemence	poison	calm	intensity
84M	mandate	palmate	command	greeting
91M	lineaments	knives	clothes	features
96T	decrepitude	strength	stealth	feebleness
104B	expatiate	talk at length	summarize	exile
114B	duped	doped	deceived	loved
125M	ebullition	abolition	repression	outburst
132M	regale	bore	entertain	crown

140M	sanguinary	bloody	timid	red
159B	execrations	spittles	curses	praises
162B	admonition	warning	praise	visage
163B	paroxysm	paradox	relaxation	convulsion
180T	acquiesced	balked	trembled	agreed
181M	imprecations	blows	profanities	prayers
187B	sullying	soiling	increasing	devouring
191B	crone	bird	queen	hag
204B	denizens	deer	residents	strangers
213B	colloquy	silence	dinner	discussion
221M	gesticulation	palpitation	movement	swearing
230B	unmitigated	lessened	covered	unrelieved
233B	solicitude	grace	questioning	concern
237B	zenith	peak	valley	dawn
247B	exonerate	blame	excuse	change
258B	dexterously	skillfully	sweetly	awkwardly
260M	credence	disbelief	charge	belief
295M	intervening	coming between	ignoring	stabbing
310M	discomposure	calm	uneasiness	decay
320B	encomiums	engines	hatred	praises
336B	contrition	hope	remorse	desire
340T	impetuosity	premeditation	pettiness	impulsiveness
342T	importunate	begging	important	wealthy
353M	viands	nightgowns	food	bedding
367M	frowsy	freezing	untidy	trim
371M	dissimulation	candor	disrobing	guile
376B	zealous	apathetic	enthusiastic	evil
382B	destitute	needy	dirty	rich
410T	indemnified	robbed	repaid	fined
413B	panacea	poison	cure-all	flat cake
417B	restitution	document	restoration	theft
434T	dissemble	feign	take apart	be natural

Answers

extant-surviving, *impertinences*-rudenesses, *pervade*-go through, *stupefied*-bewildered, *diurnal*-daily, *concurrent*-happening together, *precursor*-forerunner, *sobriquet*-nickname, *obeisance*-deference, *ingenious*-cunning, *vehemence*-intensity, *mandate*-command, *lineaments*-features, *decrepitude*-feebleness, *expatiate*-talk at length, *duped*-deceived, *ebullition*-outburst, *regale*-entertain, *sanguinary*-bloody, *execrations*-curses, *admonition*-warning, *paroxysm*-convulsion, *acquiesced*-agreed, *imprecations*-profanities, *sullying*-soiling, *crone*-hag, *denizens*-residents, *colloquy*-discussion, *gesticulation*-movement, *unmitigated*-unrelieved, *solicitude*-concern, *zenith*-peak, *exonerate*-excuse, *dexterously*-skillfully, *credence*-belief, *intervening*-coming between, *discomposure*-uneasiness, *encomiums*-praises, *contrition*-remorse, *impetuosity*-impulsiveness, *importunate*-begging, *viands*-food, *frowsy*-untidy, *dissimulation*-guile, *zealous*-enthusiastic, *destitute*-needy, *indemnified*-repaid, *panacea*-cure-all, *restitution*-restoration, *dissemble*-feign

Teaching Aids

for

PRIDE AND PREJUDICE

A clergyman's daughter living in the narrow world of a country parish, Jane Austen wrote about the people she knew—prosperous country families, pompous preachers, dashing naval officers (her brothers were in the Navy), and giddy girls and scheming women whose sole purpose in life was to reel in the social whirl until matrimony beckoned them to secure domesticity. *Pride and Prejudice* is a perfect example of Miss Austen's ability to construct a novel that is a model of exactness of structure and symmetry of form. Within the limitations of her provincial world, she managed to illuminate basic human characteristics—cynicism, pettiness, jealousy, and genuine passion.

I. *Objective Test*

In the space provided at the left, insert the *letter* of the correct choice from among those offered; for example:

....b....   The author of this book is (a) Poe (b) Austen (c) Dickens (d) Brontë

.... 1. Mr. Bennet's attitude toward his wife is that of (a) amused tolerance (b) consistent hostility (c) complete indifference (d) obvious dislike

.... 2. Mrs. Bennet's main purpose in life is to (a) please Mr. Bennet (b) climb the social ladder (c) get her daughters married (d) gossip with friends

.... 3. Mr. Darcy soon falls out of favor with the people of Hertfordshire when they discover that he (a) has an annual living of ten thousand pounds (b) doesn't know how to dance (c) is from Derbyshire (d) is too proud

.... 4. Elizabeth thinks that Mr. Bingley's two sisters are (a) ladies of impeccable manners (b) supercilious in their treatment of everyone (c) good friends of Jane's (d) important people to know

.... 5. Although Mr. Darcy is "bewitched" by Elizabeth, he does not feel he can fall in love with her because (a) he is in love with Miss Bingley (b) she always argues with him (c) she has inferior relatives (d) her mother talks too much

.... 6. Mrs. Bennet does not like Mr. Collins because he (a) is in line to inherit the Bennet estate (b) insults her daughters (c) writes pompous letters (d) invites himself for a visit

.... 7. Mr. Collins visits Longbourne in order to (a) discuss the entailment (b) play backgammon with Mr. Bennet (c) ask for money (d) choose a wife

.... 8. Elizabeth believes Mr. Wickham when he tells her he has been cheated by Mr. Darcy because she (a) knows Mr. Wickham's background (b) has seen Mr. Darcy cheat others (c) is charmed by Mr. Wickham (d) has heard the same story from Miss Bingley

.... 9. When Elizabeth turns down Mr. Collins' marriage proposal, he thinks that she (a) is just being coy (b) doesn't want to be a preacher's wife (c) is conceited (d) is in love with Mr. Wickham

.... 10. Charlotte accepts Mr. Collins' proposal because (a) her mother demands it (b) she loves him (c) he will provide a respectable living (d) she is jealous of Elizabeth

.... 11. Elizabeth is displeased when Charlotte decides

to marry Mr. Collins because she (a) doesn't want Charlotte to be able to inherit Longbourne (b) is against all marriages (c) wants Mr. Collins to continue pursuing her (d) knows Charlotte doesn't love him

.... 12. Elizabeth believes Mr. Bingley is staying away from Netherfield because he is (a) no longer attracted to Jane (b) influenced by his sisters (c) afraid of marriage (d) in love with Miss Darcy

.... 13. To take her mind off Mr. Bingley, Jane (a) visits Meryton (b) flirts with Mr. Wickham (c) goes to London (d) plays the piano

.... 14. Elizabeth is impressed by Lady Catherine's (a) interference in the affairs of others (b) good manners (c) quick wit (d) sympathetic concern for others

.... 15. When Mr. Darcy first proposes to Elizabeth, he (a) demands a large dowry (b) is fulfilling a bet with Mr. Bingley (c) is uncertain of her answer (d) expects her to accept

.... 16. Mr. Darcy's letter to Elizabeth reveals that he (a) loves her deeply (b) is jealous of Mr. Bingley (c) has not cheated Mr. Wickham (d) did not persuade Mr. Bingley to leave Netherfield

.... 17. On Elizabeth's visit to Pemberley, Mr. Darcy surprisingly asks her to (a) leave his estate (b) go fishing (c) admire his portrait (d) meet his sister

.... 18. Lydia wants to go to Brighton to (a) be with the soldiers (b) visit Mrs. Foster (c) spite Kitty (d) get away from her family

.... 19. When Mr. Bennet learns that Mr. Wickham expects one hundred pounds per annum for marrying Lydia, he (a) refuses to pay (b) thinks Mr. Gardiner has given Mr. Wickham money (c) is convinced of Mr. Wickham's great love for Lydia (d) asks Mr. Gardiner for a loan

.... 20. On her return to Longbourne after her marriage, Lydia (a) appears contrite (b) seems embarrassed (c) betrays no guilt feelings (d) is cool toward her sisters

.... 21. When Mr. Bingley returns to Longbourne, Jane (a) feigns indifference (b) welcomes him enthusiastically (c) asks him to leave (d) treats him coolly

.... 22. Lady Catherine visits Elizabeth to tell her that she (a) has news about the Collinses (b) is pleased about her nephew's attention to Elizabeth (c) does not want Elizabeth to marry her nephew (d) believes Mr. Darcy would not make a good husband

.... 23. Mr. Darcy is encouraged to return to Longbourne when he (a) gets Elizabeth's letter (b) talks to Mrs. Gardiner (c) learns of Mr. Bingley's engagement (d) hears the result of Lady Catherine's visit

.... 24. Elizabeth's family is amazed when she announces her engagement to Mr. Darcy because they thought he (a) would marry Miss de Bourgh (b) was interested in Jane (c) was detested by Elizabeth (d) would want a larger dowry

.... 25. After their marriage, Elizabeth and Mr. Darcy (a) avoid contact with the Bennets and Philipses as much as possible (b) secure a place for Wickham at court (c) keep in close touch with the Bennets (d) sever relationships with Jane and Mr. Bingley

Answers

1-a, 2-c, 3-d, 4-b, 5-c, 6-a, 7-d, 8-c, 9-a, 10-c, 11-d, 12-b, 13-c, 14-a, 15-d, 16-c, 17-d, 18-a, 19-b, 20-c, 21-a, 22-c, 23-d, 24-c, 25-a

II. *Alternate Objective Tests*

A. Matching

Before each number in the column on the left, write the *letter* of the item in the column on the right that matches:

.... 1. Mr. Bennet's favorite   a. 5000 pounds
.... 2. Miss Bingley   b. Jane
.... 3. Lady Catherine   c. soldiers
.... 4. praise of Mr. Darcy   d. Mr. Collins' patron
.... 5. Lydia's obsession   e. 100 pounds
.... 6. Mr. Gardiner's hobby   f. Charlotte Lucas
.... 7. Mr. Collins   g. Elizabeth
.... 8. Mr. Wickham   h. letters to Jane
.... 9. Lydia's dowry   i. gambling
...... 10. prettiest Bennet girl   j. servants
                                           k. fishing
                                           l. Kitty

Answers

1-g, 2-h, 3-d, 4-j, 5-c, 6-k, 7-f, 8-i, 9-e, 10-b

B. Fill-ins

From the column on the right, select the item that best completes each statement below, and write it in the space provided:

1. Mary Bennet's favorite recreation is
   _____.

2. Mr. Darcy looks down on Elizabeth's family because she has uncles who are
   _____.

3. A letter from Miss Bingley informs Jane that Mr. Bingley plans to marry
   _____.

Colonel Fitzwilliam
Scotland
London
sickly
soldiers
reading
playing cards

4. Elizabeth is pleased to see that Miss de Bourgh is _____.

5. Lady Catherine impresses Elizabeth as being very _____.

6. Lady Catherine thinks Mr. Darcy should marry _____.

7. Elizabeth learns of Darcy's interference in Jane and Mr. Bingley's romance from _____.

8. Instead of a living as a clergyman, Mr. Wickham asks Mr. Darcy for _____.

9. While vacationing with the Gardiners, Elizabeth visits _____.

10. Mr. Darcy invites Mr. Gardiner to _____.

11. Georgiana Darcy is not very talkative because she is _____.

12. Lydia is finally found in _____.

13. Mr. Wickham's debts are paid by _____.

14. Elizabeth and Jane are embarrassed because Lydia and Kitty are so _____.

15. Mr. Bennet's favorite son-in-law is _____.

attorneys
indifferent
Mr. Wickham
Miss Darcy
fish
land
Mr. Gardiner
opinionated
money
hunt
flirtatious
Lake Country
Pemberley
shy
Mr. Darcy
Miss de Bourgh

Answers

1-reading, 2-attorneys, 3-Miss Darcy, 4-sickly, 5-opinionated, 6-Miss de Bourgh, 7-Colonel Fitzwilliam, 8-money, 9-Pemberley, 10-fish, 11-shy, 12-London, 13-Mr. Darcy, 14-flirtatious, 15-Mr. Wickham

III. *Ideas for Written or Oral Book Reports or Class Discussions*

1. For the upper classes in eighteenth-century England, marriage was, in many ways, determined by financial considerations involving the man's means and the woman's

inheritance. How does this statement apply to the marriages of Charlotte to Mr. Collins and Lydia to Mr. Wickham? Mr. Bennet married because he was "captivated by youth and beauty, and that appearance of good humor that youth and beauty generally give" (p. 259B). Yet why does Elizabeth consider her parents' marriage a poor one? In your judgment, what were the strengths and weaknesses of their marriage? Based on what you know about the personality of each partner and the brief descriptions offered of the marriages, predict the future of the marriages of Elizabeth and Mr. Darcy, Jane and Mr. Bingley, and Lydia and Mr. Wickham. Support your predictions with reasons. Finally, in comparison with the marriages of the eighteenth century, what changes, if any, have occurred in the motives for and the attitudes toward marriage today?

2. Jane Austen once said of Elizabeth Bennet, "I must confess . . . that I think her as delightful a creature as ever appeared in print" (p. 433T). What traits does Elizabeth display that make her so attractive? Why does Jane Austen make such a point of Elizabeth's being "quick" (p. 3M)? What are some of Elizabeth's character weaknesses? How would you evaluate her as a daughter? a sister? a friend? a wife? In what ways does Elizabeth's involvement with Mr. Darcy bring about some changes in her personality?

3. "Vanity and pride are different things, though the words are often used synonymously. A person may be proud without being vain. Pride relates more to our opinion of ourselves, vanity to what we would have others think of us" (p. 20T). How does this quote apply to Mr. Darcy? Give examples to support your answer. How justified is the dislike of Mr. Darcy by the people of Hertfordshire and Elizabeth in the early stages of the novel? How do Mr. Darcy's attitudes change as a result of his acquaintance with Elizabeth? What actions does he take that demonstrate these changes? Develop an analysis of Mr. Darcy's character, taking into account all of the questions raised.

4. The snobbish behavior of Mr. Darcy and the two Bingley sisters at the first ball can be attributed largely to a feeling of superiority. Why do Mr. Darcy, the Bingley

sisters, and Lady Catherine consider themselves superior to the people of Hertfordshire? In what ways does their snobbery affect Elizabeth and Jane? To what extent is Elizabeth's attitude toward them a kind of reverse snobbery? Give reasons to support your answer. When *Pride and Prejudice* was written, the predisposition to dislike people of another class was, in a sense, "prejudice." How is this kind of class snobbery both different from and similar to prejudice as we know it today?

5. Often called a "novel of manners," *Pride and Prejudice* describes the social customs that governed the lives of the upper-middle classes (landed gentry and gentlefolk) in eighteenth-century England. What social class does each of the following represent: the Bingleys, Bennets, Lucases, de Bourghs? For example, how did the upbringing of Georgiana (Mr. Darcy's sister) and Miss de Bourgh (his cousin) differ from the training received by the Bennet girls? In terms of the social codes of the day, why was Miss de Bourgh considered a more suitable wife for Mr. Darcy than Elizabeth? In comparison with the roles of women in the eighteenth century, what changes, if any, have occurred in the lives of women today in terms of education, social training, future goals, and position within marriage? What social customs described in the novel are still practiced today among certain classes of people?

6. In spite of their seemingly comfortable lives, most of the characters in *Pride and Prejudice* are victims of their social status, accepting their expected roles and lessening their status as thinking human beings in the process. To what extent would you say Mr. Collins, Mrs. Bennet, Mr. Bennet, Mr. Wickham, Jane, Mr. Bingley, and Lydia are victims of their social positions? On the other hand, to what degree do you think their personality weaknesses are responsible for their problems? Give examples to support your arguments. Using the above characters as examples, evaluate the truth of the following statement by critic Duke Schirmer: "She [Jane Austen] exposes at the same time *sympathetically* and *satirically* the frustration, wronghead-

edness, honesty, simplicity, and duplicity of human beings. . . ."

7. It should be clear (see *Biographical Background*) that Jane Austen included many autobiographical details in the development of *Pride and Prejudice*. Select at least five elements of setting, narrative, or character that probably were derived from the real-life experiences of the writer. Discuss the changes, if any, that were made in detail for the purposes of fictional interest. Indicate, too, what imaginative touches can be traced to the normal dreamworld of a lonely young woman.

8. Irony, a literary device that uses characters, situations, or plot development to demonstrate the contradiction between how things appear and how they are *or* how things are and how they should be, is used in *Pride and Prejudice* to satirize eighteenth-century social conventions and expose the weaknesses of human beings. Explain how irony is used in developing the characters of Lady Catherine, Mr. Collins, Mrs. Bennet, and Lydia. What things do they say, write, or do that are contrary to how they really feel or how they would be expected to feel? Include in your discussion Collins' proposal, Lady Catherine's dinner parties, and Lydia's marriage. What instances of irony are evident in the romance between Mr. Darcy and Elizabeth? Explain why irony as used by Jane Austen was an effective device in exposing the shortcomings of the society in *Pride and Prejudice*.

9. Discuss what official position you think a women's liberation group would take on *Pride and Prejudice*. What would be their attitude toward Mrs. Bennet's constant obsession with marriage, Lydia and Kitty's passion for parties, Jane's passive acceptance of Mr. Bingley's withdrawal, Elizabeth's forthrightness? What do you imagine the women's liberationists would say about the marriages of Jane and Elizabeth? How would they react to the following remark made by W. Somerset Maugham (p. 432M):

. . . I have a notion that there is something to be said for the simple people who look upon marriage as a satisfactory conclusion to a work of fiction. I think they do so because they have a deep, instinctive feeling that by mating, a man and a woman have fulfilled their biological function. . . .

10. In satirizing the eighteenth-century social milieu, Jane Austen uses characters who clearly demonstrate the society's and their own absurdity. Consider her use of language in developing these characters. Give examples in which a character's entire personality is captured in a single phrase or sentence. How does Jane Austen use letters and conversations to further reveal a character's personality? Give examples. Why are letters and lengthy conversations appropriate vehicles for character development in *Pride and Prejudice?* Discuss whether you think the language in these letters and conversations is stilted and artificial or appropriate to the period and subject matter of the book, giving reasons to support your answer.

IV. *Vocabulary Study*

Diagnostic Test

4T	caprice	impulse	desire	judgment
8M	disconcerted	calmed	upset	separated
14T	censuring	praising	cutting	reprimanding
14T	candor	closeness	frankness	sweetness
23T	vexation	annoyance	smoothness	control
27T	propriety	ownership	correctness	defiance
28T	intrepidity	cowardice	embarrassment	courage
42M	affinity	relationship	severance	finality
42M	paltry	great	petty	sinful
54B	reprehensible	laudable	grasping	blamable
62B	propensity	distaste	inclination	protection
63T	propitious	favorable	profane	unfavorable
66B	odious	lovable	perfumed	hateful
76B	incumbent	obligatory	optional	official
82T	digressions	unifications	conclusions	deviations
86B	imprudence	primness	rashness	bigness
98M	surmise	guess	know	overlay

104T	implicit	doubtful	deep	unquestioning
105B	probity	possibility	virtue	dishonesty
107B	laity	laymen	professionals	clergy
116B	purport	whim	meaning	carriage
126M	doleful	gay	sorrowful	heavy
128M	forbearance	impatience	restraint	pain
136T	expedient	unwise	impractical	advantageous
136M	irksome	tiresome	agreeable	spirited
155B	acquiescence	refusal	agreement	decline
165B	defection	desertion	enlistment	wound
173M	affability	rudeness	pleasantness	grimness
187B	composure	self-possession	confusion	creation
196T	prudential	silly	lucky	sensible
202M	tractable	fierce	docile	tillable
215B	depravity	virtue	immorality	stealth
219M	refute	prove	refuse	disprove
220B	pecuniary	monetary	honorary	free
231M	obeisance	refusal	bow	escape
249M	encumbrance	freedom	lightness	obstacle
259B	conjugal	matrimonial	lonesome	funereal
268B	intimation	flattery	hint	contradiction
280M	embargo	release	contract	prohibition
296T	shrewish	coaxing	nagging	singing
309M	susceptibility	responsiveness	indifference	disease
313T	sanguine	mournful	optimistic	pessimistic
324M	affliction	distress	happiness	cure
345B	austerity	jollity	severity	amity
351M	compatible	suitable	unfitting	remediable
359T	abominate	loathe	crave	increase
376M	abhorrent	likable	hateful	bloody
385M	barbarous	genteel	cutting	uncivilized
399B	sagacity	stupidity	wisdom	subterfuge
410B	unabated	ended	dropped	unstopped

Answers

caprice-impulse, *disconcerted*-upset, *censuring*-reprimanding, *candor*-frankness, *vexation*-annoyance, *propriety*-correctness, *intrepidity*-courage, *affinity*-relationship, *paltry*-petty, *reprehensible*-blamable, *propensity*-inclination, *propitious*-favorable, *odious*-hateful, *incumbent*-obligatory, *digressions*-deviations, *imprudence*-rashness, *surmise*-guess, *implicit*-unquestioning, *probity*-virtue, *laity*-laymen, *purport*-meaning, *doleful*-sorrowful, *forbearance*-restraint, *expedient*-advantageous, *irksome*-tiresome, *acquiescence*-

agreement, *deflection*-desertion, *affability*-pleasantness, *composure*-self-possession, *prudential*-sensible, *tractable*-docile, *depravity*-immorality, *refute*-disprove, *pecuniary*-monetary, *obesiance*-bow, *encumbrance*-obstacle, *conjugal*-matrimonial, *intimation*-hint, *embargo*-prohibition, *shrewish*-nagging, *susceptibility*-responsiveness, *sanguine*-optimistic, *affliction*-distress, *austerity*-severity, *compatible*-suitable, *abominate*-loathe, *abhorrent*-hateful, *barbarous*-uncivilized, *sagacity*-wisdom, *unabated*-unstopped

Teaching Aids

for

PYGMALION

When George Bernard Shaw wrote *Pygmalion,* more than a half-century ago, it seemed unlikely that his little play would eventually be converted into one of the great musicals of our time, *My Fair Lady,* and a motion picture that captured numerous Academy Awards. Yet such popularity should not have been surprising, because succeeding generations of readers and playgoers find continual relevance in the story of a speech therapist who successfully molds an untutored flower girl into a darling of high society. The extraordinary wit of the master dramatist of the twentieth century has not lost its sharp edge as it cuts away at the artificiality of class distinctions and the callousness of indifference to human worth.

I. *Objective Test*

In the space provided at the left, insert the *letter* of the correct choice from among those offered; for example:

....b....   The play was written by (a) Ibsen (b) Shaw (c) Barrie (d) Rice

.... 1. Freddy's mother gave Liza money in order to (a) provide her with a meal (b) pay for all her flowers (c) chase her away (d) find out how she knew Freddy's name

.... 2. Higgins and Pickering had (a) met by chance (b) studied at the same school (c) been distantly related (d) been friends for many years

352

.... 3. Liza learned Higgins' profession and address from (a) a newspaper advertisement (b) a telephone book (c) a magazine article (d) what she overheard on the street

.... 4. The character in the play who probably most resembled the author was (a) Doolittle (b) Freddy (c) Nepommuck (d) Higgins

.... 5. The character who seemed most unconventional in the play was (a) Mrs. Pearce (b) Freddy (c) Doolittle (d) Mrs. Eynsford-Hill

.... 6. Mrs. Pearce worried about Higgins' (a) table manners (b) social appointments (c) attitude toward his mother (d) financial status

.... 7. Doolittle first called on Higgins in order to (a) threaten him (b) protect Liza (c) ask for money (d) ask for a job

.... 8. Some of Liza's personal habits were caused by her fear of (a) hunger (b) cold (c) poverty (d) disgrace

.... 9. Mrs. Higgins had apparently forbidden her son to (a) visit her before six (b) come to dinner (c) call on any of her friends (d) attend her at-home afternoons

.... 10. Judging by Shaw's example of Liza's speech lessons, we gather that Higgins taught her (a) sympathetically (b) roughly (c) carelessly (d) indifferently

.... 11. Higgins' outstanding characteristic was his (a) arrogance (b) humility (c) intellectual breadth (d) good manners

.... 12. Pickering moved to Higgins' house to (a) avoid a hotel bill (b) observe Higgins' methods (c) mingle with London society (d) learn Sanskrit

.... 13. Mrs. Higgins believed that a bad influence on Liza was her son's (a) selection of her clothes (b) dialect (c) vulgar expressions (d) luxurious habits

.... 14. Higgins seemed amazed at Liza's ability to (a) do fine needlework (b) play the piano by ear (c) write poetry (d) sing

.... 15. Liza feared taking a bath most because she thought it was (a) immodest (b) bad for her skin (c) dangerous to her health (d) only for rich people

.... 16. Pickering seemed to surpass Higgins in (a) intellectual attainments (b) musical appreciation (c) knowledge of Shakespeare (d) human sympathy

.... 17. At Mrs. Higgins' at-home afternoon, Liza reverted to her former speech habits when she discussed (a) weather (b) health (c) food (d) manners

.... 18. Higgins seemed willing to let the outcome of his bet depend on the appraisal of Liza by (a) Nepommuck (b) the ambassador's wife (c) Pickering (d) Mrs. Higgins

.... 19. Judging by their report to Mrs. Higgins, we gather that Pickering and Higgins were finding their work with Liza very (a) pleasurable (b) distasteful (c) easy (d) unbearable

.... 20. Higgins' reaction to winning his bet was that he was (a) sorry that Liza had not done better (b) glad the ordeal was over (c) happy to get the money (d) sorry that Liza had succeeded

.... 21. What Doolittle feared most was (a) work (b) liquor (c) marriage (d) lecturing in public

.... 22. Nepommuck was most nearly right in saying that Liza had (a) come from royal ancestors (b) been born of Hungarian stock (c) lived in a foreign land (d) learned English like a foreign language

.... 23. At the end, what Higgins wanted most was to (a) get rid of Liza (b) have Liza back at his house (c) marry Liza (d) help Liza marry Freddy

.... 24. Liza's great complaint about Higgins was that he (a) mistreated her (b) gave her no money (c) overlooked her (d) called her names

.... 25. Liza seemed to understand (a) her own problems (b) Mrs. Higgins' disdain for her (c)

Pickering's snobbery (d) her adoration of
Freddy

Answers

1-d, 2-a, 3-d, 4-d, 5-c, 6-a, 7-c, 8-b, 9-d, 10-b, 11-a, 12-b, 13-c,
14-b, 15-c, 16-d, 17-b, 18-a, 19-a, 20-b, 21-c, 22-d, 23-b, 24-c, 25-a

II. *Alternate Objective Tests*

A. Matching

Before each number in the column on the left, write the
letter of the item in the column on the right that matches:

.... 1. Higgins' housekeeper
.... 2. she had been rich all
       her life
.... 3. an unhappy heir
.... 4. she liked current slang
.... 5. he was infatuated with
       Liza
.... 6. her income had been
       much reduced
.... 7. Higgins' former pupil
.... 8. a researcher in India
.... 9. Liza's rented finery
...... 10. he was an unconscious
       bully

a. Clara
b. Mrs. Doolittle
c. Pickering
d. Freddy's mother
e. Higgins
f. Mrs. Pearce
g. Freddy
h. Mrs. Higgins
i. Doolittle
j. Nepommuck
k. clothes
l. jewelry

Answers

1-f, 2-h, 3-i, 4-a, 5-g, 6-d, 7-j, 8-c, 9-l, 10-e

B. Fill-ins

From the column on the right, select the item that
best completes each statement below, and write it in the
space provided:

1. Higgins seemed to be _____ of his own bad manners.
2. The person who seemed most uneasy about Liza's staying at Higgins' home was _____.
3. Higgins attributed Liza's rapid progress to her fine _____.
4. At Mrs. Higgins' at-home afternoon, Liza said her father was a (an) _____.
5. Mrs. Higgins complained that her son seemed to like _____ women.
6. The day after the embassy reception, Liza sought refuge with _____.
7. The person Doolittle asked to be with him at church was _____.
8. Liza was grateful to Pickering for calling her _____.
9. When Liza first saw Higgins, she thought he was a (an) _____.
10. Higgins had a rare ability to determine people's _____.
11. Liza liked to spend money on _____.
12. A possession that Liza treasured in her humble lodgings was a (an) _____.
13. Doolittle blamed his sudden inheritance on _____.
14. The new experience that Liza seemed to fear most was a (an) _____.
15. At the close of the play, Higgins laughed at Liza's possible _____.

Higgins
birdcage
Pickering
bath
origins
ear
thief
Mrs. Higgins
marriage
younger
detective
Mrs. Pearce
voice
older
taxis
settee
unaware
positions
Miss Doolittle
drunkard
reception
jewelry

Answers

1-unaware, 2-Mrs. Pearce, 3-ear, 4-drunkard, 5-older, 6-Mrs. Higgins, 7-Pickering, 8-Miss Doolittle, 9-detective, 10-origins, 11-taxis, 12-birdcage, 13-Higgins, 14-bath, 15-marriage

III. *Ideas for Written or Oral Book Reports or Class Discussions*

1. We hear much in our day about the importance of environment in shaping the individual. Describe in some detail the environment in which Liza had spent her eighteen or twenty years and its probable effect upon her. Then similarly describe Liza's new surroundings in Professor Higgins' household and their probable effects upon her. Explain whether you think the many years of Liza's experience in her native locale or the few months on Wimpole Street had a greater effect upon her, both at the end of the play and in future years. What satirical purpose do you suppose Shaw might have had in mind in illustrating the changes that can be wrought in a simple flower girl?

2. Liza's avowed purpose in seeking lessons from Professor Higgins was to enable her to speak well enough to secure employment in a flower shop (p. 20B). Give the reasons why you think she did or did not achieve her goal by the time the play ended. To what extent would the results have been different if Liza had come for daily lessons instead of living in Professor Higgins' house? Just what did Liza mean when she said to Higgins (p. 96M), "Why did you take my independence from me? Why did I give it up? I'm a slave now, for all my fine clothes"? Explain why you agree or disagree with her estimate of her position.

3. Despite her careful training by Professor Higgins, we see two examples of Liza's relapsing into her former speech habits: (a) her account of her aunt's death (pp. 53B–55T) and (b) her exclamation of surprise (p. 91M) at seeing her father so splendidly dressed. For each example, explain why you think Liza reverted to her former speech patterns. In the final discussion after Liza had said that she could teach phonetics, why did she return to her old form of speech to say, "Thats done you, Enry Iggins, it az" (p. 99T)? Give your reasons for believing that Liza could or could not have achieved success as a teacher of phonetics.

4. An interesting contrast is provided by Professor

Higgins and Colonel Pickering. They were probably of the same social class, both had achieved professional success, and both had a deep interest in phonetics. Their manners and habits, however, seemed to be very different. After pointing out the differences between the two men, try to explain why Higgins developed such objectionable habits and manners. Then show the effects of Higgins' habits and manners on (a) his mother, (b) Mrs. Pearce, (c) his mother's friends, and (d) Liza.

5. In his preface, Shaw says that an ordinary stage production of the play would be impossible unless the scenes separated by rows of asterisks were omitted (p. x). The scenes thus separated are the following: Liza's arrival at her home (pp. 13M–14M), Mrs. Pearce and Liza before the bath (pp. 28B–30M), the example of Liza's speech lessons (pp. 42M–43B), the embassy reception (pp. 60T–65M), and Liza's departure from Higgins' house (pp. 76M–78B). Discuss how much you think would be lost if these five scenes were omitted. You may draw some of your conclusions by assessing the effectiveness of these scenes in *My Fair Lady*.

6. When Liza lapsed into her earlier form of speech at Mrs. Higgins' at-home afternoon (pp. 53B–55T), everyone was shocked except Freddy and Clara, who were delighted and called Liza's expressions "the new small talk," or current slang. How do the reactions of Freddy and Clara reveal aspects of their characters and personalities? What comparisons can you make with the use of slang by young people today? What might have been Shaw's satirical purpose in regard to current slang?

7. As Shaw depicted him, Freddy was rather weak and pitiable. Analyze Freddy's character; include a discussion of the following topics:

a. how Freddy probably became what he was
b. why he was attracted to Liza
c. why Liza was attracted to him
d. why Professor Higgins seemed to scorn him
e. what you think would have happened to him, if you disregard Shaw's epilogue.

8. George Bernard Shaw was widely known as a satirist. Discuss the ways in which his *Pygmalion* satirizes:

a. the lower social classes
b. the upper social classes
c. the "absent-minded professor."

In your summary, explain how Shaw made his satire gay instead of bitter.

9. The interpreter, Nepommuck, says that he believes that Liza is a Hungarian princess (p. 64T–B). Analyze his reasons for that opinion. Why did the host and hostess at the embassy reception seem to agree with him? What do you suppose was Shaw's satirical purpose in having these three people come to that decision? Evaluate how Nepommuck's opinion that Liza speaks English "too perfectly" (p. 64T) reflects Professor Higgins' success or failure in achieving his goal.

10. Analyze what you think were Liza's real feelings in regard to (a) Higgins, (b) Pickering, and (c) Freddy. Illustrate your opinions by means of specific references to the play. Then give your reasons for Shaw's decision to depict Freddy as about Liza's age (p. 4T, 4B), Higgins as twice her age (p. 18M), and Pickering as even older than Higgins (pp. 6T, 96B). Finally, set forth your own reasons for your personal prediction of Liza's future.

IV. *Vocabulary Study*

Diagnostic Test

3M **preoccupied**	alert	listening	lost in thought
6M **proximity**	nearness	distance	illness
6B **deprecating**	praising	disapproving	choosing
7T **staid**	sedate	tragic	emotional
8T **molestation**	ostentation	harassment	enjoyment
9B **repudiate**	welcome	drop	reject
11M **bilious**	peevish	rosy	pleasant
12M **mendacity**	sale	untruthfulness	integrity
14M **chronically**	seldom	sickly	constantly

14M	prodigal	wasteful	thrifty	filial
17M	laryngoscope	eyeglass	hearing aid	instrument to examine voice organ
18T	mezzotint	engraving	singer	oil painting
18M	petulance	cheerfulness	ill humor	affection
19M	pathos	comedy	arousing pity	despair
23T	guttersnipe	duchess	small bird	low street person
23M	prudery	enthusiasm	primness	immodesty
23B	modulation	voice control	monotony	middle
25M	remonstrance	agreement	size	protest
27M	presumptuous	huge	arrogant	shy
28M	plaints	laments	cheers	replies
28M	scullery	bedroom	den	kitchen
29B	frowzy	neat	slovenly	sleepy
30T	formidable	causing dread	weak	stocky
30M	dogmatically	doubtfully	gracefully	dictatorially
32T	alliteration	rhyme	rhythm	repetition of sounds
32M	unassailable	helpless	invulnerable	stern
34M	audacity	boldness	fear	doubt
37M	unabashed	cowed	smashed	undisturbed
38B	pauperize	make poor	make rich	spoil
39B	deferentially	respectfully	rudely	delayingly
42M	discomposes	calms	wastes	upsets
47M	ottoman	table	armchair	armless seat
47B	caricatured	duplicated	copied exaggeratedly	painted
47B	estheticism	horticulture	art cult	society
50T	straitened	in need	free	lined up
52B	pedantic	kind	pompous	agile
53M	fender	door mat	fireplace screen	tong
57M	sanguinary	bloody	heavy	pretty
61B	voluble	withdrawn	bookish	talkative
63T	gravity	levity	seriousness	indifference
63M	somnambulist	acrobat	doctor	sleepwalker
64B	morganatic	wealthy	like royal marriage	like marriage to lower rank
75M	dudgeon	anger	joy	relief
75B	perfunctorily	gratefully	quickly	mechanically
76M	decorum	looseness	propriety	artistry
78M	oblivious	attentive	round	unmindful

83M	vehement	energetic	low	soft
92T	demean	degrade	deceive	uplift
98B	toadying	scolding	fawning	attacking
99M	millstone	gem	heavy weight	dam

Answers

preoccupied-lost in thought, *proximity*-nearness, *deprecating*-disapproving, *staid*-sedate, *molestation*-harassment, *repudiate*-reject, *bilious*-peevish, *mendacity*-untruthfulness, *chronically*-constantly, *prodigal*-wasteful, *laryngoscope*-instrument to examine voice organ, *mezzotint*-engraving, *petulance*-ill humor, *pathos*-arousing pity, *guttersnipe*-low street person, *prudery*-primness, *modulation*-voice control, *remonstrance*-protest, *presumptuous*-arrogant, *plaints*-laments, *scullery*-kitchen, *frowzy*-slovenly, *formidable*-causing dread, *dogmatically*-dictatorially, *alliteration*-repetition of sounds, *unassailable*-invulnerable, *audacity*-boldness, *unabashed*-undisturbed, *pauperize*-make poor, *deferentially*-respectfully, *discomposes*-upsets, *ottoman*-armless seat, *caricatured*-copied exaggeratedly, *estheticism*-art cult, *straitened*-in need, *pedantic*-pompous, *fender*-fireplace screen, *sanguinary*-bloody, *voluble*-talkative, *gravity*-seriousness, *somnambulist*-sleepwalker, *morganatic*-like marriage to lower rank, *dudgeon*-anger, *perfunctorily*-mechanically, *decorum*-propriety, *oblivious*-unmindful, *vehement*-energetic, *demean*-degrade, *toadying*-fawning, *millstone*-heavy weight

Teaching Aids

for

THE RED BADGE OF COURAGE

This monumental novel is one of the few undisputed classics of modern American literature and is a stunning example of Stephen Crane's writing talent, touching both the mind and the heart. It is much more than a story about the Civil War; it reveals the secret insecurities and deep-rooted anxieties of a young man as he gropes toward maturity and manhood. It delivers one of the most powerful statements against war that can be found in all of literature. It is a hymn to a special kind of courage, the ability to raise a heroic figure from the ashes of cowardice.

I. *Objective Test*

In the space provided at the left, insert the *letter* of the correct choice from among those offered; for example:

....b....   The author of this book is (a) Melville (b) Crane (c) Poe (d) Hardy

.... 1. The youth enlisted in the army primarily because (a) his mother urged him to (b) a dark-haired girl admired him (c) he dreamed of the glory of war (d) he felt great patriotism

.... 2. Prior to his first battle, the youth most feared (a) untried qualities that would cause him to run (b) the loss of close friends (c) the wrath of his officers (d) his own death

.... 3. The most difficult aspect of the early army days was the (a) monotonous waiting (b) exhausting drills (c) abusive sergeants (d) poor food

.... 4. In the first onslaught, Henry fought (a) bravely (b) fearfully (c) clumsily (d) mechanically

.... 5. Those who fled the second onslaught were (a) one or two (b) a number of men near Henry (c) nearly the whole regiment (d) several officers

.... 6. When the youth first learned that his companions had held the enemy off after his flight, he felt (a) pride (b) humility (c) shame (d) anger

.... 7. Jim Conklin, wounded, was afraid of (a) dying (b) being run over (c) being captured (d) being seen

.... 8. Symbolically, the "red badge of courage" was a (a) wound (b) medal of honor (c) hat band (d) arm stripe

.... 9. The tattered soldier left the road (a) blindly (b) from fear (c) to help Henry with Jim (d) to hide

.... 10. Henry left the tattered soldier to (a) escape his questions (b) call for help (c) avenge him (d) bury Jim

.... 11. As Henry gazed at the bodies strewn in the field, he (a) envied them (b) hated them (c) pitied them (d) felt relieved

.... 12. The youth admitted to himself that he wished the army to be defeated because he (a) thought their cause unjust (b) felt sorry for the enemy (c) wanted the generals disgraced (d) felt he would be vindicated for having fled

.... 13. Henry was wounded by a (a) 12-pounder (b) rifle butt (c) Minie ball (d) bayonet

.... 14. After he was wounded, Henry behaved (a) with senseless curiosity (b) courageously (c) hysterically (d) with complete indifference

.... 15. Safely back in camp, the youth suddenly realized that he had been befriended by a man (a) who had never spoken to him (b) who was a

Confederate soldier (c) who was from his own regiment (d) whose face he had never seen

.... 16. Upon his return to camp, Henry found the loud soldier (a) friendly and selfless (b) curious about the youth's absence (c) anxious to quarrel (d) severely injured

.... 17. Henry's self-pride was entirely restored because he (a) slept well (b) had Wilson's packet (c) knew he was really brave (d) found his rifle

.... 18. The youth first gained the admiring glances of his comrades when he (a) boasted of his desertion (b) spoke back to an officer (c) criticized army regulations (d) continued firing after the enemy had left

.... 19. The youth's reaction to hearing his regiment referred to as "mule drivers" was to (a) feel ashamed (b) curse the officer (c) feel greatly complimented (d) want to fight bravely to gain revenge on the officer

.... 20. The general ordered a charge fully expecting (a) heavy loss of life (b) very few casualties (c) total victory (d) no enemy response

.... 21. The youth grabbed the flag from the dying color sergeant because he (a) loved it as a goddess (b) obeyed an officer's command (c) longed to be a hero (d) had it thrust upon him

.... 22. In the charge against the enemy stationed behind a fence, Henry's greatest goal was to (a) capture prisoners (b) get the enemy flag (c) plant his flag on the enemy side (d) end the battle as quickly as possible

.... 23. At the end of the battle, the Union forces (a) were routed (b) pursued the shattered enemy (c) withdrew in good order (d) dug in

.... 24. In remembering his experiences, the youth felt his greatest shame for having (a) run from battle (d) deserted the tattered soldier (c) been called a mule driver (d) lied to Wilson

.... 25. The story ended with Henry's dreaming confidently of (a) a new battle (b) more decorations (c) revenge (d) peace

Answers

1-c, 2-a, 3-a, 4-d, 5-b, 6-d, 7-b, 8-a, 9-c, 10-a, 11-a, 12-d, 13-b, 14-a, 15-d, 16-a, 17-b, 18-d, 19-d, 20-a, 21-a, 22-b, 23-c, 24-b, 25-d

II. *Alternate Objective Tests*

A. Matching

Before each number in the column on the left, write the *letter* of the item in the column on the right that matches:

.... 1. the loud one	a.	Bill Smithers
.... 2. the spectral soldier	b.	Henry Fleming
.... 3. the one who saved the flag	c.	Wilson
.... 4. tattered soldier's friend from home	d.	Tom Jamison
	e.	Jim Conklin
.... 5. the one with a trodden hand	f.	Jimmie Rogers
.... 6. the young lieutenant	g.	cheerful soldier
.... 7. the one who helped Henry find his regiment	h.	Hasbrouck
	i.	fat soldier
.... 8. "fresh fish"	j.	304th New York
.... 9. the horse thief	k.	tattered soldier
...... 10. the one whom the youth deserted	l.	mother

Answers

1-c, 2-e, 3-b, 4-d, 5-a, 6-h, 7-g, 8-j, 9-i, 10-k

B. Fill-ins

From the column on the right, select the item that best completes each statement below, and write it in the space provided:

1. A folded tent served as a _____ for the youth's hut.
2. The most difficult part of camp life was the _____.
3. When the men became tired from marching, they left behind their _____.
4. Henry found a lesson from nature in the actions of a (an) _____.
5. In a chapellike place, the youth saw a (an) _____.
6. The tattered soldier was fascinated by the war stories of the _____.
7. _____ was wounded in the side.
8. The youth had no sympathy for _____.
9. Henry got his _____ from another Union soldier.
10. The challenging sentry was _____.
11. Returning to his regiment, the youth hoped no one had seen him _____.
12. Henry was amazed that Wilson was no longer _____.
13. The cursing _____ often addressed his remarks at the youth.
14. Henry wanted to capture the enemy's _____.
15. An officer called Henry's regiment a lot of _____.

corporals
flag
generals
cry
monotony
mud diggers
wound
work
Conklin
squirrel
roof
knapsacks
run
sergeant
corpse
bed
Wilson
loud
lieutenant
cowards
fox
quiet

Answers

1-roof, 2-monotony, 3-knapsacks, 4-squirrel, 5-corpse, 6-sergeant, 7-Conklin, 8-generals, 9-wound, 10-Wilson, 11-run, 12-loud, 13-lieutenant, 14-flag, 15-mud diggers

III. *Ideas for Written or Oral Book Reports or Class Discussions*

1. After running farther and faster than anyone else on the previous day, Henry Fleming proves to be one of the bravest soldiers in the regiment. According to some critics, this is an unnatural reversal of form. These critics feel that the story would be more believable if Henry developed into an ordinary good soldier instead of a hero. Such treatment, however, would have denied Henry the understanding of what it feels like to accomplish deeds of great daring, and the author would have been limited to a much smaller psychological canvas. But are the critics right? If Henry Fleming is basically a normal young man, would the memory of having run away make him braver than he could be without it? Search your own experience and knowledge for tests of physical or moral courage, resourcefulness, and resolution that afford instructive parallels. If you consider the transformation entirely believable, explain whether or not it depends on some special personal quality that is in Henry Fleming from the beginning, as it is perhaps in all of us. On the other hand, if you agree with the critics, explain, with reasons, why you do.

2. Certainly one of the dominant themes in the story is concerned with courage. What is the true meaning of courage? How important is it for one to be aware of danger in order to act courageously? To what extent is the purpose or reason of an act significant in determining the degree of courage? How do courage and foolhardiness differ? What are some of the different kinds of courage? In the light of your answers to the foregoing, consider Henry's situation. How much of his initial desertion could be attributed to inexperience and loss of control and how much to sheer cowardice? Similarly, how much of a role did each of the following play in his later heroics: shame and guilt, deceit, the heat and smoke of battle, animal instinct, luck, the reference to him as a "wild cat" and the men's looking at him as a "war devil," anger at the officer who called his regiment "a lot o' mule drivers," and greater

self-confidence? What is your final assessment of Henry's courage or lack of it?

3. Stephen Crane makes some interesting observations on the so-called generation gap in describing Henry's relationship with his mother. What indications did you find in the mother's remarks that she regarded the youth as little more than a boy? To what extent was she right? In what ways did the mother try to introduce her son to some of the realities of war? In his response to the advice, how did Henry reveal reactions typical of a teenager being lectured by an adult? How long did it take the youth to discover that much of what his mother had said made sense? What are some things he might have said to her after he returned from the war?

4. This is clearly an antiwar novel. What did the story say about the glamor of war that so strongly influenced Henry to enlist? Why did the author describe the battle wounds of some of the characters in such detail? Of what significance was it that none of the battles seemed to turn out decisively one way or another? What elements of satire might Crane have had in mind when he put such emphasis on the importance of holding up or capturing the flags? What powerful message was implied in the general's estimate of the extent of casualties to be anticipated in the charge? What other indications of the author's attitude toward war could be found in his descriptions of the behavior of the officers and the treatment of the wounded? What questions about war were raised in the book that still remain unanswered after our country's involvement in its most recent wars?

5. In addition to the war around him, the youth was experiencing another kind of war within himself, literally a struggle toward maturity. Consider each of the following in terms of the level of maturity Henry had reached at the time and the extent to which it contributed toward his growth or served as a temporary setback:

a. the dreams of glory prior to enlistment
b. army camp life

    c. the flight from the battlefield, the studied deceit afterward

    d. the contacts with Conklin, the tattered soldier, Wilson, and others

    e. the "wild cat" behavior during the charge

    f. the reactions of others toward his feats of valor

    g. the final thoughts of peace

In what respects was Henry more mature at the end of the story than he was at the beginning?

6. Many pieces of necessary information were withheld until the story was well advanced, including the name of the youth. Few of the soldiers were named, the battles were hardly identified, and the locales, though richly described, were not clearly outlined. Why do you suppose Crane used this technique? Before you answer, look up the meaning of the literary term *naturalism,* consider again what the author was trying to say about war, and think about the possibility that Crane was suggesting that most of us do not enjoy freedom of will to work out our own destinies.

7. Crane had never seen a battle before he wrote this book. To what extent does this fact affect the story? What improvements could he have made had he had actual war experience? What advantages might he have enjoyed getting his information secondhand? How can we reconcile the fact of Crane's lack of direct experience with the oft-repeated and perfectly sound advice that one writes best about what one has actually experienced? Before responding to these questions, be sure to read "Critical Excerpt Number 14" in the *Reader's Supplement* of the book.

8. No study of a work by Stephen Crane can be complete without some consideration of the author's style. Note his creation of *sound and color effects* (p. 41T), *contrast* (p. 45B), *use of dialect in the dialogue* (pp. 31–32), *unusual word combinations* ("restless guns" p. 33T), *imagery* ("shell screaming like a storm banshee" p. 34M), *variety of sentence length* (pp. 38T, 35B–36T), *development of irony* (Henry's treatment of Wilson, Chapter XIV). Find additional examples of these and other writing

techniques, indicate how Crane achieves his effects in your examples, and evaluate the contribution the vivid style made to producing an exciting narrative. To what extent do you agree with several of the critics (See "Critical Excerpts") who found serious flaws in Crane's style?

9. It should be of interest to examine Crane's attitude toward his own characters. How sympathetic is his description of Henry's mother? Of these four—Henry, the tattered soldier, Jim Conklin, the cheerful soldier—whom did Crane seem to admire most? What did the author's attitude seem to be toward the Confederate soldiers? Support your answers with specific textual references.

10. In recent years, this country has been faced with the problem of what to do about draft evaders or deserters. What are your views on the subject? If you had been one of the presiding officers during a court-martial of Henry, how would you have voted if he had been caught in the act of running away? How would you have voted if he had been tried *after* his outstanding behavior during the charge, assuming that someone had recognized him as being among those who had fled in the earlier action?

IV. *Vocabulary Study*

Diagnostic Test

1B pompously	self-importantly	helplessly	laughingly
2T hilarious	sad	merry	rugged
4T secular	holy	worldly	rounded
4B impregnable	fertile	unyielding	shabby
5M diffidently	shyly	exceptionally	forcefully
14M derided	praised	ridiculed	dismounted
18T blatant	broad	showy	quiet
18B vociferous	foxy	mute	noisy
24T impetus	check	freedom	driving force
24T perambulating	strolling	thorny	still
27T covertly	openly	lavishly	secretly
27T invulnerable	unwoundable	valid	woundable
35M banshee	death prophet	life-giver	weapon

41B	imprecations	rewards	curses	entries
41B	querulous	pleasant	raving	complaining
44T	contortions	repose	drops	twists
48M	jaded	tired	broken	refreshed
50M	livid	vibrant	ashy gray	pinkish
51B	maniacal	sensible	quiet	crazy
56M	trepidation	courage	fear	abandon
57M	trundling	bouncing	rolling	stopped
60T	perfunctory	intense	mechanical	eager
60M	ilk	kind	opposite	animal
63T	spectral	gay	ghostly	dark
63M	sardonic	cordial	southerly	bitter
74M	harangue	articulation	booth	noisy speech
77B	sinuous	curving	straight	tall
78M	malediction	disease	denunciation	speed
80B	craven	birdlike	cowardly	brave
82T	vindication	vengeance	guilt	justification
94T	redoubtable	formidable	weak	questionable
98B	crone	model	old nag	lift
101M	petulantly	sweetly	soothingly	fretfully
103M	deprecating	disapproving	endorsing	closing
106T	lugubrious	happy	mournful	hostile
109B	consternation	hope	need	dismay
115M	temerity	care	rashness	fear
123T	respite	action	wrath	rest
131T	stoic	militant	calm fatalist	heretic
132M	yokel	hick	harness	urchin
134B	imperious	submitting	domineering	royal
135T	bludgeon	wand	bandage	club
141T	proximity	place	nearness	distance
142T	tableau	table	chair	scene
144T	mimicry	imitation	change	boast
144T	swashbuckler	armor	swaggerer	dupe
150B	prodigious	tiny	gentle	monstrous
153M	expletive	curse	blessing	prayer
162T	stentorian	soft	very loud	tall
166M	bedraggled	neat	scratched	unkempt

Answers

pompously-self-importantly, *hilarious*-merry, *secular*-worldly, *impregnable*-unyielding, *diffidently*-shyly, *derided*-ridiculed, *blatant*-showy, *vociferous*-noisy, *impetus*-driving force, *perambulating*-strolling, *covertly*-secretly, *invulnerable*-unwoundable, *banshee*-

death prophet, *imprecations*-curses, *querulous*-complaining, *contortions*-twists, *jaded*-tired, *livid*-ashy gray, *maniacal*-crazy, *trepidation*-fear, *trundling*-bouncing, *perfunctory*-mechanical, *ilk*-kind, *spectral*-ghostly, *sardonic*-bitter, *harangue*-noisy speech, *sinuous*-curving, *malediction*-denunciation, *craven*-cowardly, *vindication*-justification, *redoubtable*-formidable, *crone*-old nag, *petulantly*-fretfully, *deprecating*-disapproving, *lugubrious*-mournful, *consternation*-dismay, *temerity*-rashness, *respite*-rest, *stoic*-calm fatalist, *yokel*-hick, *imperious*-domineering, *bludgeon*-club, *proximity*-nearness, *tableau*-scene, *mimicry*-imitation, *swashbuckler*-swaggerer, *prodigious*-monstrous, *expletive*-curse, *stentorian*-very loud, *bedraggled*-unkempt

Teaching Aids

for

THE RETURN OF THE NATIVE

This book has rightly been called "a work of genius." Set in the vast, brooding heathlands of England, it lays bare the frailties of human love, its warmth and self-sacrifice, its cruelty and unreasoned passions. Although written about one hundred years ago, *The Return of the Native* is in many respects a very modern novel. Its major characters meet with despair and tragedy because they attempt to impose their wills upon an unresponsive environment, thereby falling victim to forces within themselves. Young people today are sometimes tempted to echo the words of Eustacia Vye's final lament: "O, the cruelty of putting me into this ill-conceived world!"

I. *Objective Test*

In the space provided at the left, insert the *letter* of the correct choice from among those offered; for example:

....d.... The author of this book is (a) Stevenson (b) Dickens (c) Poe (d) Hardy

.... 1. In his opening description of the heath, Hardy wished particularly to impress the reader with its (a) vast scope and changing landscape (b) timeless, brooding power (c) bright and cheerful aspect (d) lack of trees

.... 2. The prevailing mood of the heath folk around the fire on November fifth was (a) thoughtful and reflective (b) silly and irresponsible (c) sad and hopeless (d) lively and jovial

.... 3. The author's primary purpose in presenting the heath folk on Rainbarrow was to (a) create a good mood (b) describe events and people necessary to understanding the story (c) celebrate Guy Fawkes Day (d) expose ignorant natives

.... 4. When Mrs. Yeobright heard that Thomasin was not really married to Wildeve, she showed (a) gentle sympathy toward Thomasin (b) calm acceptance of what was (c) outrage against both Thomasin and Wildeve (d) distress that Wildeve had humiliated her and Thomasin

.... 5. Eustacia and the heath were alike, according to Hardy's presentation, in that both were (a) bright and beautiful (b) relatively unproductive (c) entirely without feeling (d) alive with passion

.... 6. During the meeting between Wildeve and Eustacia on the first November fifth, (a) both pretended cold indifference (b) Wildeve wished to assert his love but she rejected him (c) Eustacia pleaded for Wildeve's love (d) both agreed to love each other even if Wildeve married Thomasin

.... 7. The heath folk regarded reddlemen in general with (a) friendly warmth (b) alarm as possible thieves (c) superstition as images to be used to frighten children (d) ordinary awareness of their usefulness

.... 8. Thomasin's letter of rejection to Diggory was (a) straightforward and honest (b) cleverly diplomatic (c) calculated to embarrass Diggory (d) completely evasive

.... 9. Thomasin finally decided to marry Wildeve mainly because she (a) was certain of her love for him (b) was certain of his love for her (c) was influenced by her mother (d) felt a moral obligation to marry him

.... 10. The primary reason Eustacia wanted to join the mummers was to (a) enjoy a bit of excitement (b) get better acquainted with the heath folk (c) mystify her grandfather (d) meet Clym Yeobright

.... 11. When Diggory delivered Eustacia's letter and articles to Wildeve (a) they taunted each other in a get-even fashion (b) Diggory humiliated Wildeve (c) Wildeve humiliated Diggory (d) both laughed over their being losers

.... 12. The most surprising feature of Thomasin's wedding was that (a) Mrs. Yeobright was not present (b) Wildeve was late (c) the license had to be corrected (d) Eustacia gave Thomasin away

.... 13. When Clym heard of Eustacia's being pricked with a needle in church, he (a) thought it was a good joke (b) sympathized with Eustacia (c) scolded Susan Nunsuch (d) ignored the whole matter

.... 14. From the first, Mrs. Yeobright thought Eustacia was (a) an immoral woman (b) probably a witch (c) just the woman for Clym (d) lazy, vain, and a snare for men

.... 15. Mrs. Yeobright became particularly offended when Clym (a) refused to talk about Eustacia (b) called Eustacia a "queen" (c) gave Eustacia an urn meant for his mother (d) spent too much time at Bloom's End

.... 16. When Clym and Eustacia declared their love on Rainbarrow, a hint of future trouble was suggested by the fact that (a) Eustacia had fewer reservations than Clym (b) both seemed too sure of happiness (c) both were too cynical (d) Eustacia seemed to attach special conditions to her love

.... 17. Wildeve was disturbed about Mrs. Yeobright's handling of the fifty guineas because he thought (a) the gift was too small (b) Mrs. Yeobright didn't trust him (c) Thomasin didn't want the money   (d) Mrs. Yeobright would keep the money

.... 18. One of the dramatic contrasts in the dice game was shown in (a) Diggory's calmness and Wildeve's excitement (b) the heath's darkness and the moon's brightness (c) Diggory's bad luck and Wildeve's skill (d) Diggory's anger and Wildeve's good spirits

.... 19. Eustacia was insulted during the interview at the pool because Mrs. Yeobright (a) implied that Eustacia was a liar (b) berated Eustacia for marrying Clym (c) suggested that Eustacia was a thief (d) implied that Eustacia and Wildeve had an improper relationship

.... 20. Eustacia went to the dance at East Egdon because she (a) was bored with life (b) wanted to meet Wildeve (c) needed dance practice (d) wanted to irritate Clym

.... 12. Eustacia did not open the door for Mrs. Yeobright because she (a) didn't like Clym's mother (b) thought Clym had opened it (c) wanted to protect Wildeve (d) expected Mrs. Yeobright to open it herself

.... 22. Eustacia became especially interested in Wildeve after Mrs. Yeobright's death because (a) he boasted about riches (b) Clym's attitude had destroyed her marriage (c) Wildeve had reformed (d) she realized her love for Wildeve

.... 23. Most blameworthy in the tragedy of Clym's letter to Eustacia was (a) Cap'n Vye, who kept it hidden (b) Clym, who wrote it too late (c) Timothy, who forgot to deliver it (d) Eustacia, who refused to read it

.... 24. The thought that hurt Eustacia most that final night was the realization that (a) Clym had never loved her (b) Wildeve was not worthy of her (c) she had no money (d) she would make her grandfather grieve

.... 25. Thomasin discovered Diggory's deep love for

her through (a) a rumor delivered by Cantle (b) the loss of a glove (c) her presence at a dance (d) the advice of Clym

Answers

1-b, 2-d, 3-b, 4-d, 5-d, 6-b, 7-c, 8-a, 9-d, 10-d, 11-a, 12-d, 13-b, 14-d, 15-c, 16-d, 17-b, 18-a, 19-d, 20-a, 21-b, 22-b, 23-c, 24-b, 25-b

II. *Alternate Objective Tests*

A. Matching

Before each number in the column on the left, write the *letter* of the item in the column on the right that matches:

....	1. Charley	a.	besom-maker
....	2. St. George	b.	faithless husband
....	3. Eustacia	c.	the last bridegroom
....	4. Clym	d.	manor house
....	5. Quiet Woman	e.	family home
....	6. Diggory	f.	stole pistols
....	7. Olly Dowden	g.	hour glass
....	8. Alderworth	h.	amusing furze cutter
....	9. Timothy	i.	the "native"
......	10. Blooms-End	j.	honeymoon cottage
		k.	mummers' play
		l.	a pub

Answers

1-f, 2-k, 3-g, 4-i, 5-l, 6-c, 7-a, 8-j, 9-h, 10-e

B. Fill-ins

From the column on the right, select the item that best completes each statement below, and write it in the space provided:

1. Even in the gloom of the heath, a white _____ stood out clearly.

2. The girl in Diggory's van occasionally _____ faintly.

3. Grandfer Cantle liked to entertain with a (an) _____.

4. Eustacia often carried a _____ about with her.

5. Johnny Nunsuch slid down a _____.

6. Thomasin and Mrs. Yeobright went to the loft to get _____ for the party.

7. After the dancing was finished, Mrs. Yeobright's guests were entertained by _____.

8. Clym went first to Mistover to help retrieve a (an) _____.

9. Eustacia's letter rejecting Wildeve's love was sent by way of _____.

10. A pair of _____ watched the dice game.

11. Diggory discouraged Wildeve by tying two bits of _____ together.

12. Eustacia consented to let _____ hold her hand as part of a bargain.

13. On the stormy November sixth, Susan Nunsuch prepared a _____.

14. Eustacia and Wildeve both died by _____.

15. At the close of the novel, Clym had become a _____ on Rainbarrow.

apples
drowning
heath-croppers
heather
reddleman
Diggory
road
gravel bank
wax image
ballad
grassy knoll
hanging
telescope
cried
bucket
preacher
Charley
laughed
joke
mummers

Answers

1-road, 2-cried, 3-ballad, 4-telescope, 5-gravel bank, 6-apples, 7-mummers, 8-bucket, 9-Diggory, 10-heath-croppers, 11-heather, 12-Charley, 13-wax image, 14-drowning, 15-preacher

III. *Ideas for Written or Oral Book Reports or Class Discussions*

1. In Hardy's writing, says Professor Ernest A. Baker, "Man is represented as the helpless plaything of invisible powers, ruthless and indifferent. Every exertion of individual will ends in futility." Using specific references to passages or incidents in the novel, indicate how certain elements of the setting, plot, and characters tend to support Hardy's philosophy of life. On the other hand, why would it be reasonable to say that when the author deals with the minor characters and their activities—Grandfer Cantle, Timothy, Charley, even Susan Nunsuch—his attitude is considerably more cheerful? Why, for example, does almost all the humor in the story appear when the less important characters are present? What does this fact suggest about the kind of people Hardy thinks have the best chance of happiness?

2. It has been suggested that Egdon Heath should be considered as one of the characters in the story. How is it possible for setting or background to seem like a living person? In developing your answer, consider these questions:

   a. How does the writer imply that Eustacia and Egdon Heath have much in common (pp. 57B–62B)? Of what significance is the catching of her skirt on a bramble?

   b. What far-reaching influence does Egdon Heath seem to have had on Clym Yeobright even though he was living abroad?

   c. How is Mrs. Yeobright's entire destiny wrapped up in the heath?

   c. What events occur on the heath that show how the setting is actively functioning in the lives of the villagers, Wildeve, Diggory, and Thomasin, as well as the three major characters?

3. Consider whether you agree or disagree with Eustacia's estimate of herself: "How I have tried and tried to be a splendid woman, and how destiny has been against me! . . . I do not deserve my lot! . . . I was capable of much; but I have been injured and blighted and crushed by things beyond my control" (p. 404M). Basically, who or what is most to blame for the frustrations Eustacia feels early in the story? What could she have done to change her way of life? What warnings are offered that Clym may not be her means of escape? How badly does she manage her affair with Wildeve? What is the best advice to offer to young people today who claim that they are trapped by their environment and that their failure can be blamed on "bad breaks"? What advice would you have offered Eustacia at various points in the narrative?

4. Elizabeth Bowen says of Hardy's characters in general that "the most alive of the men are creatures of intellect; the most alive of the women are creatures of passion." Defend or attack this criticism. Use specific references from the novel. Think of the behavior of Clym, Wildeve, and Venn and then of the behavior of Eustacia, Thomasin, and Mrs. Yeobright. How accurate, for example, is Hardy's comment on Eustacia: ". . . she seemed to long for the abstraction called passionate love more than for any particular lover" (p. 77B)?

5. Thomas Hardy maintained that "the human race . . . is one great network or tissue which quivers in every part when one point is shaken, like a spider's web if touched." Show the validity of this statement by referring specifically to situations in *The Return of the Native*. (Suggestion: Consider as an example Eustacia's comment [p. 312T] that Clym has altered the destinies of five people. Who are they? How have their lives changed because of Clym's return to Egdon Heath? Discuss also the "quiver" idea as it applies to the impact upon the lives of others by Wildeve, Diggory, and Mrs. Yeobright.

6. An important insight into the development of the final tragedy can be derived from an analysis of the marriage between Clym and Eustacia. Like other women before and after her, what mistake in judgment does she make when

she decides to marry Clym even though he has already said that he has no desire to return to Paris? Similarly, like other men before and after him, what mistakes does Clym make in both marrying and then handling a spirited woman who cannot be made to enjoy the kind of life he has in mind? What other factors enter into the eventual failure of the marriage? Who or what, then, is most to blame? Why? Incidentally, how accurate would it be to say that Eustacia would have welcomed modern women's liberation movements?

7. In many respects, Mrs. Yeobright is the classic example of the "mother-in-law problem." How does her behavior in the Thomasin-Wildeve marriage almost guarantee failure? How much responsibility does she bear in the failure of Eustacia and Clym's marriage? Cite specific references to support your answers to both questions. How does she, even in death, exert the crucial impact on Clym's attitude toward Eustacia? Mrs. Yeobright's treatment of others opens the intriguing problem of self-interest masquerading as selflessness. Although she insists that she is doing what is best for her loved ones, to what extent is she doing what she *wants* rather than what *needs* to be done? How does her behavior explain the fact that the mere mention of the word *mother-in-law* nowadays sometimes provokes either a laugh or a hostile reaction?

8. Diggory Venn is one of the first characters to appear in the story and one of the last before the close. In what respects can he be described as the only one of the major characters who remains relatively serene as the turbulent events swirl about him? What evidences are there of his constancy, his persistence, his conviction almost that he will prevail in the end? In what ways has Hardy used the character of Diggory as a means of contrast to that of Wildeve and Clym? Why do Mrs. Yeobright's objections to him as a suitor for Thomasin fail to discourage him? How often in real life does a person go through a destructive, unsuitable love affair before realizing the worth of a stable partner who has always been there when needed? Describe one such relationship.

9. Hardy's style of writing has been the subject of much

critical analysis. Consider each of the following in determining whether certain characteristics can be regarded as strengths or weaknesses:

a. *Coincidence:* Some have said that Hardy used too much coincidence in developing his plot, almost as if he were relying on his architectural training to diagram his narrative. A prime example, of course, is the series of events that prevent Clym's letter from reaching Eustacia toward the end. Find the numerous other turns of plot that depend on chance, and then indicate whether these coincidences were reasonably consistent with life's unexpected occurrences or revealed a weakness in plot structure.

b. *Irony:* Very typical of Hardy's handling of circumstance are his frequent examples of events that turn out opposite to what the character had hoped or expected. Eustacia, ironically, selects Clym as her husband, the man who is least likely to bring to her the freedom and romance she craves. What is ironic about Wildeve's relations with Thomasin and Eustacia? How does Mrs. Yeobright's death produce a contrary result in terms of her expectations? How effective are these contradictory plot developments?

c. *Symbolism:* Hardy often uses an object or a person to represent a concept much broader than the original. For instance, how does Susan Nunsuch, with her needle and wax image, symbolize the attitude toward morality of the heath folk? What is significant about Diggory's redness? How is Egdon Heath a symbol in the lives of Eustacia, Clym, and Mrs. Yeobright? Find other symbols and discuss how effectively Hardy used them.

d. *Descriptive power:* Where does Hardy's descriptive strength seem to lie—in dealing with the sights and sounds of nature or depicting human actions and emotions? Supply evidence to support your choice. Why is Hardy's use of light and shade in describing Egdon Heath almost akin to that of a painter's brush? How did his reference to fire —on the heath, in Eustacia's emotions—suggest the myth of Prometheus? (Look this myth up if you are unfamiliar with it.) Refer to specific passages in the story to support your views.

e. *Richness:* References to literary figures, mythology, history, and general learning abound in the text. To what extent was this a distraction in your reading? Mrs. Evelyn Hardy noted that her husband's mind "was rich with stored impressions." How does this explain the richness?

f. *Sense of drama:* In what ways does the famous dice game exhibit an excellent feel for dramatic incident? What other scenes would lend themselves to dramatic presentation, even if divorced from the rest of the text?

g. *Dialect:* What does Hardy's faithful recording of native speech and wit contribute toward rounding out the setting and providing foils for the central characters?

10. Hardy actually finished the novel at the end of Book V, but was persuaded by his publisher and serial readers to bring it to a happier conclusion. Considering what you know about the author's philosophy of life and his preoccupation with the irony of circumstance, why would the original ending have been more valid thematically and artistically? On the other hand, if you think the addition of Book VI was necessary to tie up loose ends, explain why you agree with the publisher's view. In either case, why might it be said that the "native" really "returned" after the deaths of Eustacia and Wildeve?

IV. *Vocabulary Study*

Diagnostic Test

1B	opacity	clarity	dullness	richness
3M	ascetic	indulgent	self-denying	bitter
4B	anomalous	abnormal	usual	nameless
8M	contiguity	separation	similarity	touching
12T	homogeneous	human	same kind	mixed
14M	ephemeral	short-lived	infantile	long-lived
29M	effulgence	cover	darkness	radiance
34M	perspicacity	ignorance	clearness	penalty
35T	reticence	talkativeness	stubbornness	silence
41M	ingenuous	simple	experienced	clever

50M	excruciatingly	delightfully	painfully	unhappily
59B	intermittent	steady	short	alternating
62T	incipient	commencing	catching	ending
65M	perfunctorily	emotionally	mechanically	lovingly
68M	denizens	inhabitants	travelers	caves
71M	chameleon	permanent	pretense	changeable
73B	captious	tolerant	fault-finding	imprisoned
76B	juxtaposed	snatched away	balanced	placed near
87M	peregrination	journeying	settling	greening
93B	peremptorily	timidly	decisively	slowly
99B	astute	stupid	devout	shrewd
113B	clandestine	secret	open	close
123B	myriads	weights	numberless	limits
131B	mendacity	truthfulness	lying	begging
133M	iridescent	flat	colorful	waterproof
138T	spurious	false	truthful	sticking
148B	salient	minor	prominent	aggressive
155B	idiosyncrasies	ignorances	peculiarities	performances
156B	palpable	hidden	noticeable	breathing
164T	discomfiture	embarrassment	comfort	loss
189M	anachronism	pertinent	something out of date	currentness
194B	bucolic	urbane	divine	rustic
205M	nebulous	certain	vague	cumulous
217B	taciturnity	reluctance to talk	verbosity	willingness to talk
221M	ostensibly	apparently	secretly	amusingly
237M	maligned	praised	slandered	lifted
247B	affinity	closeness	distance	repulsion
264M	imprecation	prayer	curse	involvement
272T	evanescence	visibility	fading from sight	equality
281B	excoriating	stating	lauding	scolding
293B	gyrations	whirls	machines	
306B	somnolent	sleepy	alert	wishful
331M	vindictive	conciliatory	vengeful	kind
340B	stigmatized	marked as disgraceful	brought to light	cultivated
357T	equanimity	anger	likeness	calmness
366T	embellish	rifle	adorn	ring
379B	diffidently	boldly	lightly	shyly
404B	atrophy	wasting away	strengthening	terror
407M	effigy	summary	image	live person
437B	diaphanous	clouded	double	transparent

Answers

opacity-dullness, *ascetic*-self-denying, *anomalous*-abnormal, *contiguity*-touching, *homogeneous*-same kind, *ephemeral*-short-lived, *effulgence*-radiance, *perspicacity*-clearness, *reticence*-silence, *ingenuous*-simple, *excruciatingly*-painfully, *intermittent*-alternating, *incipient*-commencing, *perfunctorily*-mechanically, *denizens*-inhabitants, *chameleon*-changeable, *captious*-fault-finding, *juxtaposed*-placed near, *peregrination*-journeying, *peremptorily*-decisively, *astute*-shrewd, *clandestine*-secret, *myriads*-numberless, *mendacity*-lying, *iridescent*-colorful, *spurious*-false, *salient*-prominent, *idiosyncrasies*-peculiarities, *palpable*-noticeable, *discomfiture*-embarrassment, *anachronism*-something out of date, *bucolic*-rustic, *nebulous*-vague, *taciturnity*-reluctance to talk, *ostensibly*-apparently, *maligned*-slandered, *affinity*-closeness, *imprecation*-curse, *evanescence*-fading from sight, *excoriating*-scolding, *gyrations*-whirls, *somnolent*-sleepy, *vindictive*-vengeful, *stigmatized*-marked as disgraceful, *equanimity*-calmness, *embellish*-adorn, *diffidently*-shyly, *atrophy*-wasting away, *effigy*-image, *diaphanous*-transparent

Teaching Aids

for

THE SCARLET LETTER

A poignant, fiery novel about a woman who committed adultery, this book has become one of the prime American classics. It remains as modern, as dramatic, as passionate, and as moving as if it had been published only yesterday. The story of a noble woman who had to live through the purgatory that only a Puritan colony could have created for a transgressor stands as an eternally current rebuke to all those who would cast the first stone.

I. *Objective Test*

In the space provided at the left, insert the *letter* of the correct choice from among those offered; for example:

....b....   The author of this book is (a) Dickens (b) Hawthorne (c) Day (d) Melville

.... 1. The story of the scarlet letter is suggested to the author by (a) a friend's tale of an interesting legend (b) some ancient documents (c) an old newspaper account (d) his personal experience

.... 2. In the first chapter, the image that suggests perhaps a moral symbol is the (a) heavy prison door (b) rusty iron work (c) rose beside the door (d) bearded men

.... 3. When Hester is first led from prison to the pillory, the predominant mood of the crowd is

(a) compassionate (b) mocking (c) vicious (d) self-righteous

.... 4. Arthur Dimmesdale's appeal to Hester on the scaffold is (a) hypocritical (b) denunciatory (c) evasive (d) courageously sincere

.... 5. Roger Chillingworth does not want to be known publicly as the husband of Hester because he (a) secretly wants to hunt down the father of Hester's child (b) feels the public will scorn him (c) knows that Hester does not love him (d) believes the community will blame him for her sin

.... 6. The oath Roger extracts from Hester in the jail is that she will (a) never see her sinful partner again (b) keep their own relationship a secret (c) live alone forever (d) always wear the scarlet letter

.... 7. Hester continues to live in the community after she is condemned because she (a) wants to purge her guilt through public shame (b) has been ordered to by the magistrate (c) is penniless and cannot leave (d) hopes to marry Arthur Dimmesdale eventually

.... 8. At Governor Bellingham's mansion, Hester's main concern is to (a) excuse Pearl's behavior (b) plead to be allowed to keep Pearl (c) ask permission to discard the scarlet letter (d) catch a glimpse of Arthur

.... 9. After a few years' residence, Roger Chillingworth is regarded by the townsfolk as a (a) worthy citizen (b) scheming fraud (c) helpless victim of circumstance (d) strange but devout Christian

.... 10. Roger is brought into close association with Arthur because of the latter's (a) desire for theological discussions (b) loneliness (c) need to win Roger's forgiveness (d) failing health

.... 11. Chillingworth's attitude in Arthur's presence is characterized by (a) cordial friendship (b)

cautious inquiry (c) abrupt ill-humor (d) strict professional detachment

.... 12. Arthur often thinks Hester is more fortunate than he because she has (a) less responsibility (b) freed herself of Roger (c) faced her guilt openly (d) Pearl to comfort her

.... 13. Roger's analysis of Arthur's illness is that it has been caused by (a) overwork (b) some mysterious germ (c) excessive exposure to cold (d) a guilty conscience

.... 14. Chillingworth's suspicion of the cause of Dimmesdale's illness is confirmed when (a) Pearl tells him (b) he pulls back the sleeping minister's vestment (c) he hears Arthur plead for Hester (d) Arthur stands on the scaffold

.... 15. Strangely, Arthur's deepening sense of guilt causes the townsfolk to (a) regard him as more saintly (b) question his sincerity (c) refuse to listen to his sermons (d) like Roger more

.... 16. Arthur goes to the scaffold in the middle of the night to (a) grieve over his lost Hester (b) meet Hester (c) somehow seek relief from his guilt (d) pray for Roger's departure

.... 17. Symbolically, the appearance of the meteor during the night Arthur is on the scaffold seems to (a) light his soul as well as the sky (b) highlight the letter *A* in the sky (c) seek to reveal Chillingworth in the darkness (d) permit Arthur to see Hester more purely than before

.... 18. A proper characterization of Pearl throughout the story would label her a (a) combination sprite, witch, and loving daughter (b) stubborn, heartbreaking little monster (c) quiet, affectionate daughter (d) chattering, gregarious girl

.... 19. As Hester pursues her lonely life, she (a) becomes more embittered (b) gradually ceases to care for Arthur (c) turns toward meditation and away from emotion (d) feels more acutely her awful sin

.... 20. Chillingworth's response to Hester's threat to reveal his identity to Arthur is to (a) plead for her not to tell (b) ask forgiveness (c) tell her to seek repentance (d) accept her decision philosophically

.... 21. Hester's gesture of triumph as she celebrates her reunion with Arthur is to (a) kiss him (b) take off the scarlet letter (c) call out to God to witness the purity of their love (d) tell Pearl about her father

.... 22. After Arthur's meeting with Hester in the forest, he feels (a) freer to be himself, but senses he is a slave to the devil (b) healthier but physically weak (c) no further need for Roger's medicines (d) a renewed love for Hester, but cannot respect her wish to leave

.... 23. On the day of the Election procession, Hester hears from the ship's commander that (a) Arthur has decided not to sail (b) Pearl will not be permitted aboard (c) Roger also proposes to sail (d) the ship has changed destination

.... 24. Throughout the story, Hester's feeling toward Mistress Hibbins is that of (a) hatred (b) admiration (c) half-awe, half-fear (d) half-love, half-pity

.... 25. The purpose of Hester's final mission to her village is to teach that (a) sacred love can be a redemptive experience (b) a rigid moral code is the only road to redemption (c) the Ten Commandments are too harsh (d) good deeds are more important than religion

Answers

1-b, 2-c, 3-d, 4-d, 5-a, 6-b, 7-a, 8-b, 9-a, 10-d, 11-b, 12-c, 13-d, 14-b, 15-a, 16-c, 17-b, 18-a, 19-c, 20-d, 21-b, 22-a, 23-c, 24-d, 25-a

II. *Alternate Objective Tests*

A. Matching

Before each number in the column on the left, write the *letter* of the item in the column on the right that matches:

....	1. the scaffold	a.	chief resident of the forest
....	2. Pearl	b.	a living confession
....	3. the prison	c.	a backwoods minister
....	4. Roger Chillingworth	d.	official authority on morality
....	5. the Black Man	e.	an ignorant quack
....	6. Arthur Dimmesdale	f.	a wolf in sheep's clothing
		g.	a gay hostess
....	7. Mistress Hibbins	h.	instrument of disgrace
		i.	a blessing from sin
....	8. Mr. Wilson	j.	a secret penitent
....	9. Hester Prynne	k.	adorned by a rose
......	10. Governor Bellingham	l.	the New England race problem
		m.	official No. 1 citizen
		n.	servant of the Black Man

Answers

1-h, 2-i, 3-k, 4-f, 5-a, 6-j, 7-n, 8-d, 9-b, 10-m

B. Fill-ins

From the column on the right, select the item that best completes each statement below, and write it in the space provided:

1. One of the gayest days of the year in old Boston was _____.   Boston   kiss

2. Hester and Arthur saw a (an) _____ when they were on the scaffold.   Roger   confession

3. Pearl was examined on the _____ when she was in the governor's mansion.

4. Hester first talked with Roger Chillingworth in the _____.

5. Dimmesdale agreed to flee after his _____.

6. _____ was regarded as an imp.

7. Hester's last days were spent in _____.

8. Arthur Dimmesdale's very last act was a _____.

9. Both Roger and Arthur were accomplished _____.

10. Throughout the novel, the letter *A* stood for _____.

11. Hester embroidered Governor Bellingham's _____.

12. Dimmesdale often placed his hand on his _____.

13. Pearl tried to wash off Dimmesdale's _____.

14. Mistress Hibbins was generally recognized as a (an) _____.

15. Hester finally revealed the identity of _____.

church
gloves
meteor
ministers
prison
Election Day
Europe
forest
scholars
witch
Pearl
robe
catechism
Christmas
gossip
heart
sermon
adultery

Answers

1-Election Day, 2-meteor, 3-catechism, 4-prison, 5-sermon, 6-Pearl, 7-Boston, 8-confession, 9-scholars, 10-adultery, 11-gloves, 12-heart, 13-kiss, 14-witch, 15-Roger

III. *Ideas for Written or Oral Book Reports or Class Discussions*

1. The problems faced by Hester and Arthur cannot be properly analyzed without considering the nature of the community in which they lived. How reasonable would it be to say that the Puritan villagers at times exhibited the

classic symptoms of a lynch mob? In what sense did public punishment in such a rigid environment often serve the needs of the punishers more than it did those of the punished? What is there about human nature that makes it almost impossible to enforce inflexible codes of behavior? In your reply, make reference to such modern issues as dress and hairstyles, interpersonal morality, and integrity in political office.

2. What are your impressions of Hester's general character, considering her reactions to the crowd, her punishment, and her sin? How deep was her sense of guilt? What extenuating circumstances existed that not only influenced the judges but seem to suggest that there was more of tragedy than guilt in Hester's plight? How do you as a modern view the situation? Where did the author's sympathies seem to lie? Give evidence to support your conclusion by referring to words, tone, or mood. (Do not confuse *your* sympathies with those of Hawthorne.)

3. Why did Hester prefer to remain in Boston after her disgrace? She might have arranged to sail away to another land where she and Pearl might have begun life anew, with no badge of dishonor and no reputation for sin. Remember that she had some means of her own (p. 81M) and that her needlework provided a living for her. How far do you go in accepting the author's explanations of her reasons for staying (pp. 79M–81T)? Why did she return to Boston after Pearl's marriage abroad? In summary, to what extent can it be said that she was a victim of her environment?

4. There are those who say that Arthur Dimmesdale was basically a hypocrite. How reasonable was his statement that he could not confess for fear of destroying his parishioners? Why might this be called a cowardly excuse, or was it? In your assessment of Arthur's possible hypocrisy, consider these additional points:

a. His only gestures in Hester's behalf were his efforts to keep her from being branded or executed.
b. He seemed obviously relieved when Hester refused to name the father of her child.
c. He, too, was a product of his environment, and it

might be argued that it took an act of courage to remain silent for the sake of his church.

d. There seemed to be ample evidence that he was suffering within almost as much as Hester was without.

5. When you first became aware of Roger Chillingworth's relationship to Hester, what did he do or say to arouse your sympathy? On the other hand, in his insistence on Hester's oath of secrecy, what suggestions of unwholesomeness or evil did you suspect? Remember, it was he who sent Hester to Boston alone, did not correspond or get word to her somehow for two years, and suddenly appeared after her disgrace. What might have been his real reasons for the pledge of secrecy? In what respects might his concepts of appropriate punishment have been even more severe than those of the self-righteous mob? In this connection, bear in mind his cat-and-mouse game with Arthur.

6. The religious person says that confession is good for the soul. The psychologist suggests that facing up to one's mistakes and weaknesses, admitting them, and learning to live with them frees the mind and the emotions from an impossible burden. From either or both points of view, evaluate the extent of spiritual freedom gained or lost by Hester, Arthur, and Roger in their struggles with proclaiming or hiding the truth. Suppose either Arthur or Roger had revealed their true relationship to Hester early in the story, how might it have changed its course? Again, keep in mind the nature of the community.

7. Some critics have charged Hawthorne with excessive use of *symbolism,* that is, the use of an object, figure, or word to represent a broad idea or concept. Hester's *A,* for example, is a symbol, as is the rose near the jail door. In what way might Pearl be regarded as a symbol? or Roger Chillingworth? What other symbols can you point to in the narrative development? Explain them. How does the use of symbols contribute to economy of writing? How do you assess Hawthorne's use of this literary device—too much or consistent with his fictional purposes? Explain.

8. Hawthorne expresses Hester's hope that a new relalationship between man and woman might be established "on a surer ground of mutual happiness" (p. 275B). Write an analysis of the man-woman relationship as Hester might have written it in her day. Continue the paper by having Hester reveal her dream of the future. Conclude the paper by comparing Hester's views with relationships as they exist today. Include your opinion of the extent to which greater freedom does or does not lead to greater "mutual happiness."

9. Pearl is depicted as a rather strange child. Indeed, old Mr. Wilson says, "The little baggage hath witchcraft in her, I profess. She needs no old woman's broomstick to fly withal" (p. 118B). Why do you suppose Hawthorne chose to give Pearl odd traits? What might this reveal about some of the author's moral prejudices? Speak to a school psychologist. What is her (his) explanation of the child's behavior under the circumstances of her birth and upbringing?

10. Although it was written well over one hundred years ago, *The Scarlet Letter* continues to be among the top five classics taught in the schools. Every year hundreds of thousands of copies of the novel, both clothbound and paperback, are sold in the educational market. How do you account for the book's continuing popularity? In your response, consider such matters as plot, style, point of view, and issues raised. If you were a teacher, would you want your students to read the book? Why or why not?

IV. *Vocabulary Study*

Diagnostic Test

48M inauspicious	faltering	unfavorable	clouded
49M indubitably	unquestionably	doubtfully	carefully
49B heterodox	devout	mixed	unorthodox
53B ignominy	fane	nomination	disgrace
57B contumely	praise	verbal abuse	relief

60B	heterogeneous	similar	related	differing
62T	iniquity	discrimination	wickedness	devotion
68T	tremulously	steadily	strongly	waveringly
71T	amenable	responsive	cold	opposed
76B	besmirch	clean	soil	smile
79M	infamy	good repute	ignorance	bad repute
80M	galling	irritating	soothing	pleasing
84T	penance	boldness	self-punish-ment	money
84M	morbid	sickly	unjust	healthful
85T	repugnance	fondness	humility	dislike
85B	exhortation	refusal	urging	leaping
89T	inscrutable	fathomable	incomprehen-sible	clear
90B	mutability	changeability	deafness	stability
91M	imbibe	reject	drink	rouse
94B	anathemas	blessing	angels	curses
96T	dearth	plenty	scarcity	seat
102B	imperious	overbearing	gentle	blocking
103B	dauntless	fearful	bold	tame
107M	panoply	curtain	wood	suit of armor
114B	constrained	yielded	compelled	sifted
115T	depravity	corruption	saintliness	want
125T	sensibility	intelligence	power to feel	reliability
129T	celibacy	single life	rite	marriage
137M	propagate	check	reproduce	isolate
145M	odious	cordial	smelly	hateful
146T	forlorn	happy	fortunate	miserable
146B	efficacious	productive	ineffective	affectionate
147M	ethereal	heavy	airy	poisonous
153M	expiation	expense	atonement	rigidity
163B	scurrilous	slanderous	formal	clean
170M	transfigured	unchanged	transformed	damned
180B	bane	benefit	joy	ruin
187B	petulant	calm	irritable	stroking
190T	asperity	harshness	gentility	medicine
203T	misanthropy	love of people	charity	hate of people
211B	machinations	mechanics	goods	plots
214T	effluence	absorption	flowing out	wealth
215B	choleric	quick-tempered	hearty	southern
221T	mollified	nagged	soothed	left
225T	vicissitude	repetition	sin	change
238B	preternatural	ordinary	extraordinary	native

270M	conjectural	guessing	proving	stating
271M	nugatory	worthless	valuable	sweet
271M	repudiate	accept	reject	insulate
276B	gules	plates	red lines	birds

Answers

inauspicious-unfavorable, *indubitably*-unquestionably, *heterodox*-unorthodox, *ignominy*-disgrace, *contumely*-verbal abuse, *heterogeneous*-differing, *iniquity*-wickedness, *tremulously*-waveringly, *amenable*-responsive, *besmirch*-soil, *infamy*-bad repute, *galling*-irritating, *penance*-self-punishment, *morbid*-sickly, *repugnance*-dislike, *exhortation*-urging, *inscrutable*-incomprehensible, *mutability*-changeability, *imbibe*-drink, *anathemas*-curses, *dearth*-scarcity, *imperious*-overbearing, *dauntless*-bold, *panoply*-suit of armor, *constrained*-compelled, *depravity*-corruption, *sensibility*-power to feel, *celibacy*-single life, *propagate*-reproduce, *odious*-hateful, *forlorn*-miserable, *efficacious*-productive, *ethereal*-airy, *expiation*-atonement, *scurrilous*-slanderous, *transfigured*-transformed, *bane*-ruin, *petulant*-irritable, *asperity*-harshness, *misanthropy*-hate of people, *machinations*-plots, *effluence*-flowing out, *choleric*-quick-tempered, *mollified*-soothed, *vicissitude*-change, *preternatural*-extraordinary, *conjectural*-guessing, *nugatory*-worthless, *repudiate*-reject, *gules*-red lines

Teaching Aids

for

SILAS MARNER

This gentle novel tells the story of how a golden-haired baby girl restored the will to live in a miserly recluse who had rejected society for its deception and greed. One of the great classics, it is a tale so rich in human understanding that it will capture hearts and minds as long as books are read. Filled with the literary excellence that made George Eliot world famous as a writer, *Silas Marner* is a narrative at once compassionate and dramatically powerful.

I. *Objective Test*

In the space provided at the left, insert the *letter* of the correct choice from among those offered; for example:

....b....   The author of this book is (a) Scott (b) Eliot (c) Dickens (d) Hardy

.... 1. When the story opens, we learn that Silas is regarded by the villagers of Raveloe as (a) one of themselves (b) a strange but useful man (c) a newcomer (d) the best of companions

.... 2. In Lantern Yard, the main evidence against Silas is his (a) gloves (b) knife (c) hat (d) jacket

.... 3. Guilt is confirmed by (a) new evidence (b) a fair trial (c) a police investigation (d) the drawing of lots

.... 4. Squire Cass is considered more important than the Osgoods because he has (a) tenants (b) more money (c) many horses (d) better food

.... 5. Godfrey needs money to (a) get married (b) cover a lie (c) buy a house (d) leave town

.... 6. Wildfire dies (a) before the sale (b) after the sale (c) during the bargaining (d) in the stables

.... 7. When Dunstan reaches Marner's cottage, he (a) has already decided to steal the money (b) has not thought about Silas at all (c) convinces himself to take the gold (d) finds Silas unwilling to part with it

.... 8. The first person Silas suspects of stealing his money is (a) Dunstan (b) Godfrey (c) Jem (d) William

.... 9. "The truth lies atween you" refers to a dispute between the farrier and the (a) butcher (b) weaver (c) clerk (d) tailor

.... 10. Just before Silas appears at the Rainbow, the men have been arguing about (a) sheep (b) land (c) horses (d) ghosts

.... 11. The villagers decide the money was stolen by (a) devils (b) a peddler (c) poachers (d) small boys

.... 12. Godfrey tells the squire he has (a) lost the money (b) spent it (c) given it to Dunstan (d) returned it

.... 13. Mr. Macey suggests to Silas that he go frequently to (a) the Rainbow (b) church (c) town meetings (d) parties

.... 14. During a visit to Marner's cottage, Dolly asks Aaron to (a) play (b) take a nap (c) sing (d) stop crying

.... 15. Raveloe's greatest annual social event takes place on (a) Christmas Day (b) Thanksgiving Eve (c) Easter Sunday (d) New Year's Eve

.... 16. The Misses Gunn are shocked at Nancy's (a) clothes (b) hairstyle (c) speech (d) hat

.... 17. Priscilla Lammeter is convinced she will be (a) an old maid (b) married soon (c) forever unhappy (d) seriously ill

.... 18. Godfrey gets a chance to be alone with Nancy at the affair when (a) the others leave (b) her dress tears (c) they take a walk (d) she faints

.... 19. The little girl enters the cottage while Silas is (a) asleep (b) weaving (c) having an attack (d) out delivering some cloth

.... 20. Marner is reminded of his lost gold by (a) the flickering fire (b) his mother's locket (c) an old watch (d) a child's hair

.... 21. Of greatest help to Silas in caring for the child is (a) Nancy (b) Dolly (c) Priscilla (d) Sally

.... 22. Eppie's name is derived from that of Marner's (a) wife (b) aunt (c) grandmother (d) mother

.... 23. When Eppie is twelve years of age, Godfrey asks Nancy to (a) befriend (b) adopt (c) teach (d) ignore the child

.... 24. Dunstan's remains are identified through a (a) scarf (b) boot (c) whip (d) pair of spurs

.... 25. For the wedding, Nancy gives Eppie a (a) ring (b) bouquet (c) bonnet (d) dress

Answers

1-b, 2-b, 3-d, 4-a, 5-b, 6-b, 7-c, 8-c, 9-a, 10-d, 11-b, 12-c, 13-b, 14-c, 15-d, 16-c, 17-a, 18-b, 19-c, 20-d, 21-b, 22-d, 23-b, 24-c, 25-d

II. *Alternate Objective Tests*

A. Matching

Before each number in the column on the left, write the *letter* of the item in the column on the right that matches:

.... 1. Jem Rodney   a. tobacco
.... 2. Mr. Macey   b. cobbler's wife
.... 3. Sally Oates   c. spaniel
.... 4. Sarah   d. nickname
.... 5. Dunsey   e. mole-catcher
.... 6. Molly   f. horse trader
.... 7. Snuff   g. "lovely carkiss"
.... 8. Bryce   h. parish clerk
.... 9. Mr. Snell   i. drunken wife
...... 10. red Durham   j. box
                                k. landlord
                                l. sweetheart

Answers

1-e, 2-h, 3-b, 4-l, 5-d, 6-i, 7-c, 8-f, 9-k, 10-g

B. Fill-ins

From the column on the right, select the item that best completes each statement below, and write it in the space provided:

1. Godfrey has misappropriated one hundred pounds of _____ money he collected.
2. Marner's money is hidden under some _____.
3. At the Rainbow, an argument arises over Mr. Tookey's _____.
4. Mr. Macey tells a story of a mixed-up _____.
5. The farrier is called a (an) _____.
6. A (an) _____ is found at the scene of the robbery.
7. When he first visits Silas, Aaron is _____ old.
8. The holiday dance takes place at the _____.

spanked
Sally
seven
coal-hole
money
voice
locket
Molly
tinder-box
attic
christened
cow-doctor
walk
Red House
ring
marriage

9. The huddled figure in the snow is _____.

10. The child in Marner's arms is immediately recognized by _____.

11. Dolly convinces Silas that the child should be _____.

12. Silas punishes Eppie by putting her in the _____.

13. One day, Silas shows Eppie the _____ belonging to his mother.

14. Silas revisits Lantern Yard after _____ years.

15. Mr. Macey's prophecy about the _____ comes true.

thirty
Rainbow
selling horses
Godfrey
boards
rent
Dunstan
bricks
twelve

Answers

1-rent, 2-bricks, 3-voice, 4-marriage, 5-cow-doctor, 6-tinder-box, 7-seven, 8-Red House, 9-Molly, 10-Godfrey, 11-christened, 12-coal-hole, 13-ring, 14-thirty, 15-money

III. *Ideas for Written or Oral Book Reports or Class Discussions*

1. Chance plays an important part in the story. Silas happens to have an attack when he sits with the patient in Lantern Yard, he happens to be out when Dunstan passes the cottage, Eppie happens to see the light in the doorway, Molly happens to die before Godfrey is exposed, and so forth. Find several other examples. Some critics say that coincidence is perfectly consistent with real-life situations. Others argue that so many accidental occurrences rob the story of true reality or even credibility. Take one position or the other, and support your ideas by references to incidents in the story and in your own experience.

2. George Eliot often makes skillful use of dramatic irony; that is, a situation in which the reader knows more than the character or characters involved. One example is the knowledge of Godfrey's secret marriage. Find several

more examples of dramatic irony, and explain whether they add to or detract from the suspense in the story.

3. In her accurate reproduction of the speech of the inhabitants of Raveloe, Eliot uses some words that no longer have the meanings she used. An example is *doubt* (p. 72M), which means in this context "suspect" or "imagine." Find other words whose meanings have changed, and, consulting a good etymological source, try to explain what brought about the changes.

4. The villagers of Raveloe have many superstitions, such as "a bit of red thread round the child's toe" or "little bags round their necks" (p. 20T). Collect other examples of these superstitions, and show how they might have originated and how they can be disproved.

5. *Silas Marner* has been called by some a sentimental story. Sentimentality consists of making a thing or an event more charged with emotion than is justified, or in so arranging incidents as to make them appeal to the emotions rather than to reason. In what ways is George Eliot sentimental in her attitudes, and in what other ways does she avoid sentimentality?

6. In the eyes of some readers, Godfrey Cass must appear to be an utter weakling, unable to manage his affairs without indecision and outright deceit. In the eyes of others, he may appear to be intensely human, with certain weaknesses common to us all. Select one of these points of view and support your conclusions by citing examples based upon people you know.

7. To what extent is it believable that Silas, pictured as he is in the early chapters of the book, could turn about and become an ideal father of an orphan girl? Compare his development with that of some person you know, have read about, or have seen in a television or motion picture drama.

8. It is thought by some that, of the two sisters, Priscilla Lammeter is more interestingly drawn than Nancy. Why do you suppose this opinion is held? How could the author have given the plain sister a more vital role in the plot?

9. Considering the kind of life the author (Mary Ann Evans Lewes Cross) led, what is revealed about her secret

longings in her treatment of Eppie from childhood to young married womanhood? To what extent is her stress on morality a reflection of her own misgivings about her private life? What part of Marner's personality may have stemmed from her own reactions to society, especially in her early years?

10. Have you ever revisited a town or neighborhood where you formerly lived? Compare your reactions to those of Silas when he saw Lantern Yard thirty years after his departure.

IV. *Vocabulary Study*

Diagnostic Test

1T	pallid	tanned	pale	friendly
1B	intermittent	regular	warm	periodic
2M	eccentric	odd	normal	circular
2M	conjuring	praying	practicing magic	declining
3T	chary	bold	burned	cautious
3T	protuberant	bulging	flat	hollow
7T	repugnance	love	dislike	force
8M	resurgent	falling	closing	rising again
14B	culpable	innocent	blameworthy	doubtful
16M	occult	secret	clear	clangorous
23T	erudite	stupid	learned	primitive
26M	unctuous	rough	balky	oily
29M	gratuitously	uncalled for	loyally	evilly
35B	rumination	blankness	thought	drink
36T	prosaic	narrative	dull	exciting
36B	compunction	revenge	assurance	remorse
44T	felicitous	suitable	extreme	strange
48T	cupidity	generosity	love	greed
49M	presentiment	review	foreboding	gift
55M	hectoring	pestering	consoling	fighting
55M	conviviality	sociability	isolation	discharge
56T	fustian	wool	cotton cloth	rayon
72T	torpid	active	brown	sluggish
76M	repudiated	accepted	rejected	defeated
83M	fluctuation	holding steady	decline	rising and falling

88B	embezzle	defraud	pay	make up
89B	duplicity	bargaining	double-dealing	imitating
93B	deprecated	applauded	belittled	disapproved
102T	imperceptibly	openly	not noticeably	thinly
107B	ogre	saint	vegetable	monster
111T	irascibility	irritability	calmness	stealth
111M	paltry	huge	trifling	stored
131T	levity	sadness	rudeness	gaiety
133M	carping	grumbling	receptive	fishing
133M	offal	distance	waste	produce
137M	premeditated	looked back	settled	thought ahead
139M	torpor	lightness	sluggishness	raciness
140M	inarticulate	clear	showy	not expressive
141B	catalepsy	reagent	fit	health
145T	volatile	steady	changeable	fast
145M	profligacy	tightness	profit	extravagance
161M	dormant	inactive	lively	roomy
163M	incompatible	suitable	not in harmony	uncovered
173T	veracious	truthful	greedy	deceitful
177T	beholden	free	tight	indebted
179T	fetishism	religion	object worship	weight
185T	rusticity	decoration	simplicity	decay
195B	retrospect	backward look	forward look	inward look
220M	repose	action	talk	relaxation
227B	renunciation	addition	giving up	proclamation

Answers

pallid-pale, *intermittent*-periodic, *eccentric*-odd, *conjuring*-practicing magic, *chary*-cautious, *protuberant*-bulging, *repugnance*-dislike, *resurgent*-rising again, *culpable*-blameworthy, *occult*-secret, *erudite*-learned, *unctuous*-oily, *gratuitously*-uncalled for, *rumination*-thought, *prosaic*-dull, *compunction*-remorse, *felicitous*-suitable, *cupidity*-greed, *presentiment*-foreboding, *hectoring*-pestering, *conviviality*-sociability, *fustian*-cotton cloth, *torpid*-sluggish, *repudiated*-rejected, *fluctuation*-rising and falling, *embezzle*-defraud, *duplicity*-double-dealing, *deprecated*-disapproved, *imperceptibly*-not noticeably, *ogre*-monster, *irascibility*-irritability, *paltry*-trifling, *levity*-gaiety, *carping*-grumbling, *offal*-waste, *premeditated*-thought ahead, *torpor*-sluggishness, *inarticulate*-not expressive, *catalepsy*-fit, *volatile*-changeable, *profligacy*-extravagance, *dormant*-inactive, *incompatible*-not in harmony, *veracious*-truthful, *beholden*-indebted, *fetishism*-object worship, *rusticity*-simplicity, *retrospect*-backward look, *repose*-relaxation, *renunciation*-giving up

Teaching Aids

for

A TALE OF TWO CITIES

In this magnificent tale of London and Paris during the bloody days of the French Revolution, Charles Dickens won for himself the greatest popularity any novelist has ever known. Few readers will fail to respond to the rich descriptive power of the author as he depicts the noble self-sacrifice of Sydney Carton, the awesome carnage of the Reign of Terror that almost destroyed France, the gentle courage of Lucie Manette, or the comic relief provided by the rib-tickling antics of Jerry Cruncher.

I. *Objective Test*

In the space provided at the left, insert the *letter* of the correct choice from among those offered; for example:

....b.... The author of this book is (a) Jones (b) Dickens (c) Stevenson (d) Hardy

.... 1. The messenger on horseback turns out to be (a) Cly (b) Jerry (c) Barsad (d) Defarge

.... 2. When Miss Pross first meets Mr. Lorry, she (a) pushes him (b) curtsies (c) smiles prettily (d) stands speechless

.... 3. After the cask of wine breaks, one man writes on a wall the word (a) Revolt (b) Treason (c) Blood (d) Freedom

.... 4. "Recalled to life" refers to (a) Dr. Manette (b) Lucie (c) Madame Defarge (d) Darnay

.... 5. Charles Darnay is accused in Old Bailey of (a) theft (b) arson (c) forgery (d) treason

.... 6. Young Jerry cannot understand why his father (a) gets angry (b) drinks (c) has rusty fingers (d) works so hard

.... 7. Carton plays jackal to the lion called (a) Lorry (b) Stryver (c) Darnay (d) Defarge

.... 8. The carriage of the Marquis kills a (a) woman (b) road mender (c) sweeper (d) child

.... 9. The nephew of the monseigneur is (a) Darnay (b) Gabelle (c) Gaspard (d) Defarge

.... 10. The man who tells Lucie he would give his life to keep a life she loves beside her is (a) Darnay (b) Dr. Manette (c) Carton (d) Stryver

.... 11. Jerry Cruncher objects to his wife's (a) nagging (b) smoking (c) singing (d) flopping

.... 12. Young Jerry learns that his father's "fishing" trips take him to a (a) river (b) graveyard (c) lake (d) stream

.... 13. Madame Defarge knits to (a) keep busy (b) make socks (c) fashion clothes (d) register names

.... 14. The revolution begins when the peasants attack the (a) Bastille (b) palace (c) soldiers (d) king

.... 15. One Hundred and Five North Tower is a (a) shop (b) house number (c) street (d) prison cell

.... 16. He dies with grass in his mouth: (a) Gaspard (b) the governor (c) Foulon (d) the turnkey

.... 17. Darnay goes to Paris after receiving a letter from (a) Defarge (b) Dr. Manette (c) Jacques (d) Gabelle

.... 18. Darnay is seized and consigned to (a) the Bastille (b) La Force (c) Guilon (d) Marseilles

.... 19. At his first trial before the Tribunal, Darney is (a) sent back to prison (b) released (c) condemned (d) helped by Defarge

.... 20. At his second trial, Darnay is set free because

of the plea of (a) Lucie (b) Defarge (c) Gabelle (d) Dr. Manette

.... 21. Darnay's second arrest is caused by (a) Defarge (b) Barsad (c) Cly (d) the wood-
sawyer

.... 22. Miss Pross turns out to be the sister of (a)
Cly (b) Carton (c) Barsad (d) Jerry

.... 23. Carton convinces Barsad to help by mentioning
(a) money (b) jewels (c) an empty coffin
(d) gold

.... 24. Darnay is finally condemned after the reading
of a paper written by (a) Madame Defarge
(b) Dr. Manette (c) Gabelle (d) Stryver

.... 25. Carton saves Darnay after giving him a (a)
blow on the head (b) glass of wine (c) drug
(d) note

Answers

1-b, 2-a, 3-c, 4-a, 5-d, 6-c, 7-b, 8-d, 9-a, 10-c, 11-d, 12-b, 13-d,
14-a, 15-d, 16-c, 17-d, 18-b, 19-a, 20-d, 21-a, 22-c, 23-c, 24-b, 25-c

II. *Alternate Objective Tests*

A. Matching

Before each number in the column on the left, write the
letter of the item in the column on the right that matches:

.... 1. Ladybird   a. Dr. Manette
.... 2. shoemaker   b. witness
.... 3. Aggerawayter   c. Miss Pross
.... 4. stone face   d. revolutionary
.... 5. Jacques   e. Madame Defarge
.... 6. Cly   f. Mrs. Cruncher
.... 7. "Shoulders his way"   g. monseigneur
.... 8. letter *de cache*   h. courthouse
.... 9. Old Bailey   i. Mr. Stryver

...... 10. woman of "red colour"

j. Sydney Carton
k. imprisonment
l. English town
m. Mr. Lorry
n. forged note
o. Lucie

Answers

1-o, 2-a, 3-f, 4-g, 5-d, 6-b, 7-i, 8-k, 9-h, 10-c

B. Fill-ins

From the column on the right, select the item that best completes each statement below, and write it in the space provided:

1. The story opens on the road to _____.
2. St. Antoine is a district of _____.
3. "Drive him fast to his tomb" is written on a note attached to the _____.
4. The "honest tradesman" calls his work _____.
5. The knife murderer is _____.
6. Dr. Manette has a relapse when he learns Darnay's real _____.
7. The "best cure for a headache" is _____.
8. Carton is helped in the prison by _____.
9. Dr. Manette's story is found in the _____.
10. Lucie appeals for her husband's life to _____.
11. Carton arranges his escape plans for Lucie with _____.
12. Madame Defarge is finally _____.

Gaspard
shoemaking
La Guillotine
disapproval
road mender
Dover
Mr. Lorry
rest
approval
marquis
Bastille
place
Paris
Resurrection
Barsad
occupation
seamstress
name
strangled
Madame
  Defarge

13. Carton's companion in the tumbril is a   Gabelle
_____.   nobleman

14. Among his final words are these: shot
". . . it is a far, far better _____   pills
I go to. . . ."

15. Dickens looks upon the bloody execu-
tions with _____.

Answers

1-Dover, 2-Paris, 3-marquis, 4-Resurrection, 5-Gaspard, 6-name,
7-La Guillotine, 8-Barsad, 9-Bastille, 10-Madame Defarge, 11-
Mr. Lorry, 12-shot, 13-seamstress, 14-rest, 15-disapproval

III. *Ideas for Written or Oral Book Reports or Class Discussions*

1. *Buried Alive* and *The Doctor of Beauvais* are names
that Dickens considered for this book, set in the period of
the French Revolution. When he finally thought of the
name *A Tale of Two Cities,* he said, "I have exactly the
name for the story that is wanted." To what extent do you
agree that he chose the best possible name? Even if you
agree that he chose wisely, what other names might he
have considered that would have been more attractive or
more representative of the theme? Support each suggestion
by explaining why you think it is as good as or better than
the original.

2. At the beginning of Book II, Chapter 21 (p. 260T),
Dickens refers to Lucie as "ever busily winding the golden
thread which bound her husband and her father, and herself . . . in a life of quiet bliss." What was the golden
thread? Why do you suppose Dickens stresses this stage
in the lives of the main characters just before he launches
into his fiery descriptions of the wild scenes that are soon
to follow?

3. At one point, when he is expounding his philosophy
of power to his nephew Charles Darnay, the marquis says,
"Repression is the only lasting philosophy. The dark def-

erence of fear and slavery, my friend, will keep the dogs obedient to the whip, as long as this roof shuts out the sky" (p. 151B). On the other hand, when Dickens is describing the reactions of the citizens of Saint Antoine when they have finally decided to revolt, he says, "Every pulse and heart in Saint Antoine was on high-fever strain and at high-fever heat. Every living creature there held life as of no account and was demented with a passionate readiness to sacrifice it" (p. 266B). How badly has the marquis misjudged the temper of the people? To what extent can the savage acts of revenge of the mobs be attributed, in whole or in part, to pent-up fury generated by the philosophy of the marquis, who stands as the symbol of many French noblemen of the time? What efforts, if any, were made in France, prior to the revolution, to institute reform movements, and why were they unsuccessful?

4. Consider the oft-repeated statement: "The end justifies the means." Does it always? If you had been a French peasant at the time of the revolution, would you have agreed entirely with the treatment of the governor of the Bastille, Foulon, Darnay, the seamstress, and others among those caught in the tide of revolt? Explain. What sometimes happens to people who become too accustomed to violence? What recent events in history can you cite to support your views?

5. What would psychologists have to say about Dr. Manette's loss of memory? About his occasional relapses? About the great strength of will he displays when he becomes involved in the fight for Charles Darnay's life?

6. After you learn the true reasons for Dr. Manette's long imprisonment, you understand better why Madame Defarge has such an implacable hatred for the Evrémondes. How does this information affect your attitude toward her? To what extent were her actions against all noblemen generally, and Darnay particularly, justified? Describe the thoughts that passed through your mind after she was killed by Miss Pross.

7. Among the characters Dickens obviously looks upon with approval are Lorry, Darnay, Lucie, Dr. Manette,

Carton, Miss Pross, and, however subtly, Jerry Cruncher. Among those he considers unworthy human beings are the marquis, the Defarges, Barsad, Cly, Mr. Stryver, and, collectively, the mobs in the streets and before the Tribunal. What does this tell us about the attitudes of the author toward good and evil, weaknesses and strengths of character, vice and virtues of mankind?

8. Coincidence plays a rather large role in the story. Darnay accidentally meets the daughter of the man whom his uncle has wronged; Carton happens to look very much like Darnay; Jerry digs up the empty coffin that later traps Barsad, who turns out to be the brother of Miss Pross! The Defarges, of course, are intimately involved in the past of both the Manettes and Darnay. How likely would it have been in real life for all these associations to have occurred as they do in the novel? What criticism would you make of the plot manipulations of Dickens in view of the many coincidences?

9. Charles Darnay is handsome, noble-minded, democratic far beyond what his background should have produced, faithful as a husband and doting as a father, courageous and loyal as a friend (to Gabelle especially). Sydney Carton is shiftless, frequently intoxicated, self-destroying, rather surly. Yet with one act of heroism, he becomes the hero, if we can call it that, of the book. What's more, he is considered to be the more interesting character of the two. What is there in our own character that makes us feel warmer toward a person like Carton than we do toward a Darnay? What is wrong with being almost perfect?

10. Suppose Dickens were alive today and was writing for television or motion pictures: How popular would he be? What are the kinds of stories he would prefer to tell? What kind of people would he write about? Who among modern writers most resembles Dickens in general style? Explain.

11. The style of a Dickens novel is so rich in technique that it has often been used as a model by fiction writers. Analyze the style by commenting on and *providing specific examples* for each of the following categories:

a. The use by Dickens of suspense, surprise, foreshadowing, caricature, irony, mistaken identity, and descriptive detail.

b. His use of humor, including dialect words and epithets like *Aggerawayter, Stryver, flopping, lion, jackal, fishing, resurrection,* and so forth.

c. His skill in developing interwoven plots, shifting locales, and contrasting points of view.

12. Dickens has been criticized for his excessive use of one-dimensional or idealized characters, to the point where the reader meets types rather than fully rounded human beings. To what extent would you say this criticism is unfair? Discuss at least two characters who are developed in reasonable depth. On the other hand, how justified is the criticism in respect to at least three other characters?

IV. *Vocabulary Study*

Diagnostic Test

3T	incredulity	belief	doubt	cause
4B	tumbril	fall	load	cart
5M	retinue	escort	guide	trail
7T	tremulous	firm	quivering	huge
14M	alienated	captured	befriended	estranged
15B	inscrutable	incomprehensible	clear	twisted
16B	cadaverous	robust	corpselike	tall
20M	sonorous	noisy	sunny	rich-sounding
20M	evanescence	brilliance	fading	darkness
22M	piscatory	of men	of elves	of fish
39T	implacable	relentless	willing	movable
40T	triumvirate	victory	three-man power	monarch
56B	lethargy	energy	toughness	sluggishness
68M	laudanum	opium mix	praise	flower
73B	aphorism	lie	proverb	demand
81T	pernicious	deadly	mild	steady
92T	antipathies	loves	medicines	dislikes
101M	terrestrial	old	earthly	planetary

113M	staid	imaginative	steady	bold
122T	culinary	raising	calling	cooking
132B	talisman	charm	giant	shawl
164M	nurtured	starved	carved	nourished
184M	transitory	fixed	fleeting	traveling
193B	acclamation	complaint	applause	demand
200M	spectral	ghostlike	statuesque	visible
203M	recompense	sale	money	repayment
214M	poltroon	hero	judge	coward
216M	ubiquitous	rare	harsh	being everywhere
221T	olfactory	sense of smell	sense of taste	machine plant
236B	apocryphal	real thing	not genuine	graceful
256M	oblivion	memory	forgetfulness	cheer
262M	turbid	clear	covered	muddy
263T	exuding	discharging	absorbing	going
270T	inundation	waste	flood	desert
285T	attenuated	thinned out	strengthened	added
289T	tocsin	song	alarm bell	antidote
291B	munificent	stingy	local	generous
313T	cockade	bird	hat badge	fort
318T	noisesome	foul-smelling	sweet	loud
322M	metempsychosis	soul transfer	insanity	medium
338T	inviolate	flowery	sacred	supreme
345B	redundancy	repetition	introduction	expiration
367M	gregarious	snobbish	sociable	single
377M	tergiversation	logic	talk	evasion
381B	ostentatious	showy	modest	stretched
399M	unimpaired	broken	undamaged	separated
452B	imbued	emptied	filled	colored
453T	inveterate	unchanging	unstable	experienced
457M	exordium	beginning	end	arena
461M	tenacity	weakness	firm hold	numbers

Answers

incredulity-doubt, *tumbril*-cart, *retinue*-escort, *tremulous*-quivering, *alienated*-estranged, *inscrutable*-incomprehensible, *cadaverous*-corpselike, *sonorous*-rich-sounding, *evanescence*-fading, *piscatory*-of fish, *implacable*-relentless, *triumvirate*-three-man power, *lethargy*-sluggishness, *laudanum*-opium mix, *aphorism*-proverb, *pernicious*-deadly, *antipathies*-dislikes, *terrestrial*-earthly, *staid*-steady, *culinary*-cooking, *talisman*-charm, *nurtured*-nourished, *transitory*-fleeting, *acclamation*-applause, *spectral*-ghostlike, *recompense*-repayment, *poltroon*-coward, *ubiquitous*-being everywhere, *olfactory*-sense of smell, *apocryphal*-not genuine, *oblivion*-forgetfulness, *turbid*-muddy, *exuding*-discharging, *inundation*-flood, *attenuated*-thinned out, *tocsin*-alarm bell, *munificent*-generous, *cockade*-hat badge, *noisome*-foul-smelling, *metempsychosis*-soul transfer, *inviolate*-sacred, *redundancy*-repetition, *gregarious*-sociable, *tergiversation*-evasion, *ostentatious*-showy, *unimpaired*-undamaged, *imbued*-filled, *inveterate*-unchanging, *exordium*-beginning, *tenacity*-firm hold

Teaching Aids

for

TESS OF THE D'URBERVILLES

Modern readers find in Thomas Hardy the forerunner of twentieth-century writers who have looked at life and found it too full of lust and avarice, selfishness and indifference to human welfare. The anguished struggles of Tess against relentless circumstance place her story among the masterpieces of world fiction. It is a tragic and beautiful tale of a woman who was forced to sin by a man she hated and was cast out by the man she loved.

I. *Objective Test*

In the space provided at the left, insert the *letter* of the correct choice from among those offered; for example:

....c.... The author of this book is (a) Twain (b) Dickens (c) Hardy

.... 1. John Durbeyfield discovered he was actually "Sir John" when he (a) visited Kingsbere (b) met Parson Tringham on the road (c) was contacted by the family solicitor

.... 2. Angel first saw Tess when he (a) met her at the dairy (b) passed through her village on a walking tour (c) wandered away from his party of friends

.... 3. In the Durbeyfield family, (a) Tess had sole responsibility for caring for the younger children (b) "Sir John" and his wife often quar-

415

reled (c) "Sir John" and Joan were both fond
of drinking

.... 4. Tess was driven to seek help from the D'Urbervilles when (a) her father became ill (b) her
brother and she lost the beehives (c) Prince
was killed by the morning mail cart

.... 5. Although she pretended to Tess that all she
expected from Mrs. D'Urberville was some
slight financial assistance, Joan actually hoped
(a) they would be paid for the use of their
name (b) Tess might become one of the old
lady's heirs (c) Mrs. D'Urberville would somehow arrange an advantageous marriage for Tess

.... 6. The job that Tess was assigned at the D'Urberville mansion was to (a) milk cows (b)
wait upon Mrs. D'Urberville (c) tend the old
woman's fowls

.... 7. Tess allowed Alec to take her off late at night
because she (a) was being attacked by the enraged females of Trantridge (b) was frightened,
lost, cold (c) was desperately anxious about
her family

.... 8. After Tess returned to her native village, her
first job was as a (a) dairymaid (b) governess
(c) harvest hand

.... 9. When the cows of Talbothays withheld their
milk because Tess had come among them, the
measure taken to correct the situation was to
(a) dress Tess in another milkmaid's costume
(b) ask Tess to go back to the house until after
milking time (c) sing to the cows

.... 10. Among his many other accomplishments, Angel Clare (a) played the harp (b) milked
better than any other man except Mr. Crick
himself (c) was a brilliant scholar at Cam-
bridge

.... 11. Because of what some of the other dairymaids
had told her, Tess was convinced that Angel
would disapprove of her (a) going to the

church she attended (b) expressed lack of faith
(c) being a D'Urberville

.... 12. The number of dairymaids at Talbothays who
were hopelessly in love with Angel was (a)
three (b) two (c) four

.... 13. When Angel returned to tell his parents about
his plan to marry Tess, he brought gifts from
Mrs. Crick, which the elder Clares (a) rejected
because of their crudeness (b) sold to local
shopkeepers (c) gave away

.... 14. Alec D'Urberville's first contact with the Clare
family came about when he (a) saw Tess, now
Angel's wife (b) was introduced to Reverend
Clare (c) insulted the elder Mr. Clare

.... 15. When Angel finally proposed marriage to Tess,
she (a) refused (b) fainted (c) wrote to her
mother

.... 16. Tess finally accepted Angel's proposal (a) on
a romantic summer evening (b) as they
skimmed milk together (c) on a wet wagon
ride

.... 17. Tess was disturbed one night by a noise caused
by Angel's (a) leaving the house (b) having
a dream about a fight (c) pacing the floor

.... 18. Angel secretly hoped to (a) impress his family
with the revelation that Tess was a D'Urberville
(b) persuade Tess to go abroad with him (c)
follow in his father's footsteps

.... 19. Tess and Angel were married on (a) Easter
Sunday (b) New Year's Eve (c) Christmas
day

.... 20. Tess first attempted to tell Angel of her past by
(a) hinting at it (b) having another dairymaid
tell him (c) writing about it in a letter

.... 21. According to the old legend, D'Urbervilles (a)
walked in their sleep (b) had to be buried in
the family vault (c) saw or heard the old
D'Urberville coach before they died

.... 22. Tess's family lost their home because (a) John

Durbeyfield died (b) they could not pay the rent (c) Alec arranged it that way
.... 23. Alec's mother was (a) crippled (b) feeble-minded (c) blind
.... 24. Angel's brothers were (a) jealous of him (b) great disappointments to their parents (c) "stuffed shirts"
.... 25. Tess first saw Alec after their long separation as the young man was (a) hunting (b) preaching (c) drinking heavily

Answers

1-b, 2-b, 3-c, 4-c, 5-c, 6-c, 7-a, 8-c, 9-c, 10-a, 11-c, 12-c, 13-c, 14-c, 15-a, 16-b, 17-b, 18-a, 19-b, 20-c, 21-c, 22-a, 23-c, 24-c, 25-b

II. *Alternate Objective Tests*

A. Matching

Before each number in the column on the left, write the *letter* of the item in the column on the right that matches:

.... 1. Izz Huett
.... 2. Retty Priddle
.... 3. Marian
.... 4. Mercy Chant
.... 5. farmer at Flint-comb-Ash
.... 6. Mr. Crick
.... 7. Marlott
.... 8. Flintcomb-Ash
.... 9. Alec D'Urberville
...... 10. Sandbourne

a. Tess and Angel's supervisor
b. tried to drown herself
c. rescued Tess from an unfriendly mob
d. fashionable resort
e. Tess's home village
f. killed Tess's horse
g. was asked by Alec to go away with him
h. almost had a fight with Tess
i. was hit by Angel
j. was expected to marry Angel
k. figured in the D'Urberville legend

l. become an alcoholic
m. Angel's hometown
n. where Tess worked with
Marian

Answers

1-g, 2-b, 3-1, 4-j, 5-i, 6-a, 7-e, 8-n, 9-c, 10-d

B. Fill-ins

From the column on the right, select the item that best completes each statement below, and write it in the space provided:

1. Tess almost had a fight with _____.
2. When Alec saw Tess after their long separation, he resolved to abandon the _____ life.
3. The Durbeyfield horse was killed by a (an) _____.
4. Tess, Joan, and the children spent their first night at Kingsbere in a (an) _____.
5. After his separation from Tess, Angel went off to _____.
6. Tess baptized the baby _____.
7. Angel's ambition was to become a (an) _____.
8. The happiest days of Tess's life were spent at _____.
9. Tess met dark Car and her sister for a second time when Tess was _____.
10. When Angel left *The Herons,* he was soon followed by _____.
11. The first person Tess met when she arrived at The Slopes was _____.
12. Tess finally settled down to live with Alec in _____.

Egdon Heath
Brazil
Tess
parson
Izz Huett
Alec
   D'Urberville
Talbothays
dancing
religious
Sorrow
inn
churchyard
mail carriage
Car Darch
'Liza-Lu
Sandbourne
reed-drawing
farmer
milking cows
playboy's
drinking
Joan
   Durbeyfield

13. Tess's departure from Chaseborough was delayed because her walking companions were busy _____.

14. Tess was assured that her baby's baptism would be effective by the _____.

15. Angel Clare walked away from Wintoncester with _____.

Answers

1-Car Darch, 2-religious, 3-mail carriage, 4-churchyard, 5-Brazil, 6-Sorrow, 7-farmer, 8-Talbothays, 9-reed-drawing, 10-Tess, 11-Alec D'Urberville, 12-Sandbourne, 13-dancing, 14-prison, 15-'Liza-Lu

III. *Ideas for Written or Oral Book Reports or Class Discussions*

1. Most authorities agree that an individual's environment is extremely important in determining the kind of person he will become. Certainly no single factor in the environment can be regarded as more significant than the person's family. By citing specific references to the events in *Tess of the D'Urbervilles,* indicate how particular traits of character in Tess, Angel, and Alec might be explained by the character's relations with his family. How, for example, would Alec's instability or lack of a moral sense be explained by his role in the Stoke-D'Urberville household? What is there about the family life in the Clare residence or in the personality of Reverend Clare that could explain Angel's domination by popular Victorian prejudices about sexual behavior? What makes Tess, who is a mere girl at the time, assume the responsibility of providing for the Durbeyfield children when she reluctantly goes off to "claim kin" with the D'Urbervilles? You should be able to identify and explore the family-life reasons to explain at least two traits of character or personality (such as determination, pride, generosity, recklessness, self-assurance, or shyness) for each of these three main figures in the book.

2. One of the most significant ways in which a gifted writer and a perceptive reader cooperate to produce an enriched reading experience is in the inclusion and interpretation of symbols in the author's treatment of his material. Hardy introduces many symbols in *Tess of the D'Urbervilles*. Discuss at least four, and explain fully how Hardy enriches the book by using them. You might, for example, cite the scene in which Tess and Angel, fleeing from their unseen and therefore impersonal pursuers, seek refuge in the ancient ruins of Stonehenge. What is the significance of the fact that Tess falls asleep on an ancient sacrificial altar? Why is society, in the persons of these faceless individuals, relentlessly "after" Tess? Another symbol is the sequence of events set in the Valley of the Froom, the richly productive land of the great dairies. Why does Tess go to that particular locality at the period in her life when she does? Why does Hardy, in describing the lush district, imply that there is just a touch of overripeness about it? When dealing with these or any other symbols, always explore as many aspects of them as possible. Additional possible sources for symbolic exploration are: Clare's sleepwalking, the locality of Flintcomb-Ash, Mrs. D'Urberville's blindness. There are many more in the book.

3. Although Hardy chooses not to discuss the events, Tess must have been tried for the murder of Alec D'Urberville. Using events, ideas, conversations, personalities discussed in the course of the book, prepare either to sum up the prosecution's case or to appeal to a jury of her peers to defend Tess. Could Tess's actions have been termed self-defense in any way? Could you support a plea that in this case the murder of Alec was "justifiable homicide"? How might the whole social structure of Tess's society have been threatened by her being given a light sentence for the crime? You might call upon your experiences with lawyers in literature or on the television screen to help you in supporting the point of view you adopt, but remember that the arguments for the prosecution or the defense must be thorough, complete, and documented from the book.

4. Much adverse criticism of Thomas Hardy has been based upon the claim that his use of coincidence in bring-

ing his plots to their climaxes is excessive. Disparaging references might be made to the fact that Alec is the first one Tess sees when she arrives at The Slopes; Alec "happens" to meet Tess on the one night when trouble develops between Tess and the tipsy merrymakers at Trantridge; the letter in which Tess tells Angel of her past slides under Angel's rug. Discuss in some detail at least five coincidences that occur in the book. Indicate why you would or would not agree with those critics who feel that Hardy has used "chance" in too many ways for the story to be completely credible.

5. a. If people such as Tess, Angel, and Alec found themselves in a situation similar to that described in this book, but were living in your community today, how might the outcome be different? Specifically, how might public opinion result in a completely different climax? To what extent would modern conventions regarding young people who have made mistakes prevent the ultimate tragedy of the book? Describe in some detail what progress we have made toward a more enlightened attitude toward the less fortunate members of our society.

b. What are the implications of the role Tess was forced to play in her family's economic life? How true is it today that large numbers of people are forced to leave jobs to seek new employment because they cannot live under the conditions of work or the low salaries? What reminders of feudal customs did you recognize in this story set in late nineteenth-century England? Discuss these and other ways in which events in the book might have been changed had they occurred in your own surroundings.

6. One of the popular literary devices used in *Tess of the D'Urbervilles* is foreshadowing. At its best, this device suggests what might happen without announcing exactly what occurrences are to be expected. It prepares the reader for later events so that the reader's reaction will approximate "Oh yes, of course!" when the event occurs. Discuss how successful Hardy is in using this technique by making specific references to at least five examples of foreshadowing in the book. Among the examples you might cite are: Angel's carrying Tess in his sleep; Tess's fears in the huge

rented coach on their wedding day; the fact that a rooster crows during the afternoon of their wedding day.

7. If you were asked to prepare an outline for a television script of an abridged version of *Tess of the D'Urbervilles,* what specific events would you regard as absolutely essential to present the spirit of the book in an hour-long show? Would you include the first wild ride Tess was forced to take with Alec? Would you feel that the tender scene during which Tess happens upon Angel playing his harp was important? What about the scene when Tess saw Alec in the unexpected role of preacher? How important would the story be of the frightened lover hiding in the butter churn (told by Mr. Crick)? Would you take time to deal with Tess's attempted visit to Angel's parents? Indicate exactly which events you would include, and provide reasons why each could not be omitted.

8. We are given only a very brief glimpse of the discussion between Tess and Alec that preceded Tess's stabbing him. The indistinct impression we get of what happened is conveyed through the muffled sounds and sights perceived by Mrs. Brooks. Reconstruct the discussion that probably occurred when Tess returned to their room and confronted Alec with the fact that Angel was back. She might have reproached him for pursuing and betraying her; Alec might have counterattacked by reviewing the favors he had done for Tess and her family. During the course of the heated argument, both participants probably would reveal much about themselves and their lives.

9. Much might be said to support or contest the selection of almost any book as a class text. State whether you feel *Tess of the D'Urbervilles* would make a good selection for study by a class in your school. Some of the points you might touch upon in your attempt to influence those responsible for making the decision are:

    a. The book is dull. Not very much happens that would serve to retain the interest of modern young people.

    b. Hardy's outlook is pessimistic. The implication that we are doomed to suffer at the hands of a basically ill-disposed fate would be depressing, bad for student morale.

c. The book is dominated by a clever but basically unbelievable plot. What happens to Tess does not seem to be a direct result of the kind of person she is. Angel and Alec are not credible characters because the first is too good and the second too completely wicked.

d. The book's theme is immoral. Tess is made a heroine in spite of the fact that she is an adulteress. Reading this book might encourage immoral behavior on the part of the impressionable young people who are exposed to it.

Although these suggestions are stated in the negative, the converse of them might be advanced as reasons why the book would make a suitable selection. Give at least five reasons for or against class use of this book, and support them by citing specific evidence from your reading experiences.

10. A classic device used by writers for the ancient Greek theater was the *deux ex machina* (the god from the machine). When a situation became so involved that natural means were insufficient to unravel it, a god would descend onto the stage and use his supernatural powers to set matters straight. This technique has been employed more recently in the form of granting wishes to certain characters or introducing a genie with special powers who offers to help. In the spirit of this device, write a detailed account of one event in *Tess of the D'Urbervilles* that you would change if you had the power. In terms consistent with the established characteristics and relationships of Hardy's people, tell why you would make this particular change. Indicate when in Tess's life you would make it. Would you prevent her meeting Alec when she first visited The Slopes? Would you send preacher Alec D'Urberville to another part of England and thus prevent their second encounter? Would you postpone her trip to the Clares until a time when Reverend and Mrs. Clare were sitting alone at home quietly discussing Angel?

Indicate exactly how the events of the book that follow your intervention would be altered. Justify your predictions by referring to what actually did happen after the event and how the variation caused by your action would modify it.

IV. *Vocabulary Study*

Diagnostic Test

XIT	protagonist	villain	main character	acrobat
118	desultory	organized	stationary	aimless
19T	appurtenances	necessities	rude questions	accessories
27M	somnolent	active	sleepy	mysterious
31B	stoically	angrily	enthusiastically	unflinchingly
57B	nascent	mature	being born	quiet
58M	ensconced	settled comfortably	displayed	cramped
58B	mien	viciousness	bearing	quality
59M	undulations	levels	complaints	waves
60T	repugnance	appetite	distaste	ugliness
63B	dyspeptic	cheerful	drugged	grouchy
66T	metamorphosed	eternal	consistent	changed
66B	nimbus	halo	insult	description
67T	discernible	recognizable	obscured	upsetting
68M	virago	girl	aunt	a scold
70B	vituperation	praise	abuse	encouragement
71T	animus	hatred	effort	enthusiasm
71T	fatuous	stupid	ample	shrewd
72M	laconically	loudly	lengthily	briefly
72B	precarious	valuable	dangerous	safe
74T	oblivion	shock	forgetfulness	activity
75B	cursory	thorough	hasty	insulting
80M	upbraiding	praising	scolding	repairing
80B	listlessly	actively	silently	spiritlessly
82B	perfunctorily	keenly	uninterestedly	noisily
84T	propinquity	nearness	success	distance
84B	copses	bodies	thickets	policemen
84B	vermilion	green	bright red	violet
85B	unwonted	abandoned	customary	unusual
85B	edification	instruction	tastiness	corruption

87M	succumbed	overthrown	conquered	surrendered
87M	adroit	awkward	clever	underhanded
88B	evanescent	fleeting	sensational	permanent
89T	spasmodic	calm	fitful	frequent
89B	innate	foreign	inborn	ungrateful
90B	attenuated	weakened	enlarged	strained
90B	accretion	growth	disintegration	expulsion
90B	flexuous	sinuous	undeviating	hasty
91M	antipathetic	friendly	sorrowful	opposed
91B	sentient	inanimate	contradicting	having feeling
93T	ephemeral	heavenly	long lasting	short lived
95T	remunerative	disappointing	rewarding	nameless
98M	counterpoises	compensations	hesitations	successes
99B	malignant	helpful	harmless	harmful
100T	lurid	sensational	obscure	noisy
102T	apotheosized	disgraced	glorified	slandered
106T	obliterated	wiped out	damaged	constructed
137B	caricature	replica	exaggerated picture	understatement
225T	sojourn	visit	quarrel	absence
230M	culpable	admirable	innocent	blamable

Answers

protagonist-main character, *desultory*-aimless, *appurtenances*-accessories, *somnolent*-sleepy, *stoically*-unflinchingly, *nascent*-being born, *ensconced*-settled comfortably, *mien*-bearing, *undulations*-waves, *repugnance*-distaste, *dyspeptic*-grouchy, *metamorphosed*-changed, *nimbus*-halo, *discernible*-recognizable, *virago*-scold, *vituperation*-abuse, *animus*-hatred, *fatuous*-stupid, *laconically*-briefly, *precarious*-dangerous, *oblivion*-forgetfulness, *cursory*-hasty, *upbraiding*-scolding, *listlessly*-spiritlessly, *perfunctorily*-uninterestedly, *propinquity*-nearness, *copses*-thickets, *vermilion*-bright red, *unwonted*-unusual, *edification*-instruction, *succumbed*-surrendered, *adroit*-clever, *evanescent*-fleeting, *spasmodic*-fitful, *innate*-inborn, *attenuated*-weakened, *accretion*-growth, *flexuous*-sinuous, *antipathetic*-opposed, *sentient*-having feeling, *ephemeral*-short lived, *remunerative*-rewarding, *counterpoises*-compensations, *malignant*-harmful, *lurid*-sensational, *apotheosized*-glorified, *obliterated*-wiped out, *caricature*-exaggerated picture, *sojourn*-visit, *culpable*-blamable

Teaching Aids

for

TREASURE ISLAND

Here is a magnificent yarn of buried treasure, lusty pirates, and mutiny on the high seas. From the opening chapters, when the mysterious captain roars his songs at the inn and old Pew comes tapping along with his stick, there is a spine-chilling fascination that carries the reader pell-mell to the end of the book. The heroes and villains of this classic tale—Long John Silver, Jim Hawkins, Dr. Livesey, Billy Bones, Squire Trelawney, and Ben Gunn—create an adventure that has become a favorite with readers of all ages.

I. *Objective Test*

In the space provided at the left, insert the *letter* of the correct choice from among those offered; for example:

....b....   The author of this book is (a) Dickens (b) Stevenson (c) James (d) Poe

.... 1. During his stay at the "Admiral Benbow," Billy Bones seems to fear most the appearance of (a) the local police (b) a seafaring man with one leg (c) the tax collector (d) the great Captain Flint

.... 2. When threatened by Billy Bones one night, Dr. Livesey responds with (a) a humble apology (b) obvious fear (c) a promise to leave (d) a scornful threat of his own

.... 3. When Black Dog appears one morning, Billy

Bones (a) greets him warmly (b) wounds him in a scuffle (c) invites him to dinner (d) pays him money

.... 4. Jim learns that the "black spot" signifies (a) permanent disgrace (b) a recall to service (c) a sentence of death (d) a secret code

.... 5. The villainous blind man, Pew, is (a) killed by a horse (b) ordered out of town (c) shot by the squire (d) captured by the villagers

.... 6. The most valuable item found in the sea chest is (a) a sack of coins (b) some stylish clothing (c) an oilskin packet (d) a priceless ruby

.... 7. Dr. Livesey expresses concern about the treasure map and the proposed voyage because (a) Jim is too young (b) the trip is too long (c) Pew's henchmen may return (d) Squire Trelawney talks too much

.... 8. At first, Long John Silver impresses Jim, Dr. Livesey, and the squire as being (a) an incompetent fool (b) a very pleasant fellow (c) an obvious faker (d) a former friend of Black Dog

.... 9. Captain Smollett enrages Squire Trelawney by (a) voicing suspicions about the crew (b) demanding a higher fee (c) speaking against Dr. Livesey (d) insisting on a share of the treasure

.... 10. Shortly after the voyage begins, the first mate (a) dies of drunkenness (b) is killed in a brawl (c) is put into irons (d) disappears overboard

.... 11. Aboard ship, Long John shows great pride in his (a) skill as a cook (b) talkative parrot (c) carved wooden leg (d) pirate mementos

.... 12. Jim accidentally overhears Long John's plot to (a) kill Captain Smollett (b) steal the map from Dr. Livesey (c) seize Jim as a hostage (d) seize ship and treasure on the voyage home

.... 13. At first sight of Treasure Island, Jim (a) hates the sight of it (b) finds a feeling of triumph (c) wants to get started digging (d) asks Long John about its history

.... 14. To avoid open mutiny, Smollett allows the crew to (a) have a shore party (b) arm themselves (c) drink all the rum (d) elect their own captain

.... 15. On shore, one of the honest men is stabbed to death by (a) Hands (b) Silver (c) Gunn (d) Alan

.... 16. In exchange for passage home, Ben promises to (a) help John (b) remain neutral (c) share the treasure (d) keep quiet

.... 17. For greater safety, the ship is abandoned by Livesey's group for (a) another vessel (b) the stockade (c) a warship (d) a secret cave

.... 18. On the trip to shore, the jolly-boat sinks because it (a) is overloaded with men and supplies (b) springs a leak (c) is struck by a cannon ball (d) hits a jagged rock

.... 19. At one point in the narrative, the events are related by (a) Squire Trelawney (b) Captain Smollett (c) Tom Redruth (d) Dr. Livesey

.... 20. Jim's trip in the coracle comes to grief against the (a) rocks (b) *Hispaniola* (c) sea wall (d) tree

.... 21. Israel Hands is killed by (a) O'Brien (b) Long John (c) Jim (d) Dr. Livesey

.... 22. Instrumental in Jim's capture is (a) a parrot (b) the moon (c) a dirk (d) a log

.... 23. To save his own skin, Silver decides to (a) shoot his crew (b) defend Jim (c) confess (d) run away

.... 24. The treasure is first dug up by (a) Ben (b) Jim (c) John (d) Merry

.... 25. At the end, Silver (a) deserts (b) gives up (c) dies (d) reforms

Answers

1-b, 2-d, 3-b, 4-c, 5-a, 6-c, 7-d, 8-b, 9-a, 10-d, 11-b, 12-d, 13-a, 14-a, 15-b, 16-c, 17-b, 18-a, 19-d, 20-b, 21-c, 22-a, 23-b, 24-a, 25-a

II. *Alternate Objective Tests*

A. Matching

Before each number in the column on the left, write the *letter* of the item in the column on the right that matches:

.... 1. "Spyglass"	a.	first mate
.... 2. Captain Flint	b.	Long John's nick- name
.... 3. O'Brien	c.	pirate flag
.... 4. Arrow	d.	Billy Bones
.... 5. Gray	e.	a tavern
.... 6. saber cut	f.	a parrot
.... 7. marooned	g.	Ben's cave
.... 8. Jolly Roger	h.	loyal carpenter's mate
.... 9. the treasure	i.	killed by Hands
...... 10. Barbecue	j.	three men

Answers

1-e, 2-f, 3-i, 4-a, 5-h, 6-d, 7-j, 8-c, 9-g, 10-b

B. Fill-ins

From the column on the right, select the item that best completes each statement below, and write it in the space provided:

1. "Fifteen men on a dead man's chest" is first sung by _____ .
2. The blind man delivers the _____ to the guest at the inn.
3. At the bottom of the sea chest, Jim finds a canvas bag of _____ .
4. The *Hispaniola* sails out of the port of _____ .

jewels
Captain Flint
old Tom
Bristol
Billy Bones
Black Spot
apple barrel
Blackbeard

5. Jim discovers the plot while hidden in a (an) _____.

6. Ben Gunn had been on the island for _____ years.

7. The loyal group included Jim, Smollett, Livesey, Trelawney, and _____ others.

8. The first of the group to be killed is poor _____.

9. In an open assault upon the stockade, the mutineers lose _____ men, leaving the odds against Jim's group about 2 to 1.

10. Jim goes back to the *Hispaniola* in a boat made by _____.

11. Much to Jim's surprise, the map with three red crosses turns up in the hands of _____.

12. Dick is uneasy over the fact that a death sign has been written on a page torn from his _____.

13. Jim, a prisoner, is amazed to see _____ pay a visit to the mutineers.

14. On their way to dig for the treasure, Silver and his men come upon a strange "pointer," a _____.

15. The pirates for a while mistake the voice of Ben Gunn for that of the spirit of _____.

four
gold coins
three
Dr. Livesey
chests
John Silver
five
Ben Gunn
Glasgow
Bible
skeleton
diary

Answers

1-Billy Bones, 2-Black Spot, 3-gold coins, 4-Bristol, 5-apple barrel, 6-three, 7-four, 8-old Tom, 9-five, 10-Ben Gunn, 11-John Silver, 12-Bible, 13-Dr. Livesey, 14-skeleton, 15-Captain Flint

III. *Ideas for Written or Oral Book Reports or Class Discussions*

1. Since the earliest beginnings of the novel, tales of adventure on the high seas have fascinated readers. This is especially true when such stories have included pirates, castaways, buried treasure, and mutiny. What is there about the nature of most human beings—young and old—that attracts them to books that deal with the heroes and villains that "go down to the sea in ships"? Why is an atmosphere of romantic excitement, indeed almost secret admiration, attached to the exploits of famous buccaneers like Captain Kidd, Sir Henry Morgan, Blackbeard, Jean Laffite, and others who were basically guilty of unspeakable crimes? Why has the lure of buried treasure figured prominently in fact and fiction? What prompted men to "Go West," join gold rushes, take off for Alaska? Why have books like *Mutiny on the Bounty* and *The Caine Mutiny* been on best-seller lists for many months, sold millions of copies, and become classics of their kind? In what respects do the same human characteristics that have kept *Treasure Island* enormously popular for about a century help to maintain interest in detective fiction, the supernatural, and real-life accounts of organized crime figures?

2. After Stevenson had drawn a treasure map to intrigue his stepson, it was necessary not only to think up a story to feature it but to create a whole imaginary world in which the story could reasonably take place. Note how quickly Stevenson establishes an appropriate atmosphere and background by introducing the intriguing name of the "Admiral Benbow" and the "saber cut" of Billy Bones (p. 3), and then goes on quickly to introduce Black Dog, the Black Spot, and the terrifying blind man, Mr. Pew. What other details in the early chapters make it clear to the reader that this will be a tale of mystery, danger, and adventure? "This is a handy cove," says Billy of his new haven (p. 4T). How does the author convince us that he knows the language of the sea and the swashbuckling

world of pirates? How important is this to the success of the novel?

3. Squire Trelawney reacts to the sealed packet in the sea chest with great interest and decides to equip a ship to sail with Dr. Livesey and Jim in search of Captain Flint's treasure. What are his motives other than money? How suited is he for such an expedition? How do you explain the fact that he "leaks" information about the projected voyage aboard the *Hispaniola* and is taken in by the devious Long John Silver and his crew? Why does he at first fail to appreciate the loyal Captain Smollett? How does the squire compare with Dr. Livesey in such characteristics as good sense, resourcefulness, faithfulness, and courage? It has been suggested that Stevenson, through the characters of Dr. Livesey and Captain Smollett, was expressing indirectly his personal preference for people who have to study and work hard for a living and more or less criticizing those, like Squire Trelawney, who inherit wealth and contribute only when some gentlemanly skill (such as excellent marksmanship) becomes useful. What do you think of that idea?

4. Stevenson, often a rebel despite his illness, made a cutthroat poet, François Villon, the hero of one of his best stories, "A Lodging for the Night." In *Treasure Island,* he created an unforgettable character in the wicked person of the pirate Long John Silver. Critic Morton Zabel said that "the sinister sea-cook" is "the dominant character" in the book, the source of "dramatic and psychological vitality from first to last." To what extent is this true? Wherein lies the fascination of Long John? Professor Zabel attributes it to "the demon of will-power and self-law." But what more appealing characteristics does Silver have than his selfishness and adherence to self-serving rules of conduct? Why might his power, despite his handicap, have appealed to Stevenson himself, a sickly man who drove on to success despite ill health? Why would this figure of a crafty adventurer appeal to all who lead ordinary lives? Find passages in the novel that highlight characteristics in Long John Silver that you wish to mention in explaining why readers delight in him. Murder, mutiny, theft, and

blackmail—add up all his crimes! Why do you think the author lets him escape as the book ends rather than delivering him to the authorities and the hanging that they would undoubtedly demand? What is the likelihood that Stevenson's reluctance to part with such a "deathless" character was prompted by a faint idea of using him to grace a sequel to *Treasure Island?*

5. If there is more than a touch of exaggeration in the character of Long John, the same is no less true of Jim Hawkins. To what extent is he too much the hero? How likely is it that a young boy today would dare to take on similar responsibilities and risks? How farfetched did it seem for Jim to take off on a mission to recapture a ship guarded by cutthroats? What are the odds that a boy could overcome the diabolical Israel Hands? On the other hand, Samuel Taylor Coleridge once said that anyone who wishes to enjoy thoroughly a work of fiction must accept a "willing suspension of disbelief," that is, the reader should not be too critical about tales of adventure and derring-do, should not ask too many questions about what is possible or not, lest he miss all the fun and excitement. To what extent do you agree with this point of view? Refer to specific episodes in the narrative to support your opinion in response to the last question.

6. For the most part, this is a first-person narrative presented from the point of view of Jim Hawkins. Why is the story picked up in Chapters XVI–XVIII by Dr. Livesey? How does this brief interlude in Jim's account add a note of variety? What are the advantages in the first-person point of view in terms of focus, economy, and human interest? However, what disadvantages are there in this treatment in terms of analyzing the characters of other people in the story, evaluating the importance of events, and determining questions of right and wrong in decisions and actions? Why do you suppose Stevenson chose Jim to be the main narrator of the story rather than tell it in the third person? How would specific parts of the story have sounded if Long John Silver had been the narrator? Dr. Livesey all the way? Squire Trelawney?

7. Although most authors of this period used a style of

writing that was very flowery, Stevenson chose to be crisp, relatively plain, and straightforward. His *descriptions* create immediate images with an economy of words, as, for example, the opening portrait of Billy Bones (p. 3M), the "January morning" (p. 10M), the scuffle (pp. 13B–14M), and our first look at Long John (p. 53B). Find other passages that show Stevenson's skill in description. Note, too, how well the author gives insights into character through *dialogue:* Dr. Livesey and Billy Bones (pp. 8M–9M, 15B–16M). Cite additional instances in which the reader can instantly judge the personality of the speaker through his words. Another strong point is Stevenson's use of *contrast* to build up *suspense.* In Chapter XXI, "The Attack," the background is set first—the hot sun, the baking sand, the jackets and coats flung aside (p. 139B)—then the stark "An hour passed away." Some talk follows, some seconds pass, "till suddenly Joyce whipped up his musket and fired." How much less exciting this scene would have been had Stevenson left out the "calm before the storm" and the breath-taking period of waiting for the attack to begin! Mention other examples of style techniques to build up suspense and excitement. In particular, show by example that Stevenson's language use is designed to *appeal to all the senses*—taste, touch, sight, smell, hearing—so that scenes of action and appearances of character create vivid impressions on the mind of the reader.

8. No story, no matter how tightly plotted, can dispense with some use of coincidence, although critics will sometimes charge a writer with having used chance to excess. Coincidence is necessary in fiction because it is present in life. A character, as is true in real life, sometimes runs into bad luck, sometimes good. Find examples of both in the story, and discuss how their presence gives the story *verisimilitude,* a lifelike quality. For instance, what chance befalls old Pew, Ben Gunn, Long John, Jim himself? When Stevenson does introduce the operations of chance, what devices does he use to make the reader accept the coincidence? Indicate how the story might have taken a different turn at certain points if chance had not dictated

otherwise. Give your estimate of whether or not Stevenson used coincidence to excess.

9. Of all the minor characters in the story, Ben Gunn is doubtless the most interesting. He appears suddenly to Jim (p. 100M) and makes a distinction between being shipwrecked and marooned. What is the difference? What purpose does Ben Gunn serve in the narrative? Since the treasure could have been located in some other way, why did Stevenson choose to include a person who had lived for three years alone on an island, after the fashion of Robinson Crusoe? Why does Ben seem to favor joining forces with Jim rather than going over to the side of the mutineers? Why could one say that the presence of Ben Gunn just about completes the picture of bold pirates and buried treasure?

10. Long John Silver, devious and daring to the last, disappears at the end (p. 239M), taking with him a sack of coins worth perhaps three or four hundred guineas. "I think," says Jim, "we were all pleased to be so cheaply quit of him." Why would everybody be so pleased? What probably happens to the peg-legged rascal? What do you suppose Jim does with all the money he brings home with him? Dr. Livesey? Captain Smollett? Assume that some years after the voyage Jim runs into Long John again. What does Jim do—report the pirate to the police, forgive him and make friends again, trust him again? Select one of the possibilities, and defend your conclusion by referring to previously mentioned character traits and events.

IV. *Vocabulary Study*

Diagnostic Test

3M	livid	lead-colored	florid	memorable
5B	diabolical	parabolic	heavenly	devilish
5B	abominable	lovely	hateful	human
9T	assizes	trials	measurements	starches
14B	scuffle	flourish	quiet	fight

21B	cowed	subdued	brave	determined
27M	repugnance	attraction	distaste	fight again
31B	formidable	threatening	trivial	shapeless
32T	shirking	attractive	poaching	neglectful
38M	miscreant	hero	villain	weakling
41T	scoundrel	rascal	cleaner	musician
49T	indomitable	beatable	unbeatable	unlivable
53B	dexterity	skill	clumsiness	determination
57B	mirth	amusement	depression	spice
61T	slight	congratulation	boatswain	insult
65M	glimmer	thief	darkness	gleam
69B	grog	food	rum	hazy
73B	derisively	happily	mockingly	clumsily
76B	maroon	save	defeat	strand
82B	agitated	worked up	calmed down	scraped off
88T	qualm	confusion	misgiving	contusion
93B	knoll	small hill	deep valley	slow stream
99B	adversary	companion	opponent	birthday
109B	stockade	larder	fort	pantry
118M	assailants	attackers	nautical men	defenders
121M	acquiescence	disagreement	agreement	knowledge
126B	missiles	projectiles	letters	prayer books
132M	morass	lake	swamp	woods
143T	impending	finished	ringing	about to happen
152B	dwindled	increased	mildewed	lessened
154M	loomed	rose up	sank down	turned over
156T	dolefully	stupidly	happily	sadly
159M	reverberations	silences	echoes	cries
166B	ironically	sarcastically	sweetly	confusingly
170T	haggard	worn out	gay	loose
177B	bulwark	support	cow pasture	undermining
181B	subsided	rose up	sank down	turned over
186T	wearisome	exciting	exhausting	tiresome
194B	furtively	secretly	understandingly	openly
200B	bungling	dexterity	clumsiness	wit
204M	gibbet	ship	gallows	food
208M	preponderance	superiority	weakness	willingness
213B	prolonged	stretched out	cut short	introduced
215T	inexplicable	clear	dry	unexplainable
226B	accomplices	confederates	competitors	relatives
227M	cache	money	hiding place	absence
234M	bland	fierce	chatter	mild
235B	diversity	variety	similarity	bad luck

| 236M | rebuffs | praises | rejections | calls |
| 240T | ample | plentiful | scarce | fruit |

Answers

livid-lead-colored, *diabolical*-devilish, *abominable*-hateful, *assizes*-trials, *scuffle*-fight, *cowed*-subdued, *repugnance*-distaste, *formidable*-threatening, *shirking*-neglectful, *miscreant*-villain, *scoundrel*-rascal, *indomitable*-unbeatable, *dexterity*-skill, *mirth*-amusement, *slight*-insult, *glimmer*-gleam, *grog*-rum, *derisively*-mockingly, *maroon*-strand, *agitated*-worked up, *qualm*-misgiving, *knoll*-small hill, *adversary*-opponent, *stockade*-fort, *assailants*-attackers, *acquiescence*-agreement, *missiles*-projectiles, *morass*-swamp, *impending*-about to happen, *dwindled*-lessened, *loomed*-rose up, *dolefully*-sadly, *reverberations*-echoes, *ironically*-sarcastically, *haggard*-worn out, *bulwark*-support, *subsided*-sank down, *wearisome*-tiresome, *furtively*-secretly, *bungling*-clumsiness, *gibbet*-gallows, *preponderance*-superiority, *prolonged*-stretched out, *inexplicable*-unexplainable, *accomplices*-confederates, *cache*-hiding place, *bland*-mild, *diversity*-variety, *rebuffs*-rejections, *ample*-plentiful

Teaching Aids

for

VANITY FAIR

When *Vanity Fair* first appeared in 1847, it shocked many Victorians who were appalled at its frank exposure of a "diseased society." In recent years, some critics have assailed Thackeray for not having been frank enough, for having been too lenient in his treatment of several of his characters. Despite the controversy that has surrounded the book from the beginning, few readers will question its stature as a masterful satire—almost definitive in its scope —of an important period of English life. As the author himself said, "What I want is to make a set of people living without God in the world—greedy, pompous, mean, perfectly self-satisfied for the most part, and at ease about their superficial virtue."

I. *Objective Test*

In the space provided at the left, insert the *letter* of the correct choice from among those offered; for example:

....b....   The author of this book is (a) Austen (b) Thackeray (c) Dickens

..........1. At the musicale, Lady Steyne (a) snubbed Becky (b) became Becky's ally (c) belittled Becky's musical talent

..........2. By a "sheep dog," Becky meant a (a) female companion (b) watchdog (c) working dog for the Crawley estate

.... 3. George Osborne's behavior at the ball on the eve of the Battle of Waterloo was (a) unfair to Amelia (b) completely ethical (c) praised by Dobbin

.... 4. To mark his complete rejection of his son, John Osborne (a) cut him off without a shilling (b) sent Amelia, George's wife, a vicious letter (c) obliterated his son's name from the family Bible

.... 5. Rawdon refused to be reconciled with Becky because he (a) was convinced she was faithless (b) realized she had constantly lied (c) was afraid she would kill him

.... 6. Amelia agreed to give up her son to John Osborne on the condition that (a) he send the boy to college (b) the boy be allowed to change his mind about staying with his grandfather (c) she be permitted to see the boy frequently

.... 7. When Sir Pitt heard that Rebecca had married his son, he was (a) furious (b) unhappy (c) delighted

.... 8. Becky won over Lady Southdown by (a) her pretended interest in medicines (b) speaking French fluently (c) claiming to be of noble birth

.... 9. Amelia felt free to love Dobbin after (a) little Georgie grew up (b) Becky showed her the note George wrote on the eve of Waterloo (c) her father died

.... 10. Dobbin wanted Jos Sedley to (a) set his father up in business (b) marry Mrs. O'Dowd's sister (c) break off his affair with Becky

.... 11. Rawdon Crawley became governor of Coventry Island because of (a) the influence of Lord Steyne (b) his fine war record (c) his talents as a diplomat

.... 12. Even though he despised Becky, Rawdon (a) permitted her to visit their son (b) paid her a good annuity (c) told her he would take her back

.... 13. Dobbin showed his high ethical standards by (a) refusing Joseph Sedley's legacy (b) saying nothing bad about Becky (c) supporting old John Osborne

.... 14. When his father's lawyer told him he had been disinherited, George Osborne blamed (a) Becky (b) himself (c) Dobbin

.... 15. Becky felt she had "arrived" socially when (a) Lady Steyne accepted her (b) she put Lady Bareacres in her place (c) she was presented to King George IV

.... 16. Dobbin's illness, which sent him back to England, was caused by (a) the cholera epidemic in India (b) a rumor that Amelia was going to remarry (c) a bullet wound

.... 17. When Amelia realized who had given her the piano (a) she lost interest in it (b) it became more valuable to her (c) she told her father to sell it

.... 18. "I think I could be a good woman if I had five thousand a year" was a statement made by (a) Amelia (b) Mrs. Bute Crawley (c) Becky

.... 19. Mrs. Bute Crawley's attitude toward Becky was (a) friendly (b) hostile (c) neutral

.... 20. Which one of these statements is *not* true? (a) Rawdon Crawley lent Pitt money to make repairs to the Crawley estate (b) Little Georgie placed a successful bet for Becky in a gambling casino (c) Jos Sedley made no attempt to support his parents

.... 21. The most generous act that Becky performed was (a) finally bringing Amelia and Dobbin together (b) returning Briggs's money to her (c) admiring her husband's manly courage

.... 22. Young James Crawley ruined his chances of getting a legacy from Miss Crawley because he (a) spoke against Becky (b) was a ladies' man (c) smoked and drank

.... 23. The guardianship of Georgie was restored to
        Amelia through (a) Miss Osborne's kindness
        (b) the efforts of Dobbin (c) Amelia's lawsuit

.... 24. The person who behaved most badly toward old
        Sedley while he was going bankrupt was his (a)
        wife (b) best friend (c) daughter

.... 25. According to Thackeray, Becky's chief aim in
        life was to (a) be a respectable woman (b)
        acquire great wealth (c) secure the love of her
        husband

Answers

1-b, 2-a, 3-a, 4-c, 5-b, 6-c, 7-a, 8-a, 9-b, 10-c, 11-a, 12-b, 13-a,
14-c, 15-c, 16-b, 17-a, 18-c, 19-b, 20-c, 21-a, 22-c, 23-b, 24-b, 25-a

II. *Alternate Objective Tests*

A. Matching

Before each number in the column on the left, insert the
letter of the item in the column on the right that matches:

.... 1. rich Creole girl without   a. Lord Gaunt
        a noble pedigree   b. Dobbin
.... 2. engaged in costly   c. Miss Swartz
        lawsuits   d. John Osborne
.... 3. married George's sister   e. Rawdon Crawley
.... 4. once loved Becky like a   f. Lord Steyne
        daughter   g. Briggs
.... 5. promoted the marriage   h. Frederick Bullock
        of George and Amelia   i. Sir Pitt Crawley
.... 6. turned on his financial   j. Miss Crawley
        benefactor   k. George Osborne
.... 7. warned Rawdon against   l. Joseph Sedley
        Becky's designs on him
.... 8. asked his brother to take
        care of his son

.... 9. told Becky to "get out of
town"

...... 10. lent the Crawleys money

Answers

1-c, 2-i, 3-h, 4-j, 5-b, 6-d, 7-k, 8-e, 9-f, 10-g

B. Fill-ins

From the column on the right, select the item that best completes each statement below, and write it in the space provided:

1. Lord Steyne and Becky arranged for _____ arrest.	George's
	annuity
2. Bute Crawley expected Sir Pitt to leave him _____.	Miss Briggs
	diamonds
3. Major Sugarplums was _____ nickname.	Miss Horrocks
	Miss Osborne
4. Becky picked up a small fortune by selling her _____ to Joseph.	James Crawley
	son
5. Old Sir Pitt installed _____ as his housekeeper at Queen's Crawley.	Rawdon's
	Rawdon
6. _____ fell out of favor with his aunt.	Crawley
	30,000 pounds
7. The Crawley estate finally went to _____.	Mrs. Bute
	Crawley
8. Becky lived happily "ever after" on a (an) _____.	horses
	Young Rawdon
9. _____ was responsible for the death of Becky's husband.	Crawley
	Lord Steyne
10. It was Dobbin who gave the _____ to Amelia.	Dobbin's
	Sir Pitt's sister
11. Becky neglected her _____.	yellow fever
12. Gaunt House was the name of the London home of _____.	dueling
	piano
13. Becky's chaperone was _____.	father

14. _____ was a master of billiards.
15. The old lady who gave George a gold
watch and chain was _____.

Answers

1-Rawdon's, 2-30,000 pounds, 3-Dobbin's, 4-horses, 5-Miss Horrocks, 6-James Crawley, 7-Young Rawdon Crawley, 8-annuity, 9-yellow fever, 10-piano, 11-son, 12-Lord Steyne, 13-Miss Briggs, 14-Rawdon Crawley, 15-Miss Osborne

III. *Ideas for Written or Oral Book Reports or Class Discussions*

1. "The characters of Amelia and Becky and their respective fates make the chief pattern in the structure of the book," points out Elizabeth Drew. "The contrast between an active and a passive nature, between villainy and virtue, between brains and muddleheadedness, between heartlessness and devotion are simple and obvious." Show to what degree these statements are true by discussing typical attitudes of Amelia and Becky (as each woman rises or falls in the novel), such as those toward relatives and friends, money, social position, motherhood, class loyalties, their dependence on reason as opposed to emotion, and their analysis of themselves. (Suggestion: Consult, for example, pp. 252T, 254B, 325T, and others for this last item.)

2. Among the characteristics that mark Thackeray's style in *Vanity Fair* is the frequent and effective use of irony. Irony is a literary device that suggests subtly, but in a most cutting manner, the discrepancy between an immediate, apparently factual statement of a situation and a real interpretation of the situation. An author uses restraint, humor, or a tongue-in-cheek attitude to convey the irony. The opposite meaning is the true one that an intelligent reader is intended to deduce. For example, we read that the smart, graceful George Osborne is a "gentleman,"

while clumsy, halting Dobbin is only the son of a grocer. Yet we soon realize that Dobbin is the real gentleman, not faithless George. Or, on p. 308M, we read that Rebecca "bore the parting from her husband with quite a Spartan equanimity" when we know the parting from Rawdon meant little to her. Perhaps one of the greatest ironies in the novel is that Rawdon Crawley, as Edward Wagenknecht notes, is purified through his love for the worthless Becky. Find several additional passages or situations in *Vanity Fair* that show Thackeray's use of irony, and explain wherein lies the irony in each illustration.

3. Early nineteenth-century England in general was motivated by snobbery. Wealth was challenging birth as a contender for social position. "Snobbery, the jockeying for social position and the pretense to a status rather higher than the person's true one [Thackeray] saw as the main driving force of man in society," Walter Allen observes. This driving force obsessed Becky, and she sought fiercely to combine her pretended noble birth and her grabbing for wealth to secure status. Consider her comments about social position (p. 13M), George Osborne's criticism of her (p. 58T), the "blood is everything" passage (p. 89M), George's advice to Amelia (p. 207M), old Osborne's thoughts about Dobbin (p. 655M), and other illustrations. What additional evidence of snobbery or of the preoccupation with it can you cite in *Vanity Fair?* Where are there hints in the novel that Thackeray himself might have been a snob or that he had prejudices against certain groups of people?

4. In the tradition of novelists like Henry Fielding and Lawrence Sterne, Thackeray makes many comments on the actions of his characters in side excursions that are little essays, sermons, or general observations on human behavior. Some readers feel that Thackeray's asides or *obiter dicta* are intrusions that detract from the flow of his narrative; others feel that they add something to the novel. Thus, he discusses husband-hunting (p. 19M), female gossips and "catty" remarks (pp. 108B–109M), or old letters (pp. 192B–193M). Find several instances of these

asides, and tell whether you think they detract from or add to the novel. Are the author's comments interesting or valuable? Do they help explain plot or character? Or are they gratuitous and unnecessarily interruptive? Explain.

5. The subtitle of *Vanity Fair* is "A Novel Without a Hero." If you believe this is true, explain why. If you believe, on the other hand, that Dobbin is its hero, defend your belief. Before you discuss this question, consider the suggestion of David Cecil that there is no hero because there is "no character through whose eyes we are to survey the . . . story . . . and with whose point of view we are meant wholly to sympathize."

"If this is a novel without a hero," wrote Thackeray of *Vanity Fair*, "at least let us lay claim to a heroine." Who do you think it is? Who do you think Thackeray thought it was? The historian of the English novel, Ernest A. Baker, claimed that "It cannot be the humdrum Amelia; it must be Becky Sharp." What do you think of this assertion? What would Thackeray have thought of it? Defend your answers with reference to the text.

6. Because *Vanity Fair* was written in early Victorian times in a period of great outward morality, we might expect that sin would be punished and virtue would be rewarded. Yet this is not always the case. Analyze the lives of some of the leading characters, and determine whether Becky, Sir Pitt, Amelia, Dobbin, George Osborne, John Osborne, Joseph Sedley, Rawdon Crawley, and Lord Steyne received fitting punishment or reward for their actions. Give reasons for your answers.

7. Select one of the following statements that various commentators on *Vanity Fair* have made, and discuss the validity of the statement by specific references to the novel:

a. The society in *Vanity Fair* is a predatory society from top to bottom, presenting a glittering surface, while below is a loveless void.

b. Amelia is the only character in the book who really matures and who achieves a measure of self-knowledge.

c. Thackeray generalizes and moralizes too much.

d. As a novelist, Thackeray was completely inhibited where the portrayal of women and of sex were concerned.

e. Becky Sharp is a unique and permanent figure in literature, a subtle embodiment of duplicity, ambition, and selfishness.

8. The tone of *Vanity Fair,* Lionel Stevenson feels, is the result of the mixture of sympathy and bitterness experienced in Thackeray's own life. Accordingly, some readers get the impression that Thackeray is simultaneously inside the action of the novel as a participant and outside it as a neutral observer of the scene before him. For example (p. 672T), he speaks autobiographically: "I first saw Colonel Dobbin and his party" in Pumpernickel. On occasions he uses loaded phrases like "even such a hardened little reprobate as Becky" (p. 712B) that suggest his own view of her. On the other hand, he is the neutral observer when in his comments on Osborne's hatred of old Sedley, he analyzes the psychological process that makes a debtor hate his creditor (p. 179T). Generally considered, when is he the participant and when is he the observer? With what facts can you support your answer?

9. Despite his many acts of kindness and consideration, the self-effacing, long-suffering Dobbin is treated badly by Amelia. Does he "deserve" to win her? Is she worthy of him? Refer to specific incidents in the novel in your answer. (If you have read Hardy's *The Return of the Native* or Dickens' *A Tale of Two Cities,* you might want to compare Dobbin with Diggory Venn or Sydney Carton.)

10. When *Vanity Fair* was published, some readers were unhappy about the lack of Thackeray's moral vision. He seems to take no strong position against the unethical or improper behavior of an imperfect society. What parts of the novel seem to indicate to you a moral or spiritual bankruptcy? Are you led to admire "a creation that is as seductive as it is evil"? Do you conclude after reading the novel "that nothing is real but folly and perfidy"? How can you justify Thackeray's apparent cynical indifference to morality? Remember that Thackeray tells us in the "Be-

fore the Curtain" section that Vanity Fair is not "a moral place" and that a "profound melancholy comes over him in his survey of the bustling place." Support your answers by specific references to the people and events in the book.

IV. *Vocabulary Study*

Diagnostic Test

4T	disconsolate	contented	individual	sad
5T	filigree	lacelike metalwork	little horse	railing
10M	propensity	huge size	inclination	dislike
12B	reprobate	refund	scoundrel	hero
28M	equanimity	anger	generosity	calm temper
31B	allegorical	symbolical	specific	assumed
38B	bruited	dampened	rumored	hurt
51T	cursorily	hastily	ill-mannered	intensity
57B	milksop	sissy	toast	strong man
65T	perquisites	energies	losses	extra gains
85M	pettifogging	clouding	trivial dishonesty	revealing
105B	paragon	villain	model	figure
117M	liaison	linking up	wound	separation
121M	ambrosial	valuable	fragrant	ill-smelling
128T	colloquy	isolation	brutality	conference
146T	scutcheon	pinpoint	scratch	shield
154B	commiserate	mix	sympathize	shun
159M	impetuosity	rashness	emptiness	extreme care
190B	homilies	sermons	ugliness	hints
213M	gimcracks	jewels	showy, useless things	burglars' tools
227M	eschew	seek	late	avoid
245M	peregrinations	shut-ins	games	wanderings
248B	cajoleries	commands	coaxings	jokes
258B	imperious	feverish	masterful	timid
266B	tawdry	gaudy	rusted	tasteful
283B	assiduity	sharpness	diligence	laziness
286B	pristine	fussy	dirty	unspoiled
288B	rapacity	greed	speed	generosity

314M contiguous	infectious	solitary	touching
331B débâcle	disaster	type of boat	success
353B recant	sing	affirm	renounce
386M parvenue	newly rich person	thirst	miser
411T harridans	young girls	flowers	old hags
423B sycophantic	sincere	falsely flattering	syringelike
435B chancel	part of a church	tent	raffle
440T anathemas	songs	compliments	curses
449B tribulation	misery	clan	comfort
482B incumbent	climbing	obligatory	entering
508M desideratum	unnecessary item	purpose	something needed or wanted
524M patrician	owner	aristocrat	commoner
540B descanting	commenting on	deciding	reserving
546M comestibles	wood chips	food	cosmetics
549B strident	tuneful	towering	harsh-sounding
551B reticules	open ends	mocks	handbags
599B emendations	corrections	buildings	errors
616T querulous	feverish	complaining	satisfied
703M factotum	analyst	handyman	clumsy worker
719M cicatrized	smoothed over	hissed	scarred
735B gormandize	eat greedily	crush	moderate
740B scapegrace	eraser	rascal	holy man

Answers

disconsolate-sad, *filigree*-lacelike metalwork, *propensity*-inclination, *reprobate*-scoundrel, *equanimity*-calm temper, *allegorical*-symbolical, *bruited*-rumored, *cursorily*-hastily, *milksop*-sissy, *perquisites*-extra gains, *pettifogging*-trivial dishonesty, *paragon*-model, *liaison*-linking up, *ambrosial*-fragrant, *colloquy*-conference, *scutcheon*-shield, *commiserate*-sympathize, *impetuosity*-rashness, *homilies*-sermons, *gimcracks*-showy, useless things, *eschew*-avoid, *peregrinations*-wanderings, *cajoleries*-coaxings, *imperious*-masterful, *tawdry*-gaudy, *assiduity*-diligence, *pristine*-unspoiled, *rapacity*-greed, *contiguous*-touching, *débâcle*-disaster, *recant*-renounce, *parvenue*-newly rich person, *harridans*-old hags, *sycophantic*-falsely flattering, *chancel*-part of a church, *anathemas*-curses, *tribulation*-misery, *incumbent*-obligatory, *desideratum*-something needed or wanted, *patrician*-aristocrat, *descanting*-commenting on, *comestibles*-food, *strident*-harsh-sounding, *reticules*-handbags, *emendations*-corrections, *querulous*-complaining, *factotum*-handyman, *cicatrized*-scarred, *gormandize*-eat greedily, *scapegrace*-rascal

Teaching Aids

for

WAR AND PEACE

Some critics have referred to *War and Peace* as the greatest novel ever written. Ivan Turgenev, a contemporary of Tolstoy, said the book "will never die as long as the Russian language lives"; nor is it likely to die in any of the numerous other languages into which it has been translated. Whether it is read as an epic of the Napoleonic Wars or as a scathing attack on war itself, whether as a defense of aristocracy or as a criticism of Tsarist Russia's treatment of the lower classes, the book has attracted enthusiastic admiration from countless readers throughout the world. The century since its publication has only added to its stature as a timeless masterpiece. The subject of the novel is the gigantic canvas of all life, a teeming panorama of willful aristocrats and humble peasants, heroic battles and vainglorious soldiers, cowards, sages, and fools.

I. *Objective Test*

In the space provided at the left, insert the *letter* of the correct choice from among those offered; for example:

....b.... The author of this book is (a) Pushkin (b) Tolstoy (c) Gogol

.... 1. During the war of 1805, Russian high society (a) stopped all normal social affairs (b) continued balls and parties (c) completely disregarded the battle of Austerlitz

.... 2. The alliance between Russia and Austria in 1805 was (a) cordial and lasting (b) an agreement between rivals (c) an accidental arrangement of allies

.... 3. The Kurágin family can best be described as (a) openhearted and generous (b) self-seeking and unreliable (c) patriotic and quick-tempered

.... 4. The first military success of Nicholas Rostóv was achieved by (a) accident (b) well-planned action (c) heroism

.... 5. Russian aristocratic officers often proved (a) especially interested in impressing the Tsar (b) unreliable in combat (c) unusually concerned for their men's safety

.... 6. Prince Andrew Bolkónski's attitude toward his wife was one of (a) reverence (b) toleration (c) contempt

.... 7. Prince Andrew admired Napoleon until (a) they met at Austerlitz (b) Napoleon invaded Russia (c) Tsar Alexander declared war on France

.... 8. Pierre Bezúkhov attracted the Kurágins' attention because (a) he was wealthy (b) his conversation was intelligent (c) he was thoughtful of others

.... 9. Prince Andrew's first great vision of peace came when (a) his first wife died (b) Pierre introduced him to Masonic ideas (c) he was wounded at Austerlitz

.... 10. Pierre's experiments with his serfs and landholdings can be described as (a) unrealistically idealistic (b) scientific agriculture (c) anarchistic

.... 11. Natásha Rostóva and Prince Andrew separated for a year to (a) test their own endurance (b) please Prince Andrew's dictatorial father (c) await peace with France

.... 12. The private betrothal was ended because (a) Natásha attempted to elope with Anatole Kurágin (b) Pierre prevented Andrew from returning in time (c) Andrew returned to army life

.... 13. The Rostóv family's wealth (a) was largely lost by the old count's mismanagement (b) grew substantially through the marriages of family members (c) was safe because it was far removed from Moscow

.... 14. The Rostóvs used their influence to keep Pétya out of danger (a) reluctantly (b) naturally, as a matter of right (c) at great cost to the fortune

.... 15. Count Nicholas Rostóv gave up his engagement to Sónya to (a) reestablish his family's fortune (b) prevent Princess Mary from being despondent (c) free himself of a nuisance

.... 16. Tsar Alexander's visit to Moscow showed that the people (a) loved the emperor (b) feared him (c) were awaiting a chance to rebel

.... 17. The peasants at Bald Hills (a) protected Prince Andrew's grain (b) looted and stole his goods (c) welcomed the French

.... 18. Kutúzov, the Russian commander, was successful because he (a) developed new tactics (b) employed his subordinates well (c) was a finer general than Napoleon

.... 19. According to Tolstoy, Moscow was burned (a) by Russian incendiaries (b) by Kutúzov's orders (c) accidentally when authority was removed

.... 20. Tolstoy regarded the battle of Borodinó as a (a) disaster (b) Russian victory (c) battle of little importance

.... 21. Pierre, imprisoned as an incendiary, actually planned to (a) assassinate Napoleon (b) become a hermit (c) lead the Russian partisans in Moscow

.... 22. Karatáev can best be described as a (a) dedicated soldier (b) philosophical peasant (c) rebel, though a prisoner

.... 23. Princess Mary and Natásha became friends because of (a) the flight from Moscow (b) their common care for Prince Andrew (c) their many common interests

.... 24. Tolstoy regarded war as (a) a heroic activity (b) a colossal blunder (c) inevitable in human society

.... 25. After his marriage to Natásha, Pierre (a) lost all interest in public affairs (b) devoted himself to scientific farming (c) became interested in constitutional reform in Russia

Answers

1-b, 2-b, 3-b, 4-a, 5-a, 6-c, 7-a, 8-a, 9-c, 10-a, 11-b, 12-a, 13-a, 14-b, 15-a, 16-a, 17-a, 18-b, 19-c, 20-b, 21-a, 22-b, 23-b, 24-b, 25-c

II. *Alternate Objective Tests*

A. Matching

Before each number in the column on the left, insert the *letter* of the item in the column on the right that matches:

.... 1. Prince Andrew Bolkónski
.... 2. Natásha
.... 3. Bald Hills
.... 4. Vilna
.... 5. Austerlitz
.... 6. Otrádnoe
.... 7. Dólokhov
.... 8. Anna Pávlovna
.... 9. Pierre Bezúkhov
...... 10. Kutúzov

a. leader of Moscow merchants
b. Russian commander-in-chief
c. city used as Russian headquarters
d. attempted to kill Napoleon
e. eventually married Pierre
f. member of Kurágin family
g. home of Bolkónski family
h. victory of Napoleon
i. artillery officer (Russian)
j. retired to monastery
k. country seat of Rostóvs
l. social power in Russian court

m. French field marshal
n. reckless partisan leader
o. Natásha's rejected suitor

Answers

1-o, 2-e, 3-g, 4-c, 5-h, 6-k, 7-n, 8-l, 9-d, 10-b

B. Fill-ins

From the column on the right, select the item that best completes each statement below, and write it in the space provided:

1. Kutúzov's plan was to use _____ to defeat the French.
2. Alexander roused great enthusiasm in the city of _____.
3. Anatole Kurágin was deceitful to _____.
4. Nicholas Rostóv became an officer of _____.
5. Many Russian officers were actually _____.
6. The author derides the idea that war can be _____.
7. Alexander replaced _____ as the French fled.
8. Pierre attempted to improve and educate his _____.
9. Prince _____ returned to military life after his betrothal ended.
10. Andrew's sister, _____, eventually married Nicholas Rostóv.
11. As they fled Moscow, the _____ lent their carts to wounded soldiers.
12. The elder Prince _____, Andrew's father, was tyrannical.

Denísov
Sónya
Russian
French
Andrew
Hélène
Germans
Natásha
patience
Cossacks
Karatáev
Borodinó
scientific
hussars
Kremlin
serfs
Kutúzov
promoted
Moscow
Rostóvs
Mary
Bolkónski

13. Pierre's friend while a prisoner of war was _____.

14. The French retreat was harassed by _____.

15. Tolstoy pictures the eventual _____ victory as inevitable.

Answers

1-patience, 2-Moscow, 3-Natásha, 4-hussars, 5-Germans, 6-scientific, 7-Kutúzov, 8-serfs, 9-Andrew, 10-Mary, 11-Rostóvs, 12-Bolkónski, 13-Karatáev, 14-Cossacks, 15-Russian

III. *Ideas for Written or Oral Book Reports or Class Discussions*

1. In *An Introduction to Russian Literature,* Helen Muchnic says, "Tolstoy's ideal characters, Andrew, Pierre, Kutúzov, Natásha, form a hierarchy with respect to their consciousness of themselves. The most self-conscious is Andrew, the least, Natásha. And Andrew is at his best when he is least self-conscious and Natásha at her worst when she is most self-conscious. What Pierre learns is to forget himself; what makes Kutúzov great is a natural self-forgetfulness." By specific references to the text, indicate the extent to which each of the characters mentioned behaves badly when he or she is acting under the influence of an overawareness of self and preoccupation with inner analysis. On the other hand, give examples to demonstrate greater nobility of character when each functions selflessly and naturally. In summary, select one of the four as the major protagonist of the story (hero or heroine). Give reasons to justify your choice.

2. One of the chief interests in reading historical novels is in seeing how closely they agree with history, what kind of light they throw on historical events. What do you think of Tolstoy's interpretation of the character of Napoleon Bonaparte? What evidence do you find that a Russian viewed the events of European history differently from the

way Americans, Frenchmen, or Englishmen viewed it?

3. Russia, as shown in *War and Peace,* was an empire run very completely by its aristocracy. What evidence is there of how Tolstoy felt about the aristocratic management of Russian affairs? How do you feel about the presentation of the serfs and peasants in the novel? Did Tolstoy seem to sympathize with them or to prefer the aristocrats about whom he wrote? Explain. How does the character of Karatáev influence your views on this matter?

4. Many of the social and military activities of early nineteenth-century Russia are paralleled in our own day and time, despite the changes in manners and language and country. For instance, in what ways do our own social entertainments parallel those of the Rostóvs and their circle? In what ways do the modern problems of supplying men and materials for an army match those of Napoleon and Kutúzov? How does Russian partisan warfare parallel the guerilla tactics used in the twentieth century?

5. Modern ideas of patriotism and national pride differ in some important ways from those pictured in *War and Peace*. For instance, what would we think of officers who tried to get themselves honors for carrying news from one place to another or those whose parents "arranged" for them to get quiet assignments? What do you think of the Russian custom of speaking in French, even while fighting a French invader? What do you think of the treatment of prisoners of war as described in the book? Give examples to support your ideas about these points.

6. Tolstoy wrote his book over a rather long period of time, and it first appeared in several parts. Can you suggest parts of the work that would make ideal or suitable individual publications? What does Tolstoy do to "round off" certain parts of *War and Peace,* and yet keep up interest in the future portions of the work? What differences do you find between the ending of the Epilogue and the endings of the subordinate parts of the book?

7. We often feel that an author should not intrude his own comments, or editorialize, on events that he describes in a book. Many readers prefer to draw their own conclu-

sions and inferences. Yet Tolstoy frequently includes his own philosophy of history, of character, of life in *War and Peace*. What effect does this philosophy have on your reading of the book? To what extent does it help or hinder you in understanding and following the story line?

8. Over the years covered in the book, the leading individuals not only grow older, but often their characters change and develop. Write one short paragraph describing each of the following character changes:

    a. Prince Andrew, between his arrival at Bald Hills to leave his wife in 1805 and his seeing Natásha outside Moscow, while on his deathbed

    b. Pierre Bezúkhov, between his introduction to Russian society as heir to the Bezúkhov fortune and his visit to the Rostóvs at Bald Hills

    c. Natásha, between her debut in society and her establishment as Pierre's wife

    d. Nicholas Rostóv, between his departure from home as a cadet officer and his tenure as master of Bald Hills.

9. A successful work of literature usually requires a highly credible plot (or story line), an attractive and well-developed set of characters, and a suitable setting, effectively presented. Considering *War and Peace,* which one, if any, of these three aspects appears to dominate the work? Are there parts in which one or the other dominates for a major section of it? Point these out, and indicate whether this interferes with or heightens the effect of the book.

10. Many historical novels have been compared with *War and Peace* when critics sought to compliment the other books. Perhaps you could compare the book with another major historical novel you have read: two famous English novels of the same approximate period are Dickens' *A Tale of Two Cities* and Thackeray's *Vanity Fair*. How do these English authors use historical setting to develop characters and to indicate their own philosophies?

IV. *Vocabulary Study*

Diagnostic Test

1B	complacently	actively	calmly	angrily
2M	impetuosity	rashness	silence	determination
6M	magnanimity	selfishness	large size	generosity
8T	imbecility	sagacity	disturbance	mental deficiency
13B	egotists	misers	braggarts	pessimists
14T	naïve	artless	clever	native
17T	debauchery	virtue	impurity	fluency
18M	languor	strength	wisdom	faintness
19B	brigands	officers	speakers	outlaws
30M	manifesto	explanation	permission	published order
37M	conspicuous	evident	very small	secretive
42M	crestfallen	victorious	defeated	beheaded
52T	aghast	elated	horror-struck	indignant
52M	veneration	reverence	venality	greenness
57M	choleric	calm	windy	wrathful
74B	rife	ripe	plentiful	unknown
95T	stubble	grain stumps	trip	permanent
98T	effrontery	construction	pleasantness	boldness
99T	delirium	happiness	derangement	warmth
102T	tremulous	agitated	tremendous	peaceful
125B	billet	money	quarters	dance
133B	presentiment	illness	prejudice	anticipation
150B	incomprehensible	evident	narrow	unintelligible
164M	rapturous	ecstatic	victimized	skeptical
166T	ottoman	backless sofa	hostile	heretic
183M	repellent	sorrowful	repugnant	defensive
185M	indolence	laziness	sorrow	suffering
189B	alms	weapons	charity	misers
193M	pedantic	troublesome	foolish	displaying narrow learning
219T	temerity	willingness	careful	rashness
220B	affable	gracious	tardy	irascible
227M	penitent	regretful	prisoner	unbending
230M	deference	pride	submission	exemption
241B	superfluous	flowing	unnecessary	essential
295T	carousals	drunken revels	surroundings	merry-go-rounds

319M mundane	everlasting	spiritual	worldly
325T corpulent	fleshy	bloody	earthy
365B foment	rest	instigate	froth
394T reticent	willing	friendly	reserved
436M disinfected	prescribed	sterilized	inoculated
443B miscreant	villain	unbeliever	peddler
504M expound	explain	extrude	drill
509T phenomena	stars	secrets	observable facts
532M tantamount	excessive	equivalent	elusive
543M cauldrons	witches	kettles	fires
550B edifices	examples	structures	lessons
562M inexhaustible	worthless	poisonous	limitless
563T indubitable	wrong	powerful	believable
567B pacify	level	make peaceful	agitate
573B reproach	blame	return	draw near

Answers

complacently-calmly, *impetuosity*-rashness, *magnanimity*-generosity, *imbecility*-mental deficiency, *egotists*-braggarts, *naïve*-artless, *debauchery*-impurity, *languor*-faintness, *brigands*-outlaws, *manifesto*-published order, *conspicuous*-evident, *crestfallen*-defeated, *aghast*-horror-struck, *veneration*-reverence, *choleric*-wrathful, *rife*-plentiful, *stubble*-grain stumps, *effrontery*-boldness, *delirium*-derangement, *tremulous*-agitated, *billet*-quarters, *presentiment*-anticipation, *incomprehensible*-unintelligible, *rapturous*-ecstatic, *ottoman*-backless sofa, *repellent*-repugnant, *indolence*-laziness, *alms*-charity, *pedantic*-displaying narrow learning, *temerity*-rashness, *affable*-gracious, *penitent*-regretful, *deference*-submission, *superfluous*-unnecessary, *carousals*-drunken revels, *mundane*-worldly, *corpulent*-fleshy, *foment*-instigate, *reticent*-reserved, *disinfected*-sterilized, *miscreant*-villain, *expound*-explain, *phenomena*-observable facts, *tantamount*-equivalent, *cauldrons*-kettles, *edifices*-structures, *inexhaustible*-limitless, *indubitable*-believable, *pacify*-make peaceful, *reproach*-blame

Teaching Aids

for

WUTHERING HEIGHTS

Set against the dark and rugged moorlands of northern England, this novel presents two of the most memorable characters in all literature: Heathcliff, the unfathomable mixture of savagery and devotion; and Catherine, the woman he loved but drove to a tragic end. The swirling passions that emerge from Emily Brontë's powerful narrative create a nightmare of supernatural horror that envelops what has been called "the strangest love story ever told."

I. *Objective Test*

In the space provided at the left, insert the *letter* of the correct choice from among those offered; for example:

....b....   The author of the book is (a) Charlotte Brontë (b) Emily Brontë (c) Charles Dickens (d) Branwell Brontë

.... 1. When Mr. Lockwood was attacked by the dogs at Wuthering Heights, Heathcliff (a) apologized profusely (b) had a servant tenderly dress the wounds (c) took the matter very calmly (d) was not informed of this inhospitable reception of a guest

.... 2. On Mr. Lockwood's second visit to Wuthering Heights, the servant Joseph set dogs on the guest because (a) he thought Mr. Lockwood was stealing a lantern (b) Hareton Earnshaw was in danger (c) Mrs. Heathcliff demanded protection (d) Heathcliff ordered the attack

.... 3. Mr. Lockwood, badly shaken, was consoled and tended by (a) Heathcliff himself (b) the surly Joseph, now repentant (c) Zillah, the housekeeper (d) his wife

.... 4. Snowed in at Wuthering Heights, Mr. Lockwood had a strange dream in which he saw (a) the dead Isabella Linton (b) the ghost of Ellen Dean (c) the child-face of Catherine Linton (d) a gigantic dog that haunted the moors

.... 5. Mr. Lockwood received much information about the past from Ellen Dean, who (a) came from London to investigate (b) was a relative of the Heathcliffs (c) had read old papers of the family (d) had lived at Wuthering Heights as a child

.... 6. When Mr. Earnshaw brought the fourteen-year-old Heathcliff from Liverpool to Wuthering Heights, the boy was at first regarded as (a) a useful worker for the farm (b) the heir of the Earnshaws (c) a pitiful orphan (d) a wild gypsy who bore watching

.... 7. When Hindley Earnshaw returned from school, he brought home to his father's funeral a (a) pack of hunting dogs (b) great fortune earned at gambling (c) new wife (d) school friend with a mysterious past

.... 8. Catherine, after a tramp over the moors with Heathcliff, had to stay five weeks with the Lintons because (a) there was a plague at Wuthering Heights (b) her father threw her out (c) she had been attacked by a dog (d) she was pregnant

.... 9. Heathcliff became jealous and ill-tempered because (a) Hindley refused him money (b) he was drinking excessively (c) he was badly treated by Hindley and insulted by Edgar and

Isabella (d) he discovered the identity of his gypsy father

.... 10. Frances, Hindley's consumptive wife, died (a) soon after the birth of their son (b) as a result of her son's cruelties (c) when she learned her dowry had been squandered (d) in America, having left Hindley in despair

.... 11. The death of his wife made Hindley Earnshaw (a) turn to heavy drinking (b) more interested in life (c) hostile to Heathcliff (d) eager to travel

.... 12. Catherine Linton's love for Edgar Linton was (a) the great passion of her life (b) not really sincere (c) the cause of his suicide (d) engineered by Ellen Dean

.... 13. When Heathcliff overheard a conversation between Catherine Earnshaw and Ellen Dean, he (a) set fire to the house (b) attempted suicide (c) attacked them both in a rage (d) disappeared for years

.... 14. Heathcliff's eventual return led to trouble between (a) Edgar and Catherine (b) Ellen Dean and Joseph (c) the vicar and Mrs. Bond (d) Hindley and Frances

.... 15. Hindley invited Heathcliff to live at Wuthering Heights because he (a) wanted a boon companion (b) wished to avoid gambling and drinking (c) was planning to steal Heathcliff's inheritance (d) wanted to keep an eye on him

.... 16. Heathcliff eloped with Isabella (a) for her money (b) to disinherit Hindley (c) to avenge himself and provoke Edgar (d) because she was his childhood sweetheart

.... 17. When Heathcliff and Isabella returned to Wuthering Heights, Edgar (a) welcomed them with open arms (b) refused to recognize his sister and her husband (c) made them live in a remodeled stable (d) decided to forgive and forget

.... 18. The shock of Heathcliff's sudden return caused Catherine to (a) divorce her husband (b) seek reconciliation with Isabella (c) have a premature delivery (d) find new energy to live

.... 19. Isabella found Heathcliff unbearable and (a) tried to take poison (b) fled to London (c) ran away with an officer (d) went back to Edgar's house

.... 20. The marriage of Cathy and Linton was (a) prevented by Linton's ill health (b) arranged by Heathcliff (c) demanded by Edgar (d) recommended by Hareton

.... 21. Cathy became (a) a widow dependent upon Heathcliff (b) a compulsive drinker (c) the second wife of Heathcliff (d) the wife of a wealthy squire

.... 22. Mr. Lockwood returned from London and found Wuthering Heights (a) in the possession of Cathy and Hareton (d) inhabited only by Heathcliff (c) completely ramshackle and decayed (d) full of mysterious strangers

.... 23. Heathcliff died (a) by his own hand (b) at the hands of Edgar (c) from a gunshot wound (d) after brooding on an old love

.... 24. In the little cemetery, Mr. Lockwood found (a) a ghost that haunted it (b) no trace of any of the family (c) tombstones for Catherine, Edgar, and Heathcliff (d) Edgar Linton's missing will

.... 25. Shepherds and travelers in the district reported that (a) Wuthering Heights had burned down (b) the ghosts of Catherine and Heathcliff roamed the moors (c) Linton Heathcliff had been seen in America (d) Thrushcross Grange was haunted

Answers

1-c, 2-a, 3-c, 4-c, 5-d, 6-d, 7-c, 8-c, 9-c, 10-a, 11-a, 12-b, 13-d, 14-a, 15-a, 16-c, 17-b, 18-c, 19-b, 20-b, 21-a, 22-a, 23-d, 24-c, 25-b

II. *Alternate Objective Tests*

A. Matching

Before each number in the column on the left, write the *letter* of the item in the column on the right that matches:

.... 1. Heathcliff	a. had a baby in London
.... 2. Zillah	b. built in 1801 by the Earnshaws
.... 3. Mr. Lockwood	
.... 4. Isabella	c. a housekeeper
.... 5. Wuthering Heights	d. heavy debts
.... 6. Joseph	e. consumption
.... 7. Linton	f. taught to read
.... 8. Hindley	g. Lascar
.... 9. Frances	h. savage dogs
...... 10. Hareton	i. Kenneth's diagnosis
	j. stole Edgar's beloved Bible
	k. mean busybody
	l. Thrushcross Grange
	m. secret visits by Catherine
	n. killed a pet springer spaniel

Answers

1-g, 2-c, 3-l, 4-a, 5-h, 6-k, 7-m, 8-d, 9-e, 10-f

B. Fill-ins

From the column on the right, select the item that best completes each statement below, and write it in the space provided:

1. Heathcliff was named by Mr. Earnshaw after his _____.
2. After the death of _____, Heathcliff became the master of Wuthering Heights.
3. A tree branch seemed to become a small, ice-cold hand to _____.
4. Heathcliff made a final visit to Catherine with the reluctant assistance of _____.
5. Hareton was regarded by Heathcliff as naturally superior to _____.
6. Heathcliff declined after a self-imposed _____.
7. "Wuthering" was a local word that suggested a (an) _____.
8. One snowy night, Hindley attempted to _____ Heathcliff.
9. Of two natures—a savage who could assume ladylike ways to gain personal ends—was _____.
10. Hareton was so cruel he was able to kill _____.
11. The only person to grieve for Heathcliff was _____.
12. Consumption was the cause of death of _____.
13. Cathy made peace with Hareton by offering _____.
14. Bitter, unrelenting, and narrow-minded piety was personified by _____.
15. As her mother had rejected _____, young Catherine at first rejected Hareton.

shoot
starvation
Ellen Dean
storm
Catherine Earnshaw
Frances
Edgar
dead son
Joseph
instructions
Heathcliff
grandfather
Lockwood
drought
Hindley
Hareton
Linton
puppies
poison
small birds

Answers

1-dead son, 2-Hindley, 3-Lockwood, 4-Ellen Dean, 5-Linton, 6-starvation, 7-storm, 8-shoot, 9-Catherine Earnshaw, 10-puppies, 11-Hareton, 12-Frances, 13-instructions, 14-Joseph, 15-Heathcliff

III. *Ideas for Written or Oral Book Reports or Class Discussions*

1. One of the earliest discoveries we make about *Wuthering Heights* is that, quite unusually, it is going to have two narrators, not one. The stormy story is told by conventional people: Mr. Lockwood and Ellen Dean. How does the rather fussy, typical bachelor, Mr. Lockwood, serve as a foil to Heathcliff? How does he place Heathcliff's passion in perspective? Ellen (or Nelly) Dean plays her part in giving us details of the past, as Mr. Lockwood presents the present. How does her personality put in perspective the wretched lives of the people who dwell on the moors? How do her memories enhance the telling of the tale? What advantages and (if any) disadvantages result from this method of narration? How does it compare to a first-person presentation by a major character or an omniscient approach by the author? What does the method of narration contribute to the movement and to the mood of the novel?

2. Emily Brontë was a young woman whose one novel made her world-famous because it embodied all the imagination she had developed in her lonely life on the remote moors of Yorkshire. Cite specific instances in the book that bring character or action to life and enable us to *see* the people, places, and things that make the story. Why is this of particular importance in a novel as "gothic" as *Wuthering Heights?* (Look up "gothic novel" in a good handbook of literary terms, for *Wuthering Heights* contains many important elements of this genre.) Where, and for what motives, does the author decide to make things less concrete, more obscure? What does this add to the book? Where does she use quick description for thrilling effect, slow revelation for impressiveness and mystery, forceful diction to fix a point securely, even humor? For humor, for instance, note that Mr. Lockwood asks whether Catherine's favorite pet is a dead rabbit (p. 10B), how Mr. Lockwood's nightmare is mocked (p. 27M), how the author very occasionally makes comments of her own, such

as "The spectre showed a spectre's ordinary caprice: it gave no sign of being" (p. 32B). What place does humor have in a novel of this sort? Does the novelist employ it as "comic relief" from her tragic themes, or does it more directly reenforce the pathos and terror? Explain your answer. Discuss other elements of style, such as irony, and explain how they are used in a book that, fraught with passion, has to deal in inner turmoils as well as mere appearances. Comment on the author's skill in writing dialogue, which comprises the major part of the text. To what extent do the spoken words reveal character, conflict, and passion? How natural do the various dialects (Hareton, Joseph) seem? How does the extensive use of dialogue contribute to the dramatic effect of the novel?

3. In a footnote to "What Is the Matter with Emily Jane? Conflicting Impulses in *Wuthering Heights*,"* critic Thomas Moser says that Heathcliff and Cathy are "both associated with trees. The pine bough scratching the window, in Lockwood's dream, becomes Cathy's fingers, and her marriage to Edgar resembles putting 'an oak in a flower pot' . . . When Heathcliff leaves Wuthering Heights a branch strikes the roof, and he beats his head bloody against a tree trunk at Cathy's death. The lovers become a single tree in Cathy's image: whoever tries to separate them will 'meet the fate of Milo' . . . the Greek athlete caught by the tree he was trying to split and torn to death by wolves." This small point stresses a larger issue: the great importance of symbolism in the novel. What other symbols are associated with these two major characters, and how do they function? How are symbols used to make points quickly and effectively about more minor participants in the story? What objects or places seem to be invested with special significance? For instance, speak of the desolate moor or the ancient house itself (whose name means "stormy heights," perhaps the heights of stormy passion). Discuss the uses of symbolism in general and in

* In *Nineteenth-Century Fiction*, Vol. XVII, No. 1 (1962), pp. 1-19, reprinted in Ian Watt's *The Victorian Novel: Modern Essays in Criticism* (Oxford University Press, 1971), pp. 181-199.

this novel in particular, citing and analyzing specific symbols.

4. "The theme of the moral magnificence of unmoral passion," writes Mark Schorer, "is an impossible theme to sustain," and yet this, he says, is the theme on which Emily Brontë set out to write her great novel. Assuming she did indeed begin with this intention, what difficulties did she run into? Why? How did she overcome them? To what extent did she modify her original theme? In fact, to what extent were her principal characters modified? Clearly, the Heathcliff and Cathy who lie buried at the end of the story are not the same people as they were at the start. What has happened to change their natures? Who else and what else are changed as the story unfolds, and by what forces or events? What *is,* in the long run, the theme of *Wuthering Heights?*

5. Nelly Dean considers herself "a steady, reasonable kind of body" (p. 73M). "I have undergone sharp discipline," she explains in the same breath, "which has taught me wisdom." She is quite proud of the way she questioned the elder Catherine about her love for Linton: "For a girl of twenty-two," she tells Lockwood, "it was not injudicious" (p. 92M). And yet her silly lie that Heathcliff was "about his work in the stable" (p. 91T) led Catherine to inflict an ultimate injury on him by saying, in his hearing, that marrying him would degrade her (p. 95B). Another lie, this a cowardly one, prevented Catherine from repairing the harm caused by her words (p. 96T). Is Nelly Dean later on equally imprudent in her reactions to the younger Catherine's secret association with Heathcliff's invalid son? Why? What differences would there have been in the story if Nelly Dean had been as wise in fact as she was in her own fancy?

6. Philip Stevick, in the preface to the anthology *The Theory of the Novel* (Free Press, 1967), states that "when a character, Heathcliff in *Wuthering Heights* let us say, becomes 'larger than life,' we legitimately cease calling the work which contains such a character a novel, calling it a romance instead." In what ways is Heathcliff "larger than life"? What is, as Professor Stevick would call it, his

"mythic level" in the story—what does he stand for, what elemental force (for instance) might he be said to embody? How does the author invest him with greater magnitude than the other characters possess; or suggest, somehow, that he has greater than human powers or force? What in his life made the simple country people imagine that he "walked" the moors after his death? To what extent is Heathcliff so exceptional a human being that *Wuthering Heights* is given an unreal quality? What other elements of romance ("a fictitious narrative in prose of which the scene and incidents are very remote from those of ordinary life") do you find in *Wuthering Heights?* How credible are the formative influences on Heathcliff? His later actions?

7. Bliss Perry says there are seventy-five characters in Dickens' *Our Mutual Friend* and sixty in Thackeray's *Vanity Fair.* Especially in nineteenth-century novels, intricate relationships in a complex plot, featuring many major and minor characters, are the order of the day. Look at *Wuthering Heights.* How many characters has it? Which are the major characters? Which are the minor ones? Look for patterns in their relationships. (There are two love triangles, for example.) To what extent are the main actions of the plot paralleled and commented upon by subplots? To what extent are subplots detachable from the action? How are narrators and other devices (such as family relationships stressed by names, and so forth) used to unify the whole? Point out any characters or details you think superfluous. Are relationships made clearer or more obscure by such devices as foreshadowing and flashbacks? Explain your answer with details drawn from the text.

8. When his Catherine is dying, Heathcliff bitterly blames her for having been untrue to her feelings for him and thus guilty of the situation resulting in her death. Reread pp. 194B–195T. How much is she really guilty and how much is Heathcliff himself to be blamed? How much is he merely complaining of his own pain, and how much has he a point in that Catherine has compromised her integrity? Where in the novel do you see that integrity was threatened by the warring sides of Catherine's nature?

What elements are struggling within her? When do we first learn of "the two Catherines" (as the critics put it), and how is the conflict developed? To what extent is she a more "divided personality" than Heathcliff, who grew up to be a raging man, having been a child who was capable of tears at the death of old Mr. Earnshaw? (Or do you interpret those tears another way? See p. 50B.) Where do we see Catherine being sweet and considerate, and where do we see her remarkably callous and cruel (as when she mocks Isabella's feelings for Heathcliff, pp. 125B–127B)? Where is she straightforward and where hypocritical or devious? Does this divided character constitute a weakness or an enhancement of the novel? Defend your opinion. Compare and contrast the younger Catherine with the elder one, for in that sense, too, there are "two Catherines" in the book. To what extent is she both tender and bitter? How does her handling of Hareton compare to her mother's treatment of Heathcliff, and, in the end, how does it suggest the way the elder Catherine should have treated Heathcliff?

9. It has often been remarked that the great novelist Jane Austen wrote novels in the time of the Napoleonic Wars and yet never mentioned them in any of her works. The last few years of the story of *Wuthering Heights* also are those of the Napoleonic Wars, but Emily Brontë doesn't mention the fact either. What points does this make about the remoteness of the Yorkshire moors where the story is set and about the isolation and timeless way of life of the people there? What do loneliness and remoteness contribute to *Wuthering Heights?* To what extent does the "outside world" intrude upon the story? Who goes to or comes from urban centers? What is the effect of this? To what extent is it to be attributed to the circumscribed life of the author and to what extent has it artistic effect in the novel?

10. Writing about romantic diction, Séan O'Faolain tells of a theatrical producer who said to him: "I'm doing a French play. Every time one of the characters makes a speech I want to make him stand with his back to the audience. Otherwise he seems as if he were about to take

off in an airplane." *Wuthering Heights* and its characters have often been described as more or less *soaring*. To follow the image, at what places in the text (and why) do you think Miss Brontë "got it off the ground"? What speeches or dramatic gestures of the characters help them to "take off"? How does she manage to make the novel an exciting (we might say "uplifting") experience that is moving and serious rather than wild and fantastic? In addition to its gothic qualities, the story contains elements that are characteristic of the Romantic period in literature, which began at the close of the eighteenth century. By specific references to the text, identify the elements of Romanticism: stress on nature, the importance of the individual, an optimism closely tied to a spirit of revolt, an interest in the supernatural, "the addition of strangeness to beauty," and a passion for lofty idealism. How do these elements make *Wuthering Heights* soar? What special pleasures does a reader find in a novel like this that are absent in the more modern novels of what has been called "pedestrian Realism"?

IV. Vocabulary Study

Diagnostic Test

1T	misanthropist	plant-lover	people-hater	food-lover
4B	morose	kindly	gentle	gloomy
6T	physiognomy	face	leg	arm
7B	laconic	wordy	clever	concise
16B	reprobate	hero	scoundrel	lover
19M	miscreants	cowards	villains	helpers
19B	virulency	friendliness	calmness	bitterness
23T	homily	temptation	abuse	sermon
24B	lachrymose	tearful	drunken	cheerful
33M	querulous	forthright	ill	complaining
38M	indigence	wealth	poverty	anger
57T	execrations	curses	prayers	predictions
61M	skulk	charge	slink	cover
62B	embellishment	ornament	paint	defect
79T	antipathy	compassion	medicine	hatred

83M	imperiously	arrogantly	softly	diffidently
87M	vagaries	experiments	fancies	errors
92M	injudicious	prudent	unwise	spontaneous
99T	protracted	drawn out	shortened	peeled
101M	audibly	silently	out loud	secretly
107M	dearth	abundance	supply	scarcity
119M	alleviation	lightening	worsening	indictment
127B	mitigating	harassing	increasing	lessening
131M	malignity	cordiality	ill will	generosity
137M	ignominious	famous	nameless	disgraceful
142M	livid	pink	lead-colored	brown
144B	apathetic	eager	cruel	indifferent
161T	recompense	bribe	repay	steal
172M	adjuration	rejection	settlement	entreaty
184M	quiescence	silence	cooperation	release
192T	scintillating	coping	sparkling	rousing
200B	proximity	nearness	distance	length
209M	orisons	oaths	prayers	commands
215M	malefactors	benefactors	losers	evildoers
224T	pertinacious	wavering	persistent	vulgar
236B	propitiate	appease	defy	offer
240M	sanguine	despairing	hopeful	bloody
246T	obviate	assist	defend	prevent
261T	languid	active	sluggish	forceful
272B	incorporeal	vivid	joined	without substance
286B	odious	loving	hateful	smelly
294M	usurped	seized	yielded	crowned
307B	interdict	agreement	ban	trial
313T	avaricious	careful	greedy	proud
320B	supplicating	rejecting	beseeching	holding
321T	enigmatical	clear	poisonous	puzzling
322B	cogitating	forgetting	pondering	grabbing
333M	derelections	acceptances	abandonments	lost souls
378B	scowled	smiled	stared	frowned
394B	admonition	caution	threat	disclaimer

Answers

misanthropist-people hater, *morose*-gloomy, *physiognomy*-face, *laconic*-concise, *reprobate*-scoundrel, *miscreants*-villains, *virulency*-bitterness, *homily*-sermon, *lachrymose*-tearful, *querulous*-complaining, *indigence*-poverty, *execrations*-curses, *skulk*-slink, *embellishment*-ornament, *antipathy*-hatred, *imperiously*-arrogantly, *vagaries*-

fancies, *injudicious*-unwise, *protracted*-drawn out, *audibly*-out loud, *dearth*-scarcity, *alleviation*-lightening, *mitigating*-lessening, *malignity*-ill will, *ignominious*-disgraceful, *livid*-lead-colored, *apathetic*-indifferent, *recompense*-repay, *adjuration*-entreaty, *quiescence*-silence, *scintillating*-sparkling, *proximity*-nearness, *orisons*-prayers, *malefactors*-evildoers, *pertinacious*-persistent, *propitiate*-appease, *sanguine*-hopeful, *obviate*-prevent, *languid*-sluggish, *incorporeal*-without substance, *odious*-hateful, *usurped*-seized, *interdict*-ban, *avaricious*-greedy, *supplicating*-beseeching, *enigmatical*-puzzling, *cogitating*-pondering, *derelictions*-abandonments, *scowled*-frowned, *admonition*-caution